HEALTHY WORK

HEALTHY WORK

Stress, Productivity, and the Reconstruction of Working Life

ROBERT KARASEK

AND

TÖRES THEORELL

Basic Books, Inc., Publishers

NEW YORK

T
60.8
K37
1990

Library of Congress Cataloging-in-Publication Data

Karasek, Robert.
    Healthy work: stress, productivity, and the
reconstruction of working life / Robert Karasek
and Töres Theorell.
        p. cm.
    Includes bibliographical references.
    ISBN 0-465-02896-9
    1. Work design.   2. Work—Psychological
aspects.   3. Job stress.   4. Stress, Psychological.
I. Theorell, Töres.   II. Title.
    [DNLM: 1. Employment.   2. Models,
Psychological.   3. Occupational
Diseases—prevention and control. WA 440 K18h]
T60.8.K37   1990   658.5'42—dc20
DNLM/DLC
for Library of Congress   89-42514
                                                        CIP

CONTENTS

PREFACE

This book is both very narrow and very broad in its focus. It examines a very simple theme about workplace control and psychological demands, but does so in the context of a broad range of intellectual disciplines. We are attempting to find ways to bridge what we feel are dysfunctionally wide gaps between medical science, psychology, sociology, industrial engineering, and economics. Such interdisciplinary spans are necessary to achieve the ultimate goal of the book: the redesign of work organizations to make them more psychosocially humane than those upon which our economy is now based.

Our aspiration has been to make the book readable by a wide audience. The real audience would be workers and managers if we could successfully integrate enough specialized issues to illuminate new problems in a way that helped promote solutions relevant to their daily lives. Failing that, the book is designed to be a readable presentation of our perspective on psychosocial job design and its health and productivity consequences, integrated with relevant materials from the related disciplines, for a broad range of practicing professionals and university students in the medical sciences, industrial psychology, industrial engineering, organizational sociology and managerial behavior, and job design and organizational change. We have also tried to contribute to public policy debate, since government policies for and against the positions we advocate have had an important impact on their success in many countries.

In spite of its breadth, the book includes much specialized material. Many general readers might wish to be spared such details, but because these discussions are often our own syntheses, new in this book (see, in particular, the second half of chapter 2 and the middle sections of chapters 5 and 6), they require the detailed support more usually found in academic journal articles. Lesser methodological support would weaken our case unacceptably for a number of important audiences. To experts in each of these areas, the coverage will still undoubtedly seem insufficient, but there is no alternative given our own restricted capabilities and our hope of reaching a more general readership. While the limited treatment of topics itself could inspire criticism, we hope to generate more interdisciplinary critiques: rival approaches that link the facts and logic of our diverse fields in a manner different than our own.

The book is divided into two parts. The first (chapters 1 through 4) presents the model of psychosocial job structure and stress-related illness and the findings from our heart disease research. These have been our own most intense areas of research over the last decade. The second half of the book attempts to translate these findings into a set of guidelines for the redesign of work by examining the productivity implications of our psychosocial model of work. Here, of course, we must also address issues of group processes, organizational change, impacts of technology, interoccupational political conflict, and finally in the last chapter, the impact of the market and the economy as a whole on stress and skill utilization.

Health-oriented readers and psychologists might find the first half of the book most relevant, while managers, job design professionals, organizational sociologists, and engineers might be more interested in the second half. The book's interdisciplinary goals would be served better by *reversing* those reading suggestions, however: it is what health professionals can bring to the process of job design and what managers and organization designers can bring to health and well-being that will be most important for the future of work design.

Robert Karasek is responsible for writing most of the book, developing its intellectual syntheses, and placing our heart disease research within the framework of the work environment, productivity, and job change processes. The heart disease research, which lies at the core of the book, has been truly a joint effort, with equal contributions by Karasek and Töres Theorell, working in both Sweden and the United States. Even the writing has occurred within the spirit of a joint partnership, with both authors contributing to theory, evidence, exegesis, and editing. Specifically, Karasek has been the substantial author of chapters 1, 2, 5, 7, 8, 9, and 10. Chapters 3 and 6 have been joint efforts, with Theorell taking the lead in chapter 6 and Karasek in chapter 3 (with roles reversing at the ends of those chapters). Chapter 4, the core evidence around which the other material has been organized, is a joint product not only of Karasek and Theorell but, happily, of a growing group of other major contributors. Joseph Schwartz and Carl Pieper (who made major contributions to the research for chapter 2, chapter 4, and the appendix), Lars Alfredsson and Anders Ahlbom, Jeffrey Johnson, Andrea LaCroix, and Peter Schnall, among many others too numerous to mention, have all spent many hours laboring over the research described in chapter 4 (and, we hope, in many other publications still to come).

Major gratitude for research support goes to the Swedish Work Environment Fund and the U.S. National Institute for Occupational Safety and Health and to the workers and industrialists who through their struggles for and against these issues have provided us with a foundation of critical issues as well as resources. The institutions that have directly or indirectly supported this research include our own universities: the University of Southern California, Columbia University, the Karolinska Institute, the National Institute of Psychosocial Factors and Health, and Stockholm University.

A very special debt is owed to our colleagues, who had the fortitude to read the earlier drafts of this manuscript and who managed to generate constructive criticism from that rough material: James House for his constructive synthesis and critique, and Jon Turner, Michael Frese, and Eli Glowgau for their vital comments and encouragement. For additional assistance and critiques of the book's content and text we would also like to thank Bryce Nelson, John Hadi, Mandy and David Li, Gunnar Aronsson, Anastasos Sioukas, Mar Preston, Harry Silberman, Ellen Hall, Jeff Johnson, Michael Cooley, James P. Henry, Fred Emery, Allan Leonard, Catherine Leonard, Jerry Ledford, Joel Fadem, Gerry Nadler, Jeff Dumas, Gert Graversen, and Martin Belmore. Also invaluable were the contributions of Martin Kessler and Cheryl Friedman of Basic Books, and the conscientious editorial effort of Nina Gunzenhauser.

PART I

THE PSYCHOSOCIAL WORK ENVIRONMENT, HEALTH, AND WELL-BEING

1

Health, Productivity, and Work Life

Economic logic tells us that material affluence should bring psychological well-being. But is this happening? In many ways, working populations in industrial countries such as the United States and Sweden, who should be experiencing the highest levels of satisfaction in history, are showing increasing signs of stress. People born in the United States during the last thirty years are more than three times as likely to experience depression than were their grandparents (Seligman 1988; Robbins et al. 1984); the number of mental health professionals more than quintupled between 1947 and 1977 (Mechanic 1980); worker's compensation claims related to stress have tripled since 1980 (Grippa and Durbin 1986); and losses to the U.S. economy associated with job stress are currently estimated to be as large as $150 billion per year (Freudenheim 1987). Clearly, our models of modern industrial organization, designed to yield the greatest good for the greatest number, have omitted much that is important. These models appear to be forcing us to trade off our psychological well-being for material affluence, instead of enhancing both.

Is stress from our work environments serious enough to cause heart disease, the major cause of death in industrial societies (World Health Organization 1984)? Could the same aspects of the work situation that cause stress also reduce productivity? If the answer to both these questions is yes, there would seem to be good reason to change our conventional views about how to organize and manage work activity. Yet most of the solutions currently advanced to reduce stress—relaxation therapies, for example—address only its symptoms. Little is done to change the source of the problem: work organization itself. While we recognize that stress is damaging, we act as though its sources were inevitable.

The alternative view presented in this book is that damaging job stress is not inevitable, that its causes can be found in the conventional models of work organization in Western industrial society, and that its cure lies in the transformation of the workplace. This solution is based on attention to psychological and social aspects of work that have been consistently omitted in conventional economic and technological calculations of how best to design work. The overlooked psychosocial side of work would also appear to be a logical place to search for solutions to the unintended consequences of modern industrialization related to lost "productivity": the decline in the quality of goods, the impersonality of services, and the emphasis on short-term profits at the expense of the ingenuity and long-term utility of products. We will argue that it is possible to reorganize production in a manner that can both reduce the risk of stress-related illness and increase aspects of productivity associated with creativity, skill development, and quality.

We contend that change in the workplace is not only desirable but essential. If the models of work organization that we use every day are so clearly connected to stress development, then we may be in the process of creating even more stressful environments—now on a global scale—that are totally incompatible with human physiological capabilities. The magnitude of the problem expands as work outside the home becomes more central to family life, involving two wage earners instead of one and overturning previous community and regional traditions. Unless many present models of economic and production organization are changed, the future will see not only a progressively poorer trade-off of health for productivity but many situations in which both are needlessly lost.

The first step toward solving the problem will be to develop new models of the psychosocial work environment, addressing both stress and productive behavior. A clearer understanding of this "soft" side of industrial production, we believe, will turn out to be the most successful pathway to the eminently "hard" and practical goals of reducing the risk of heart disease and ensuring the long-term survival of growth-oriented sectors of the industrial economy. Although the research on which this book is based actually covers only a narrow range of illnesses and restricted components of productivity, we believe that these will be increasingly important aspects of work experience in the future.

The impetus for this book came from a new set of findings relating job structure to psychological stress and then to heart disease and, separately, relating job structure to productivity. Our work has been a collaborative effort involving engineering, medical, and social researchers from several countries, who are attempting to formulate new methodologies for associating social and psychological aspects of work structure with the outcomes of coronary heart disease (CHD) and productivity change. In this book we attempt to extend the utility of these developments by integrating them with existing contributions from the fields of occupational health, industrial democracy and quality of work-life practice, industrial psychology, and organizational change.

The data have been gathered both in the United States and in Sweden, two countries different in their cultures relating to work organization (although less different than the United States and Japan). But there are also substantial similarities between the economies of the United States and Sweden: in level of technological sophistication, in the proportion of service to manufacturing employment, in standard of living (among the two highest in the world), and in the importance of individual rights. Both are private economies with substantial public sectors (albeit with higher funding levels in Sweden). Sweden's labor force, however, enjoys a much higher level of union representation and a generally more positive climate toward employee-oriented workplace reforms, particularly those involving job stress. Thus, the findings from these two countries have given us the advantage of testing the generality of our hypotheses. Many other industrialized countries might see themselves fitting somewhere between the United States and Sweden in terms of risks of psychosocial problems at work and the potential for alternative job designs.

Health and the Psychosocial Structure of Work

The goal of promoting well-being at work is not new; it has been the purpose of the occupational health movement since its modern inception in the late 1960s in both the United States and Sweden. These movements have been politically conscious attempts to roll back the residual destructive aspects of modern industrialization with scientific evidence of problems and scientifically formulated solutions.

The U.S. Occupational Safety and Health Act of 1970 and Sweden's comparable act in 1974 were both outgrowths of public reaction to longstanding physical hazards in some of the most dangerous industries and their consequences, such as the coal mining disaster in Tennessee in 1969 (see Ashford 1973) and the miners' strikes in northern Sweden in 1969 (Dahlström et al. 1971). Essential support for the enactment of these laws came from labor unions in both countries—the fight led by Anthony Mazzochi of the Oil, Chemical, and Atomic Workers' Union to protect workers from the ill effects of working with toxic chemicals is a prime example—and, in the United States, from institutional funding by the Ford Foundation (see Ashford 1973). Considerable resistance came from management (Dahlström 1965) and still continues in the United States, although now some of the largest corporations in both the United States and Sweden are staunch supporters of health and safety programs. For each step in the battle for expanded worker protection, medical research, such as Selikoff's study of asbestos (Selikoff, Chung, and Hammond 1964), has been the crucial starting point.

There has been no natural bridge, however, between this initial attention to the physical causes of occupational illness and the concerns regarding the psychosocial hazards of work. Research in the psychosocial area has involved a separate group of scientists, social scientists such as Kornhauser (1965) in the United States and Dahlström (1965, 1969) in Sweden who have studied the alienating and dehumanizing conditions of work. The U.S. and Swedish Quality of Work Life movement was also based in the social sciences but had a pragmatic program of work redesign to eliminate work dissatisfaction and increase productivity. This movement, along with the Scandinavian Industrial Democracy movement, developed some of the most important examples of new social organization of work that now exist.

New jobs and organizational structures were designed to replace the skill-fragmenting and socially-isolating industrial bureaucracies of the post–World War II era. The changes first took root as Industrial Democracy in Norway in the early 1960s with the help of pioneers such as Eric Trist, Einar Thorsrud, and Fred Emery (see Trist et al. 1963; Emery and Thorsrud [1964] 1969), and were picked up in Sweden in the late 1960s. In the United States, Lou Davis and colleagues built a parallel Quality of Work Life movement on a platform of principles of job enrichment. Enlightened managers, experimenting with new social organizations at work and new interfaces to technology, particularly in Scandinavia, cooperated with unions demanding democracy in the workplace to construct many important demonstrations of a new industrial order (see chapter 7).

Unfortunately, these results had little impact on the occupational health community. The practical realities of managing the work redesign process and concern for productivity left little energy for doing the sophisticated medical research on health effects that had been done in the case of physical work hazards. The result was that these two bodies of research on the hazards of work remained almost entirely separate.

In the 1970s, however, the social scientists joined forces with occupational health and safety institutions to undertake two vigorous decades of research on psychosocial work hazards. In Sweden, such researchers as

Frankenhaeuser (1980) and Levi (1971) did pioneering research on the physiological consequences of adverse psychosocial work settings. In the United States, Kohn (1977; Kohn and Schooler 1973) studied the impact of job structure on personality, and Gardell (1971b) did innovative work in developing processes of work reorganization to reduce psychosocial hazards. In Norway, Gustavsen (1985, 1987) helped translate this psychosocial research into new forms of occupational health legislation. Such work has been the most immediate precursors of our own research described in chapters 2, 3, and 4.

The challenge raised by the occupational health movement—that modern work environments caused serious illness and injury—was now presented to the psychosocial researchers. Did the social organization of work also cause serious physical illness? Without scientific evidence of such associations (evidence of job dissatisfaction would not suffice), the same political will to redress workers' hazards could not easily be mustered. This evidence was to be much more difficult to accumulate, however. In the case of physical occupational health hazards, such as in coal mining, the cause of injury was often obviously environmental, but for psychosocial risks work-related and nonwork-related factors were interlocked. Still more challenging would be the solutions: alternative models of the organizational structure of work, and not just substitution of a chemical in a manufacturing process, would be required.

With these challenges in mind, the research illustrated in figure 1–1 was undertaken (Karasek et al. 1981). Figure 1–1 shows the prevalence of heart disease symptoms in approximately 1,600 randomly selected Swedish working men who were interviewed in 1968 about their work and about heart disease symptoms. Symptoms were most common (with 20 percent of the workers affected) among those who described their work as both psychologically demanding and low on a scale measuring latitude to make decisions. The specific component of decision latitude that was measured—the worker's discretion over use of skills on the job—is an important part of the process of gaining control on the job: if the worker's skill is being utilized and developed, the worker is more likely to feel in control of the many different situations that may arise. By contrast, there were no heart disease symptoms among the group of workers who reported low psychological demands and a high level of skill discretion. Their jobs were associated with much better state of health than that enjoyed by the average worker. Is this the psychosocial "fountain of youth"? We will discuss a broad range of similar findings, including associations between job conditions and heart disease risk factors, in chapters 2, 3, and 4. For example, findings for measures of psychological strain, such as de-

FIGURE 1–1

Job characteristics and heart disease prevalence
(Swedish males, 1974, N = 1,621; see p. 123)

Number on vertical bar is percentage in each job category with symptoms.

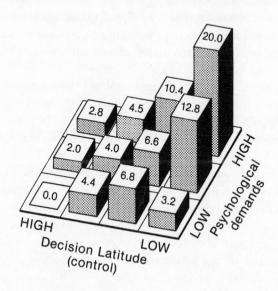

SOURCE: Redrawn from Karasek et al. 1981. Reprinted by permission of the *American Journal of Public Health*.

pression, that could be a broad precursor to a range of physical illnesses have now been demonstrated for a consistent set of job conditions in many occupations and in a number of countries.

However, we must have more information before we can assess the implications of these findings for health-oriented job redesign. First, any contribution of the work environment to physical illness must be shown to be independent of the worker's personal characteristics, including both personality and physiology. All the phenomena discussed in this book—from stress-related illness to productive behavior—are affected by individual characteristics such as age, education, and personality. Nevertheless, it is our position that these outcomes are not determined solely, or even primarily, by personal factors. Moreover, the psychosocial impacts must be the result of aspects of the structure of work that are changeable and redesignable; we must demonstrate that it is not just the inevitable demands of work that cause illness but that alterable policies for organizing task and social relationships play a major role. More important, we must show that any such changes are consistent with productivity requirements of work in the modern world. We must also consider *how* jobs are to be changed: addressing the process of organizational change requires us to build interdisciplinary bridges to aspects of organization and technology that constrain the job change process. Our models of work organization, health, and productivity must be relevant to the broad range of scientists, practitioners, and workers who will both assess the validity of the findings and attempt to translate them into solutions—a difficult challenge. We must also understand the political implications of change within and among different occupational groups. Finally, we must develop methodologies that can be used for health-oriented job redesign—that is, true health promotion in the workplace.

THE PERSON AND THE ENVIRONMENT: TWO BASES OF STRESS-RELATED ILLNESS

For decades, the medical, social, and management sciences have debated the extent to which stress-related illness can be attributed to the individual and how much should be attributed to the environment. The focus of one such current debate is the contribution of Type A behavior to heart disease via stress responses. These debates have tended to be divisive, separating medical professionals and psychologists, whose focus is on analysis and treatment of the individual, from job designers and industrial sociologists, who examine social environmental factors, with managers and engineers falling somewhere in the middle.

This book's primary emphasis on an environmental perspective is unusual. In the United States, the concern for stress-related illness has brought forth more research examining characteristics of the individual (personality, genetics) as causes of illness, which in turn have led to overwhelming numbers of person-oriented cures. There are high-priced relaxation therapies, "humor" therapies for corporations, and self-awareness therapies tending toward mysticism. These solutions seem to offer an easy alternative to complex and difficult labor/management negotiations over workplace control. To avoid the more difficult underlying issues is to deal with the symptoms instead of the causes, however. For that reason we suspect that at best such solutions will be only temporary. Certainly they will be expensive—according to one estimate, a $15 billion industry in the next ten years (Miller 1988). Even worse, they will lead to victim blaming and a tarnished reputation for any attempts to redress job stress.

If the individual is the only possible target for action, change efforts must concentrate on altering his or her biology, psychological traits, and individual behavior. Indeed, these are presently the most commonly recommended practices for reducing risk of heart disease. In the case of biological factors, they involve lowering lipids (cholesterol and other blood lipids) or blood pressure by means of pharmaceutical drugs or changes in diet. In the case of life-style, the focus is on changing eating and smoking habits. Efforts are made to change psychological traits by means of behavior modification programs, although these are yet to be thoroughly validated. Behavior change by means of pharmaceutical drugs has even been discussed (Rosenman 1984). Aside from the costs and personal side effects, such as loss of concentration and depression, here we can imagine solutions whose social consequences are worse than the disease itself. For instance, it has been claimed in the *New England Journal of Medicine* (Relman 1980) that sixty million Americans should be treated for mild hypertension by the medical professions. What magnitude of interventions by well-meaning but "elite" medical professionals in our daily lives is desirable? How much is healthy from the perspective of a democratic society?

One of the most intense preventive health efforts in the United States, Scandinavia, and other industrial societies today is targeted on smoking, as much because of claimed associations with heart disease as because of clearly confirmed associations with lung cancer. The goal of reduced smoking is, of course, to be applauded. Almost the entire anti-smoking effort, however, is aimed at personal behavior change. Layman's wisdom tells us that people light a cigarette more often during stressful periods on the job. In the recent past in many occupations, the smoke break was one of the few legitimate reasons for a worker to take any rest break on the job. Tense employees may not stop smoking even if they know it is dangerous to their health, as anti-smoking campaign research tells us (Caplan et al. 1975). Some of our own research findings, described in chapter 4, imply that job stresses are one cause of smoking. Work environment tensions represent forces that cannot be made to disappear through individually oriented coping strategies, such as stop-smoking campaigns. We argue that a more effective approach would be to set up health care teams to educate employees about how tensions at work affect smoking behavior, about alternative ways of coping with stress, about techniques for monitoring physiological and medical changes, and about the skills for critiquing work design solutions from a health viewpoint. Smoke cessation campaigns could work more effectively if the broader goals of psychosocial preventive medicine were advanced.

We do not attempt to argue that personal factors are unimportant for either health or productivity. It is rather our contention that the extraordinary breadth of the existing literature on psychosomatic causes of illness argues for integration of our understanding of environmental causes at work with the research on psychological and physiological mechanisms of individual response to the environment. Our approach is to link causes based in the environment and causes based in the individual, but with environmental causes as the starting point. We present a staged model in which personal causes are linked to environmental factors in stepwise fashion, an idea that has had many previous advocates. These stages of explanation are linked to appropriate stages of job redesign action. We will introduce two mechanisms from the core of our basic model to help link the individual and the environmental levels of analysis. The first mechanism is that job stress may inhibit learning, via effects of accumulated strain. The second is that job-induced learning may, in the long term, reduce stress response through development of confidence and self-esteem.

THE REDESIGNABLE ORGANIZATION OF WORK AND STRESS-RELATED ILLNESS

The argument for restructuring work environments would be impractical if the conditions of work that cause illness were inevitable (or avoidable only at great costs in terms of lost output to the society). Inevitability is assumed in the research tradition that explains illness in terms of "life-stressors." Stressful events—such as death of a spouse—that increase the risk of illness cannot be prevented. If the inescapable demands of work, from the farmer's labors to the social worker's burden of caring for the unfortunate, are the primary contributors to the psychosocial illness burden of work, we can expect few advocates for eliminating its contribution to stress. But this is precisely what we do not find.

Our findings show that social and psychological aspects of work situations are indeed significant risk factors for coronary heart disease, but not in the manner that might initially be supposed. While the psychological demands of work, along with time pressures and conflicts, are found to be significant sources of risk in many of our studies, work that is demanding (within limits) is not the major source of risk. The primary work-related risk factor appears to be lack of control over how one meets the job's demands and how one uses one's skills. In many cases, elevation of risk with a demanding job appears only when these demands occur in interaction with low control on the job. Other research has shown that regular physical exertion has positive effects on cardiovascular health in many situations (although physical hazards can of course pose major health threats beyond our stress perspective). Thus, in our research findings it is not the demands of work itself but the organizational structure of work that plays the most consistent role in the development of stress-related illness. Since this organizational structure is an eminently "designable" aspect of our industrial society, we are optimistic that new job redesign solutions can be found.

Productivity and the Psychosocial Structure of Work

Several generations of modern management theorists have documented the need to go beyond our present conventional (that is, hierarchical) organizational models in order to understand productivity. Almost as soon as Max Weber had clearly defined his model of the hierarchical bureaucracy ([1922] 1947) as the most efficient organizational form in growing industrial societies of the early twentieth century, critics of that model arose. Starting in the late 1920s, an entirely new direction in management theory, the Human Relations School, illustrated the importance of social interaction patterns, not just economic rewards or skill specialization, in determining the actual productivity of work. Organization theorists, from Merton (1940) to Melman (1984) and including Selznick (1949) and Gouldner (1954a), have criticized bureaucratic hierarchy as dysfunctionally rigid and easily co-opted by power structures to serve ends other than economic efficiency. The most recent generation of critics, such as Peters and Waterman (1981) and Swedish industrialists Carlzon (1987) and Gyllenhammar (1979), highlight the fact that simple, short-term economic criteria used to justify the hierarchical model in its original form can no longer be the sole validation of an organization's performance. But if short-term profitability is not sufficient, what should be the measure? One theme common to these critiques has been the underutilization of creative resources at all levels: workers' skills are insufficiently developed or not utilized. Organizations rigidly reject rather than facilitate creative adaptations to their environments. There is new pressure, visible in many management and business-oriented journals, to develop new management strategies for innovation, research and development, and other growth-oriented productive activities.

It is this theme of lost productivity that we are addressing with the skill underutilization associations shown in figure 1–2. In a nationally representative sample of the male U.S. work force we found an association between psychosocial job characteristics and a measure of skill underutilization: the difference between a worker's formal education and the amount of skill the worker's job actually required, assessed in terms of years of training. The diagram clearly shows that jobs low in decision latitude—jobs that gave little opportunity to make decisions or to decide which skills to use—were highly wasteful of the worker's actual capabilities. By contrast, jobs high in decision latitude (as in managerial and professional occupations) actually pushed workers beyond their training—possibly a good strategy (within limits) to encourage new learning. If such

FIGURE 1–2
Job characteristics and skill underutilization
(U.S. males, 1972, 1977, N = 1,749)

Number on vertical bar is underutilized skills
in terms of years of education (see p. 175).

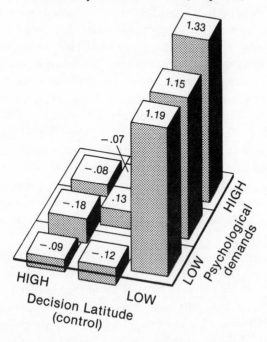

NOTE: Cell sizes, reading from left to right, are as follows (see p. 49n)—high demands: 225, 177, 174; medium demands: 146, 221, 137; low demands: 162, 255, 202.

SOURCE: Data from Quality of Employment Surveys.

extra challenges are motivators for those jobholders, it is hard to imagine that the jobs low in decision latitude and with wasted skills can be anything but unmotivating and unproductive. Indeed, in chapter 5 we shall examine further evidence that increased job demands lead to productivity increases only when the demands are combined with high decision latitude. When possibilities to control were perceived to be small, high levels of demands were associated with low productivity and stress symptoms.

It is truly ironic that just such low-decision-latitude jobs have been recommended in the conventional management models of the last two centuries, as we will see at the end of this chapter. Added to the business costs of the productivity losses resulting from this conventional wisdom are, of course, the economic costs of job-related illness discussed earlier. General Motors' biggest supplier is Blue Cross (Sloan, Gruman, and Allegrante

1987). Health care is becoming one of society's biggest budget items, in the United States increasing from 7 percent to over 11 percent of the gross national product in just ten years (Ginzberg 1987), while Sweden devotes 9½ percent to it (Swedish Central Bureau of Statistics 1987). Consumption of this part of the GNP is rarely associated with much happiness.

Could the solution to the productivity problems of work be the same as the solutions that enhance employee health? Can we get both health and productivity, and if so, how could we do it? Here we recall that the low-decision-latitude jobs that carried the highest risk of heart disease in figure 1–1 are also the ones that waste employee skills in figure 1–2. Thus, if we combine the results of the heart disease and the skill utilization studies, we might speculate that much more desirable jobs could be designed by avoiding low levels of decision latitude, where increasing output demands results in increased stress and even heart disease but no increase in productivity. If instead jobs could be redesigned with high decision latitude—that is, opportunities for taking responsibility through participative decision making—demands would be seen as challenges and would be associated with increased learning and motivation, with more effective performance, and with less risk of illness.

Of course, such findings could only represent the beginning of a new strategy for work redesign, for many reasons. For one thing, the process of work redesign would certainly involve more than isolated changes to two dimensions of the task structure: it would necessitate a detailed understanding of interrelated economic and technical effects of task design, organizational-level opportunities for and constraints on participatory decision making, and institutional forces at the level of the market or national policy that might affect job structures.

A strategy based on the joint search for worker well-being and productivity has, indeed, been the core of the entire Quality of Work Life movement, at least in the United States (Katzell, Bienstock, and Faerstein 1977). The most common connection between productivity and well-being, however, has been the supposition that work redesigned to be more satisfying to employees would also be more productive. We believe that this construction, while refreshing to managers, is flawed in its justification of employee health primarily as a pathway to profitability. Productivity cannot be considered the sole justification for a healthy workplace. Workers' health must be a separate goal in its own right. From the standpoint of the worker as consumer, health is the obvious prerequisite to obtaining satisfaction from material consumption: it is hardly possible to be a happy consumer in the evening after being an unhealthy worker all day long.

To avoid this difficulty, and to enhance the scientific validity of research with a joint focus, our proposed mechanisms for predicting productive behavior are separated from those that predict illness. This approach also allows us to consider separately the maximization of individual benefits and of firm benefits when job design strategies are analyzed. These dual mechanisms for health and productive behavior, however, will turn out to be different combinations of the same basic parameters of the psychosocial structure of work. It is therefore possible for an integrated set of job design principles to be developed in the later chapters of the book.

Our model for productive behavior is based on evidence for the importance of decision latitude in the learning process. At that point in the book (chapter 5), we can integrate our model with productivity evidence from several decades of Quality of Work Life and Industrial Democracy experiments. Our addition of psychological demands to the models most widely used in industrial psychology (such as Hackman and Oldham's Job Diagnostic Survey [1975]) allows us to describe two previously overlooked long-term inhibiters of productivity: job-induced passive withdrawal and lowered ability to make successful long-range plans. The potential of stress to inhibit the learning of new skills at both the individual and the organizational level is a phenomenon we will use to understand the linkage between individual tasks and organizational processes.

An important corollary of our arguments on productivity is the need for a new definition of productivity itself for many of the fastest-growing sections of the industrial economy. Our goal of simultaneous health and productivity enhancement may be obtainable only in a subclass of industries and outputs, those outputs most associated with customer-adaptive services, innovative technical development, and high reliability and quality. Our primary examples involve enhancement of long-term productive capabilities: enhanced skills for the worker and enhanced product lines and service potential for firms. These issues fall outside the conventional economic definitions of productivity that have dominated our industrial policy making: definitions that have increasingly been criticized for encouraging short-sighted cost cutting. We propose a new skill-related productivity definition in chapter 5. It implies new social structures for production, not only at the task level but also at the market level. We recommend new and often direct linkages between producer and customer in order to monitor and satisfy customers' needs and to facilitate growth of producers' skills. While they are not universally applicable, we feel that such new definitions of productivity are well justified by the actual behaviors recently observed in the most rapidly growing and innovative industrial sectors.

The Work Reconstruction Process

The process of arriving at a new organizational structure of work may be as important as the form of the resulting organizational structure itself. This is the message of the Industrial Democracy movement in Scandinavia in the 1960s and 1970s. Results of recent experiments in the design process have shown that in order to work effectively, a model must be adopted as its own by each workplace—a "local theory" (Elden 1983; Gustavsen and Hunnius 1981). A new organization of tasks that is imposed from above may not work because it lacks the necessary worker and staff advocates. More importantly, it fails to reflect the democratic value structure that was the major goal of the Industrial Democracy movement—that is, a structure that ensures self-determination in workplace organization for employees at all levels, particularly low-status employees, who so clearly lack these rights otherwise.

The very fact that our approach is based on the psychosocial structure of work should make it more relevant for the inherently social process of work redesign than models that focus only on the physical reality or the impersonal financial rewards of work. We believe, however, that the true potential of our model lies in the centrality of the concept of control: influence by employees in the work process decision. Changing the distribution of control opportunities, a close correlate of the decision-latitude construct that we use to predict health and productivity, is the central strategy for changing the structure of an organization. Patterns of control are central features of an organization's social groupings, reward structures, and information structures. The involvement of control in both the nature of our solutions and the process of obtaining them means that it will be difficult to separate the ends from the means in our model. In our perspective, the job design process and its ultimate design goals are inextricably linked.

The models we use must be broad and flexible. They must address several salient issues for each type of participant among the many groups needed to build new job structures. These groups include not only managers and workers but professionals with diverse backgrounds: medical professionals, social scientists in psychology and sociology, and engineers. In order to serve as the basis for a dialogue, the models must also be simple enough to be understandable to all. They must be generally applicable across intellectual disciplines as well as across the different perspectives of labor and management. The need to address multiple scientific disciplines requires a multilevel model, one that deals with phenomena at the level of the person, the task, and the organization. Because of our concerns with health and job design, we begin our discussions at the micro level, interactions between the individual and the environment. We then move up to the level of the organization and finally beyond the organization to occupational groups and their job design interrelationships. Finally, these task and organizational changes must be translated into changes in the management policies that have led to our present work situations—a grand feedback loop that will now include health effects as well as productivity.

The process we have described is called *work reconstruction*. Although it clearly develops out of the other work transformation strategies discussed above, it differs from them in several significant respects. Work reconstruction implies a broader social, economic, and political process than *job redesign*. In particular, it includes more precise measures of health and well-being. On the productivity side, conventional economic measures are supplemented by more humane measures of production output. It thus brings a more varied group of professionals into contact with workers and managers. Work reconstruction can be undertaken at the firm level since representatives for all these viewpoints exist within the microcosm of a single company. However, to be fully successful, work reconstruction will require redefinition of existing political agendas (see chapters 9 and 10). Although it is consistent with broad goals of Industrial Democracy, work reconstruction does not fit as neatly into the existing labor-relations structures of many countries—which would have to be expanded to include our new issues.

Work reconstruction ultimately may be more broadly diffusable than Industrial Democracy precisely because it is not as tightly dependent on the specific institutions of a country. The new measures of productivity, as well as the attempt to universalize some conceptions of psychosocial well-being at work, may make work reconstruction more easily generalizable. Finally, in contrast to most existing "work-site health promotion" strategies, work reconstruction involves environmental as opposed to personal behavioral change, addressing what we consider the causes rather than the symptoms of health problems.

Because of a lack of direct data on each individual's job, we have sometimes relied on occupational groups and their average job characteristics to test our hypotheses. Ultimately, this occupational-level analysis has provided us with a useful frame of reference for comparing health conditions and job conditions among sectors of the work force that were previously examined in isolation. From this perspective, many of the job redesign experiments of the last decades are seen to be surprisingly limited, primarily using the same basic solutions over and over again in limited sectors of the modern industrial work force. On the other hand, they have been surprisingly powerful, bringing about changes in job characteristics far beyond the boundaries of single occupations and indicating the feasibility of major restructuring of occupational boundaries.

One straightforward example of the political implications of such job changes is illustrated in figure 1–1. The high incidence of health problems with low-decision-latitude jobs shows that it is not the bosses but the bossed who suffer most from job stress. The most common problem is not executive stress (although some executive jobs are certainly stressful) but stress among low-status workers who bear equally heavy psychological demands but lack the freedom to make decisions about how to do the work. For most people, decision-making freedom appears to aid in coping with the heavy psychological demands of work, but for high-level managers, it represents an additional job demand. These findings suggest a simple solution: equalize the decision-making opportunities of managers and workers within work organizations, thus both reducing an unhealthy burden on high-level executives and professionals and providing health enhancement and skill development opportunities for lower-status workers.

Obstacles to Work Reconstruction

Redesigning work with these new goals will not be an easy task. Part of the hesitancy to address stress at the workplace is obviously political. There are national priority disagreements over the importance of occupational health, clearly illustrated by the divergent policies of the United States and Sweden. During the early 1980s in the United States, the National Institutes of Health eliminated research sections of the National Institute of Mental Health that were studying work stress and dramatically cut funding for research at the National Institute for Occupational Safety and Health (NIOSH). The U.S. government's denial of the importance of work stress was dramatically illustrated in the firing of the U.S. air traffic controllers. The U.S. Office of Management and Budget has deleted job stress measurements on some occupational health questionnaires (Cimons 1987).

In Sweden, the situation has been different. Over the last decade, workers and experts alike have become increasingly aware of the importance of psychosocial factors in the working environment. More and more courses on work stress, including its relationship to work organization and structure, are being organized for occupational health personnel. The Swedish Work Environment Fund (which has a budget equal to that of its U.S. counterpart NIOSH, despite the 25-fold difference in size of the national populations) directs more and more of its money to research on psychosocial factors. Although the actual pace of job restructuring has been slow, more and more leading Swedish company managers publicly acknowledge that participatory processes in the workplace are an important goal for a democratic society and may also be related to job stress problems.

Surprisingly, there is also resistance from institutional groups and universities. While the general public widely believes that psychosocial work stress is important to cardiac health and productivity, this relationship has been largely unrecognized and even denied by many experts. The Danish National Confederation of Management (Brøchner 1983a, 1983b) several years ago demanded the elimination of national funding for occupational stress research as too politically provocative among workers, although it ultimately reversed its position because of professional and public protest. In the area of education, job stress is almost universally ignored in the engineering curricula of all industrialized countries, and engineering courses routinely teach work design principles that if rigorously applied would be almost certain to increase job stress. The training of physicians also devotes little attention to issues important for understanding environmental stress.

We believe that there is also an underlying intellectual problem stemming from an expanding scientific gap in multidisciplinary knowledge, a gap that is visible in both countries. There is a deficit in comprehensive understanding, caused by the ever greater specialization that each scientific discipline develops in the advancement of its own field. The resulting "collective myopia" about real work problems can totally prevent the undertaking of coordinated solutions to modify the structure of work. There is at present little agreement on any aspect of the psychosocial redesign of work that can unite the full range of experts and workers needed to bring about the solutions. Many of these already unreconciled perspectives have become even more isolated in recent decades. We see several underlying issues that are causing the gap in multidisciplinary knowledge to widen. For example, as we have seen, while occupational medicine has been a cornerstone for our research, much of medical science has largely been preoccupied with individual-level causes of and cures for illness. When environmental factors are addressed, they are rarely the social organizational factors that could provide a pathway for prevention as well as an explanation of illness. And while some pragmatically oriented social scientists involved in experiments in Industrial Democracy and Quality of Work Life have been our teachers, many other academic social scientists are involved in much less helpful debates on narrowly specialized topics that indirectly diffuse energy for the common solutions we advocate.

The greatest barrier to redesigning work, however, is in the world of conventional business philosophy. While a large number of business school professors in organizational behavior are researching new management approaches similar to ours—and we must acknowledge our debt to them—there is still an increasing emphasis in the business and economic community on easily quantified, short-term productivity results. And in the United States there is still much implacable reluctance to sharing of enterprise control either with workers or with the medical or social science experts—in spite of much sloganeering to the contrary (Lawler, Ledford, and Mohrman 1989). This is the primary source of resistance to our suggestions.

The Development of Contemporary Patterns of Work Organization

The political complexity of changing the organization of work suggests that we would do well to understand how jobs came to be the way they are today. A brief look back at the past justifications for work designs shows that the problems in work organization today are deeply rooted in the conventional economic and management theories of the last two centuries.

We believe, along with Piore and Sable (1984), that the choice of one work organization over another cannot be justified by inevitable natural or economic laws. Production organizations are ultimately justified by social decisions and by the state of technological development. As technology and society's goals evolve, so does what is considered logical in terms of work organization.

In many ways, work organization as a science is now in a transition period. Old patterns are deeply entrenched yet appear more vulnerable than ever. New models exist but have not yet won widespread acceptance. There are major changes in how optimal work organization is intellectually justified. Indeed, many of the interdisciplinary conflicts we have noted can be related to transition in the very choice of sciences we apply to work organization. This century has witnessed a dramatic change in the rewards and difficulties of work, from hard to soft science in nature. The physical and economic outputs and occupational hazards at the beginning of the century were analytically amenable to hard scientific measurement. They required progress in the quantitative sciences for solution. The emerging challenges in societies like the United States and Sweden require a new scientific synthesis on the soft, psychosocial side of work for their solution, if both the new health and the new productivity goals are to be achieved. These shifting perspectives may well be a major source of the tensions that exist between today's hard and soft scientific perspectives on work organization and the major discrepancies between the reality of new psychosocial job design experiments and the still-dominant theories inherited from the earlier era of heavy industry. Let us first trace the source of the older, conventional models.

The extraordinary increases in material standards of living in the industrialized world in the last century have clearly been based on technological innovations with origins in the physical sciences: the steam and internal combustion engines, electrical power, the telephone, the automobile, the computer chip. A close look at the social history of the end of the nineteenth century reveals that the hard sciences were also the key to solving the health problems of that era. The primary problems then were the daily debilitations faced by physical laborers: physically exhausting working conditions and life-threatening hazards such as those faced by mine workers (and described vividly in Émile Zola's *Germinal* ([1885] 1952) and slaughterhouse workers (revealed by Upton Sinclair [1906]). The economic and physical deprivations of these workers were easy to measure and simple to understand (now, at least) and were thus good candidates for solutions according to the model of hard scientific analysis. To the list of physical oppressions Karl Marx added his economic analysis of the easily measurable injustices of labor's meager share of production rewards and forecast a decline in the system if workers lost the income necessary to buy the goods that kept capitalism's industries afloat (1867).

The hard science–based industrial revolution of the nineteenth century also changed the social structures of work. Swept away were the old small-scale shops of independent artisans and their craft guilds and unions. By the turn of the century, these forms of traditional work organization yielded to the political and economic power of enterprises based on new technologies—but not without a struggle. Violence often accompanied the destruction of traditional social structures of work, in which fiercely independent tradesmen had powerful control over their work processes and over passing on their skills. These changes in work organization occurred earlier in England, Germany, and the United States and later in Scandinavia and Japan, but they were always accompanied by enormous social protest. In some countries, there were socialist revolutions; in others, battles were waged by captains of industry against workers, as in the Homestead Strike at Carnegie Steel in Pennsylvania in 1892. Craft groups were replaced by lower-skilled (previously agricultural) labor that was in plentiful supply. The new labor supply, along with new machine-driven production technologies, resulted in a drop in the production skills required, from the high craftsman level to medium and low levels. The companies acquired control over job training and removed the responsibility for planning production from the workers (see Stone 1973 for a well-documented discussion of these processes in the U.S. steel industry). The downgrading of production workers' skill levels eventually left a gap at the middle skill level in the work force where numerous self-managing craftsmen had been. This resulted in the need to develop a smaller "middle-elite" of technical managers and foremen and a whole new breed of engineers to manage the newly retrained workers and their machines (Piore and Sable 1984).

It was this vacuum of the missing "middle-elite" that Frederick Taylor addressed with his *Principles of Scientific Management* in 1911 in the United States. Scolding the managers of his day for their lack of technical understanding, and banishing the old craftwork methods as hundreds of years out of date with the requirements of the new technologies, he laid the foundation for training a new profession: industrial engineers were to be educated at universities where they could "scientifically" identify and analyze the basic elements of a worker's task and recombine these elements into new task structures that could accommodate the new machines filling every corner of the shop. Precise division of labor facilitated the development of mechanized equipment to perform operations automatically, which in turn justified further division of labor.*

According to Taylor, workers' tasks were to be simplified into the elemental skills required and then reorganized in minute detail by plans drafted by engineers. Physical labor was to be reduced by elimination of wasted motions. The pace of work was to increase substantially, and workers were to be isolated from each other and individually evaluated, to avoid "time-wasting" habits and the development of social groups that might resist management plans. Taylor made encouraging promises to both labor and management: to traditional managers who had refused to interfere with old craftwork structures, he promised dramatic improvements in profits; to the new (often immigrant) workers, he promised major increases in wages. This dual largesse was to be made possible by the huge increase in overall output and productivity that would occur under what he called *scientific management*—the new scientific method of systematic work measurement, systematic review of data, formulation and testing of genera-

---

*"Once a human task has been decomposed into its elementary motions, it became possible to build a device that would perform these motions, automatically; and as one step in the manufacturing process was thus mechanized, the preceding and following steps had to be correspondingly reorganized, to keep pace with the new machinery" (Piore and Sable 1984, p. 22).

lized theories, conclusions on the basis of evidence, and finally unwavering application of the solutions—to workers—by management.

Taylor's recommendations were actually only the task-level consequences of a much more general set of principles for organizing an industrial economy dating back to Adam Smith's *Wealth of Nations* ([1776] 1976). That book, along with Jeremy Bentham's (1794) "Utilitarian" philosophy of economic measurement for all individuals' pain and pleasure (the source of the economic logic on psychological well-being from the opening line of this chapter), are the cornerstones of Western "free-market" economic thought and quantitative (i.e., "bottom line") social decision processes. Adam Smith started the very first chapter of his book with the fundamental proposition that productive social organization of work is built upon the division of labor: productivity is maximized when workers are assigned to jobs with tasks as small and as specialized as possible, to promote dexterity, and to eliminate wasted motions. These benefits of specialization, however, could only be obtained by trade in the marketplace. Here the producer efficiently specializing in production of one good could obtain more "welfare" by trading with its profits than he would have obtained if he had (inefficiently) produced all goods he needed himself—what Smith called the principle of comparative advantage.

Smith acknowledged only one limitation to his principle of maximum specialization of labor leading to maximum economic profit: the size of the market for the product. Only a large market could justify the highest levels of labor specialization. Almost as a corollary, conventional management wisdom holds that large-scale markets and enterprises (hence corporate expansion) are economically efficient because of the high levels of specialization possible (of course, economies of scale in capital equipment also lead to collateral savings).

However, specialization of labor leads almost inevitably to restricted power for workers. This is so because a set of managers and engineers must be hired to control the workers' behavior in a way that recoordinates their specialized activities—Taylor's contribution. Ironically, in democratic Western industrial societies one of the only "legitimate" justifications for limiting equality of power is the "necessity" of achieving maximum economic efficiency, as a first priority. According to Smith and Bentham this will lead to the "greatest [economic] good for the greatest number." However, the tendency to evaluate all decisions on the basis of economic measurements can also adversely affect workers. The actual impact of Bentham's Utilitarian penchant for economic evaluation may be to benefit some groups at the expense of others: the quantifiable physical output of the firm becomes the primary basis for decision making, while non-quantifiable behavioral phenomena at work, like control, are easily overlooked. Obviously, our later discussions will have to examine the distribution of both quantifiable and nonquantifiable production consequences.

Two major changes in working life, then, were wrought by the introduction of what we are calling the conventional theories of production organization. However, these changes were often invisible in hard economic or physical terms. The most obvious change was that onerous, concrete physical labor was relieved by new machinery. It was replaced by very high, but hard to measure, psychological work loads, the most salient characteristic of our new psychosocial work environment. The second change was the application of the division of labor principle, with its theoretically separate but closely related impacts on skill usage and control over the work process. These two transformations are closely related to the two dimensions used to categorize the psychosocial job structure in figures 1–1 and 1–2 and will form the basic analytic model used in the book.

A number of factors beyond the two-dimensional model may also significantly affect stress at work. One set of issues relates to the impact of the division of labor on social relations in the company—and outside it. Market transactions (which, according to Smith and subsequent economists of the still dominant neoclassical tradition, were to occur between "strangers") are the means to augment, evaluate, and distribute all production output. They also carry the negative consequences of disrupting the previous community-oriented production processes and further increasing workers' feelings of powerlessness. As markets increased to global scale, workers' job opportunities were affected by distant factors beyond their understanding and influence, and job insecurity became a problem.

Nevertheless, we will begin our analyses with just two primary dimensions, the division of labor and psychological demands, for the same reasons that Adam Smith did: he considered the division of labor in society to be the cornerstone upon which all his other principles of economic organization rested. This preliminary set of principles of work organization has remained intact to a remarkable degree almost to the present day; in some ways it is stronger than ever. Refinements added since the First World War have largely reinforced the resulting patterns of social relations at work. Scientific management's restriction on the power of labor in the work process can be seen in the fact that the primary tactic for increasing profits under the model is to search for ways to cut wage costs (using short-term measures of cost-effectiveness), while the costs of coordination and management (indirect costs) have gone relatively untouched. One recent enhancement of Smith's argument for the efficiency of large-scale enterprises was that large scale could ensure predictable operations. Easily repeatable operations came to be considered an additional requirement for high productivity: unexpected variations could lead to waste, inefficient mixes of resources, and less-than-optimal use of new production technologies. This argument led to further justification for management's need to control all factors in its operating environment—not only labor behavior but even customer demand, which can only be manipulated if market share is large enough. Another new factor is, of course, the computer, which allows centralized monitoring and coordination of operations that were previously integrated by worker discretion, increasing the interdependence and complexity of the production system and the need for more coordinators.

The search for predictability and machine-like determinacy has also been evident in the design of new machinery to be operated, of course, by human beings. As Lund and Hansen (1986) recently pointed out, engineers (particularly in the United States) have often adopted simplified views of human requirements that focus on the quantitatively modelable "human machine" but usually overlook people's proactive, goal-oriented social and political needs. Conventional management's "profits only" orientation and the computer's data-processing potential have further reinforced information-gathering strategies that collect only hard, easily quantifiable data on economic outputs and inputs, hours of work, and material requirements, rarely measuring the pain or pleasure of psychosocial working conditions.

What have the consequences been? The historical impact of these policies on material productivity was often dramatically positive in the industries of the early twentieth century. The new industrial engineers often radically speeded up the pace at which the task was accomplished. For instance, Gilbreth (1909) describes the redesign of a bricklayer's job that produced a 300 percent increase in efficiency and also resulted in higher wages for the workers. Under Henry Ford in 1913, jobs became even more restricted in skill and authority as the mechanically controlled auto assembly line moved each car chassis through its sequence of worker operations. Ford offered workers double wages, and his offer was finally accepted by labor in spite of early walkouts and a turnover rate of 300 percent. Although organized labor resistance to the methods of scientific management was not insignificant (Hoxie 1920), these work methods were eventually almost universally accepted by major unions by the early 1950s in the United States and the 1960s in Sweden. Indeed, Walter Reuther's strategy for United Auto Workers was to give up control over the work process in trade for wage increases, a policy which has been significantly reversed only very recently with renewed worker interest in decision participation. No less a champion of worker interests than Vladimir Ilyich Lenin was a supporter of Taylor's methods for the U.S.S.R. in 1921, as an appropriate building block of scientific socialism (Lenin [1917–1923] 1976). Taylor's principles are still at the core of industrial engineering curricula when it comes to the design of the worker's task. In spite of the entirely different and glitteringly successful examples of alternative work design in Western Europe, Japan, and the United States, Taylor's principles still probably represent the predominant direction of job design change in the modern world (for examples, see Gardell and Gustavsson 1979; International Labour Office 1979; U.S. Department of Defense 1985).

The Forces for Change I: A New Generation of Psychosocial Problems

Over time, the new solutions of Taylor and his followers gave rise to an entirely new set of worker deprivations and management problems, problems that have now created a need for a new set of work design principles for the future. Consider the profile that has been found to characterize the job at high risk for psychological stress: the job is low in task decision freedom, low in skill level, but high in psychological demands; it is also, as we will see, low in physical exertion and socially isolated from workmates. This stressful job fits, embarrassingly closely, the specific job design *goals* of Taylor's scientific management. Thus, psychological stress may easily be the direct, if unintended, outcome of application of these job design philosophies. Of course, Taylor's conscious goal was not to increase psychological stress; the word is never mentioned in his texts and did not even exist in its present meaning. Indeed, the stress consequences might be viewed as an innocent oversight, if only Taylor's crusade to transfer control over work processes from tradesmen to the new class of managers had not been waged with such dogmatic vigor (which ultimately resulted in his being called before Congress in 1921).

The three major oversights in Taylor's prescription for job design related to psychological demands, control, and social support. First, the worker was left with little possibility for psychological relaxation. The promised increase in work pace did indeed occur, and many motions that had served as the workers' only rhythmic respites from the pressures of production were eliminated as "wasted." Second, the worker was freed from the "burden" of making decisions about how to perform a job, a change usually resented by workers as a loss of control. The transformation was so thorough that workers were deprived of almost all possibility of self-pacing and self-initiated improvements to the work process. To craftsmen, the ultimate loss was the loss of mastery of a trade capable of rendering a complete service to a customer. The divide-and-conquer aspects of job fragmentation placed labor at the mercy of the new market middlemen (Thompson 1963) and of engineers' and managers' "planning requirements." Job security became dependent on a new set of uncontrollable factors. Third, the social isolation of workers that was explicitly and rigidly enforced in Taylor's system had negative consequences not only for the workers but, in the long term, for work effectiveness. Eliminating group work, in which Taylor saw exaggerated dangers of loafing and featherbedding ("soldiering") as well as the power to resist work structures imposed by management, undercut not only the social support of the work group but the potential for easy cross-training of skills and ultimately the flexibility to restructure work processes to meet constantly changing markets and technological demands.

During the first half of the twentieth century, psychosocial work hazards such as loss of control, greater psychological demands, and social isolation were less important to workers than increased wages and reduced physical demands. Now, however, there is evidence that these psychological and social factors are gaining in importance in comparison with the physical burdens of work.* The nationally representative (1:1,000) Swedish Level of Living Surveys in 1968, 1974, and 1981 showed a clear increase in reports of psychologically demanding work, from 29 percent in 1968 to 42 percent in 1981 (Swedish Central Bureau of Statistics 1982). There is now a higher percentage of psychologically demanding jobs than of jobs involving heavy lifting, which dropped from 36 percent in 1968 to 28 percent in 1981, and jobs involving dirty work (noise problems have not changed significantly). Of course, part of this increase in reports of psychological job demands may be due to increasing worker awareness of these problems, but that would simply confirm our point. We suspect that similar tendencies are true in the United States, although comparable national statistics have unfortunately not been collected by the U.S. Department of Labor since 1977.

In the last decade or two, a new wave of critical literature on the work environment has emerged documenting these psychosocial problems (Edwards 1979; Gordon, Edwards, and Reich 1982; Howard 1985a, 1985b; Noble 1977; Shaiken 1984). Inappropriate use of computer technology and video display terminals, which can combine demands for concentration with socially rigid, deskilled job structures and monitoring, can build be-

---

*For lack of a new vocabulary to describe these phenomena, many authors (for example, Sennett and Cobb 1972) speak of stress and illness as "costs" and discuss the dollar value of these losses, relying on the symbol of the previous era of physical and economic deprivations, as though the new problems could also be neatly fitted into Adam Smith's marketplace model.

havioral prisons and restrict hopelessly the development of human potential in working life. These critics illuminate new debilitations of psychological job stress and show the powerlessness of segments of the work force
who fear their skills will be made obsolete by new waves of automation.
These criticisms of our present implementations of computer technology
are all the more striking when we note that the computer is often a very benign technology that in the right circumstances leads to skill development
and creativity.

Changes in health care delivery and its costs are also challenging the
conventional approaches to work organization. The cost of illness attributed to the work environment is increasing in the psychosocial areas,
with worker's compensation claims for stress-related causes rising to 14
percent of all claims, up from only 5 percent in 1980 (Grippa and Durbin
1986). The overall magnitude of these costs, while difficult to estimate
precisely, as we shall see in chapter 5, has now come to represent a significant fraction of health care costs overall, which in turn continue to
rise as a proportion of the gross national product. The potentially preventable health care costs thus run to many tens of billions of dollars
every year.

"Preventive health care" is in fact becoming more and more common in
the workplace, with over 66 percent of U.S. companies with more than 50
employees offering some kind of program (U.S. Office of Disease Prevention and Health Promotion 1987). The importance of the work site as a location for health care delivery is trivialized, however, if the prevention activity does not target hazards that exist at the workplace itself. At present,
the work site health promotion programs almost never address such issues
but instead focus on changing workers' life-styles, leading workers to question management's motives for sponsoring them (Canton 1984). In light of
the magnitude of prepaid medical expenditures by third-party health care
organizations such as private health insurance plans and the United States
government (over $360 billion a year in the United States in 1987 [U.S. De-
partment of Health and Human Services 1988]), it is surprising that these
organizations devote so little funding to prevention that actually changes
jobs. By contrast, over the last decade social expenditures in Western Europe have risen, often to cover the costs of work-related adjustments in
areas of occupational health, employment maintenance, humanization of
technology, and skill retraining. These expenditures represent preventive
medicine against future health care problems and long-term productivity
losses. What happens if the United States fails to pay these costs? The bill
for omitted prevention will come due in the future, and it will be higher
than the costs of prevention.

The Forces for Change II: A New Industrial Revolution

Ultimately, the strongest forces for job change are the transformations—fully as dramatic as those of the original industrial revolution—that production and technology themselves are undergoing. In many ways, these changes undermine core assumptions of Smith's, Taylor's, and Weber's conventional models of production organization. They imply the need for change in the most basic concepts, including development of new measures of the value of output from productive enterprises that transcend simple Utilitarian approaches.* Many of these changes imply new economic paradigms and social structures for work that may, with the proper design goals, be consistent with jobs with lower risks of stress.† If on the other hand psychosocial well-being is overlooked as a goal, we may confront more intractably disturbing psychological and emotional consequences than those of the first industrial revolution. While full elaboration of such new socioeconomic models is far beyond the scope of this book, we will review evidence for some of the job design implications of these models in chapters 5 through 10. But the evidence for changes is also contradictory. Some transformations, such as the globalization of the economy, appear to reinforce the impact of Adam Smith's original model—with market scale enlarged to its maximum extent.

We first review the several major transformations that challenge the basic assumptions of conventional economic models: they are wide-ranging. In general, the social relationship components of production output are becoming more important while its physical components are becoming increasingly limited. The primary example is the expansion of the service industries, where social relations between the client and the server are of paramount importance. These already employ more than twice as many workers as the manufacturing sector. The true nature of output in these industries must often be described as unknown, because it is beyond the analytical capabilities of the old scientific management and productivity analysis to describe. The difference between these new service outputs

*New forms of productivity measurement focusing on growth and development are becoming more important. Management literature has recently criticized the myopic concern for short-term cost reductions, showing ultimately that it can lead to disastrous failures to invest adequately in new capital equipment or human capital. The short-term focus, based on conventional economic models, is also inconsistent with innovation, which yields uncertain but essential future benefits.

†Important syntheses have emphasized the importance of creative involvement of workers, but without taking into account the social structural prerequisites for humanized work that labor unions would emphasize (Naisbett 1984; Naisbett and Aburdene 1985; Toffler 1981).

and the conventional outputs of Adam Smith's world is fundamental. In our definition (Karasek 1989a), the production of goods involves adding value to inanimate objects, whereas services involve adding value to a person or to an organization, both entities that can grow. Since goods production involves the use of physical resources that are strictly limited, such as forests and fossil fuels, and poses a risk of catastrophic pollution at present scales of production, new forms of production emphasizing social relationships and development of human capabilities—rather than material output—could be an important contribution to an environmentally healthy planet.

Biological needs alone no longer generate sufficient demand to keep populations constructively employed. In much of the industrialized world, the previously hungry-for-products mass of consumers has now been replaced by a population that often needs to be persuaded to buy something (with advertising expenditures that for many popular products exceed production costs) and taught how to "need" the products that technology can make available (for example, home computers). The world's chief economic problems at the turn of the century often involved developing new production technologies to keep pace with increasing demands for basic industrial commodities such as steel and coal. Now the most pressing economic problem for the industrial economies of the world may be how to keep their populations employed in the face of overcapacity in everything from ships to computer chips, a problem that each country tries to solve by increasing its own relative productivity—and thereby, of course, producing greater overcapacity.* Desirable products for the future will be those that stimulate demand in a constructive way, not satiate it, completely reversing the previous model of economic satisfaction. Labor has become an item of consumption (in the sense of the need for a job), instead of just an input to production, and creative challenges at work are an important aspect of well-being.

Skill utilization and development are also becoming more important, and the education levels of the human resources of populations are increasing. The work forces in the industrialized countries have dramatically higher levels of educational training and more experience in democratic participation than the rural immigrant laborers discussed by the early production theorists. Skill surpluses, when combined with rigidly hierarchical organizational systems, lead to dissatisfaction, boredom, or disengagement from work. Furthermore, the present base of installed capital equipment

*We acknowledge that redistribution of income both within countries and between countries—an international Keynesianism discussed by Meade (1987) and Piore and Sable (1984)—would reduce the overcapacity problem, but we think our argument would still be relevant.

cries out for workers skilled enough to obtain the maximum yield from this expensive investment. The productivity of capital in the United States has not increased for decades (U.S. Office of Technology Assessment 1986); most of the effects of automation in this country have merely been to replace expensive labor with expensive equipment.

At the same time that these developments have been taking place, there has been a contrasting change in the form of a major expansion of the first industrial revolution, driven by the dramatic consolidation of enterprises around the world. The global economy has created a division of labor on an international scale. Ironically, many of the new technologies that have made global communication possible (such as software, computer chips, and sensor systems) are themselves suited to small-scale production and often do not technically require the vast organization or expenditures for production that mass automobile production, steel mills, or railroads require. A growing number of management theorists see small organizations, often combined in networks, as a more effective form for production in areas of future economic growth (Piore and Sable 1984; Starr 1989). The goal of market domination by global multinational corporations, however, and the international competition for job opportunities are leading to enterprise consolidation regardless of the costs to productivity or psychosocial well-being.

Overall, it is remarkable that our conventional principles for work organization have been successful to a fault. They have yielded productivity increases that have so far outstripped demand that for many they have led to job insecurity. Extreme division of labor has limited skill development, autonomy, and social relationships to the point of creating some very undesirable new environments. When the original principle of endless division of labor is seen in the light of its production of psychosocial outcomes, the need for alternative models of organizing work becomes clear.

We believe that significantly increased importance for the psychosocial aspects of work is common to all the transformations just described. To produce new models of work organization for these new conditions that will be genuinely useful in practice, there will need to be not just separate breakthroughs within disciplines such as medicine, engineering, and the social sciences, but coordinated changes around new tools developed using the combined wisdom of multiple disciplines. Our own attempt in this direction will begin in chapter 2, with presentation of an initially simple model formulated from the two most salient characteristics of the psychosocial work environment for predicting the health and behavioral consequences of work: specialization of labor and psychological work demands. A model based on these aspects of work could be a means of communication for the major professional groups who must be involved in future job redesign processes. The inclusion of the demands of work addresses issues raised by productivity-oriented engineers and health-oriented physicians and other medical professionals, and the issues of task authority and skill use address concerns of organizationally conscious managers, industrial psychologists, sociologists, and job redesign professionals. We do not claim that our theoretical model explains everything, and indeed we have been obliged to make a number of expansions of its original formulation since the 1970s. Nevertheless, we will defend both its scientific validity and its use as a tool to encourage the first stages of communication between the groups of problem solvers mentioned above. Ultimately, its defense is that it is at least one attempt at developing a new vocabulary for the psychosocial side of work that is suitable for beginning policy discussions in an area where most issues are still not clearly articulated.

After presentation of the basic model in chapter 2, the topics in the book proceed in an order that moves from the micro level to the macro level. In chapter 3, we draw connections between the environmental perspectives discussed in chapter 2 and the psychological and physiological processes that explain our heart disease findings reported in chapter 4. The second half of the book is devoted to work reconstruction. The sequence of the topics we address in the second part of the book is determined by the level of the work reconstruction strategy involved. We start with task-level job redesign issues in chapter 5 and move to successively larger-scale work transformation challenges in chapters 6 through 10. In addressing issues of how to change work, we integrate our own findings with the products of two decades of job redesign experience and with currently emerging strategies of preventive health care at the work site. In chapter 5, we examine the economic consequences of job stress, review models of motivation, examine evidence for the effectiveness of these models as a basis for the redesign of work tasks, and develop a new definition of productivity. Chapter 6 reviews job redesign processes from the point of view of health promotion. What can the occupational health team do to improve job design? Chapter 7 examines methodologies for job redesign at the organizational level. Chapter 8 considers the effects of new technology on humane job redesign. Chapter 9 examines political strategies for different groups of occupations. Finally, chapter 10 explores the broader social and market context of our original task-based model and speculates on the implications for the nature of the future economy of implementing—or failing to implement—our models of work reconstruction.

2

The Psychosocial Work Environment

In this chapter, we demonstrate how a model based on the psychological demands of work, skill use, and task control can predict a broad range of health and behavioral consequences of the structure of work. Our management models in chapter 1 outlined the organizationally determined relationship between the breadth of skills workers could use on the job and their authority over decision making. We call these two concepts skill discretion and decision authority and combine them into the single measure—decision latitude—used in the figure below, along with psychological demands. Later in the chapter, we augment this model with measures of physical demands and social interaction at work, to complete our description of what we call the psychosocial work environment.

Psychological Demands and Decision Latitude:
The Demand/Control Model

We begin with the two-dimensional model shown in figure 2–1. Four distinctly different kinds of psychosocial work experience are generated by the interactions of high and low levels of psychological demands and decision latitude: *high-strain* jobs, *active* jobs, *low-strain* jobs, and *passive* jobs. We will look at each of these types of experience in more detail.

HIGH-STRAIN JOBS

Our first prediction, now familiar, is that the most adverse reactions of psychological strain (fatigue, anxiety, depression, and physical illness)

FIGURE 2–1
Psychological demand/decision latitude model

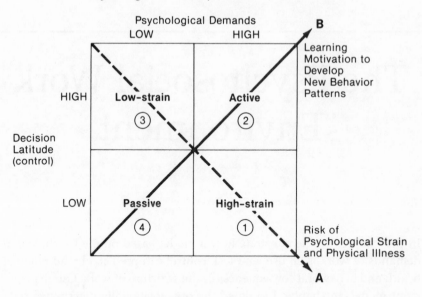

SOURCE: Karasek 1979. Used with permission of *Administrative Science Quarterly*; © 1979 by Cornell University.

occur when the psychological demands of the job are high and the worker's decision latitude in the task is low—the lower right-hand cell in figure 2–1. A simple descriptive example can illuminate the two-stage process by which environmentally induced psychological strain develops. One of the authors used to get his lunch at a sandwich shop across the street from Columbia University, in New York City. The street was on a steep hill with fast, heavy truck traffic. On the way to lunch, he would start to dash across the street, at the same time taking the precaution of checking for trucks that might be heading toward him. If he saw a truck out of the corner of his eye, it represented a new, very high-priority psychological demand (or *stressor*) and put him in an alert state of arousal (*stress*). Such a state, of course, is biologically essential to ensure the immediate physical and psychological response necessary to avoid being injured—in this case to get out of the way of the truck.

Consider now a second element of the situation. Suppose that just as the researcher notices a fast truck dangerously close and is alerted to get out of its path, his environment introduces a *constraint* on this optimal course of action—for example, his foot slides into a pothole, throwing him off balance and foreclosing his escape strategy. In this situation, our researcher would experience the dramatically more extreme response of *psychological strain*, the result of high demands combined with low control over environmental circumstances. The result is a psychological state of acute fear or terror and a sharp increase in heart rate and adrenaline response. In most cases the story would end as a near miss, with the truck driver swerving to avoid the researcher. The psychological strain experienced by the researcher, however—a distinctly unpleasant, unproductive, and in the long term unhealthy state—could last for hours. This residual strain (see diagonal A, figure 2–1) reaction contrasts with and is of much longer duration than the normal arousal reaction. A normal reaction would have occurred if the researcher had caught a glimpse of the truck and rapidly dashed out of its path, unhindered by the pothole. This latter, totally functional "fight/ flight" arousal and response would have effectively used up the potential energy supplied by psychophysiological mechanisms by translating it into action, soon leaving the researcher back in a state of equilibrium, unstressed and ready to enjoy lunch and go back to work. The implied model of the high-strain situation is that the arousal energy is transformed into damaging, unused residual strain because of an environmentally based constraint on the person's optimal response (see Henry and Cassel 1969), processes we will discuss in greater detail in chapter 3.

We hypothesize that the strain phenomenon occurs, albeit in less acute form, in too many jobs in the modern world. For example, the assembly line worker has almost every behavior rigidly constrained. What occurs in a situation of increased demands such as speed-up is not just the constructive response of arousal but the often hopeless, long-lasting, and negatively experienced response of residual psychological strain, often appearing as aggressive behavior or social withdrawal (Terkel 1972). In Whyte's classic study of restaurant workers (1948), during a heavy lunchtime rush, it was the waitresses who could not control their customers by "getting the jump on them," or who had no possibility of letting off steam at other employees, who experienced the greatest burden of strain, sometimes leaving the floor in tears.

Kerckhoff and Back (1968) described garment workers under heavy deadline pressure and the subsequent threat of layoff, concluding that when the actions normally needed to cope with job pressures cannot be taken, the most severe behavioral symptoms of strain—fainting, hysteria, social contagion—occur. The same might be true of the white-collar telephone service representative, who operates under bureaucratic rules that rigidly limit the responses that may be given to an irate customer. When a higher output quota is imposed, the responses go beyond arousal to psy-chological strain and in the long term, we claim, to stress-related illness such as heart disease.

When the objective requirements of a situation cannot be routinely dis-charged, any one of a full range of unintended outcomes may occur, depend-ing on the severity of the requirements, from simple symptoms of fatigue in the case of low-level stressors to basic personality breakdown in the case of inescapable wartime trauma, which was studied by Grinker and Spiegel (1945). It is not only freedom of action in accomplishing the formal work task that relieves strain; it may also be the freedom to engage in the informal rituals—the coffee break, the smoke break, or even fidgeting—that serve as supplementary tension release mechanisms during the work day (Csikszentmihalyi 1975). These are often social activities with other workers (as will be seen in an expansion of this two-dimensional model with a third measure, social support, later in the chapter)—precisely those activities elim-inated as "wasted motions" and "soldiering" by Frederick Taylor's methods. Lack of freedom for informal activity or relaxation, one form of constraint, may be the reason for the high frequency of psychological complaints re-ported by workers who have no freedom to engage in informal coping pro-cesses on machine-paced jobs (see diverse perspectives in Salvendy and Smith 1981). Displeasure with rigid rhythms of working life on the tradi-tional auto assembly line was reported by Walker and Guest (1952) and Kornhauser (1965). Shaiken, Kuhn, and Herzenberg (1983a), however, found that the unpredictable and uncontrollable stops on the assembly line at a highly computerized automated auto body production facility also pro-duced complaints. In the words of one worker, "What you're doing is you're going and stopping, going and going, running and going. You know what that does to your insides? It changes your whole system" (p. 49).

Firth (1939), studying Polynesian fishermen, found that the periodic spiritual rituals and chants that punctuated their working routine alleviated strain at times of high anxiety, such as when fish were scarce and food re-serves were low. The rituals occurred in a social context, during a relatively unconstrained portion of the fishing task. When these internal coping mechanisms were delayed, there was a massive increase in the fishermen's anxiety. When such rituals were prevented altogether (for example, when Christianity was introduced) in a neighboring primitive tribe of the Maori in New Zealand, Firth found a comprehensive collapse of their production process. It took almost a century to rebuild the spirit of communal coopera-tion to the point where it could again sustain large-scale economic activity. Others have also found that without periodic returns to equilibrium through relaxation activities, no additional work can be effectively accom-plished and disorganized activity results (Dement 1969).

ACTIVE JOBS

Some of the most challenging situations, typical of professional work, call for the highest levels of performance, but without negative psychological strain. These are the active jobs in the upper right-hand corner of figure 2–1. Examples are provided by surgeons performing difficult operations, or rock climbers struggling to scale an unmastered mountain peak, both described by Csikszentmihalyi (1975), or by professional basketball players when both they and their opponents are at their best, described by Russell and Branch (1979). Such situations, while intensely demanding, involve workers in activities over which they feel a large measure of control, the freedom to use all available skills. Csikszentmihalyi describes this kind of activity as flow. Bill Russell describes how it was experienced by a professional basketball player:

It usually began when three or four of the ten guys on the floor would heat up. . . . The feeling would spread to the other guys, and we'd all levitate. . . . The game would be in the white heat of competition, and yet somehow I wouldn't feel competitive. . . . I'd be putting out the maximum effort, straining, coughing up parts of my lungs as we ran, and yet I never felt the pain. The game would move so quickly that every fake, cut and pass would be surprising, and yet nothing could surprise me. . . . During those spells I could almost sense how the next play would develop, and where the next shot would be taken. . . . My premonitions would be consistently correct and I always felt then that I not only knew all the Celtics by heart, but also that I knew all the opposing players, and that they all knew me. There have been many times in my career when I felt moved or joyful, but these were moments when I had chills pulsing up and down my spine. (p. 40)

We call this kind of job, in which control is high and psychological demand is also high, the *active job*, because research in both Swedish and American populations has shown this group of workers to be the most active in leisure and popular activity outside of work, in spite of heavy work demands (Goiten and Seashore 1980; Karasek 1976, 1978). From such jobs we predict an optimistic set of psychosocial outcomes—learning and growth—that are conducive to high productivity. Of course, there must be some limits to this phenomenon: simple fatigue ultimately provides an upper limit, as we shall see in chapter 3. While even the professional basketball player and the surgeon (see also Payne et al. 1984) may have extreme peaks of stimulation only rarely, we suspect that the most challenging jobs contain them to a greater degree than average, leading to the high levels of job satisfaction we find in high demand, high control jobs (Karasek 1979), as we discuss in chapter 5.

Because much of the energy aroused by the active job's many stressors (the challenges of the job) is translated into action through effective problem solving, there is little residual strain to cause disturbance, and we predict only average psychological strain. This conversion of energy into action is also one necessary prerequisite of an effective learning process. Given the freedom to decide what is the most effective course of action in response to a stressor, the individual can test the efficacy of the chosen course of action, reinforcing it if it has worked or modifying it if it has failed.

Low-Strain Jobs

It is interesting to note that the highly desirable state just described is hardly a situation of relaxation, as necessary as the latter is. Relaxation is more closely represented by the third quadrant of figure 2–1, situations with few psychological demands and high levels of control. This sounds idyllically leisurely for the workplace, almost too good to be true, yet it does characterize certain jobs, such as the jobs of repair personnel (see figure 2–2). For this group of workers we also predict lower than average levels of residual psychological strain and risk of illness, because job decision latitude allows the individual to respond to each challenge optimally, and because there are relatively few challenges to begin with. This *low-strain* job category marks the other end of the residual psychological strain diagonal, labeled A in figure 2–1.

This quadrant implies that there may be a sort of low-stress utopia of healthful jobs that have escaped the critical eyes of journalists and academic researchers concerned with documenting society's problems. These people are actually made both happier and healthier than average by work. Not only should this be a point of praise for industrial society, but it might be a source of solutions for problems of psychological strain. Of course, the existence of unknown heavens at the opposite end of the spectrum from the job-stress hells we have described serves to illuminate the huge potential for inequitable distribution of the psychosocial rewards of work, in much the same way that the economic rewards are unequally distributed. It is not, however, the same pattern of unequal distribution, as we see at the end of this chapter.

Passive Jobs

Seligman, in his book *Helplessness* (1975), describes another set of situations that are associated with very nonenergetic responses but that have none of the desirable aspects of relaxation of the low-strain jobs we have discussed. The following is his account of a professional-level employee, previously involved in very active jobs, whose current unemployment has lead to apathetic behavior because of challenges that seemed completely beyond his control:

> Mel [who was usually outgoing and persuasive] had been a rising business executive [with twenty years of high executive achievement]. Up until a year ago, he had been in charge of production for a multimillion-dollar company involved in the space program. When the government decreased its financial support of space research, he lost his job, and was forced to take a new executive position in another city, in a company he described as "backbiting." After six miserable and lonely months he quit. For a month he sat listlessly around the house, and made no effort to find work; the slightest annoyance drove him into a rage; he was unsocial and withdrawn. Finally his wife prevailed on Mel to take some vocational guidance tests. . . . [The test results] revealed that he had a low tolerance for frustration, that he was unsociable, that he was incapable of taking on responsibility, and that routine, prescribed work best fit his personality. The vocational guidance company recommended that he become a worker on an assembly line. (p. 75)

The last cell in figure 2–1 represents situations of low demand and low control—what we call a *passive job* in a work context—in which a gradual atrophying of learned skills and abilities may occur. While Mel's situation, described above, is again extreme, its demotivating elements occur with disturbing frequency in the U.S. and Swedish work forces, as the findings on skill underutilization in chapters 1 and 5 indicate. It must be noted that Seligman uses the example of Mel to illuminate the rapidly induced but long-lasting consequences of high-strain situations; the initial situation was highly demanding, with an uncontrollable threat of job loss. We have observed similar consequences, however, in many cases in which the worker was not only not required to meet significant challenges but also not allowed to pursue any activity energetically (for example, to write a great epic novel during slack time at work) or encountered a long series of rejected initiatives on the job. These two different interpretations of passive response highlight the difference between dynamic and static model predictions. We will try to reconcile these perspectives in chapters 3 and 5.

The passive job setting is the second major psychosocial work problem we can describe with our model. Neither the nature of the injuries it induces nor the strategies for eliminating it are the same as for the high-strain job. We predict that the phenomenon of negative learning or gradual loss of previously acquired skills will lead to lower-than-average levels of leisure and political activity outside the job (Goiten and Seashore 1980; Karasek 1976, 1978). Furthermore, lost skills, lack of job challenges, and environmentally rigid restrictions preventing workers from testing their own ideas for improving the work process can only mean an extremely unmotivating job setting and result in long-term loss of work motivation and productivity. Shaiken, Kuhn, and Herzenberg (1983a) provide an example in the de-skilling of trained machinists who have become "machine-tenders," waiting to repair broken machines in automated computer-based manufacturing firms. In the words of one worker,

> You don't have to think anymore. You lose touch with what you're actually doing because everything's been told. You're not a set of documents, you're not your tapes, and you're not a set of instructions as to how to set the machine up and run it, and I believe you yourself become a robot because you don't get to use your mind. (p. 28)

For the passive job, we hypothesize only an average level of psychological strain and illness risk (as in the case of active work). Although each stressor exposure would result in substantial residual psychological strain (just as in the high-strain circumstance), the low demands of this work situation mean that fewer stressors are confronted.

The four simple situations described in the last several pages are just combinations of high and low job-decision latitude and psychological demands, yet each has significant implications for this book's main themes of health and productivity. The active and passive jobs, taken together, trace diagonal B on figure 2–1, which maps the likelihood of learning and increased motivation. The position of diagonal B implies that these skill acquisition mechanisms are independent of (that is, orthogonal to) the residual psychological strain mechanism discussed in our first hypothesis, diagonal A. Overall, we now have a model with two major psychological mechanisms, utilizing just two broad dimensions of work activity (what Southwood [1978] calls an interaction model). The goal of the examples above has been to illuminate the importance of combinations of psychological demands and decision latitude in predicting health and behavior.

By contrast, many of the traditions of research in industrial sociology, industrial psychology, and epidemiology upon which our research has been built have dealt with simpler unidimensional models. Literature reviews of the mid-1970s (Karasek 1976, 1979) showed that the great body of research predicting work stress was based on the psychological demands of work alone and gave relatively little mention to control at the workplace. (One exception was the work of Kornhauser [1965].) Control received relatively little attention in the "life stress" research tradition (Dohrenwend and Dohrenwend 1974) and in the widely utilized perspective on "role overload, role ambiguity, and role conflict" (Kahn et al. 1964), and it has not been emphasized in the current "burnout" literature (Maslach 1982) in the United States.

The importance of control at the workplace had been clearly recognized in the job satisfaction literature (reviewed by McCright 1988), but here too the emphasis had been narrow, especially in U.S. industrial psychology. The closely related measures of task autonomy and skill variety were mainly used to predict job satisfaction, absenteeism, and productivity, with limited additions reflecting the worker's social relationship to the job. The job satisfaction literature had made little mention of the demands of work, and thus health outcomes were rarely addressed as a central concern. A major complaint was that this research tradition did not have a strong theoretical foundation. For example, Turner and Lawrence (1965), who began much of this work had no explicit unifying theory but merely tried to categorize the most necessary elements of a task. Hackman and Oldham's widely used measure of perceived task characteristics, the Job Diagnostic Survey (1975; Hackman and Lawler 1971), had a more elaborate theory. It was based upon expectancy theory, which means that the task attributes would be most important for predicting outcomes when they were most congruent with one's "needs," but this begged the question of determining needs exogenously. A variety of critiques have claimed that the theoretical basis of this research was too vague and the findings too narrow (Aldag, Barr, and Brief 1981; Karasek 1976, 1979; McCright 1988; Taber, Beehr, and Walsh 1985).

What research findings could be used to bridge the gaps between theories to construct broader models? One unifying finding, which led to Karasek's development of the demand/control model (Karasek 1976, 1979; Karasek, Russell, and Theorell 1982), was Dement's (1969) observation that vital relaxation related to REM dreaming was inhibited if animal subjects were placed on a treadmill, with actions as constrained as they are for assembly line workers after periods of exposure to extreme psychological stressors. Such a combination of environmental circumstances eventually led to mental collapse. The combined actions of environmental stressors and environmental control were essential in producing these effects. Another unifying finding was that demanding job situations involving high levels of control seemed to encourage competency building outside of work, as Meisner (1971) observed for carryover of job responsibility to active leisure and Kohn and Schooler (1973, 1982) observed for the development of intellectual capabilities. This is, of course, an entirely different behavioral outcome.

Because challenge, or mental arousal, on one hand clearly seemed necessary for effective learning and on the other was a clear contributor to psychological strain, control became a crucial moderating variable that determined whether positive learning consequences or negative strain consequences would accompany environmental demands. Control was not the only moderator; the level of psychological demands also "moderated" effects, determining which of two significantly different types of problems would result from low control: passive withdrawal (discussed by Maier and Seligman [1976]) or psychological strain. A model combining these two dimensions was clearly needed. Frankenhaeuser and Gardell's study of sawmill workers in 1976 had also explored the effects of demands and control, but they utilized Kahn's (1981) framework of qualitative and quantitative "underload and overload" to retain a unidimensional perspective on stress occurrence, in keeping with the early traditions of Levi (1972a) and Selye (1976).

There was also ample political support for the broader scope of the demand control model from several countries. In 1974, at a major German union conference on humanization of work, Schumann claimed that beyond wages and job security the two most important issues in working life were stress in the workplace and the possibility of developing new skills at work. These priorities have also been reflected in a booklet issued by the Swedish Metal Workers Union on the future goals for working life (Metallarbetarförbundet 1985). House and Cottington (1986) also presented a listing of job dimensions necessary to predict a broad conception of health that included task control, psychological demands, physical stressors, and social interactions.*

Occupational Distributions of Psychosocial
Job Characteristics

We can make our model of job characteristics more concrete by associating different levels of decision latitude and psychological demands with well-known occupations such as butcher, baker, or teacher. Such associations could also help confirm the objective validity of our job dimensions and identify more specifically populations with desirable and undesirable job situations. Occupations, like guilds or unions, represent relatively homogeneous and distinct social realities in the world of work (Lysgaard 1961), because of the finite number of labor markets and the institutional structures for apprenticeship and career development. Occupational categories can

*In the four available U.S. governmental job classification systems based on expert ratings, job control is included in all four, while psychological demands and social relations are each included in two of the four (Karasek, Schwartz, and Theorell 1982).

therefore efficiently aggregate a great deal of information about jobs. A category such as "baker" offers a gestalt of easily remembered, if diverse, information about baking: heated ovens with pleasant aromas, skilled but repetitive work, appreciative direct customer contacts, early hours and long days, and so on.

A joint analytic system based on job dimensions and occupational categories requires two elements: first, sets of occupational categories that are widely accepted by researchers, and second, large, nationally representative empirical data bases with job characteristics information to measure the job dimensions. In the first occupational plot below, the decision latitude dimension is composed of an equally weighted combination of decision autonomy and skill discretion questions (see p. 58 for a discussion of this combination). Typical questions include: "Do you have a lot of say on your job?"; "Do you have freedom to make decisions?" (decision authority); "Do you keep learning new things?"; "Is there variety in your tasks?" (skill discretion). Psychological demands are measured by questions such as: "Is there excessive work?"; "Must you work fast (or hard)?" For our job characteristics data base in this chapter and for some of the studies noted in chapters 3 and 4 we use what is still the largest U.S. national survey of detailed job characteristics: the combined sample of individuals surveyed for the U.S. Department of Labor's Quality of Employment Surveys (QES) in 1969, 1972, and 1977 by the Institute for Social Research at the University of Michigan (Quinn and Staines 1979). For our analysis we use a modified version of the 1970 U.S. Census occupation codes, which provide over 200 categories at the detailed three-digit level (an analogous Swedish system used in chapter 4 is based on a version of the international occupational codes). More detailed information on the composition of the job dimension scales, the occupational codes, and the detailed plots of all occupations are provided in the appendix. (The occupational plots in this chapter are based on thirty-eight occupations, selected to be broadly representative, and covering about 33 percent of the work force [Karasek 1989a; see also p. 279].)

In figure 2–2 we plot decision latitude and psychological demands for men and women in a variety of jobs, using data from the QES and U.S. Census occupation codes just described. These dimensions are plotted using interpretable scale units: one unit equals one standard deviation of variation on that job dimension at the individual level of the U.S. national population in the nationally representative QES surveys. The origin point for each plot corresponds to the individual-level population means on each dimension. These scales also give us a much needed reference standard for variations in psychosocial job characteristics (the full U.S. population variation), allowing useful quantitative comparisons to be made. The dot size reflects the number of people in that occupation in the QES sample. The accuracy of the occupation locations is discussed in the appendix.

We find major differences in the psychosocial character of people's occupational experiences in each demand/control quadrant of figure 2–2. The upper right-hand quadrant, where psychological demands and decision latitude are both high, clearly seems to be the locus of high-prestige occupations (the active jobs): lawyer and judge, nurse, physician, teacher, engineer, managers of all kinds—and farmer. We also find a predominance of male occupations in this quadrant. The research above showed that these people "burn the candle at both ends" with active work and active leisure but maintain average health; they even reported less tiredness than the high-strain group. They receive higher incomes and enjoy the highest psychic rewards from work; they have by far the highest job satisfaction (Karasek 1979; Kauppinen-Toropainen 1981).

Low- and middle-status occupations may be found rather uniformly dispersed among the other three psychosocial quadrants. In the high-decision-latitude/low-demands quadrant (that is, leisurely work), we find self-paced occupations such as repairman, lineman, and natural scientist—again a predominance of male jobs. While these occupations are a relative psychosocial paradise with low levels of psychological strain, as we see in the next section (p. 47), there is one sobering note: in spite of all the freedom from fatigue, our research showed only average levels of participation in political and leisure activity and low levels of mass policy and labor activity in Sweden (Karasek 1976). This group with few problems appears to have little motivation to promote active social change through collective means, either for their own sake or for the sake of others.

In the low-demand/low-decision-latitude quadrant, the passive jobs, we find sales clerks, billing clerks, transport operatives, and some nonpublic contact service personnel, watchmen and janitors. In both Swedish and U.S. data, these jobs are associated with social and political withdrawal. Interestingly, this group in national Swedish data bases (Karasek 1976) has by far the lowest level of sleeping problems (1.9 percent versus 8.0 percent for the full male working population). The person in the passive job may inhabit a stimulation-deprived world that allows the development of one capability almost to perfection: the ability to sleep.

Finally, we examine the high-strain quadrant that we hypothesize to be highest in psychosocial health risk (see p. 47). The occupations with low decision latitude and high psychological work load are found to be machine-paced operatives (assembler, cutting operative, inspector, freight handler), as well as low-status service operatives (such as waiter and cook). Most notable are the large numbers of occupations populated primarily by

FIGURE 2–2

The occupational distribution of psychological demands and decision latitude
(U.S. males and females, N = 4,495)

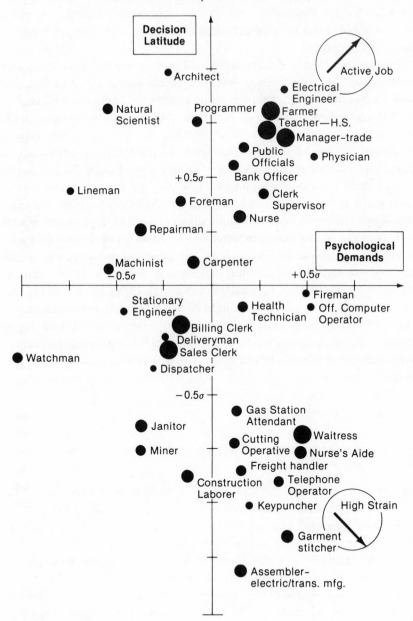

SOURCE: Data from Quality of Employment Surveys 1969, 1972, 1977. Figure reprinted from Karasek
1989a; used with permission of Baywood Publishing Co.

women (garment stitcher, waitress, telephone operator, and other office automation jobs). The assembly line worker in the automotive and electrical equipment industries is so low in decision latitude that publications of our materials have occasionally omitted this occupation—Charlie Chaplin's classic symbol of the stress of industrial automation—to maintain the symmetry of the diagram.

Our quadrant analysis certainly would not predict that executives and professionals have the highest levels of psychological strain in the U.S. work force, and the national population studies we cite in the next section empirically confirm that they do not. Their active jobs place them in a middle psychosocial risk category. "Executive stress" exists, of course, but it is the bossed, not the bosses who experience the most stress in our society in general. The classic reason advanced for executive stress is the burden of decision making (Janis and Mann 1977), but we find that constraints on decision making, not decision making per se, is the major problem, for most jobs. While the problem can certainly affect executives, it primarily affects workers in low-status jobs with almost no freedom for decisions (Zaleznik, de Vries, and Howard 1977). We have also observed, however, that at the very highest status levels decision making may become a significant contributor to strain instead of a moderator (Karasek 1979). In view of the fact that the vast majority of workers might be better off with more decision opportunity and at least some executives would be better off with fewer stressful decisions, the implication of these dual findings is that both executives and workers would be better off with a more nearly equal sharing of decision power.

A Comparison of Men's and Women's Jobs

In general, the evidence cited in this book is more often derived from male subjects. While research on women in occupations is rapidly developing, it still has not generated as much theory and evidence as has been accumulated for men, particularly in the occupational health area. This omission must be rectified in the future, however, because we can see major differences in typical male and female work experiences in our QES data.

We can make a simple comparison in sex differences in the distribution of job characteristics in the United States by examining the compacted plot of U.S. Census occupational means for men and women separately in figure 2–3. A comprehensive and scientifically precise comparison of men's and women's job characteristic profiles for the same occupation is difficult,

FIGURE 2–3
*Comparison of psychosocial job characteristics
for males and females in the U.S. population*

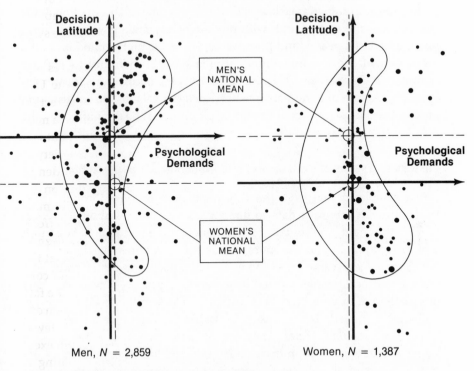

Men, *N* = 2,859   Women, *N* = 1,387

SOURCE: Data from Quality of Employment Surveys 1969, 1972, 1977.

because there are relatively few occupations with large proportions of both sexes. This disparity itself suggests that the recruitment or allocation process by which men and women come to occupy particular jobs may be the major cause of the sex differences we observe in job characteristics. A more detailed discussion of demographic differences can be found in Schwartz, Pieper, and Karasek (1988).

Women's average level of decision latitude is markedly lower than men's. Women's mean relative to the men's scale is shown in figure 2–3; it confirms similar results from other studies on job authority (Wolf and Fligstein 1979a, 1979b). Men are far more likely than women to have high control over their work process at the task level. Psychological demands at work do not differ markedly for men and women, although they appear somewhat higher for women. A major sex difference shown in figure 2–3 is the negative correlation between decision latitude and demands for women ($r = -.24$): the majority of women's high-psychological-demand jobs also have low decision latitude. By contrast, men's high-demand jobs are generally accompanied by somewhat higher decision latitude, with a small positive correlation ($r = .08$). Thus there is a much higher proportion of high-strain jobs, and a lower proportion of active jobs, in the women's population than in the men's (Cranor, Karasek, and Carlin 1981). The full occupational distribution resembles a peanut, with predominantly male jobs in the active upper end of the peanut and predominantly female high-strain jobs in the lower end of the peanut. Similar results have been found in Finland (Kauppinen-Toropainen 1981). Since many of the occupations for women in the high-strain quadrant are newly created clerical jobs, this distribution raises a warning signal about the future psychosocial health impacts of the office automation revolution.

HISTORICAL TRENDS IN JOB CONTENT AND INDUSTRIAL DEVELOPMENT

Our sample, drawn from the U.S. population in 1969 through 1977, hardly provides us with data to directly test hypotheses about historical trends in changing job content.* Examination of the occupational distribution in figure 2–2 (and the more detailed plot in appendix figure A–1), however, suggests some impressionistic clues about long-term trends. Several current occupations (circled in appendix figure A–1) were certainly more common in preindustrial times: sailor, blacksmith, peddler, forester, millwright. Indeed, this group sounds like a cast of characters from Chaucer's *Canterbury Tales*. They are leisurely jobs in our modern-day frame of reference: high in decision latitude and low in psychological demands, although the physical demands of most of these occupations were probably quite high in earlier times. On the other hand, we find the newer jobs of the industrialized era in the high-strain quadrant, diagonally opposite in figure 2–2. The new high-strain industrialized proletariat is located here: punch press operators, assemblers, garment stitchers, office machine operators, and freight and material handlers. These occupations are undeniably newer than the group above and were often designed in the context of the rigid task specification and time pacing of Taylor's *Principles of Scientific Management*. Many of these occupations are lower in decision latitude and higher in demands (that is, higher in psychological strain) than even the traditional peasant occupation of the past, whose modern counterpart is the farm laborer (circled in the "passive" quadrant in appendix figure A–1). Of course, these rough observations about historical changes are only conjecture, because much has changed in conditions of work that transcends these two task characteristics and even the job content of occu-

*For limited computations of such job content changes from 1969 to 1977, see Schwartz, Karasek, and Pieper 1982. For skill discretion, where questions are the same in all three QES surveys, there is essentially no change from 1969 to 1977 (see footnote, p. 336).

pations may change over time. Nevertheless, the observed differences are substantial: they span our entire occupational spectrum.

These observations are empirically congruent with the theoretical discussion in chapter 1 of job evolution due to our conventional models of production organization, which has led to higher psychological stress. Physical exertion appears to have been replaced, as expected, by higher psychological demands, one trade-off of the industrial revolution. The substantial overall decline in decision latitude, in spite of increasing formal education (Braverman 1974; Dubnoff 1978; Eriksson and Åberg 1984; Spenner 1979), we would attribute to the effects of the division of labor. Such historical changes may have diminished the incidence of some diseases in society by reducing the risk of physical exhaustion and injury, but they may actually have increased others (Sterling and Eyer 1981), although again, lack of data from earlier eras makes such inferences highly speculative. Cardiovascular illness may have increased since the nineteenth century because of such factors, particularly since several types of dynamic physical exertion that appear to be protective for cardiovascular illness have also disappeared. It should be noted that such changes in the psychosocial character of work would also be largely missed in the most common current historical analyses of occupational mobility, which focus primarily on income-related changes.

Findings for Psychosocial Health and Behavior with the Demand/Control Model

Does the empirical evidence support the demand/control model? We will first examine the findings that relate to the two hypotheses expressed as diagonals A and B in figure 2–1.

Evidence for the Psychological Strain Mechanism

Evidence confirming the psychological strain hypothesis has been found in a number of industrialized countries in studies using nationally representative data bases. Using random national samples of the male work force in both the United States and Sweden, Karasek (1979) found that the model was associated with a fourfold variation in depression in the United States in 1972 and Sweden in 1968 (figure 2–4d) and with similar variations in a longitudinal study of the Swedish population from 1968 to 1974. Figure 2–4a and b show that similar depression associations exist for males

FIGURE 2–4(a-e)
Job characteristics and psychological strain:
multiple symptom indicators

Number on vertical bar is percentage in each job category with symptoms.

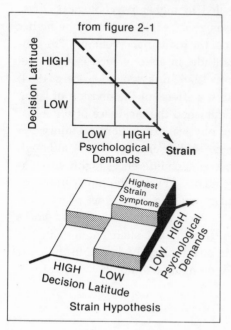

Strain Hypothesis

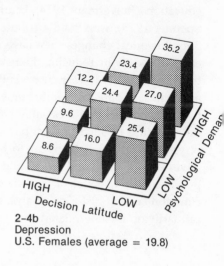

2–4b
Depression
U.S. Females (average = 19.8)

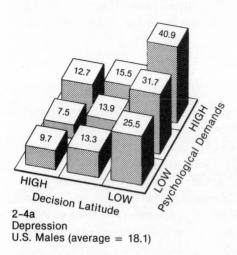

2–4a
Depression
U.S. Males (average = 18.1)

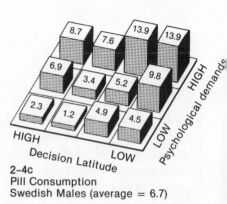

2–4c
Pill Consumption
Swedish Males (average = 6.7)

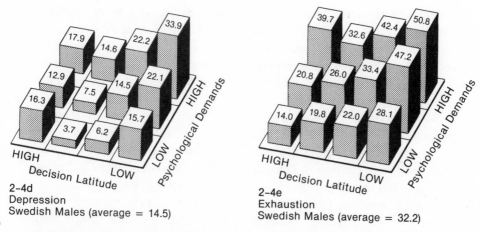

2–4d
Depression
Swedish Males (average = 14.5)

2–4e
Exhaustion
Swedish Males (average = 32.2)

NOTE: For discussion of depression indicator used in 2–4a and 2–4b, see p. 49*n*. For U.S. males, *N* = 1,769; for U.S. females, *N* = 925; for Swedish males, *N* = 1,896. Cell sizes, reading from left to right, are as follows (see p. 49*n*), for U.S. males—high demands: 228, 181, 174; medium demands: 199, 223, 139; low demands: 65, 250, 204; for U.S. females—high demands: 90, 94, 102; medium demands: 104, 135, 85; low demands: 117, 131, 67; for Swedish males, see Karasek 1979.

SOURCE: Data for U.S. males and females from Quality of Employment Surveys, 1972, 1977. Data for Swedish males from LNU 1968. Figures 2–4c, 2–4d, and 2–4e redrawn from Karasek 1979. Figures 2–4c, 2–4d, and 2–4e used with permission of *Administrative Science Quarterly*; © 1979 by Cornell University.

and females in the U.S. national QES data in 1972 and 1977 using the decision latitude and psychological demand scales discussed in the previous section.* Men and women are combined in later analyses; see p. 72. Similar associations for exhaustion and job satisfaction were found in a large representative sample of male and female workers in Finland (Kauppinen-Toropainen 1981) and for a combined measure of exhaustion and depression for both males and females in a nationally representative study of men and women in the Federal Republic of Germany (Braun and Hollander 1988). Figure 2–4 illustrates the breadth of the psychological strain findings: moderately severe forms of depression, exhaustion, pill consumption (as well as absenteeism and job dissatisfaction [Karasek 1979]). A subtle but consistent distinction has emerged in our review, however. Symptoms of exhaustion (figure 2–4e), rushed tempo, or simply reports of "feeling stressed" are more strongly related to psychological demands and thus relatively high for executives and professionals, while the more serious strain symptoms such as depression (figure 2–4a,b,d), loss of self-

*The depression indicator used here (Quinn and Staines 1979) is only one of the three measures from Karasek (1979). It measures response to eight pairs of life descriptions which if trichotomized as "good," "fair," and "poor" would indicate an average condition of fair to poor (interesting, enjoyable, worthwhile, friendly, full, hopeful, rewarding, brings out my best; versus boring, miserable, useless, lonely, empty, discouraging, disappointing, doesn't give me a chance). The decision latitude and psychological demand scales are trichotomized at .5 standard deviations above and below the mean for the male, female, and male plus female populations respectively. These cutpoints are also used in figure 1–2 on skill underutilization.

esteem, and physical illness are more strongly associated with low decision latitude, a problem for low-status workers. The majority of these national studies are cross-sectional and relate self-reported questionnaire responses about jobs with self-reported measures of psychological strain, but some of the studies are longitudinal, and some also include more objective observer assessment of work situations.

Do these associations hold in more restricted groups, such as single occupations, or for white- and blue-collar workers separately?* Kasl (1989) and Ganster (1989) have reviewed the literature. There are a number of studies that specifically confirm the model across a wide variety of occupational groups: 1,500 mortgage loan clerical workers in seventy New York savings and loan associations (Turner 1980); 2,600 U.S. workers in three manufacturing assembly plants (Freeman and Jucker 1979, for some symptoms); 7,000 Danish slaughterhouse workers (Søndergaard-Kristensen and Lønnberg-Christensen 1983); German metal workers in a longitudinal study (Semmer and Frese 1988); and Swedish postal workers (Wahlstedt 1988).

The decision latitude measure is correlated with education and other measures of social class. The job strain construct is almost orthogonal to most social class measures, however, as we discuss at the end of this chapter, so social class confounding does not appear to be responsible for the above findings. Karasek (1976) found that controls for demographic and social class factors did not significantly reduce these associations in Sweden. This finding was confirmed for Swedish white-collar workers (Karasek, Gardell, and Lindell 1987). Confirming associations have been observed within both white-collar and blue-collar groups in the United States, Sweden, and other countries, although one group or the other often shows stronger associations in a particular study. Overall, it still remains unclear whether job strain associations are stronger among white-collar or blue-collar workers.† One reason why the associations might be weaker for high-level white-collar workers is given in Karasek (1979): for the very highest-status managers and professionals, decision making may become a significant demand in itself, as does skill acquisition (both "qualitative overloads"), a point further discussed by Aronsson (1987), Frese (1987), and for physicians by Theorell et al. (Om den psykosociala arbetsmiljön för

*When the investigations are narrowed to the point where the jobs investigated are exactly the same—for example, with garment stitchers all using the same machines in the same plant—then the variance in task-level decision latitude diminishes to zero and correlations disappear, just as would be predicted. Macro measures of workplace control remain important (Johnson, personal communication, 1986).

†Karasek (1981d) shows U.S. and Swedish white- and blue-collar confirmation; Karasek, Gardell, and Lindell (1987) show Swedish white-collar confirmation; Semmer and Frese (1988) show German blue-collar confirmation. Johnson (1986) finds substantially stronger blue-collar associations in Sweden, while Orth-Gomér et al. (1986) find stronger white-collar associations (both for heart disease).

läkare, 1988). So far the evidence is somewhat unclear. Among twenty-one white-collar occupations in Sweden, policeman, teacher, and local public administrator are the only ones that show substantial qualitative overloads (Lindell 1982). Weak associations have indeed been found for the model with teachers (Payne and Fletcher 1983) and cardiothoracic surgeons (Payne et al. 1984) as is predicted.

There has been substantial research on the related white-collar professional concern known as burnout (Paine 1982; Maslach and Pines 1977). There is general agreement that burnout has much in common with exhaustion and depression measures (Shinn, Rosario, and Chestnut 1984), but the effects of decision latitude are only beginning to be addressed. The primary focus has been on the social-emotional demands of client contact that service professionals face, which lead to depersonalization. Psychological demands and lack of social support were the primary predictors investigated. Until recently, levels of control were rarely initially addressed in this research on professional groups, who for the most part have relatively high levels of decision latitude. However, a study of Swedish physicians has shown that burnout indices are higher in physicians who report higher demands and lower control than in other physicians (Arnetz et al. 1987). Female general practitioners, who are closer to the lower clerk role than other physicians, interestingly show the highest burnout indices in this study. Similar findings for health care personnel have been made by Kanner, Kafry, and Pines (1978), who also emphasize that lack of positive job factors per se is an antecedent of burnout. A number of researchers (for example, Shinn, Rosario, and Chestnut [1984]) conclude that the professional's burnout problem cannot be solved by personal coping strategies alone and must involve organization policy changes. A common focus for change is bureaucratic rigidity, which is common in service industries and which certainly restricts decision latitude. In chapter 9 we try to compare job redesign strategies for professionals to those for other occupational groups.

Evidence for the Active Behavior Mechanism

Our second hypothesis concerns the learning of new patterns of behavior and skills on the basis of psychosocial job experience, learning for adults that would presumably accrue over a lifetime of work experience. Such experiences should be very important determinants of labor motivation and productivity on the job, and we will explore that association in chapter 5. We begin our empirical investigations in another area, however: leisure and political behavior that might be molded by years of job experience. This classic focus of adult socialization research (Frese 1982) has the advantage of pro-

FIGURE 2–5
Job characteristics, leisure, and political participation
(Swedish males, 1968, N = 1,466)

Number on vertical bar is percentage in each job category
with low active participation.

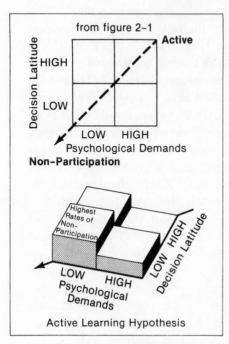

from figure 2–1

Active

HIGH

LOW

Decision Latitude

LOW   HIGH
Psychological Demands

Non-Participation

Highest Rates of Non-Participation

LOW   HIGH
Psychological Demands

LOW   HIGH
Decision Latitude

Active Learning Hypothesis

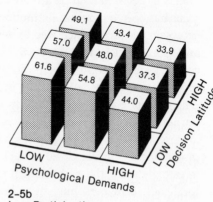

49.1
57.0   43.4
61.6   48.0   33.9
54.8   37.3
44.0

LOW
Psychological Demands   HIGH

HIGH   LOW
Decision Latitude

2–5b
Low Participation
in Political Activity

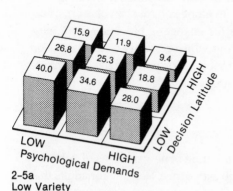

15.9
26.8   11.9
40.0   25.3   9.4
34.6   18.8
28.0

LOW
Psychological Demands   HIGH

HIGH   LOW
Decision Latitude

2–5a
Low Variety
in Leisure Activities

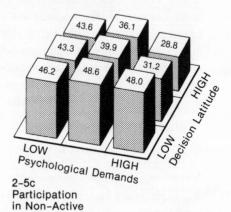

43.6   36.1
43.3   39.9   28.8
46.2   48.6   31.2
48.0

LOW
Psychological Demands   HIGH

HIGH   LOW
Decision Latitude

2–5c
Participation
in Non–Active
Leisure

NOTE: For discussion of non-active leisure indicator used in 2–5c, see p. 53n. Cell sizes, reading from left to right, are as follows—high decision latitude: 110, 191, 314; medium decision latitude: 194, 316, 154; low decision latitude: 52, 84, 50.

SOURCE: Redrawn from Karasek 1976, 1981e. © 1981 by John Wiley and Sons, Ltd. Reprinted by permission.

viding a look at behavior patterns when people are free to be themselves, unconstrained by work rules.

Figure 2–5 shows the findings of a test of the job strain and active-learning hypotheses using seven Swedish leisure indicators and two Swedish political activity indicators from the same national random sample discussed on p. 48 (Karasek 1976; Johansson 1971). The three graphs indicate the percentage of workers of each job type with a non-participation problem: low "total political activity," and low "variety in leisure" (participation in only one out of seven activity categories: culture, sports, entertainment, religion, home activities, elite and mass political leisure). The figure shows that the active job situation with high psychological demand and high decision latitude is significantly associated with high rates of participation in socially active leisure and political activities. Thus, workers do not compensate for passive jobs with active leisure but instead appear to carry over socialized patterns of behavior from work to leisure. While only 9 percent of workers with active jobs reported low variety in leisure, 40 percent with passive jobs reported such restricted leisure behavior (Karasek 1976). This finding is consistent with other findings of job socialization (Kohn and Schooler 1973, 1982; Mortimer and Lorence 1979) and leisure and political activity findings in the United States (Goiten and Seashore 1980). It is noteworthy that psychologically demanding work is associated, as predicted, with more active leisure, rather than less active leisure, as might be expected. The finding for the "total political activity" measure confirms a dismal vision of severely restricted political participation for workers whose jobs permit little exercise of judgment and no opportunity for challenge (Elden 1981a).* A wide variety of demographic and social class measures are correlated to these leisure and political activity indicators, but controlling for them does not substantially change the findings. For example, substantial job-related leisure and political activity associations were observed in the 60 percent of the Swedish population with the statutory minimum education.

These findings are corroborated by longitudinal analyses using panel data from 1968 and 1974. Swedish workers whose jobs had become more

---

*There are several elaborations and one important exception to this basic picture of active jobs–active leisure. Participation in adventure magazine reading and window shopping ("mass cultural leisure") is lower for workers with more active jobs, and, indeed, those activities do appear to reflect relatively little use of judgment by participants (this is the only activity with a negative loading on the active factor in a canonical correlation analysis). Workers with high-strain jobs (that is, jobs with high demands and low decision latitude) generally have intermediate levels of leisure and political participation, but they are the most active participators in "mass political activity." The mechanisms for coping with unresolved strain seem more important than those relating to job socialization in this case. This finding suggests that mass political activity is, in every way, a protest reaction. Workers with the most demanding and restrictive jobs are most active in labor and political organizations, which in Sweden have a record of success in improving working-class conditions.

passive during this period became more passive in their leisure and political participation, and workers with more active jobs became more active. These findings were significant in eight out of nine subpopulations controlled for education and family class background.* Figure 2–6 shows relative leisure participation rates for different work experience cohorts in the 1968 cross-sectional population. Young workers, just beginning their occupational careers, show no significant job-related differences in leisure participation rates. Workers with forty years' experience, however, show job-related participation differentials of two and three to one. These relationships are congruent with an explanation that children begin their lives with relatively equal tendencies toward active and passive life-styles, are tracked into different life-styles during adolescence (Rosenbaum 1976), and then are further socialized as adults in the work environment, society's most heavily deterministic sphere of life. The job is the classroom, particularly for the 60 percent of Swedish adults with lower levels of formal education.

While we may have thought that stress was the major unintended cost of modern work environments, here we see a problem that could be even worse. The finding that political participation declines as jobs become passive is disturbing, for it implies a gradual withdrawal from political participation by the majority of workers and an increasingly dominant role in social decision making by the few who retain active work opportunities in their jobs. The task of instilling democratic values that is now given to the educational systems of modern democratic societies should also be given to their work environments. And what about consumers whose leisure is too passive to require consumption of the products of our modern economy? Passive jobs may simply not support an active economy. Income allocation is clearly not the only work-related distributional problem in modern society.

Developing the Demand/Control Model

The evidence introduced so far has provided consistent support for the validity of our model as a simple description of causal factors operating in the psychosocial work environment. As with any theory, however, empirical questions remain to be answered. And like most models, ours has evolved over time. Important questions have motivated an expansion of the model, first with more detailed elaboration of the existing dimensions, and second with the addition of several dimensions, which were foreshadowed in our

*A weakness in these data was that age was not controlled. This factor could weaken the findings somewhat but probably not change the main trends (Karasek 1978).

FIGURE 2-6
Testing for job socialization
(Swedish males, 1968, non-rural employees, age 18 to 66, N = 1,451)

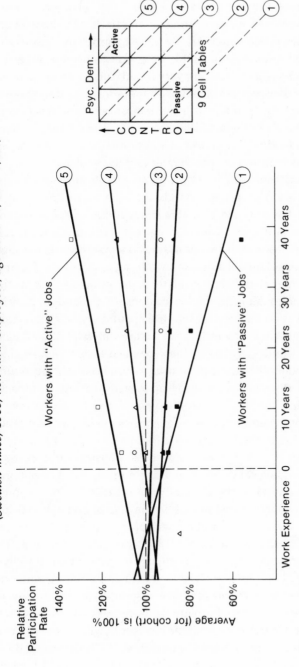

NOTE: Relative participation in Total Active Leisure (five "active leisure" categories).

SOURCE: Redrawn from Karasek 1976.

historical discussion. These refinements will be discussed in the remainder of this chapter and a more ambitious multilevel expansion will be discussed in later chapters. A variety of detailed methodological questions have been raised regarding the existence of interaction effects and the magnitude of explained variance, and these are discussed further in Karasek (1989b). Another current question relates to the precise meaning of each of the model's main dimensions; both are very broad constructs. Decision latitude combines discretion over use of skill with measures of social authority, and questions are arising as to which has the most potent effects (Frese 1989; Ganster 1989; Kasl 1989—see discussion p. 58). The important question of the effects of individual differences in questionnaire-based responses is addressed at the conclusion of this chapter and in chapter 3.

The most common criticism, which we agree is its most serious defect, is that the model is too simple as it stands and omits some important aspects of the job. We have argued that this simplicity is essential for practical interdisciplinary applications and for the first stages of scientific research. But the problem of simplicity arises in several ways. In some investigations, the demand/control model alone shows strong associations (Freeman and Jucker 1979; Sauter et al. 1983), but later analyses involving a much larger number of variables diminish the associations for demands or decision latitude. Since task specialization and control are underlying general factors in workplace design, they may well cause a wide variety of other detailed job circumstances. Controlling for all these detailed factors in a single model could certainly diminish decision latitude associations. The introduction of many explanatory variables can also lead to statistical indeterminacy (Robins and Greenland 1986). The problem could also be substantive. Social support has been seen to compete for variance with decision latitude in samples of clerical workers using VDTs (Sauter et al. 1983) and health care workers (Rafferty 1988). We also suspect that physical stressors may often affect both psychological demand and decision latitude associations.

How shall we expand the demand/control model? Suggestions come from the most widely utilized models in the area of occupational stress research: the multivariate path and moderator models from the University of Michigan, such as Katz's and Kahn's (1966) four-stage path model (see figure 6–2a). This model is built on a chain of associations: the objective work environment leads to the perceived psychological environment, which in turn leads to behavioral and affective responses, which finally lead to physical and mental disease. Individual differences and social relationships on the job moderate these associations between stages, often with feedback loops to the main effects. An entire generation of scholars using the Michigan model has proved the major importance of these multistage associations, and many of the most fruitful psychosocial research pathways have developed from these leads. Unfortunately, this common approach to analysis of the work environment suffers from the opposite problem of our model: overcomplexity (and even then productivity is omitted completely as an outcome and no specific job characteristics are recommended for analysis). Tests of the fully developed four-stage Michigan model, with multiple reciprocal linkages tested by large regression models, can become a maze of coefficients, very difficult for the lay person to translate into consistent policy recommendations. Even the statistical validity of one model structure versus another is difficult to confirm unless the data are very robust. Rather than long lists of variables entered into regression analyses, we prefer a sequence of smaller models that are more rigorously specified in terms of variable definitions, directionality of effects, and interaction mechanisms. But we cannot omit the associations shown by the Michigan model and they form a basis for our discussions in chapter 3.

Our previous complaint about unidimensional research also does not apply to the practically-oriented Scandinavian job design and Industrial Democracy traditions which by the late 1960s had gone beyond skill and autonomy measures to identify social support and affiliation at work, career development security, and meaningfulness of the job as additional task measures necessary for good job design (Emery and Thorsrud [1964] 1969). While workplace demands—vital for our occupational health perspective—were missing, the emphasis on social relations at work (see chapter 5) reinforced the lessons of the Michigan model about the importance of these issues.

Our basic model, built upon individual-level psychological demands and decision latitude, cannot address all the relevant scientific issues from the Michigan model or the job redesign approach directly. Our claim is that the model does address that small number of job dimensions that lie at the core of management theory in our industrial society, and therefore can serve as a useful basis for beginning a dialogue about job change and its social policy implications. However, the demand/control model occupies an intellectual "middle ground" equidistant from two major scientific belief areas and can serve as a reference point for expansion in two directions. First, task-level attributes can serve as a micro-level reference point for psychologists, medical scientists, and personnel managers in assessing the relative contributions of individual personality (or physiology) and environment, allowing integration of individual concerns with a task-level model (as we see in chapter 3). Second, task-level attributes serve as building blocks anchored in individual well-being for managers, organizational and job designers, sociologists, and workers who are concerned with policy implications that affect entire organizations or have impacts on society, allowing integration of group and organizational concerns with a task-level model, as we will discuss in chapters 5, 6, 7, and 8. In both directions the two mechanisms of stress-affects-learning and learning-affects-stress serve as bridges between the levels.

We will start by partially integrating in the basic model two additional dimensions that were foreshadowed in chapter 1: social isolation/support and physical demands at work. (A third dimension—job insecurity—will be added in chapter 10.) Physical demands still represent the primary factor in many blue-collar jobs and will also help us understand the limiting contexts of the model historically and the linkages to social class. Social support captures some of the market-related effects of the conventional production organization models and also adds the social relational aspects of participatory decision making that accompany decision latitude changes in the job redesign process. In addition, for compelling practical and theoretical reasons related to work redesign strategies, the components of the demand/control model are discussed more precisely and partially integrated with additional variables in the sections that follow.

DECISION LATITUDE: A COMBINATION OF TASK AUTHORITY AND
SKILL DISCRETION

There is a close practical linkage between the two theoretically distinct concepts of the breadth of skills usable on the job (Adam Smith's specialization of labor, our *skill discretion*, or task variety) and social authority over making decisions (our *decision authority*, or autonomy). We have claimed that these are mutually reinforcing aspects of work that often appear together in the workplace, in a combination which we call *decision latitude*. Because in our opinion a high level of skill gives the worker control over which specific skills to use to accomplish the task, we refer to such a measure as skill discretion, and often loosely label the decision latitude combination: "control." Skill utilization and decision authority are so closely related in empirical studies (Karasek 1989b) that they are often combined for analytic purposes in the job design research. Examples are the two most empirically important components of Hackman and Oldham's Motivating Potential Score (1976)—the closely related measures of task autonomy and skill variety; Gardell's freedom and qualification level scale (1971a); and two subcomponents of Kohn and Schooler's occupational self-direction scale: closeness of supervision and substantive complexity (1973). In the U.S. QES data used in this chapter, the decision latitude scale is an equally weighted combination of six skill discretion questions and three decision authority questions (see Schwartz, Pieper, and Karasek 1988; and the appendix for further details). But theoretical and practical distinctions between skill discretion and decision authority are just as important as the similarities, as can be understood by reviewing four occupations below that represent high and low combinations on these two dimensions.

The mutually reinforcing relationship between these dimensions derives from the fact that acquisition of skills over the long term is what gives workers influence over the work process. An example is a management trainee for an insurance company who is allowed to spend a month in each service department to gain an overview of its operation so that she can participate in decisions about departmental reorganization. Here, increased skill will lead to increased authority, but she is given these skills because of the authority of her role. Reinforcement can also occur in a negative manner. Consider the clerk typist in the same company who is never trained broadly in the use of the computer system, precisely so that she will not deviate from the predetermined work procedures. The difficulty of having one aspect of decision latitude without the other is illustrated by Ehn's (1988) example of the frustrations associated with developing "empowering" new computer programs even for craftsmen such as typographers and repairmen when the company authority structures are hostile to participation. In this case it is the authority structure that determined the possibilities for skill development. For Adam Smith, the specialization of labor is the causal factor: workers with specialized tasks are inevitably coordinated by managers with higher authority levels. Indeed, this linkage is the fundamental operating principle of our modern Weberian ([1920] 1947)—that is, bureaucratic—organizational hierarchies in which the highest levels of knowledge legitimize the exercise of the highest levels of authority.

However, two other sets of occupations illustrate the need for keeping these concepts distinct. While examples of occupations high on skill use and low on authority are rare, they can be important (just how rare is shown in Karasek 1989b, figure 3, showing the QES occupations plotted by decision authority and skill discretion with a correlation of .77). Frankenhaeuser and Gardell's lumber graders (1976) were highly skilled inspectors who worked under rigid time and method constraints. An even more extreme example are highly skilled orchestra musicians who have no authority to play the score their own way. The opposite combination—high authority and low levels of skill use—can be found in delivery personnel with much freedom from direct supervision. This latter example raises the question about what is being controlled: only one's own behavior (important for our strain hypotheses) or some significant output of the company—a potentially important source of feedback relevant for further skill development (Bazerman 1982).

Distinctions must be maintained between skill discretion and decision authority for a variety of theoretical reasons as well (more detailed discussions of the control concept can be found in Aronsson 1987; Frese 1989; Karasek 1989b; and Kasl 1989). The question now being raised is whether skill discretion or task autonomy is more important, for low levels on both measures have been separately shown to have significant impacts on a broad spectrum of psychosocial strain, health, and behavioral consequences, controlling for social class (Caplan et al. 1975; Karasek, Gardell, and Lindell 1987; Kornhauser 1965).* Theoretical distinctions between these dimensions will have to be more carefully considered in future research, however (see, for example, Kasl 1989). M. Smith (1985) observed that since machine-paced work involves both (as well as lack of control over time pacing), the true cause of strain responses is difficult to isolate. Frese (1987) noted that intellectual complexity acts as a stressor, not a stress moderator, in an expanding number of jobs (although as we have noted, the effects of such qualitative work loads have so far been salient in only a few high-status jobs). Our theoretical discussions in chapter 3 also suggest distinct effects for skill discretion and decision authority. For psychological strain, constraint at very low levels of task authority may be most important, while for motivation and learning of skills, influence over the flow of rewards and challenges (the reinforcement sequence, more closely related to skill discretion) may be primary, as we shall discuss in chapter 5. The implications would be that freedom from rigid constraint has more basic physiological effects and that skill acquisition opportunities are salient only after basic psychophysiological well-being has been attained.

Our concept of decision latitude is interpreted as the worker's ability to control his or her own activities and skill usage, not to control others, although that is also a potentially important construct (Thibault and Kelly 1959). This focus is in keeping with our original goals of modeling the effects of individual-level outcome measures. Macro-level sources of control, however, such as organizational policies, are of daily concern to many managers, organizational designers, and industrial sociologists who design policies for macro-level control at either the work group or organizational level. Union membership and membership in influential work groups must also affect the decision latitude available to the worker. These social factors will have direct effects on health and productivity as well as indirect effects through changes in the possibility of task control at the individual level. Several studies have found that the worker's possibilities for control at the macro level—participation in major production planning and personal decisions—are preconditions for increased levels of decision latitude (Frese 1987; Karasek 1989b). Macro control measures have also been found to

*One of the broadest findings by Kohn and Schooler (1973, 1982) is that "occupational self-direction" (substantive complexity and intellectual flexibility) affects individual behavior as much as personality affects selection of work.

contribute directly to psychological well-being (Gardell and Svensson 1981; Semmer 1982). Unfortunately, many of our analyses in this chapter and in chapters 4 and 5 are made without these sources of organizational-level control. Some of these components have been included in our new Job Content Questionnaire (see the appendix), however, and will thus be a component of our future research. We will also discuss them as elements of strategies for solutions to work redesign problems at the work group and organizational levels in chapter 7.

Other macro-level factors that affect control in the workplace are often the result of broad economic and business conditions related to the market mechanisms of the conventional models. They are generally perceived by workers to be beyond their control. We discuss these measures of uncertainty in chapter 10 as constraints on job redesign policies. They may arise from such diverse causes as management instability from mergers and takeovers—certainly a major problem in the United States and other Western countries in the 1980s—product market instabilities in a world market with a few large-scale producers, or technological change. Some other measures of uncertainty, such as the often-discussed "role conflict" and "role ambiguity" (Kahn et al. 1964), are similar to low decision latitude in that they imply conflicting authority structures at the task level that the worker is powerless to resolve.

CLARIFYING CONTROL AND DEMAND DEFINITIONS

Could control be more easily conceptualized as a negative stressor, rather than as a separate type of psychosocial job characteristic? This is the implication of the "resources" perspective in which different environmental factors can be viewed as simple additions or subtractions to the risk of stress.* However, the distinction between decision latitude and psychological stressors must be retained with our model, because the model predicts both learning and stress consequences from two different combinations of demands and control. Our initial hypothesis predicts that having decision latitude over the work process will reduce a worker's stress but increase learning, while psychological demands will both increase learning and increase stress—an asymmetrical relation. These demands and challenges associated with lack of control are not associated with increased learning; they are thus not positive challenges. For example, uncertainty over market changes that might lead to job loss would be considered a stressor by many people. Following our criterion, however,

*The "resource" perspective has the advantage of breadth to accommodate factors beyond those discussed in the model section above, but infers inappropriate analogies to "zero-sum" economic behavior models (see chapter 5).

these are not the type of challenges that one can easily learn from, because they are unpredictable and beyond one's control. Thus, this type of uncertainty would be lack of control. Of course, job insecurity could simply be considered a separate dimension that need not be forced into a simple model; we agree, as we indicate on p. 305. Our criterion remains germane in one sense, however; chapter 1 showed that the effects of the division of labor (and the switch from physical production) underlie many other aspects of the work environment.

We feel that failure to distinguish among the clearer examples of psychological demands and decision latitude has led to significant confusion. One problem has been the tendency to classify all organizationally determined aspects of work as demands and, in the next logical step, as stress-inducing. Ritti (1971) has observed that engineers' "qualitative" intellectual demands (Kahn 1974) were satisfying but that "quantitative" time pressure demands were not. Of course, the intellectual demands of the engineer's task may actually allow the engineer to choose from several highly intellectually challenging strategies for task performance. This type of "qualitative" intellectual demand might therefore be better labeled "decision latitude," because it really measures both the degree of constraint and choices over learning opportunities.

Another unfortunate mixture occurs when measures that appear to reflect control also include a demand component. Time-paced tasks have been cited by Kasl (1989) as one confusing example; piecework is shown to lead to higher levels of psychological strain than salaried work, in spite of the increased levels of control that piecework presumably implies. Here, a weekly salary is actually a source of security for a worker who might otherwise be exposed to all manner of management-initiated output pressures, such as competition among co-workers and new production goals. Piecework's "freedom" to work harder is rather like the freedom of the poor to sleep under bridges: it brings with it a set of new demands for adjusting to the environment that may more than offset the salubrious effects of control. Another example is "responsibility", which we think actually means high demands combined with high decision latitude. Indeed, according to the management canard, "authority should be commensurate with responsibility." Of course, the fact that demands and control are often not commensurate is one of this book's main themes. One simplifying device we have used in some of the Swedish studies is to look at the ratio of demand to control (using standardized variables), which measures the discrepancy between demands and control. In summary, whenever it is possible, it is important first to distinguish between psychological demands and decision latitude and then to examine their joint effects at the workplace.

PSYCHOLOGICAL JOB DEMANDS

Examples of the psychological demands of work ("how hard you work") include deadlines, how many widgets you make per hour, and how many reports are due this week. Obviously, these have an effect on productivity. There is also substantial evidence that psychological job demands have a major impact on health outcomes of work activity, in many ways (Caplan et al. 1975; House et al. 1979; Karasek, Gardell, and Lindell 1987). Indeed, psychological demands on the job remain difficult to conceptualize and measure because of the diversity of subcomponents and because of some theoretical problems that are as yet unresolved. Even the psychological burdens of the work task itself can come from several sources: the mental arousal or stimulation necessary to accomplish the task, coordination burdens, or even psychological arousal associated with physical exertion. Of course, we are explicitly trying to differentiate physical and psychological stressors, but there are problems in doing even this. For example, "static physical loading"—holding the body's mass in an uncomfortable position, such as when painting a ceiling—is associated with many of the same psychophysiological responses as purely psychological demands.

Other components of psychological job demands are stressors arising from personal conflicts that may have begun because of task pressures but soon take on a life of their own. Skill obsolescence or the fear of losing a job may also be a source of job-related strain. (We will discuss this issue separately in chapter 10 as part of our discussion of macro strategies for job redesign.) A common research perspective associated with job-related stress has been to use Kahn's "role overload, role conflict, and role ambiguity" (Kahn et al. 1964). Of these, role overload, of course, corresponds to our concept of psychological demands; role ambiguity was mentioned with respect to control; and role hostility will be discussed in combination with social support (p. 71).

In spite of the diversity just described, "task requirements" (work load) are the central component of psychological job demands for most workers, as Buck (1972) notes. A task's mental work load has been one of the most difficult concepts for human-factor engineers to specify and measure, even in highly controlled laboratory experiments. The central concept is that of the mental alertness or arousal (Bainbridge 1974; Welford 1976) needed to carry out the task. We can imagine the number of mental tasks per unit of time (for example, the rate at which defective parts are sorted out by an inspector or the number of project status reports prepared by an engineer) as one obvious measure of work load, and thus time pressures could increase the magnitude of mental work loads. We might also define mental work load in information theory terms, as the amount of disorganization in the work task that the worker is required to place in an organized state (for example, a chaotic office that the supervisor must manage). Imposing this external order requires imposition of internal organization over the worker's own cognitive functioning—intense concentration, without distracting thoughts. This is a costly process in terms of mental energy expended. O'Hanlon (1981) has discussed the burden of constant vigilance even when response demands are rare, as for an operator in an automated process plant waiting for a breakdown. This type of intermittent control, in which the operator must still impose the same internal order on his thoughts, is called "passive supervision" by Sandén and Johansson, Aronsson, and Lindström (1987), who observe that it occurs for 80 percent of operators in paper pulp processing plants. In such jobs, which are still a rarity but are growing in number, human mental activity has become residual, needed only when machines break down—a parallel of the changes in physical exertion on the job. This passivity may lead to skill degradation but no relief from strain. Other unintended aspects of a task increase demands—for example, the stress felt when a task in process must be broken off for another job and returned to later, the effect Ziegarnik described in 1927. Still another theoretical component of task demands is the dependency created by technology such as computer-aided machinery, where to accomplish tasks workers must depend on other operators or staff resources beyond their control (Turner 1980).

One reason for the conceptual difficulties addressed by human factors research is that while some level of demands (such as challenge, interest, or importance) is necessary to effective performance and job satisfaction, too high a level of demands can obviously be disastrous. This has implied a U-shaped association between demands and performance (or stress), which in turn implies the need to determine an optimal level of demands, a subject we will discuss further in chapter 3.

It might seem that a measure of hours worked would be a simple and appropriate psychological work-load dimension. Unfortunately, mere hours of work are not consistently related to stress or health measures; indeed, negative relations with illness are observed in some cases in chapter 4. One working hours measure, however—shiftwork, especially rotating shiftwork—is associated with substantial social problems as well as increased illness (Åkerstedt et al. 1984; Baker 1985; Frese and Semmer 1986). Since shiftwork is often introduced to increase the economic productivity of facilities (that is, to increase the utilization of expensive capital equipment), this is clearly an aspect of work that may force workers to trade health for productivity. Indeed, almost all work demands at very high levels (although not at moderate levels) force this unfortunate bargain.

THE PHYSICAL DEMANDS OF WORK

The rush to develop models relevant to the new "service" or "information" society (and we are certainly a part of that) can bias explanations toward the white-collar world and make them less relevant for many blue-collar workers whose health is jeopardized by their work. The physical demands of work are still important to almost as many workers in the United States and Sweden as the new psychological demands. Furthermore, our model of psychological demands and decision latitude must be expanded, even at the individual level, if it is to be acceptable to medical scientists who must use it to explain and treat job-related illness. In most occupational health and safety research, the focal causal factors are physical stressors and hazards, not psychological demands. While we have no intention of duplicating that approach, we recognize that even cardiovascular pathology (and other psychosomatic illness) is clearly influenced by the effects of physical exertion.* Of course, the interaction between psychological stressors and physical hazards may also be an important issue, as Ebeltoft (1986), Karlsen and Naess (1978), House (1981), and Ashford (Hattis, Richardson, and Ashford 1979) have pointed out. We shall discuss this issue in chapter 4.†

Physical exertion on the job, necessary for production in preindustrial settings, was often of a rhythmic, self-paced variety, with few exceptional peak loads. In today's machine-powered work, however, human labor is rarely a direct major component of output. Now it is usually a residual component, involving lower magnitudes of exertion but also less predictability and perhaps less comfort. While the assembly line carries the heavy car chassis, the worker must now bend over to work in awkward positions and has no control over pace. We therefore need to be concerned not only about overall level of exertion but about other aspects, such as regularity of exertion, the level of impulse loading (Fredriksson and Voight 1979), and static loads imposed by spending long periods in uncomfortable positions (Milvy, Forbes, and Brown 1977; Tichauer 1973). The complexity of the effects of physical demands is illustrated by the negative associations between physical exertion and heart disease found in field studies of longshoremen (Paffenbarger and Hyde 1980) and the opposite finding in a study of concrete workers (Theorell, Olsson, and Engholm 1977). Positive

*Other physical hazards such as noise have been suspected of being causative in the development of cardiovascular illness (Berglund, Berglund, and Lindvall 1984; Hattis, Richardson, and Ashford 1979; Jonsson and Hansson 1977).

†Evidence of complex interactions exists in analyses with our QES data. These show that physical exertion is significantly correlated with our high-strain jobs. However, controlling for physical exertion does not diminish the associations between our depression measure and decision latitude and psychological demands—it increases them, especially in males and females who do physically demanding work.

associations are also, of course, found between physical exertion such as lifting and musculoskeletal disorders.

It is obviously also important to distinguish between physical exertion and other physical stressors such as exposure to toxic substances, for the pathways by which they might affect health are very different. This book cannot review the extensive and rapidly growing literature on the illness effects of exposure to diverse hazardous physical and chemical agents at work (Berglund, Berglund, and Lindvall 1984; Stellman and Daum 1973; Vågerö and Olin 1983), but many current examples highlight their obvious importance such as asbestos exposure and lung disease, pesticide exposure and a variety of cancers. A separate and older tradition in the occupational health field involves safety hazards at work, such as dangerous work methods and risk of burn or shock. Of course, most of these hazardous conditions lead to specific injuries, unlike the generalized illness risk implied by psychological stress. Nevertheless, the clearly demonstrated presence of such confounding etiological agents should be controlled for in any analysis of stress-related illness (see scale discussed in the appendix).

DISTRIBUTION OF OCCUPATIONS BY DECISION LATITUDE AND
PHYSICAL EXERTION

Figure 2–7 shows the distribution of occupations by physical exertion in combination with decision latitude, using the U.S. QES data for males and females. This occupation distribution is particularly useful for understanding the political and social status divisions in the U.S. (and Swedish) work forces. This two-dimensional job characteristic distribution clearly captures the classic Marxist class conflict between factory machine operatives and factory management. These groups can be found in the lower right- and upper left-hand quadrants of the diagram, respectively. The fact that relatively few occupations are in the central portion of this axis reflects the still-present reality of class divisions with respect to these measures; a less polarized distribution would have been expected because of the normality of the distributions of each dimension. It is interesting that self-employed farmers—in the upper right-hand quadrant—fall outside this conflict. Groups such as the Kulaks in the Soviet Union in the 1930s and American farmers in the 1910s have been hard to recruit to such political struggles. The fact that the overall correlation between these dimensions is negative shows that while the industrial revolution may have diminished the physical demands placed on workers, in general there is little compensation: in the population overall, workers with low decision latitude also have high physical demands.

FIGURE 2–7

The occupational distribution of physical exertion and decision latitude
(U.S. males and females, N = 4,495)

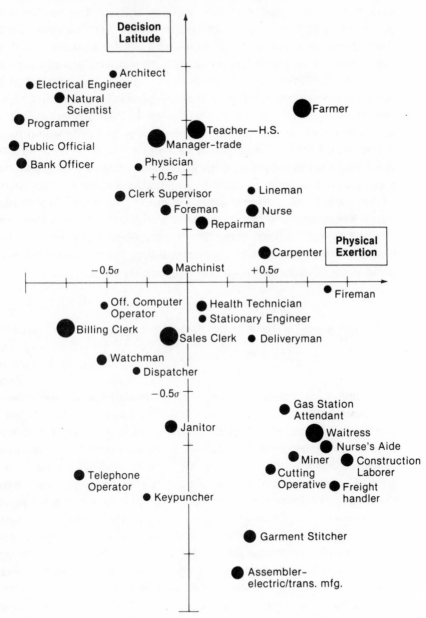

SOURCE: Data from Quality of Employment Surveys 1969, 1972, 1977. Figure reprinted from Karasek 1989a; used with permission of Baywood Publishing Co.

Figure 2–7 also reveals another reality about these basic facets of social class that until recently has received relatively little notice: the blue-collar class is split. Not all low-control/low-status workers have heavy physical demands. Some, notably clerical workers and workers rendering non-professional services, such as dispatchers, have light physical demands. They therefore experience a fundamentally different social reality from that of the classic factory-based industrial proletariat. Certainly these social differences are important for political affiliations. This overlooked blue-collar experience involves low control, low physical exertion, and high psychological demands. While less oppressed in the conventional physical sense, this new class of low-status worker is more oppressed in terms of psychological stress-related problems—and probably represents a high-risk group for heart disease, as we shall see in chapter 4. No future working-class political strategy could be formulated without an understanding of the psychosocial work realities of this group. The current U.S. public debate is beginning to recognize the "new working class" (Trost 1986) of service and clerical workers, but to date the discussion has usually referred to income differentials only. We hope it will broaden to include the psychosocial work environment in the future (see chapter 9).

Expanding the Model: Social Support at Work and the Participatory Work Process

Up to this point our examination of *social* processes at the workplace has only been indirect. The effects of the organization's control structure are manifest, for example, through the decision latitude of the individual worker. An expansion of the model in this area is needed, but poses a major challenge because of the diversity of relevant workplace social relationships. The most basic of all workplace social relationships—that between the worker and the customer—is much affected by Adam Smith's principle of labor specialization: most workers in large-scale enterprises are specialized out of customer contact roles altogether. While this could be our starting point we will instead hold this discussion until chapter 5. We also hold discussion of work groups and organizations until chapters 6 through 8. This leaves the worker's close personal relationships with co-workers and supervisors as the subject of this section.

Since the Hawthorne experiments in the 1920s, it has been obvious that social relations with co-workers and supervisors determine productivity directly through "norms of fair performance," as Homans described them in

1950. Lysgaard (1961) saw the cohesive work group as the worker's main defense against unreasonable management pressures. Recent research on work groups and productivity (reviewed in Cummings 1978) has focused on group autonomy, group leadership, and the nature of individual-level feedback generated by the group. Indeed, one of the most common themes concerning worker/supervisor relationships in the popular press recently has been the stress caused by an overly demanding or unsympathetic boss. Many U.S. studies (for example, Quinn and Staines 1979; U.S. Department of Health, Education and Welfare 1973) have found that supervisor support is the most important correlate of job satisfaction and low psychological strain, although this is less clear in Swedish studies. While workplace control issues are certainly reflected in all these studies, the social interaction itself is obviously a major component of health and behavioral reactions. We must therefore expand our original demand/control model to include social support as a third dimension, as seen in figure 2–8. In practice, when the model is applied to job redesign, we find that changes in social relations between workers (such as initiation of autonomous work groups) and changes in decision latitude are almost inseparable strategies. This linkage has led House (1981) to refer to "participatory work design processes" as a combination of control and social support changes.

The Nature of Social Support at the Workplace

Much recent research (such as Cohen and Syme 1985; House 1981; House and Cottington 1986; Johnson 1986) has focused on how social-support relations on the job affect psychosocial health. Social support at work refers to overall levels of helpful social interaction available on the job from both co-workers and supervisors. The mechanisms by which social relations at work might affect well-being are diverse, however. First, social support can refer to buffering mechanisms between psychological stressors at work and adverse health outcomes, recently elaborated in a number of studies (Berkman and Syme 1979; Karasek, Gardell, and Lindell 1987; Karasek, Triantis, and Chaudhry 1982; LaRocco, House, and French 1980; Marmot and Syme 1976). Second, in all higher animals, including humans, social contacts and social structure affect the basic physiological processes important to both maintenance of long-term health and acquisition of new knowledge, as the work of Henry and Stephens (1977a) demonstrates. Third, social support can facilitate active coping patterns that not only affect health through second-order effects, as we shall see in chapter 3, but could affect productive behavior as well (Pearlin and Schooler 1978). Although evidence is lacking, we believe that a fourth mechanism is particu-

FIGURE 2–8
A 3-dimensional model of the psychosocial work environment

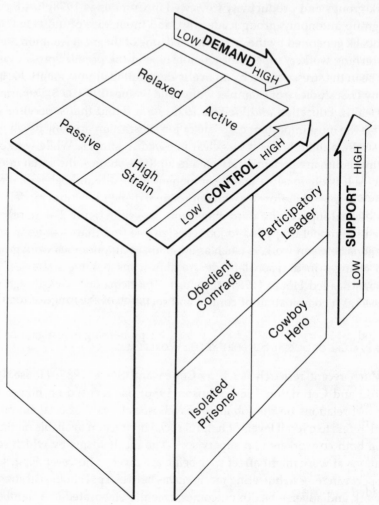

larly important in the development of active behavior patterns: a positive sense of identity, based on the socially confirmed value of the individual's contribution to the collective goals and well-being. This mechanism is linked to the market relationships of jobs, as we will see in chapter 5.

Several types of social support in the workplace have been identified. Socioemotional support is support that buffers psychological strain. It may be measured by the degree of social and emotional integration and trust between co-workers, supervisors, and others. It may also be measured by the degree of social cohesion and integration in the overall work group. In the latter case, it would be a measure of the strength of norms that may foster new behavior patterns in the work group (Homans 1950). A second type of social support—instrumental social support—measures extra resources or assistance with work tasks given by co-workers or supervisors.* Task interdependency, the necessary coordination of workers performing complex tasks, can become a source of stress (Turner 1980), so not all social interaction at work is supportive. The same is obviously true of hostility, which might be considered a negative level on support scales. In spite of these distinctions, however, there is a high correlation among these components in large population studies such as our U.S. QES data base. For this reason, the analysis below is based on an equally weighted combination of co-worker and supervisor support.

In figure 2–9, social support is added to the original job strain model in the U.S. nationally representative population (QES 1972, 1977) using the same depression measure and scale intervals discussed in figure 2–4a and b. Social support is associated with dramatically lower levels of depression in the combined male and female populations. We also see a clear job strain (that is, demand/control) association within each level of social support, bolstering the independent validity of the original demand/control model. Together, these three dimensions of work activity—demand, control, and social support—are capable of predicting much of the range of total variation in depression symptoms in the U.S. population, from a 6 percent likelihood to a 41 percent likelihood. Johnson's pioneering investigations (1985, 1986) of the combined demand/control/support model have explicitly developed statistical measures of these separate and interactive effects. He has confirmed a similar pattern of joint risk for a random sample of the Swedish national population, with a 131 percent increase in age-adjusted mental fatigue from low-strain to high-strain jobs under conditions of high work support and a 225 percent increase for the high-strain jobs under conditions of low work support. Payne and his colleagues (Payne et al. 1984; Payne and Fletcher 1983) also discuss a model in which support is added to a demand/control–like model, although "constraints" are substituted for control and operationalized differently, and "qualitative work load demands" are often used (see p. 62). Prediction seems less successful in this form.

DISTRIBUTION OF OCCUPATIONS BY SOCIAL SUPPORT AND DECISION LATITUDE

Figure 2–10 displays the distribution of occupations by social support and decision latitude, using the U.S. QES data for males and females. The differ-

*In addition to separating co-workers and supervisors as sources of social support (French, Rodgers, and Cobb 1974; LaRocco, House, and French 1980), the empirical literature consistently documents the dichotomy between instrumental and emotional support, particularly when it comes from supervisors. Bales and Slater's (1954) role dichotomy is similar.

FIGURE 2–9 (a-b)
Social support, the demand/control model, and depression
(U.S. males and females, N = 2,679)

Number on vertical bar is percentage in each job category with symptoms.

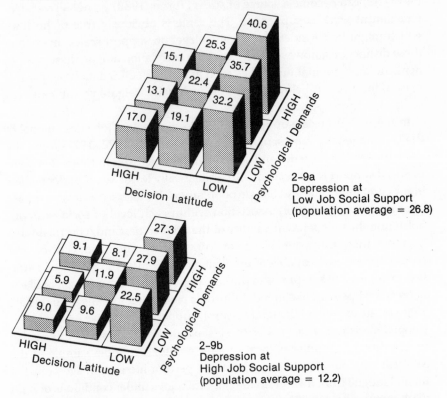

2–9a
Depression at
Low Job Social Support
(population average = 26.8)

2–9b
Depression at
High Job Social Support
(population average = 12.2)

NOTE: For discussion of depression indicator, see p. 49*n*. Cell sizes, reading from left to right, are as follows (see p. 49*n*), for low support—high demands: 126, 158, 244; medium demands: 99, 152, 129; low demands: 53, 120, 121; for high support—high demands: 208, 99, 66; medium demands: 222, 160, 86; low demands: 234, 251, 151.

SOURCE: Data from Quality of Employment Surveys 1972, 1977.

ences between the quadrants are at least as rich in implications as those in our demand/control quadrants. We label the high-decision-latitude/high-social-support quadrant the *participatory leader* quadrant, reflecting House's (1981) point (p. 69) that decision participation and social support are an important force for work environment change (see figure 2–8). Of course, not all workers in these occupations are necessarily leaders in a conventional sense, but in general they share power, have influence, or at least have some chance of affecting collective decisions. The occupations we find in this quadrant are professions: scientist, teacher, therapist, manager—even barber. There appear to be several processes that may facilitate professional co-

FIGURE 2–10
The occupational distribution of social support and decision latitude
(U.S. males and females, N = 4,495)

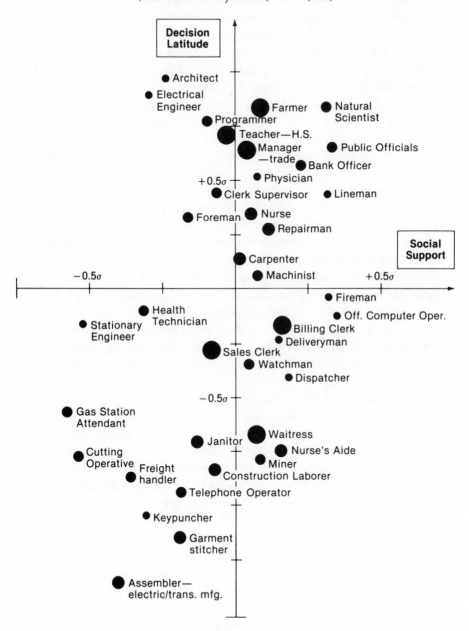

Source: Data from Quality of Employment Surveys 1969, 1972, 1977. Figure reprinted from Karasek 1989a; used with permission of Baywood Publishing Co.

hesiveness among workers in these occupations, from ongoing joint training experiences to engaging in community political activities.

At high decision latitude and low social support, we see a significantly different picture. Because of the positive correlation between decision latitude and social support, there are relatively few occupations of this type: architect, lawyer, engineer, artist, professor, and manufacturing manager (most of which are not shown in figure 2–10). The image is of Ayn Rand's genius of the Howard Roark type—very skilled, but operating in isolation, almost in opposition to conventional social authority. The label of *cowboy hero* (Gary Cooper in *High Noon*) illustrates how significant the exercise of control unfettered by social authority is in American culture. Comparable images are not as important in Swedish, Western European, or, certainly, Japanese society.

At low decision latitude and low social support, we find assemblers and machine operatives in a variety of industries. Among women, keypunch operators and telephone operators are included. These groups more clearly than any other in the society represent the automated, machine-paced worker on the assembly line; they embody Taylor's job design principles. However high their wages, the psychosocial nature of their work is undesirable in the extreme. We have labeled this quadrant *isolated prisoner*. This combination of psychological characteristics appears to have no clear analogue in most animal societies and there is evidence that such jobs represent a clear sociobiological misfit with human physiological capabilities.

The last quadrant, with high social support but low decision latitude, is labeled—for want of a better term in American usage—*obedient comrade*. The first characteristic of this group is its antithesis to the American cowboy hero ideal. Such occupations involve many social resources and obligations but have little freedom of action. This group may even seem hard to conceptualize in an American context, but as we examine the occupations in it we find that these are the behind-the-scenes, low-status service workers who keep U.S. society (or Swedish society) operating: dispatchers, delivery personnel, switchmen, mail workers, stock clerks. This group has been relatively overlooked in job redesign activities. Their location in this quadrant suggests to us the importance of further examining the associations between these workers and the customers they serve.

We can compare U.S. and Swedish occupational distributions on these dimensions of decision latitude and social support (Swedish occupations from Johnson 1985). There are major overall similarities for decision latitude (twenty of twenty-three occupations are in approximately the same position), but for social support there are a number of differences (only fourteen out of twenty-three occupations are in similar positions). In the

U.S. QES data, there is a substantial positive correlation between decision latitude and social support, observable in the upper right to lower left distribution of the occupations in figure 2–10; it is stronger than the correlation obtained between decision latitude and psychological demands.* This clear U.S. correlation is almost absent in the Swedish data (Johnson 1986)—an indication of a fundamental national difference in social relations at work. The decision-latitude/social-support correlation is an important issue, because it reflects the participation linkage. The primary difference is that machine operator jobs (isolated prisoners) have a high percentage of unionized workers in Sweden but not in the United States. Unionization does provide social support. Examples of such groups that report higher social support in Sweden than in the United States are assembler and switchboard operator. While some of these differences may reflect the very high measurement error for social support at the occupation level (see the appendix) and the more limited coding precision of the low-status Swedish occupations, they also seem to reflect fundamental differences in the industrial relations systems in the two countries. Swedish unions may not have greatly changed the occupational distribution of decision latitude, but they appear to have changed social relationships on the job substantially.

There is also a correlation, but a negative one, between social support and psychological demands in the U.S. data. This negative correlation is consistent with Taylor's job design policies of preventing social interaction as work rates increase, but it is very inconsistent with conventional psychophysiological research on the psychological demands of complex social settings, as we shall see in chapter 3. The natural link between the burden of social demands and the palliative of social support seems to have been broken only by the explicit introduction of Taylor's scientific management, which left workers powerless in isolated but demanding jobs.

SOCIAL SUPPORT BEYOND THE WORK GROUP

Probably over half (a pure guess) of the social interactions important to workers' lives in Sweden and the United States are not reflected by the social support measures we have discussed so far. We have not yet mentioned social interactions at the organizational level, which will be taken up in chapter 7, or career development issues, which we will have to omit (see Spillerman 1977). The effects of social relations on learning and productiv-

*The U.S. QES correlations for males between decision latitude and social support are .28 for individuals and .47 for occupations; between decision latitude and psychological demand, .08 for individuals and .30 for occupations; between social support and psychological demands, −.27 for individuals and −.30 for occupations.

ity have also not been discussed; these will be considered in chapter 5. We
have not addressed the market-based changes in social relations that occur
between producer and consumer in the division of labor (see chapters 8
and 9). Most important, of course, are social interactions with family and
friends, which are beyond the scope of this book. Henry and Stephens
(1977b) emphasize the fact that social structures are the source of family responsibilities (that is, demands) in all higher-order mammals. Clearly there
are reciprocal effects of the family on work behavior. Some of these relationships are discussed in classic sociological works such as Young and
Willmott's *Family and Kinship in East London* (1957) (see also *The Symmetrical Family* by Young and Willmott [1973]) and a more recent work by
Piotrokowski (1979). Karasek, Gardell, and Lindell (1987), however, have
shown that for full-time Swedish male and female white-collar workers,
the psychosocial situation at work appears to have a greater impact on psychological well-being than do family situations. Finally, our list of omissions includes all community social relationships and their work interactions, interactions that clearly have been important for understanding the
psychosocial effects of plant closings, for example (Cobb and Kasl 1977) or
company–union relationships.

Issues Affecting the Objectivity of Psychosocial
Job Characteristics

Our interest in measuring jobs is to assess the objective working environment, which must be the basis of job redesign activities. Two important
substantive issues are closely related to the objectivity of the psychosocial
job characteristics we have been describing. The first is social class. Are our
job measures limited by—or in some way affected by—the worker's social
class? This is implied by the literature from the 1960s that claimed that
blue-collar workers did not want decision latitude in their jobs, even
though white-collar workers did (Hulin and Blood 1968). The second issue
is whether individual characteristics such as personality affect the impact
of the psychosocial work environment. The answer to the second question
is obviously yes, to some degree (the extent is estimated later in this section). We shall attempt to account for these effects in the next chapter.

PSYCHOSOCIAL JOB CHARACTERISTICS AND SOCIAL CLASS

We have, of course, already controlled for social class in many of the
analyses above. A related question is whether our dimensions represent a

better way to predict the rewards of work than do conventional social class measures, which are derived from the income rewards from work or the potential for income rewards, measured by education (or the combination of income and education in the Duncan Socio-Economic Index [SEI] [1961]). These social class measures are unidimensional: ownership of surplus value is the implied single dimension that ultimately predicts all other social phenomena. This classic Marxist view (1867), however, contradicts the more psychosocial foundation of Marx's early critique of capitalism, in which alienation in the work process was seen as the main problem. Such an alienation could certainly be the result of factors such as low control, heavy work demands, and job insecurity.

To test whether our psychosocial work environment dimensions relate to psychological strain in the same way as the conventional status measures, we ran multiple regression tests with the U.S. QES data (Karasek, Schwartz, and Theorell 1982). We found that decision latitude, psychological work load, and physical exertion predict five times the variance in a composite measure of psychological strain as the conventional occupational status scale—33 percent versus 7 percent for the Duncan SEI. Thus, our job dimensions represent a dramatic improvement in prediction over the conventional class measures for psychological strain. Occupational-level multiple regression analysis is used here, because class status is measured at this level and because it reduces the possibility of personal response bias in linking job characteristics and psychological strain.

The low control that is characteristic of low-status jobs appears to be a more important contributor to psychological strain than the distinction between mental and physical work load, the conventional determinant of status. Indeed, the physical exertion common in many blue-collar jobs appears to be protective for psychological strain. The protective impact of physical exertion could partially suppress the aggravating effects of low control and thus could account for the poor predictive ability of conventional social class measures that aggregate both measures (with differing signs) into a single scale. While the signs of the associations between psychological and physical demands are the same for both social status and strain, there is a dramatic switch of sign in the case of decision latitude, from a positive association for status to a negative association for strain.* This implies that the combination of psychosocial work measures that predicts conventional social class is different from the combination that predicts psychological strain; in fact, the two constructs are almost orthogonal. The groups at highest risk are still at the low end of conventional social-status scales, but now we can identify them more precisely: workers with

---

*These standardized regression coefficients are, respectively, .20 and .24 for psychological work load; −.55 and −.19 for physical exertion, .41 and −.67 for decision latitude.

low decision latitude, low social support, low physical exertion, and high psychological work load.

Thus, our analysis defines a psychological strain–risk dimension that is almost independent of the conventional social-class measures. This finding certainly helps to explain why conventional social-class measures fail to find associations with mental distress outcomes (for a discussion of the poor performance of social class as a predictor of psychoactive impairment, see Dohrenwend and Dohrenwend 1969). Even for the leisure and political-activity indicators, which certainly are correlated with social class, the psychosocial job measures do better than conventional class. Our nationally representative Swedish study (Karasek 1976) showed that 76 percent of the variance in leisure and political participation measures that could be apportioned between psychosocial measures and conventional social-class measures was explained by the psychosocial measures.* Of course, conventional white-/blue-collar distinctions still capture many important life phenomena, particularly with respect to material well-being and exposure to physical hazards. The fact that so many contemporary behavioral health and well-being phenomena are not captured by conventional social-class models, however, makes a strong case for new conceptions.

In general, the conventional status measures appear to be too narrow in their conceptualization of occupational experience to delineate accurately the mechanisms by which stress-related illness is caused (Ferrarotti 1980). Perhaps the greater precision of our still very imprecise psychosocial dimensions will provide advantages over the measures of status scale, wages, or education in predicting productivity in work organization, as they do in predicting active leisure. Ultimately, our dimensions imply an entirely different conception of the distribution of work's rewards—that is, a psychosocial conception of social class (Karasek 1989a; Marmot and Theorell 1988). In chapter 9 we use this new frame of reference and all three of our occupational maps, together with conventional social-class measures, to define new sets of advantaged and disadvantaged workers and to target new sets of job design strategies.

PSYCHOSOCIAL MEASURES AND INDIVIDUAL DIFFERENCES

Self-report questionnaires administered to workers have certainly been the most common method of gathering data on the psychosocial charac-

*Mortimer and Lorence (1979), in a longitudinal study, found that work autonomy also influences value systems, with conventional class held constant. In the area of political participation (possibly reflecting learning at the community level), job decision authority and skill level are associated with political participation, controlling for social status (Elden 1981a,

teristics of work, for both researchers and practitioners. The measures are simple to administer and have had great appeal for tapping core concepts in the work redesign efforts of Quality of Work Life research in many countries; for example, Hackman and Oldham's Job Diagnostic Survey (JDS) (1975), our own Job Content Questionnaire (Karasek 1985), and the Swedish Örebro Job Survey Instrument (Yrkesmedicinska Kliniken Örebro 1983). The primary problem with all such instruments, of course, is that as measures of the objective environment they are far more subject to bias than instruments traditionally used in the physical sciences, (thus, the advantage of our national reference standards in figures 2–2, 2–7, and 2–10). Although they are designed to measure the job objectively, such questionnaire instruments inevitably measure job characteristics as perceived by the worker, which may be biased by individual personality differences and may therefore not reflect the objective task accurately. The problem of self-report bias is further aggravated by the nature of the dependent variables we have used in this chapter. Depression, exhaustion, and dissatisfaction are difficult to verify precisely, and if measured by questionnaires along with job characteristics may overestimate the associations between them (Kasl 1979). This latter problem disappears, however, when we investigate an objective dependent variable, heart attack, as we do in chapter 4.

Almost all researchers agree that it would be better to have more objective measurement strategies, particularly if job redesign is the goal, but few good ones have been suggested for psychosocial aspects of jobs. Even expert ratings of jobs present problems. Is an expert's dispassionate (and very costly) fifteen-minute observation a more accurate measure of supervisor interactions, for example, than a worker's questionnaire response (albeit biased) based on years of experience? Moreover, the repetitive jobs of assembly line workers are much easier to observe than the diverse tasks of managers or professionals, which could take a week to understand—an expensive measurement requirement. Finally, expert ratings in general underestimate job-characteristic variance that is associated with psychological strain (for a discussion, see Frese and Zapf 1988).

Our own first step toward this demonstration of objective content was the development of occupational maps such as figures 2–2, 2–7, and 2–10 that demonstrated that occupations could plausibly be located using a given dimension: occupations that we would expect to be high in

1981b; Karasek 1976; Meisner 1971), with evidence of socialization in longitudinal studies (Karasek 1978). Similar job characteristics show association with leisure behavior in cross-sectional studies (Goiten and Seashore 1980; Karasek 1976; Meisner 1971) and also in longitudinal studies (Karasek 1978), even when social class is held relatively constant.

decision latitude, such as manager, are indeed high on our scales, while assembly line worker is low. Other researchers have noted that a number of the JDS scales have good convergent validity—that is, different raters produce substantially correlated measures, which are also highly correlated with workers' self-reports (Aldag, Barr, and Brief 1981; Dunham, Aldag, and Brief 1977; Hackman and Lawler 1971; Pierce and Dunham 1976; Sims, Szilagyi, and Keller 1976). Measures similar to decision latitude are usually most reliable, with correlations between self-report and expert observation usually .70 or higher. Other confirmation of the objective validity of verbally reported task measurements comes from Griffen et al.'s (1987) and Thomas and Griffen's (1983) reviews of experimental manipulations in laboratory studies, where social influence could bias self-reported job characteristics. These studies were based on a joint model in which social information from others about the job influences reported job characteristics, according to Salancik and Pfeffer's (1978) social information processing model. It concluded that all the experiments found self-reported job characteristics to be significantly affected by objective task characteristics, as well as by social information. Kahn's "role overload, role conflict, and role ambiguity" research (Kahn et al. 1964) has also used questionnaire measures. In spite of potential self-report bias difficulties the utility of questionnaires to measure even such difficult scales as psychological job demands has been demonstrated by many researchers (Brass 1985; Kemery et al. 1985; McCright 1988; Miles 1976; Rizzo, House, and Lirtzman 1970; Rousseau 1978), if appropriate reliability assessments are included (Bainbridge 1974). Frese and Zapf (1988) have shown similar associations between work demands and strain for objective and self-report questionnaire assessments (but correlations are lower than for decision latitude, about .35).

We would like to obtain a more precise estimate of just how much of the variance in our scales is due to the environment and how much is due to the person. Fortunately, we can approximate this using the between-occupation variance estimates from our occupational analyses, graphically represented in the occupational maps. The simplest estimate of the individual variance is the remaining variance. It is certainly an overestimate, however, since a substantial fraction of objective variance is lost because of the roughness of the occupational categories themselves. A baker is still a baker in the occupational categories, regardless of whether he or she works in an upscale French pastry boutique in Manhattan or supervises the slicing machine at a mass-production bread factory in Brooklyn. Appendix table A–2 shows the percentage of reliable between-occupation variance for each job characteristic. There are substantial differences in these variances between dimensions. The between-occupation variance is 35 to 45 percent for the decision-latitude measures and roughly 25 percent for the physical exertion and job insecurity scales. These statistics may seem low, but they are actually quite strong: they compare favorably with the 21 percent between-occupation variance of income from the job, which is conventionally considered to vary drastically across occupations. The implication here is that decision latitude, hours of work, job insecurity, physical demands, and hazards all are better discriminated by an occupational title than is take-home pay—a strong indication of the potential validity of job dimension analysis and the utility of inferences based on occupation. On the other hand, psychological demands and social support are discriminated very poorly between occupation (with only 7 percent and 4 percent, respectively, between-occupation variance). Some further estimate of the impact of individual differences can be assessed by examining how much additional variance in the QES scales is added by truly important individual differences such as age, education, and race. This amount is usually between 2 and 7 percent—significantly less than the between-occupation variance, except for psychological demands and social support. Thus while we do have clear evidence for objective validity of some dimensions, it is weak for others. The contribution of explicitly measured individual differences to the self-reported job scales is not large.

Conclusion

This chapter has attempted to provide a conceptual road map for the psychosocial world of work, based on decision latitude, psychological and physical work demands, and social support. Although we feel we have been able to demonstrate substantial validity and practical importance for our view of these issues, no doubt there will be other attempts to define this structure in the future. We have attempted to confirm the utility and the objective validity of psychosocial measures of work by reviewing the plausibility of the overall picture they provide of working life and by establishing congruency among findings from many areas of research. This is still only a partial picture of psychosocial work life, however. We must address more directly the point raised by many researchers that psychosocial reality of work is substantially influenced by individual characteristics. To cause heart disease, psychosocial work characteristics must interact with individual mechanisms of perception, coping, and physiological functioning, and the effects obviously must vary among individuals. The challenge of understanding how this happens, in a manner that also leaves us in a position to design more effective work environments, is the subject of chapter 3.

3

The Environment, the Worker, and Illness: Psychological and Physiological Linkages

How do personality and physiology interact with the psychological work environment to produce, on the one hand, illness such as coronary heart disease or, on the other, productive behavior? Our ultimate goal will be to understand whether we have created social environments that are maladjusted to human psychological and physiological functioning, and if so, what is needed to correct them.

To answer these questions, we must explore hypotheses linking the obvious effects of personality and physiology on health and behavior with environmental causes at the level of the work task. As we review the literature, we find that the vast majority of research in this area to date has focused on the individual alone; relatively little attention has been given to the linkage to the environment. In this chapter, therefore, we will engage in some additional theory building and synthesis.

In the United States today, newspapers, magazines, and books are filled with an ever-growing discussion of personal "stress cures." Whole industries purvey improved health through changes in personal life-style, from yoga, transcendental meditation, and positive thinking to jogging and special diets; and stress has become a growth industry for practitioners who treat stress symptoms (Miller 1988). The individual focus of many of the contemporary stress solutions probably results at least in part from American cultural patterns emphasizing individual initiative, which also places responsibility for health on the individual. The cure for stress is seen to lie in changes in personal styles of behavior or personality: they are the intermediate variable between inevitable stressors and illness. This view is reflected in McGrath's (1970) "overload" definition of stress as the result of environmental demands that are too heavy for the individual, given the individual's resources and capabilities. The full burden of moderating life stressors is placed on the individual, instead of being shared with the environment. In Sweden, there is less emphasis on individual blame and more emphasis on social causes of illness.

One problem is that this individual-focused view can be used to the political disadvantage of employees suffering from work stress, in a form of victim blaming. One classic example is found in the U.S. Federal Aeronautics Administration training materials for air traffic controllers that were in use at the time of the 1981 strike and lockout. During the previous decade, substantial grievances about work stresses had been expressed by the controllers. The FAA answer to these complaints was to issue a 1½-hour training film that claims to summarize relevant scientific information on job stress. Specifically, the film calls on air traffic controllers to question the belief that events in the work setting are a cause of stress reactions. It is not real work-load events themselves that cause stress, the film stoically states, but the employee's own interpretation of events. In an example showing a disagreement between an air traffic controller and his superior, the controller's interpretation of the situation, rather than a management error, is claimed to cause his stress. Controllers are also told that their "unrealistic" expectations of "fair treatment" are often "irrational" in a modern setting and lead to further unnecessary stress. Finally, controllers are told to correct their "must thinking" (for example, "I must be perfect") in a politically damaging way: if they acknowledge that their own personal fallibilities are the cause of problems on the job, they will experience less stress than if they blame outside forces, such as management policy. In the context of the controllers' objectively very demanding work situation before and after the strike, accepting the full burden of responsibility would have represented a tragic weakening of the controllers' bargaining position—and would probably have increased their personal stress problems. The training film's further suggestions for alleviating stress (visualizing babbling brooks, making diet changes, and doing finger exercises) are also exclusively individual-focused. The entire film represents a lopsided validation for shifting the full responsibility for stress problems from FAA management to the workers. An environmentally based model of job stress would have come to much different conclusions. Of course, an exclusively environmental perspective can be just as distorted; there are obviously individual differences in response to stress, as we shall discuss later in this chapter. A joint theory is needed (Karasek 1984).

The Evolution of Stress Theories

The dominance of the focus on the individual probably derives from the fact that many of the stressors studied in the early research in this field were environmentally uncontrollable. Most existing stress theories were developed to describe not the chronic effects of poorly designed work but the reactions to acute stress in situations threatening biological survival. The first research goal for Walter Cannon, one of the first physiologists in the field (1914), was to illuminate the nature of quasi-instinctual animal fight/flight responses. When an animal is attacked by a predator, the stressors are acute and the cost of faulty response mechanisms is enormous: loss of life.

The next stage of research was triggered by Hans Selye's impatience, as a student, with a medical curriculum that rarely focused on the complaints that most often brought patients to doctors' offices, generalized low-level problems such as nausea, depression, dizziness, and fatigue ([1936] 1976). These responses were ultimately associated with his concept of the "generalized stress syndrome." The bulk of Selye's research in the 1930s and 1940s, however, involved exposing animals to acute stresses that human experience seldom provides: unexpected plunges into ice-cold water, cuts in body tissue, and toxic implantations. The first human "life experience" stress research involved reactions of soldiers to battlefield traumas during the Second World War (Eitinger 1971; Grinker and Spiegel 1945) and, later, reactions of populations to natural catastrophes such as floods and fires. In the early 1960s, this research broadened somewhat to include catastrophes that sooner or later arise in almost everyone's life—divorce, death in the family, loss of a job—represented by Holmes and Rahe's (1967) schedule of recent experiences to predict illness. Nevertheless, the focus remained on acute, catastrophic stressors. More important, most of these were stressors that could not be prevented by human intervention. The uncontrollability of the stressors meant that the most interesting question was how the individual could cope with or bear this inevitable burden.

Our theoretical perspective is developed for an entirely different context: the work environment where stressors are routinely planned, years in advance, by some people for other people. These stressors, while much lower in severity, may occur day in and day out for decades. In this context, the controllability of the stressor is a very important new component of a theoretical model. The issues of control have become more acute as we develop ever more complex and integrated social organizations, which bring ever more complex limitations on individual behavior. These effects are of course aggravated by the fact that our work stresses now are not related to the need for rapid fight/flight physical reactions for which we are physiologically adapted. Instead, our demands are for long-term psychological arousal (combined with no physical exertion), where environmental constraints on response play a much more important role.

THE BASIC ELEMENTS OF A STRESS THEORY

Stress theory is not so much a single theory as an umbrella term referring to a relatively new basic scientific approach to problems in human behavior and health (we revert to common usage of the term "stress" until the demand/control model is reintroduced). Extremely diverse concepts, all called stress theories, have been developed by different groups of scientists, with apparently totally contradictory predictions. In spite of the diversity, all stress models have one distinguishing feature that allows their recognition: the environment is the source or the cause (albeit not the sole source), and the individual is the target or locus of effects. The tendency to focus cures for stress on the individual is ironic in light of the inevitability of an environmental source when a stress process is implied. Most medical science has not traditionally taken an environmental perspective; while an individual illness is clearly the problem manifestation, medicine most often searches for causes in malfunctions of that individual's own physiology or psychology. Thus, stress theory really represents a new paradigm for scientific explanations of health and behavior.

Another common characteristic of stress theories is that the nature of the causal link between environment and effect on the individual is less easily determined than is usually true for the physical sciences or for conventional medical science. Instead of a single unambiguous cause-and-effect linkage, as in the hard sciences, in stress models many causes may accumulate to produce a single effect (Levi 1972c).* On the other hand, a single

---

*Indeed, there is evidence (Karasek 1976, addendum p. 224a) that the effects of stressors are more clearly deterministic when aggregated over all causes, and over all kinds of effects. The impact of individual differences is to distinguish *what kind* of response will occur for the individual. For workers with no childhood stressors, job strain was associated most strongly with tiredness; for those with one such reported problem, job strain and depression were associated most strongly; and among those with several reported childhood problems, job strain and physical illness symptoms were associated most strongly. The aggregate response of all individuals across all symptoms was much more constant than the response to any particular strain symptom.

cause (stressor) may manifest itself in many quite different effects. Furthermore, there is usually a significant time delay between the cause and the effect. This means that stress effects may often appear to be unintended results where lack of professional observation of the phenomena makes it still harder to isolate the true causes. Of course it must also be noted that when deterministic physical models are applied to human illness or even to very complex physical systems, prediction is also very far from complete. The ambiguity of stress theory need not be mistaken for non-science or sloppy science; it is merely another form of cause-effect rationality. This form of rationality is probably very well suited to complex systems of all sorts that involve multiple, interacting subsystems.

STRESS IN COMPLEX SYSTEMS: CONTROL-SYSTEM DISEQUILIBRIUM

It is probably in the context of complex systems that the concept of stress is most relevant. A system as a whole can be said to be in the state of stress even though we cannot pinpoint any single diseased or defective sub-mechanism that accounts for all the disruption. If this state lasts for a long time, any further—even minor—disruption of one part of the organism is likely to send ripples of disruption to the other parts. Stress is a systemic concept referring to a disequilibrium of the system as a whole, in particular of the system's control capabilities. Biological control systems include the brain, the heart muscle, and the psychoendocrine systems. Control systems also occur at the level of cognitive functioning and at interpersonal levels. All organisms must have control mechanisms to integrate the actions of separate subsystems, each of which has a different responsibility in ensuring the organism's effective functioning within its environment. Psychosomatic diseases, including hypertension, are increasingly regarded as disorders of regulation in which the process of attaining system equilibrium (*homeostasis*) is disturbed (Henry and Stephens 1977b; Page 1976; Weiner 1977). Most stress models—including Selye's, which we will discuss in the next section—have focused on maintenance of homeostasis; our attempt to explain these phenomena, however, builds on two disequilibrium mechanisms: strain and learning.

Returning to our demand/control model terminology we can speculate on how strain and learning processes might work in a systems context. Strain is an overload condition experienced by an organism's control system when it attempts to maintain integrated functioning in the face of too many environmental challenges. Imposing order on a chaotic environment is work; it takes energy (a lesson from the second law of thermodynamics in physics). This formulation is quite consistent with information-systems theory.* To impose order on its environment, the control system must push itself out of equilibrium (the rest state) and do work. Such proactive, goal-oriented actions can go to extremes and lead to strain or fatigue. The system's state of disorder (entropy) must be restored before further information can be organized. Thus, all living organisms must return their control systems to the rest state (actually a state of relaxed disorder—high entropy) periodically in order to be capable of undertaking the next round of order-imposing tasks. Without sleep or relaxation periods, for example, no further work can be done, by anyone. The coordination processes or the attempts to relax may be inhibited if the controlling bodily organ cannot follow its own optimal course to coordinate action—that is, if it has low decision latitude. One classic inhibitor of relaxation is unstopping and demanding treadmill work, which clearly prevents random, relaxing activities. Experiments have shown the destructive effects of treadmill-type activity on animals (inhibition of REM sleep or REM rebound [Dement 1969; Watson and Henry 1977]), which may roughly correspond to adverse effects of highly demanding assembly line work for humans. Weiner (1977) observes that psychosomatic diseases are increasingly regarded as disorders where complex feedback linkages that are needed to return to the rest state are disturbed. In this case it may be constraint of the possibilities to take needed relaxation periodically that is crucial to strain development.

Of course, systems can grow in their capacities to organize their environments, by developing new meta-organizational strategies that accomplish the same amount of organization with less work. This is a skill development process. But such activities make heavy use of the system's internal organizational capacity, and such learning activities therefore cannot occur when the system is exhausted or out of equilibrium. Welford, Brown, and Gabb stated in 1950 that subtasks cannot be organized into larger plans by chronically stressed or fatigued individuals. More recent experiments show that deprivation of REM sleep inhibits learning of complex tasks (C. Smith 1985).

In summary, we can deduce two principles of system disequilibrium that will be important for linking work activity both to personality and to com-

*The system disequilibrium concept is not the most common form of environmentally based stress theory. Energy-based theories are more common, and we have made use of this formulation ourselves. In chapter 2 we referred to the demand/control model as a *potential for action* model, because the implied operation is that a potential for environmental action is aroused when an environmental stressor is recognized. We can label this aroused state *stress*. Such a model format is quite common in the physical sciences, where potential energy is stored up and then released to do work as kinetic energy, or even in Freudian psychology, where the repression of disturbing incidents provides the motivation for later shaping of individual behavior. Our reinterpretation of system and information theory given here provides more insight into the system control implications of action potential models. Excess environmental demands or response restrictions can ultimately lead to disturbance of the individual's internal control system that organizes its environmental response.

pany organizational structures in this and later chapters: (1) increased skills allow the system to face its challenges with less effort: *learning inhibits strain*; (2) systems in a state of strain have little capacity to learn: *strain inhibits learning*.

We can find examples in large-scale human organizational control systems where system-strain leads to irrational, disorganized, and non-productive behavior and to an inability to coordinate subsystems in usable plans. One example was the New York power grid failure that resulted in the city blackout of July 1977 (Federal Energy Regulatory Commission 1980). A small lightning strike in an overworked municipal power system led to the collapse of the entire system because of completely unresponsive and uncoordinated communication patterns between the controllers of each member power system in the grid. In spite of repeated, clearly communicated warnings to each other of impending catastrophe, the controllers were unable to agree on a coordinated plan of action to cut system loads, and the entire system collapsed, leaving the world's most complex city without electric power and in a state of chaos for over a week. We can see the damage done when separate power systems cannot coordinate; is there an analogous result when complex human physiological processes are out of coordination?

The Demand/Control Model and Other Stress and Learning Models Compared

While some level of demands (in the form of challenge, interest, or importance) is necessary for effective performance and job satisfaction, too high a level of demands can obviously be disastrous. This fact has implied a U-shaped association between demands and performance (or stress) and in turn the notion of an optimal level of demands, in Selye's well-known general adaptation syndrome ([1936] 1976) and related, classic theories by Yerkes and Dodson (1908) and Wundt (1922), on stimulation and performance that still form the basis of much contemporary stress theory. It also implies the existence of equilibrium-maintaining processes that the individual can employ to maintain optimal arousal, maximizing performance and minimizing strain. For example, the worker can develop new skills or strengths or switch to simpler conceptual strategies when facing a complex task, in order to maintain a constant level of engagement (Bainbridge 1974). The problem with this formulation is that disequilibrium processes, such as we hypothesize in our strain and learning mechanisms, receive less

attention. Minor levels of disequilibrium associated with fatigue have indeed been clearly found to lead to decreased accuracy, slowed response,
and disorganization of task strategies (Welford 1976), but the premise is
that recuperation and renewed performance follow easily with rest. It has
also been found, however, that extended disequilibrium is related to system
destruction or to system growth. Irreversible physical damage and long-
term degradation of behavior, as well as expansion of capabilities, obviously do occur and must be reflected in theory development.

The Strain Hypothesis

We will begin by comparing our demand/control model with the general
adaptation syndrome of Selye. With the appropriate redefinition of some
terms, the two theories have some common predictions. Selye's "eustress"
and "dystress" distinction maintains that a certain amount of stress
(arousal) is considered good ("eustress"); whereas too much stress represents "dystress" and can result in pathology—the classic U-curve in figure
3–1. This model reflects the homeostatic approach, where any displace-
ment from the optimum level of arousal, in either direction, represents an
undesirable departure from the equilibrium state. Unfortunately, the level
at which arousal switches from good to bad is not specified in Selye's theory; one can determine that the stress is too much only if it produces bad
consequences. Our two-dimensional theory, however, tries to specify the
necessary condition that determines whether the consequences of stressor
exposure will be good or bad: the individual's level of control over his or
her responses in the stressful situation. Translation between our two-
dimensional model and Selye's single-dimensional model is then possible
(figures 3–1a and 3–1b).

We consider Selye's arousal (or stress) continuum to be equivalent to the
unresolved strain (diagonal A) dimension of our two-dimensional model
(figure 3–1b). In our model, this diagonal represents the difference between stressors and control possibilities; in the corner near label A,
stressors exceed control possibilities. To help confirm our interpretation, we
note that in Selye's experiments the laboratory animal's control over
stressors was not usually incorporated as an experimental variable, and
control was always very low. That is, the laboratory rats were not supposed
to try to escape when the stressor was applied, and if they struggled they
were undoubtedly restrained even more. At high demands and low control,
our two-dimensional theory and Selye's theory yield the same prediction:
physiological and psychological stress, and possible disease. This interpretation is consistent with results obtained by Weiss (1971); when he explic-

FIGURE 3-1 (a-b)
*Comparison between psychological demand/decision latitude model
and other stress models*

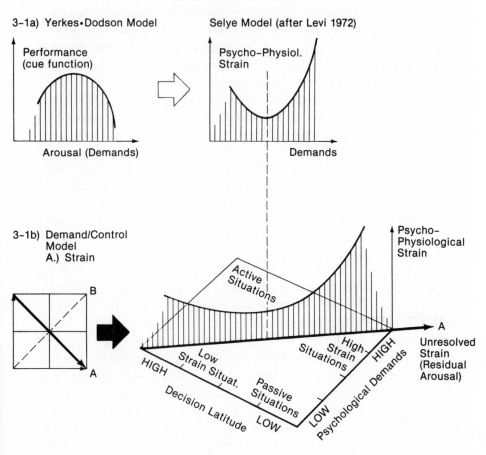

SOURCE: Redrawn from Karasek, Russell, and Theorell 1982.

itly restricted control for animal subjects facing stressors, severe stomach ulceration occurred.

THE ACTIVE LEARNING HYPOTHESIS

There is another emerging tendency in social-psychological literature, quite different from our strain model, that views some of life's taxing situations as challenges and opportunities for growth and learning rather than as burdens. A classic statement of this position can be found in Robert White's article on "The Concept of Competence" (1959), which describes how the psychological state of people in challenging circumstances is enhanced, rather than disrupted, by increasing demands—up to a point. White calls his observations a new theory of motivation based on environmental circumstance rather than innate needs. There is also a substantial literature on children's play suggesting a motivation to increase the stressfulness of play, up to a certain point (Gilmore 1971). Similar perspectives have been reported by industrial psychologists attempting to broaden their conceptual frameworks to include activation theory (Scott 1966) and stimulation theory (Schwab and Cummings 1976).

The fact that environmental demands can thus be conceptualized in both positive and negative terms is, fortunately, not a contradiction for our joint model. We simply take it as evidence that at least two separable mechanisms must be used to describe psychological functioning on the job. Indeed, the existence of these two distinct areas of stress findings is one of the primary validations of our more complex demand/control model structure.

In our model, learning occurs in situations that require both individual psychological energy expenditure (demands or challenges) and the exercise of decision-making capability. As the individual with decision-making latitude chooses how best to cope with a new stressor, that new behavior response, if effective, will be incorporated into his or her repertoire of coping strategies; that is, it will be learned. The expanded range of solutions to environmental challenges raises the person's potential activity level in the future. The individual can risk more and attain more; motivation is increased. Thus, incremental additions to competence (that is, learning) are hypothesized to occur most often when the challenges in the situation are matched by the individual's control over alternatives or skill in dealing with those challenges (see Csikszentmihalyi 1975). Under these circumstances, opportunities for constructive reinforcement of behavior patterns are optimal: the situation will not be unchallengingly simple (thus unimportant) nor so demanding that appropriate corrective actions can neither be determined nor invoked because of high anxiety level (the latter situation will simply result in psychological strain). There is much evidence that active behavioral changes are indeed induced in challenging situations (Cooper and Marshall 1976; Marris 1975); we shall discuss this point further in chapter 5. Seligman (1975) observed that unless a young person confronts anxiety, boredom, pain, and trouble *and* masters them by actions he will have impoverished the sense of his own competence. In mastering them, the individual experiences an increased range of responsibility for exercise of choice. The importance of learning to exercise choice in a responsible manner was also discussed for childhood socialization settings by Piaget (1932). In summary, the phenomenon of growth that often occurs in situations of environmental challenge (diagonal B in figure 2–1) illustrates that a high level of demands is not necessarily harmful (at least up to a point).

It must be noted that the concept of control implied by these decision-making mechanisms may differ somewhat from that involved in the strain mechanism discussed in the previous section, which emphasized constraint on opportunities to relax, and rigid behavioral restriction. In learning theory, the crucial issue is whether the individual has continuing control over the reinforcement sequence (Rotter 1966)—that is, the latitude to decide what new strategies to invoke after strategies succeed or fail. There is also congruency between this theory and social learning theory (Bandura 1977), which we further discuss in chapter 5.

We can also compare the predictions of the demand/control model with Selye's theory of optimal activity level—for example, optimal job performance by workers—and with Yerkes and Dodson's earlier predictions. Again, Selye's optimal activity range is defined tautologically as occurring in the middle of his stress continuum, whereas we can list the conditions for motivated, optimal activity more specifically: demands and control are matched at high levels. Our model predicts that the shape of the optimum activity curve broadens (implying greater adaptability) or narrows as a function of the level of the stressor/control match or equilibrium. Moving into the "active" quadrant of our model (toward label B in figure 3–1b), the curve of optimal function broadens. This means that the individual is capable of maintaining a state of equilibrium while confronting a much larger range of stressors (that is, effectively able to tackle greater challenges—or even endure greater boredom). The challenges can, of course, be more easily faced because the individual has developed more skills through the trial/failure/success learning process that these high control–high demand environments permit. Welford (1976) and Fiske and Maddi (1961) have also observed that at higher levels of equilibrium (for us, stressor/control match), optimal activity occurs over a broader range of stress exposure.

The process that we have described above—"broadening the range of confrontable challenges"—is also consistent with our information theory–based system disequilibrium model. While systems models were previously considered closed (always tending to return to a fixed homeostatic state), recent developments in the thermodynamics of self-organizing physical systems (Prigogine 1980) illustrate a congruent set of mechanisms for growing systems that expand the range between their most energetic, organized state and their true resting state. Energy added to the system from the exterior environment (so-called "dissipative systems"), enables it to reach equilibrium at a higher level of complexity. The growing system develops new patterns of functional operation congruent with a higher state of organizational capability (see also Volpert 1974). Such growth may require periods of relaxation in biological systems, as Watson and Henry

(1977) and Henry and Stephens (1977b) have pointed out. For instance, women sleep more during pregnancy, and young people require far more sleep than do adults.

Of course, a negative possibility also exists: demands and control may be matched at a *low* level. This passive situation, which unfortunately appears to be present in many jobs (such as routine clerical jobs in older bureaucracies, as we saw in chapter 2), could be associated with the reverse process of skill atrophy and unlearning. A resulting very narrow curve of optimum performance would mean that even moderate demands are perceived as causing strain; consider the totally unoccupied clerk in a large telephone or postal bureaucracy who "can't possibly" do us a favor and solve our small problem. Even stressor-free periods would easily lead to uneasiness, restlessness, and anxiety, rather than to the expected relaxation, because the acceptable range of demands is so narrow. This negative growth possibility has been demonstrated in the growing literature on "learned helplessness" in terms of skill usage in human subjects. The evidence is further discussed in chapter 5.

An important unexpected implication of our theory is that situations conducive to relaxation are distinct from situations conducive to active development, although in both situations the individual has a high level of control. In the active case, environmental challenges are also present. This distinction makes clear our contention that a truly healthy situation is one that contains challenges for the individual. Of course, relaxation and active regeneration may also occur together in many growth processes. In an active job, control may allow the individual to take short periods of relaxation at self-determined, physiologically optimum times, even if the job situation is one of intense overall activity and challenge. However, according to Kern and Schumann (1984), a new type of active job has become increasingly common in industry, where activity is too intense and very little relaxation is allowed. In these jobs any ameliorative impact of an increased variety of tasks to be done is overwhelmed by the sheer magnitude of intense loads— leading to strain. This condition forces us to consider limits on the model with respect to skill utilization at very high work loads.

Integrating Personality and Environmental Factors

Perhaps the most common strategy for linking personality and environmental aspects of stress response is through a theory of environmental adaptation or growth, such as we have described above. Most such explanations, however, differ from ours in one crucial respect. For example, the Person-Environment Fit model (see French 1974) states that the individual's background and capability should be matched with the demands of the environment. In many cases this is a very useful approach, but it has often been used primarily to reassign persons to different jobs. That is, the individual must bear the burden of adjustment to the work setting (Baker 1985). In the "interactionist" approach introduced by Cox (1978) and further developed by Hingley and Cooper (1986), the supremely adaptable human species can adjust to adversity by developing "coping skill" and often become stronger as a result of this adjustment. But individuals (and systems) can fail to adapt successfully, as in the case of long-lasting strain.* The interactionist approach is seen by its proponents as humanistic because it keeps the proactive individual in the center of attention and emphasizes "free will." It is certainly true that striving in the face of environmental adversity is an irresistible theme in most cultures, not least the American. When these models speak of the positive mechanisms of growth and adaptation, however, they often place a disproportionate burden of adapting on the individual. Just the opposite critique might be made of our model. While correctly illuminating the "costs" of some environments, it appears to shackle the individual's strivings for creative adaptation with environmental determinism. A model that considers both individual and environmental factors is clearly necessary to avoid this problem. In the next section, we will utilize a stepwise approach in which personal characteristics are introduced in a dynamic two-stage process derived from the interaction between the environment and the individual. We believe that this approach will be much more practical for job redesign situations in which both workers' personalities and the impact of work on their personalities must be understood in order to organize effective change processes.

Many factors compel us to address individual characteristics when explaining stress, health, or behavior. Individuals do have true inborn differences in their potential for adaptation, although this book focuses on those aspects of behavior that are not determined by such unchangeable factors. More relevant for our discussions is the well-demonstrated fact that not all individuals perceive an objectively similar situation as equally threatening

---

*One such alternative perspective views long-lasting "stress" as the burden of the process of adaptation itself—Selye's own construction. Energy must be expanded to readjust to changing realities, and each such adjustment diminishes the individual total lifetime reserve of adaptation capability (a limit that is actually contradicted by recent systems theory predictions on self-organizing systems [Prigogine 1980]).

Strain may be viewed as the discrepancy between the individual's desire to cope with a challenge and reality. Implicitly this type of strain can be eliminated by a reduction in expectation level: the person would be happier not even trying to succeed in the face of difficult challenges. This approach, however, can justify repressive environments.

or conducive to action and thus stressful in our definition. This difference could affect our self-report job measures, as we saw in chapter 2. Lazarus (1966) concluded that individual personality characteristics mediate between stressors of the objective external environment and individual symptoms of stress. Lazarus and others have shown that the magnitude of psychological stress actually perceived (as measured by physiological reactions such as skin resistance and hormone secretion) is a function of the stressful event, anticipatory worrying, and the individual's tendencies toward defensive denial and avoidance. This emphasis on the individual's self-appraisal of stressors has been further enhanced by the last two decades of theoretical development in psychology which has emphasized *cognitive* processes: the individual's interpretation of his or her environment. The time pattern of stress response is another individually controlled phenomenon of importance (Lazarus 1966). Janis and Mann (1977) have discussed the extra burden of anxiety faced after major surgery if the patient has not done the "work of worrying" beforehand. Anticipatory worrying may shift the impact of the perceived stress to an earlier time and thus level out the impact of the stressor.

Although the impact of personality is undeniable, there is a major problem in determining what personality characteristics are important. Decades of research have still not reliably identified *the* personality variables.* Indeed, views about the permanency of personality traits is changing. More recently, joint personality/environment theories have been strongly advocated by personality psychologists (see Mischel 1973). One logical starting point for building a joint personality/environment model would be a simple congruence principle in which a dimension of environmental control would imply a personality measure related to control and the same would apply for demands. For example, Kobasa's (Maddi and Kobasa 1984) concept of "hardiness," which emphasizes personal feelings of control, commitment, and desire to accept challenges as a personality measure, could be easily related to our measures of control at work. Frankenhaeuser and her co-workers (Frankenhaeuser, Lundberg, and Forsman 1980) have also developed a two-dimensional framework based on "effort" and "distress" which yields four categories of emotional response that are congruent with the four cells of the demand/control model. Difficulty in specifying the precise environment/person linkage carries over into difficulty labeling the specific emotions that might trigger particular psychophysical reactions.

*For instance, a NIOSH report (1975) that devoted one chapter to personality characteristics as causes of accidents and illness found no reliable indices except that subjects with a high score of stressful life events are more accident prone than others. Caplan et al. (1975), in their comprehensive study of 2,000 American workers, concluded that their findings did not support the hypothesis that personality predicts illness. In much of our research in this chapter and chapter 4, it has been difficult to identify crucial personality factors.

Work environment researcher Fred Emery has hypothesized loss of self-esteem (shame) as the negative emotion which could translate the effects of restricted control and respect in the workplace into illness. Such a suggestion is not inconsistent with Henry and Stephens' (1977b) contention that feelings of defeat and social detachment are the pathways between undesirable social environments and psychophysiological response.

In spite of the above examples, however, the main themes that appear relevant for description of industrial work environments do not seem to be the same themes that appear in the literature on personality and personal coping style. While control and demands serve as a basic platform for models of work environment, the most common theme in the personality literature is *affiliation*—emotionally interdependent relationships between individuals—with control coming second. Henry (1988) observed that intimacy and power are the most common themes raised by several recent personality reviews (Kiesler 1983; McAdams 1985; Wiggins and Broughton 1985). He further observed that these seem to be identical to the psychophysiologist's drives for control and attachment. *Control* is the physiologist's term for defense against a threat. *Affiliation* is the mammalian mother-infant attachment (see, for example, Bowlby 1969). These themes are also reflected in Frankenhaeuser's (1980) discussion of stress coping styles.

One major reason for the salience of affiliation in the personality and physiology perspective is that psychological demands are considered to result primarily from the social responsibilities of mothering the young, defending kin, and finding food and shelter for the family. Much of the support for this conception, however, comes from animal studies and human parent/child studies; few studies address the work activity that we described in chapter 2. That type of work is a unique activity in the animal kingdom, occurring only in modern human societies. What is unfortunately special about this human world of work is that demands can occur without social affiliation. Indeed, according to Frederick Taylor, increasing work demands often *had* to be done in isolation, or the workers would either revolt against the process or return to time-wasting socializing. In the animal world, the situation of enforced demands combined with enforced isolation is rare. Indeed, this behavior seems equally rare among our hunter-gatherer ancestors (Turnbull 1972), to whose behavior we are probably best adapted physiologically (Henry and Cassel 1969). What seems to be missing in the modern world is relaxed affiliative behavior, such as the grooming activities displayed in other mammals. This difference, along with the discrepancy between demands and control, seems to be the source of a major potential misfit between human physiology and modern social institutions.

In our opinion, the discrepancy between the control/demand approach and the control/affiliation approach cannot be resolved in the work environment without the development of a three-dimensional model such as we presented at the end of chapter 2: control/demand/social support. Unfortunately, we cannot extend this three-dimensional model through this chapter (the literature to be integrated is almost limitless), so in the discussions below we will continue to emphasize our demand/control model and look for individual response measures congruent with its mechanisms.

THE INTEGRATED MODEL: WORK ENVIRONMENT AND LONG-TERM PERSONALITY EVOLUTION

Our attempt to graft personality measures utilizes the two basic composite mechanisms of our model: strain and learning, rather than a direct correspondence to the demand and control dimensions. Figure 3–2 illustrates the two hypotheses from our earlier discussion of system disequilibrium: stress inhibits learning, and learning inhibits stress. Our first hypothesis is that high anxiety level may inhibit the normal capacity to accept challenge and thus may inhibit new learning. High anxiety level, in turn, may be the result of psychological strain accumulated over time (see the diagonal arrow #3 from accumulated anxiety intersecting the extension of the active-growth arrow, diagonal B). Second, we hypothesize that new learning may lead to reduced perception of events as stressful and to increased success in coping. Accumulated learning experiences, stimulating the long-term development of the feeling of mastery or confidence, may be important in this process (see the diagonal arrow #4 from feeling of mastery intersecting the extension of the strain arrow, diagonal A). We will use this broad frame of reference to organize our review of the literature linking personality theory with the accumulated effects of environmental circumstances. Not all important findings will fit neatly into such a model, of course, notably Type A behavior, which will be discussed separately at the end of this chapter.

We should note that our perspective on personality is an unusual one, much more global and environmentally based than most research on personality, which the scope of this book does not allow us to review in other than a cursory manner. The two dynamic mechanisms linking the person and the environment in our model require two personal-response orientations that result from accumulated environmental exposure. This need in turn leads to our evolution of two global categories of personality: *feeling of mastery* and *accumulated strain* (figure 3–2). Both of these should probably be considered broad response orientations, not specific personality mea-

FIGURE 3–2
*Dynamic associations linking environmental strain and learning
to evolution of personality*

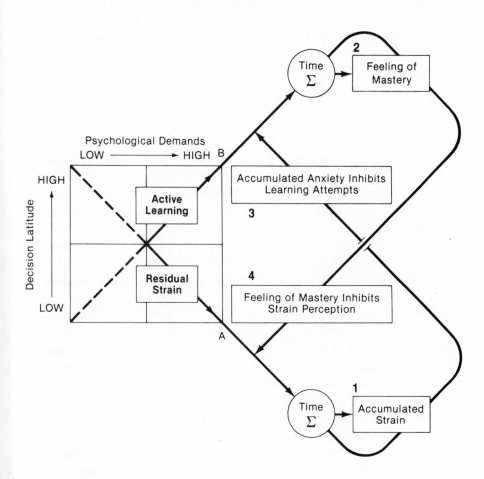

sures, from the perspective of current psychological research. Our interest
is primarily in personality modifications that occur in adulthood, but the
same processes might link childhood experiences and adult personality orientations. In the sections that follow, we briefly discuss the congruence of
the broad implications of our model with several current measures in the
research literature: feelings of environmental mastery, denial, alexithymia,
trait anxiety measures, cumulative life stressor implications, and finally
Type A behavior—a set of measures not unlike those proposed by Kahn
and Quinn (1970) to link environment and stress response.

STRAIN INHIBITS LEARNING

Our first hypothesized mechanism (arrow #3 in figure 3–2) is that accumulated level of unresolved strain (or anxiety level) appears to restrict a person's ability to learn solutions to new problems (Lader 1969).* Miller and Swanson (1960) hypothesized that people with stressful life histories avoid perceiving current problems, diminishing their level of active engagement in the environment and thus the likelihood of learning. We recall the impact of two job traumas on the coping orientation of the once-successful executive described by Seligman in chapter 2: he became incapable of addressing even the simplest of challenges. This example also showed the difference between short-term effects—the experience of intense job strain—and the long-term effect of passivity (theoretically linked in the learned-helplessness research). The literature on burnout has also demonstrated that prolonged job stress is associated with a decline in initiatives at work (Maslach 1982). Finally, there is confirmation from experimental studies: animal studies by Watson and Henry (1977) show that forced participation in a stressful treadmill exercise after a potential learning experience (instead of a rest break) inhibits retention of the new learning. C. Smith (1985) has demonstrated similar effects: lack of REM sleep restricts learning of complex tasks.

A possible personality trait[†] measure that could be related to unresolved strain in our model is the level of accumulated anxiety (arrow #1 in figure 3–2). Studies of life stress and mental health (Brown 1973; Langner and Michaels 1963; Paykel 1973; Theorell, Flodérus, and Lind 1975) have documented the significance of accumulated demands for adaptation on general health and predisposition to illness. In Karasek's (1976) analysis of the Survey of Level of Living in Sweden, the total number of traumatic life events faced through adolescence moderated the later relationship between job strain and kinds of symptoms reported (see p. 86n). Longitudinal studies of life events have shown that the adrenaline output increases during periods of accumulated events (Theorell et al. 1972, Chadwick et al. 1979). Findings for illnesses closely related to the psychoendocrine system, such as the Cushing syndrome (Gifford and Gunderson 1970), are of particular interest; they indicate that such an accumulated demand for adaptation may influence not only temporary behavior but even the long-term functioning of the endocrine system.

*Sensitivity to role conflict is higher for workers with a high level of neurotic anxiety, a factor with which unhappy childhood is correlated (Kahn et al. 1964). The more the residual strain is internalized, the less capacity there is to tackle new challenges.

†A large number of personality tests have been developed with scales of "trait" anxiety: a permanent orientation to the environment as opposed to transient response to stressful settings.

LEARNING INHIBITS STRAIN

Our second hypothesized mechanism (arrow #4 in figure 3–2) is that the cumulative result of newly learned behavior patterns is to increase skills and feelings of mastery, which in turn are associated with a reduced perception of stress. We saw such an example clearly in chapter 2 in Bill Russell's description of his most demanding basketball challenges: after years of successful competition, even in the most demanding contests he felt totally in control and elated, not strained. In a more common job situation, described in chapter 8, when workers at the Almex manufacturing plant experienced increased autonomy with the introduction of autonomous work groups, which allowed them to solve their own job-related problems, their feelings of self-confidence grew and they perceived their work to be less stressful even after demands increased. Reviews by Kasl (1989) and Jackson (1983) show that perceptions of control and mastery are consistently associated with lower levels of psychological strain. Bandura's (1977) work with "cognitive appraisal" coping strategies also confirms such associations.

A possible personality trait measure that may be associated with accumulated learning experience in our model is a feeling of mastery (arrow #2 in figure 3–2). Many current psychological research themes could be related to mastery feelings, such as flexibility or rigidity of response. Kohn (1985) documents the impact of rigid, low-control work environments on personality at the macro social level: parents in rigid jobs pass on to their children the personality orientation of rigidity in coping styles and obedience to authority. Several researchers in the field of learned helplessness maintain that the crucial dimension that prevents passivity is perception of mastery, even if the subject lacks actual control (Glass and Singer 1972). Of course, when it is time to test reality, only true control over the situation will allow a feeling of control to be maintained (Buck 1972).

A personality measure that fits the mastery orientation in our model is Rotter's (1966) "locus of control" measure, which is cited as a determinant of the degree of behavior change toward passivity in the learned-helplessness literature (Seligman 1975). Rotter's "external" is a person who has little feeling of mastery over situations and attributes control to factors outside his influence—that is, to "fate." Kobasa's "hardiness" concept, noted above, also measures perception of success in meeting workplace challenges. Another related concept has been introduced by Antonovsky (1987), who emphasizes the importance of the individual's sense of coherence for active coping and has created the "sense of coherence scale" (SOC).

There is also evidence for the converse process: the ineffectiveness of coping behavior (passive coping) when mastery attitude is low (Dohrenwend and Dohrenwend 1974; Seligman 1976). A very low perception of mastery can also lead to the tendency to deny the problem's importance, through cognitive dissonance and devaluation of alternatives. Denial diminishes stress in the short term, but it has very undesirable long-term effects and seems very dysfunctional (see p. 114). Some authors cite denial of stressful reality or denial of socially unacceptable behavior as the crucial characteristic through which people modulate their reactions to events in their external reality (Funkenstein 1956; Kerckhoff and Back 1968; Knox et al. 1988; Miller and Swanson 1960). Thus, a high tendency to deny problematic reality may operate in a manner roughly opposite to feelings of mastery, with respect to strain perceptions (Knox et al. 1988). A third concept, related to denial, is alexithymia—the inability to express emotions (Lesser 1981). One important methodological aspect of denial, alexithymia, and low levels of mastery is that people with these tendencies may describe their job situations in a distorted way. Because they do not easily complain about emotional problems at all, they may not be able to analyze and describe psychosocial conditions in the workplace.* The inhibition of emotional expression may be associated with an increased risk of stress-related illness, as we see on p. 114.

THE COMBINED SECOND-ORDER IMPACTS

The two mechanisms can be combined into an integrated model, because the personality characteristic hypothesized to be the output of one of the mechanisms is an input (a moderator variable) in the other. In the residual psychological strain mechanism, accumulated unresolved anxiety level is the output (a personality output), but anxiety level is an input (moderator) for the learning mechanism. In the active learning mechanism, an accumulation of learning experiences leads to a feeling of mastery as an output, but mastery is also an input (moderator) for the residual psychological strain mechanism.

Thus, a model combining both mechanisms yields an important dynamic perspective on personality and environment. First, environmental factors over the long term partly determine personality, and later, environmental effects are moderated by these previously developed personality orientations. The combined model yields the possibility of two long-term dynamic spirals of behavior—one positive, based on the inhibition of strain by learning, and the other negative, based on the inhibition of learning by

*A poor ability to describe the characteristics of a job environment may be a consequence of the environment itself, as Hacker (1978) and Volpert (1989) have pointed out. Even underutilization of skill may lead to underreporting of problems.

strain. In the positive behavioral dynamic, an active job setting and its successful learning opportunities lead to an increased feeling of mastery and confidence. This feeling in turn helps the person to cope with the inevitable strain-inducing situations of the job. The result is reduced residual strain and thus increased capacity to accept still more challenging situations, which promote still more learning and positive personality change, ad infinitum. The second, undesirable behavioral dynamic begins when a high-strain job setting leads over time to a high anxiety level (accumulated residual strain). This strain in turn restricts the person's capacity to accept the positive challenges that the job may also offer, leading to less learning of new coping strategies and a diminished feeling of mastery over situations. This reduced feeling of mastery in turn restricts the capacity to cope with job strain and leads to still higher residual strain levels, ad infinitum.

The model as a whole is still an untested extrapolation of the mechanisms above, and even the mechanisms are quite broad. There is substantial evidence, however, for the theoretical and empirical independence of demands and control presented in chapter 2, and substantial evidence that new learned patterns induced by the job are theoretically and empirically independent of stress-related health outcomes (Karasek 1976). On the positive side, we hope that such an integrated model gives us a conceptual framework broad enough in scope to be useful to professionals outside the field of psychology—the workers, managers, engineers, and physicians who must constantly work with the whole reality of the work situation, the person, and the job.

Job Structure and Physiological Response

To make plausible the argument that job characteristics can cause heart disease, we must take one additional theoretical step: we must connect psychological strain to physical illness with appropriate physiological linkages. Again, our initial demand/control perspective on environmental factors will be used to synthesize theoretical perspectives. Is human physiology organized, with respect to its environmental response, in a manner congruent with the mechanisms of our model? In this section we will show how some recent findings in work physiology by job stress researchers have bolstered the case for a dissociation or split between two fundamental types of physiological response. We believe that this split is congruent with the dichotomy between the strain and learning mechanisms of our demand/control model (Karasek, Russell, and Theorell 1982).

PSYCHOPHYSIOLOGICAL LINKAGES

In expanding our initial demand/control model into the physiological sphere, we hypothesize that two categories of physiological responses, *catabolic* (metabolic consumption) and *anabolic* (restoration), are linked, respectively, to the two mechanisms of our joint psychological model of the previous section, strain and learning. We argue that catabolic phenomena, which are associated with taxing metabolic processes, are more likely to occur when stressors are combined with low control. Catabolic response is therefore the physiological analogue of our psychological strain mechanism (diagonal A, figure 2–1). We further suggest—and here the evidence has been quite speculative until recently—that situations in which high stressors are coupled with high control are conducive to anabolic psychophysiological response (Karasek, Russell, and Theorell 1982). Anabolic response is associated with physiological repair and regeneration and thus is a health-promoting response. It is the physiological analogue of our psychological active learning mechanism (diagonal B, figure 2–1). Of course, the complexities of physiological processes make it impossible to fit all phenomena into such simple categories, but we hope that this environmentally based review of physiological mechanisms will lead to new insights.

Mason (1968) was one of the first to challenge the one-dimensional stress concept and emphasize the complex physiological balance between energy-providing catabolic processes and regenerative anabolic processes. Evidence has been accumulated by Frankenhaeuser and her group of researchers (Lundberg and Frankenhaeuser 1978) that the combination of control as an environmental moderator with psychological stressors in human subjects can lead to dissociated functions of the adrenal medullary and adrenal cortisol systems, the two major hormonal control systems commanded from the brain. Typically, when fast pace is coupled with low control, as in our high-strain jobs, secretion of both cortisol from the adrenal cortex and adrenaline from the adrenal medulla is elevated, whereas in a situation where the subject has a controllable and predictable stressor, adrenaline secretion alone is elevated (Frankenhaeuser, Lundberg, and Forsman, 1980) and cortisol secretion is low. Adrenaline secretion, when associated with a quick return to baseline level, may be evidence of an active behavior pattern that is perfectly healthy, indeed even health-enhancing, as we shall see. Cortisol secretion, on the other hand, may represent a type of uneasy, depressed reaction to a high-strain psychological situation. This is consistent with an interpretation of the demand/control data made by Henry and Stephens (1977b), who link it to the original stress ethological distinctions of fight, flight, feigning death, and dominant/

submissive role in social relations. According to this perspective, activation to conquer a threat or respond to other major stressors engages the adrenal medulla, while loss of control and attachment is associated with adrenal cortex activity.

CATABOLIC RESPONSE: RESIDUAL STRAIN

The central nervous system's control over many of the human body's metabolic processes is operated through two major hormone systems, the adrenal medullary and adrenal cortical systems. The most extensively studied catabolic processes involve the catecholamines (noradrenaline and adrenaline) and cortisol. Adrenaline secretion into the bloodstream occurs in the early stages of arousal to a stressor. When the organism is responding actively to a challenge, the blood provides the muscles and the brain with fuel in the form of glucose and lipids. Glucose is mobilized from glycogen deposits, and lipids are mobilized from lipid deposits. These processes, which transform stored energy into fuel for the potential muscular or neural action, are labeled *catabolic.* Cortisol may be more important in later stages; it is more associated with feelings of distress and depression. Long-standing arousal may cause chronic excess production of catecholamines. It should be emphasized, however, that catabolic and anabolic processes cannot be translated directly into individual hormones. Cortisol as well as adrenaline may facilitate anabolism under certain conditions.

The complexity of theoretical generalizations in this area is shown by the fact that in many cases a cortisol reaction is clearly healthy. It has been associated with desirable coping processes (Rose, Hurst, and Jenkins 1978; Theorell et al., changes in job strain, 1988; Theorell, Häggmark, and Eneroth 1987), in spite of the fact that it occurs during times of distress.* The biological function of cortisol may be to make difficult situations more easily tolerated, but high levels of cortisol over an extended period of time may lead to a health threat.

The timing of the very common plasma adrenaline responses may determine whether their effects can be considered anabolic or catabolic. Frankenhaeuser's (1980) "economic" adrenaline response, characterized by quick return to baseline levels following short-term exposure to stressors,

---

*A marked elevation of morning plasma cortisol level during a crisis has been shown to be associated with healthier coping during follow-up in a study of relatives of cancer patients and also in air traffic controllers (Rose, Hurst, and Jenkins 1978; Theorell, Häggmark, and Eneroth 1987), as well as in workers during increasing job strain (Theorell 1989). Theorell et al. (changes in job strain, 1988) observed that men who have a positive family history of hypertension and a tendency to deny stressful reality (see p. 114) had a significantly lower morning plasma cortisol level than comparable men during periods of peak strain, despite the fact that their systolic blood pressure during working hours was markedly higher that day than on days with less strain.

may be considered regenerative. A slow return to baseline represents an undesirable overreaction that mobilizes resources no longer demanded and is therefore considered catabolic. In addition, it contributes to chronic elevations in catecholamine levels that may result in pathology. Vacations appear to facilitate a rapid return to the catecholamine excretion level characterizing normal off-work hours (Rissler and Elgerot 1978). This finding is consistent with our system disequilibrium hypotheses above: the more relaxed the system, the more easily it can handle new loads.

When searching for linkages between these daily physiological response mechanisms and coronary heart disease, one must distinguish between effects of chronic levels of arousal (stress) and more temporary acute arousal. Acute arousal, such as during periods of psychosocial work load (Theorell and Flodérus-Myrhed 1977) or bereavement (Parkes, Benjamin, and Fitzgerald 1969), may precipitate episodes of myocardial infarction in vulnerable persons. Psychosocial strain that accumulates over a lifetime may significantly contribute to such irreversible diseases as the late stages of hypertension and coronary atherosclerosis. Chronic excess plasma catecholamine levels have been correlated with hypertension (Kjeldsen et al. 1983; Theorell et al., Psychosocial and physiological factors, 1985). It has also been suggested that they are linked to the progression and development of atherosclerosis (Carruthers 1969)—occlusion and hardening of the arteries—with a possible direct toxic effect on the inner part of the blood vessel walls (Haft 1974). Changes in the synthesis of catecholamines with resulting hypertension (Henry et al. 1971), changes in blood-clotting mechanisms (Gertler and White 1976), and changes in lipoprotein production that accelerate atherosclerosis (Chadwick et al. 1979; Friedman, Rosenman, and Carroll 1958; Siegrist et al. 1988) may be pathways to these serious illnesses.

The work environment has been clearly shown to contribute to catabolic responses involving both acute and chronic catecholamine reactions. Increased urinary excretion of catecholamines (including adrenaline) has been observed when job demands increase, such as during periods of overtime work (Rissler and Elgerot 1978), during precision work combined with sleep deprivation (Levi 1972c), when the tempo is rushed (Johansson, Aronsson, and Lindström 1978), when piecework replaces regular salary (Levi 1972a), and when rushed tempo is combined with lack of control (Timio, Pede, and Gentili 1977). Blood catecholamine levels have also been observed to rise when a subject, particularly one who shows signs of Type A behavior, is exposed to long-term situations of rushed job tempo combined with lack of control (Lundberg and Forsman 1979). Cortisol, both in urine and in plasma, has been followed in several field investigations of job stress, particularly in situations of low control or low predictability, as in the studies of Timio, Pede, and Gentili (1977). The plasma cortisol levels were observed to be higher in workers with a combination of assembly line jobs and piecework than in comparable workers with other job designs. This difference remained in workers who became accustomed to the job design during a six-month period. Friedman, Rosenman, and Carroll's classic study (1958) of income tax accountants found significant increases in both triglycerides and serum cholesterol before the April 15th income tax deadline. Prison guards have also been studied in stress research. The guards, whose work is frequently perceived as meaningless, complain that they have a very low degree of skill discretion and authority over decisions. A Swedish study of four contrasting prisons showed that guards at the prison with the lowest employee decision latitude had the highest mean urinary excretion of noradrenaline, particularly at night after work (Härenstam and Theorell 1988).

ANABOLIC RESPONSE: REGENERATION AND HEALTH PROMOTION

Respectable literature on physical regeneration ("the fountain of youth") is scarce, and our hypotheses in this area must therefore be speculative. Yet the importance of this activity is attested to by the sheer volume of cell regeneration that is known to occur. In the active functioning adult, the cells in several bodily systems have a short life expectancy and must be constantly reconstructed. Polymorphonuclear leucocytes (white blood cells), for example, which are essential in the defense against infections, have a life span of eight days, and the body's supply must be totally replaced in that time span. Cells of the epithelial lining of the digestive system that are essential in the defense against ulcer development have a life span of two to five days, and red blood cells, which transport oxygen in the blood, circulate for an average of 120 days. Because of these limited cell lifetimes, this process of regeneration and repair called *anabolism* becomes absolutely necessary in the survival process. If it does not keep pace with catabolism, vulnerability to ulcer development, skin disease, infection, and cardiovascular disease may increase (Bajusz 1965; Raab 1970).

The hormones most closely associated with anabolism are insulin, testosterone (within limits), and, usually, growth hormone (for further discussion, see Karasek, Russell, and Theorell 1982). In addition to its essential roles in long-bone growth and the maintenance and adaptability of normal liver function, growth hormone has anabolic functions, facilitating the incorporation of cellular amino acid for protein synthesis, particularly in skeletal muscle. Its regenerative role is illustrated by the fact that the highest secretion of growth hormone takes place during deepest sleep. Testosterone and growth hormone have been demonstrated to contribute to the protein synthesis of the heart muscle itself (Hjalmarson, Isaksson, and Ahren 1969; Williams-Ashman 1979). The hormones associated with anabolism usually function independently of those associated with catabolism and sometimes even directly counteract their effects (Ensinck and Williams 1974; Fain, Kovecev, and Scow 1965; Leaf and Liddle 1974; Manchester 1972; Tata 1970; Topping and Mayes 1972; Williams and Porte 1974). The facts that anabolic and catabolic processes operate relatively independently and that they correspond to our strain and learning hypotheses fairly well help confirm the relevance of the dual-mechanism system disequilibrium model of basic physiological functioning presented earlier in the chapter.

Our regenerative physiological hypothesis states that physiological growth and regeneration are promoted by work environments high in control and high in challenges. A jogger, for example, is facing high levels of stressor but is totally self-paced and in control of the response to demands, unlike the assembly line worker facing a speedup. Similarly, children's muscular development occurs in situations that challenge them to run faster or jump higher than they had previously done. The regenerative effects of physical exercise have been found to include the reversal of some hormonal and metabolic effects of mental stress (Pyörälä et al. 1971); these could be seen as further examples of regenerative activities that take place during the nonrestful condition of active behavior. We do not yet have a large body of evidence for analogous results from psychologically active behavior, but we do find evidence in one case study of nursing home patients (see chapter 5, p. 194). We also found, in our study of working men who experienced spontaneous variations in job strain, that plasma testosterone levels dropped when job strain (demand divided by decision latitude) increased, and vice versa. This effect was much more evident in those men who did not have physical activity in their jobs (Theorell, Karasek, and Eneroth in press).

Another reason why physical exercise is health promoting may be that anabolism may also influence lipoprotein metabolism—regular physical exercise is associated with long-term elevation of the high-density lipoprotein (HDL) cholesterol that protects against atherosclerosis (Hartung et al. 1980; Paffenbarger and Hyde 1980). At the same time it lowers the serum triglycerides that are harmful to the arteries (Martin, Haskell, and Wood 1977). The anabolic effects of physical exercise may also influence the defense against bacterial infections. It has been shown, for instance, that regular physical exercise is associated with improved glucose utilization in monocytes—white blood cells circulating in the blood (Koivisto et al. 1979; Soman et al. 1979).

The most obvious physiological manifestation of environmental demands is, of course, heart rate. The association between arousal and increased heart rate, as well as between relaxation and decreased heart rate, has been extensively documented (Light and Obrist 1980). Interestingly, regular exercise (Graveling 1980) as well as daily relaxation exercise (Bali 1979; Patel, Marmot, and Terry 1981), clearly self-controlled activities, can lower baseline levels of heart rate and blood pressure and possibly increase tolerance to stress—further evidence that regenerative activity may take place during both active and relaxed states.

Linkages to Coronary Heart Disease

The final link in our causal chain from psychosocial work structure to illness is in the nature of heart disease itself. Coronary heart disease (CHD) has several manifestations, all greatly accelerated by narrowing of the coronary arteries due to atherosclerosis. Coronary atherosclerosis is known to be influenced by hereditary factors, dietary intake of saturated fat, high blood pressure, and cigarette smoking. Except for heredity, all these factors could enter into the work environment hypotheses we have presented above. Siegrist, Siegrist, and Weber (1986) have described the process of evolution of coronary heart disease in the individual, which they divide into three stages: vigilance, immersion, and overt illness. During the vigilance phase, the individual is fighting for achievement in the job situation. At this time, excess reactivity to environmental challenges may be recorded. During the immersion phase, the person is immersed in a situation with overwhelming demands in which there is a constant threat of loss of control. Elevation of the levels of several standard risk factors for coronary heart disease may be observed during this phase. Overt illness may take one of the several forms described below.

Heart attack (myocardial infarction) is a necrosis—death—of part of the heart muscle; the heart muscle is replaced by scar tissue. A myocardial infarction usually gives rise to dramatic symptoms, such as severe pain in the middle of the chest that lasts for several hours and radiates to the arms, the back, or the jaws; fainting; or severe breathing difficulties. *Angina pectoris*, in which no tissue death occurs, also involves chest pain of several minutes' duration but is actually a transient state of oxygen deficiency that may also result from atherosclerosis. Several mechanisms that could be related to work activity may increase the risk of myocardial infarction. The first is *total occlusion* of one of the coronary arteries, which prevents the corresponding part of the heart muscle from getting sufficient oxygen and induces the death of that part. Total occlusion of a coronary artery could be the final stage in a chronic atherosclerosis that has developed over several years, even decades, and that might in part result from chronic job-related catabolic physiological processes such as we have discussed in the preceding section. Indeed, psychosocial factors may be involved in the atherosclerosis process itself. A recent longitudinal study by Langosch, Brodner, and Borcherding (1983) showed that progression of coronary atherosclerosis was more frequent among young men whose jobs (according to external observer ratings) were characterized by strain. Occlusion can also occur suddenly because of clot formation, sudden bleeding within an atherosclerosis formation inside the wall of a coronary artery, or nervous system–induced arterial spasms (neurogenic vasospasm). All these mechanisms, with the possible exception of the bleeding in the atherosclerosis formation, could in part be the consequence of psychological arousal of the nervous system.

Metabolic necrosis is death of the heart muscle, which may occur without total occlusion of a coronary artery. In this case the infarction arises from excessive oxygen consumption in the heart muscle—because of physical exertions or emotional reactions that make the heart beat faster and harder, for example—over an extended period of time. Long-term elevation of certain hormones such as cortisol may make the heart muscle much more vulnerable to necrosis formation in a situation demanding hard work by the heart muscle, possibly because catabolic hormones have a tendency to deplete the heart muscle of desirable mineral salts, such as potassium and magnesium. This factor would be important in our theories, because the production of hormones in the cortisol group is sensitive to excessive psychological stress. Other factors may also be important in making the heart muscle vulnerable to necrosis formation. During periods of excessive work demands with a low decision latitude, the production of some of the anabolic hormones may be inhibited (Theorell, Kasarek, and Eneroth in press). As a result, new heart muscle protein may not be built up to a sufficient extent for long periods of time (Hjalmarson, Isaksson, and Ahren 1969; Williams-Ashman 1979). Because cell elements in the heart tissues are constantly wearing out, this failure may contribute to increased vulnerability. The relative importance of the latter factors, however, is largely unknown.

Arrhythmia refers to disturbed cardiac rhythm. A disturbance associated with a fast heart rate is called *tachyarrhythmia*. The most extreme tachyarrhythmia is ventricular fibrillation, which is a cause of death: the heart rate is so fast that the heartbeat becomes inefficient. There are three established factors that may increase the risk of tachyarrhythmias. First, scars in the myocardium (possibly caused by previous myocardial infarction) may disturb the natural flow of electrical currents in the heart. Second, lack of oxygen, caused by overwork of the heart muscle and/or narrow coronary arteries, may trigger the onset. Finally, adrenaline may lower the threshold at which arrhythmias occur. The importance of environmental stress in triggering the onset of serious arrhythmias has been discussed by many researchers, and work could play a very important role.* Ventricular tachycardia and sudden cardiac death are more likely to occur when premature ventricular contractions (PVCs) are high. Lown, Verrier, and Corbalan (1973) have also shown that PVCs are more common in situations of low control (the inescapable shocks to animals) and that in humans they are associated with the feelings of depression and entrapment. In view of the fact that such irregularities of the heart's own control system seem to occur after periods of great environmental stress, we may speculate that perhaps the heart's control system is manifesting its need to return to a state of baseline relaxation, where irregular events, analogous to the violent irregularities of REM sleep, can occur harmlessly. For the heart, however, such occurrences may be unavoidably harmful.

Several researchers have explored whether stability of the heart rhythm itself is associated with stress-related catabolic job conditions. Of particular relevance are studies of premature ventricular contractions associated with arousal (Lown, Verrier, and Corbalan 1973). Twenty-four-hour recordings of electrocardiograms (ECGs) have indeed indicated associations between the job environment and the prevalence of PVCs. In an example from our own research (Härenstam et al. 1987), PVCs were studied in 24-hour recordings of ECGs in prison personnel. This group is of particular interest because some of the personnel, in particular the guards working at night, may have very low decision latitude. Sixty-two men were studied in four different prisons, deliberately selected to represent a wide range of prison environments. In a univariate analysis, decision latitude explained a statistically almost significant ($p = .07$) number of arrhythmias. The less authority the guard had over decisions and skill utilization, the more PVCs were recorded, both at work and during leisure. In the same study, night work was shown to correlate with a significantly increased prevalence of arrhythmias.

In summary, psychosocial factors at work play some role in three different pathways to heart disease: (1) They may contribute to several long-term physiological processes such as hypertension and atherosclerosis. (2) They may be involved in the acute triggering mechanisms for coronary heart dis-

---

*A tendency to develop arrhythmias may be a manifestation of, rather than the cause of, coronary heart disease.

ease. (3) Finally, they may aggravate the effects of conventional risk factors. For example, the effect of excessive sodium intake in the diet is aggravated when high strain increases production of cortisol, which induces salt retention and elevation of blood pressure. They may also aggravate the risk factor pattern itself (for example, the habitual smoker may smoke more during periods of adverse job conditions). Of course, a myocardial infarction that occurs in the final stage of a chronic atherosclerosis process may have very little to do with psychosocial processes at work; it may, for example, be the consequence of a complex interplay between hereditary, dietary, and toxic factors in the environment. Psychosocial factors must therefore be considered contributing causes, not the sole cause, of myocardial infarctions.

Type A Behavior and Heart Disease

The most widely recognized individual trait that has been explored in the case of myocardial infarction is Type A behavior. Type A behavior does not fit cleanly into our model, and little of the research into it has been based on what we feel is the promising joint environmental-personality perspective that examines work settings simultaneously. The sheer magnitude of the research efforts under way means that the research cannot be overlooked, however, and we review below several important studies associating Type A behavior patterns directly to heart disease. These efforts have still not identified the particular psychological traits or the physiological mechanisms that could lead to coronary heart disease.

Type A behavior was initially described as a constant, exaggerated struggle against obstacles toward undefined, unattainable goals (Friedman and Rosenman 1959). Actually, Type A behavior is not defined by its authors as a stable personality trait but as a pattern of responses elicited by an adverse environment. Nevertheless, it is almost always measured as a personality trait. In several large-scale prospective studies (reviewed in Matthews and Haynes 1986), this behavior pattern has been associated with increased risk of development of myocardial infarction. Several groups have studied the psychophysiological reaction patterns in acute situations in persons with marked Type A behavior. For example, Johansson and Lindström (1975) observed that young men with Type A behavior react more vigorously than others, both psychologically and physiologically, when they are exposed to psychologically demanding situations that are outside their control. Furthermore, men with Type A behavior have been shown to be more likely to exhaust themselves to extreme degrees in physically demanding situations such as the ergometer bicycle or treadmill.

The last two decades of research have certainly confirmed that instruments aimed at measuring Type A behavior identify a cardiovascular risk factor in a broad sense. In fact, Type A is such a common behavior pattern in the most highly industrialized societies that it may even be difficult to find a sufficient number of non–Type A subjects for research (David Glass, personal communication, August 1979). The core concept underlying Type A, however, is still the subject of intense debate. To some, the original and most useful concept is the Sisyphus pattern. This concept, derived from the Greek myth of the king condemned to roll a large stone uphill, only to have it roll down again, means endless striving without ever obtaining true satisfaction (Wolf 1969). Other researchers note that certain Type A measures, such as the Framingham Type A scale used by Haynes and her colleagues (Haynes, Feinleib, and Kannel 1980), are highly correlated with anxiety-proneness, a personality trait that could actually be the long-term result of stressful environments. Still other researchers, such as Glass and Singer (1972) and Siegrist (1984), have emphasized the Type A individual's need to control the environment as the core of the construct. The most recent research emphasizes the hostility component of Type A behavior (Matthews and Haynes 1986). It is likely that such a trait is also affected to some extent by the environment; a demanding, constrained job situation lasting for many years without emotional support from fellow workers is likely to create or aggravate hostility, anxiety, or a desire for more environmental control.

The conflicting literature on the Type A concept makes it hard to integrate Type A neatly with our joint model, for Type A could measure both of our major personality categories, the feeling of (or need for) mastery and overall anxiety level. Type A is also related to both of our environmental variables, control and demands. One of the very first studies made by the researchers who defined Type A behavior was of a highly demanding work situation, not a personality trait: income tax accountants facing the April 15th tax deadline in the United States.

Several studies have shown that Type A behavior is statistically associated with self-reported work stress (Kornitzer et al. 1982; Theorell et al., Psychosocial work conditions, 1987). This correlation could mean that there is large overlapping person/environment effect—for example, that people with Type A behavior suffer more than others when the work conditions are frustrating. There is also the possibility, as we have noted above, that long-term frustrating job demands may generate Type A behavior, which would create difficulties in interpreting associations between job conditions and heart disease: what is cause and what is effect? The effects of behavior that are now primarily attributed to a personal trait may actually be the effects of environment. Other causally complex associations between type of job behavior and heart disease risk could arise if people with Type A behavior, for example, were more likely than others to stay in strain-filled jobs. To our knowledge no one has explored this possibility. It seems hardly likely, however, that people with Type A behavior who dislike being deprived of control would actively try to stay in demanding, uncontrollable, and boring jobs, which have the highest heart disease risks, as we shall see in chapter 4. Thus, while Type A behavior may be an important risk factor in its own right, it seems unlikely that it could explain away the environment-based associations with heart disease.

A substantial number of studies have also examined denial and the related phenomenon of alexithymia in relation to heart disease, a direction that may be promising and more clearly defined than Type A research. The risk of suppressing emotions is illustrated by a study of Finnish policemen who were tested psychologically and then followed for several years (Nirkko et al. 1982). Those who died sudden, unexpected cardiac deaths were more likely than others to have expressed overly optimistic and denying attitudes. The least serious manifestation of heart disease—angina pectoris without infarction—was more likely among policemen who over-reported their emotions. Hypertension may also be associated with denying tendencies. An underdeveloped ability to analyze one's own emotions (alexithymia) in a frustrating situation may induce long-lasting and pronounced physiological reactions even in young workers. In our study of 28-year-old men (Knox et al. 1988), an exploratory interview technique was designed to assess lack of ability to differentiate feelings; the results indicated that men with a high diastolic resting blood pressure were more likely than others to lack this ability.*

Does Personality Determine Career?

A common belief invoked to support the supposition that the person, not the job, causes the illness is that the psychological traits of people in different kinds of jobs are systematically different from one another. To some extent this must be true, but there are actually few rigorous scientific studies that adequately test this common presumption. Of course, employees in many jobs are selected on the basis of certain skills and experience, but that does not necessarily mean that personality characteristics relevant to heart disease are highly correlated to job type. In fact, most of the evidence is to the contrary. Costa, McCrae, and Holland (1984) have summarized research on vocational preferences in relation to personality. They found that

*An association between underreporting of work problems and a denying attitude has also been found in young subjects without hypertension but with a positive family history of hypertension and with cardiovascular hyperreactivity (Jorgensen and Houston 1986).

a person with an extroverted personality tends to take extroverted jobs, but apart from this clear finding, no other personality traits were consistently associated with vocational preference, and extroversion is not in itself associated with heart disease risk in any obvious way (Flodérus 1974).

In our own study of 28-year-old Swedish men, we recorded all the jobs that each of the 88 men had had during his whole work career (Theorell et al. 1984) by means of a classification system for occupations based upon Swedish national surveys (described in chapter 4). This system enabled us to calculate the lifetime weighted amount of exposure to hectic, monotonous, noneducational, uncontrollable, and heavy-lifting job experiences. These objective (that is, not self-reported) measures of jobs were then related to personality characteristics calculated from responses to a standardized personality inventory. The results of this analysis indicated that men who described themselves as "monotony avoiders" were indeed less likely to have had monotonous work careers. Apart from this result, however, no other significant associations were found.* Also, because the study had a longitudinal design, we were able to explore whether blood pressure at age 18 had any association with work career up to age 28. No such associations were found.

Another issue that is frequently raised is the extent to which personality traits are biologically inherited. An extreme argument would be that individuals with genetically determined personality traits associated with increased heart disease risk would select high-strain jobs and that therefore the association between environment and risk is simply a noncausal one. Recent epidemiological studies of twins reared apart and reared together refute this possibility. While it is true that some Type A behavior—probably around 30 percent—may be biologically inherited (Lichtenstein et al. 1988), it probably has little relevance to job selection in the association between job and heart disease. Furthermore, most of "locus of control" is environmentally determined (Pedersen et al. 1988).

Thus, only very limited conclusions can be drawn about how personality is associated with work activity and cardiovascular strain. There is still substantial uncertainty about what is really being measured in this research. The associations between personality and initial work career would not appear to be strong enough to be responsible for the associations between work environment and heart disease risk that we describe in chapter 4. But several of the personality dimensions that we have discussed (denial,

---

*Thus, Type A behavior, socialization, verbal aggression, indirect aggression, alexithymia (which was measured by means of a standardized interview), muscular tenseness, and various aspects of neuroticism were unrelated to type of work career in these 88 young Swedish men. In particular, we were interested in any possible association between personality and a career in jobs characterized as highly demanding and with a small decision latitude, for any such associations could have had implications for our research. No such findings were made.

alexithymia, and Type A behavior) have one thing in common: people with these traits are likely to work very hard and not complain in their work situations. They are therefore attractive to an employer and are likely to stay employed—as long as they are healthy, which may not be very long.

Conclusion

We have taken the reader through a long, comprehensive path of explanation that has sequentially covered at least four separate levels of scientific inquiry. We have first examined in detail a new model of how the psychosocial work environment could affect psychological stress and behavior. Second, we have discussed how individual personality might affect these hypotheses. Third, we have extended our model to predict the physiological consequences of the job-related effects from our original model. Finally, we have briefly discussed the manifestations of heart disease that could be related to these physiological mechanisms. These four areas are usually dealt with separately, by rather separate scientific disciplines. Our attempt to synthesize these findings can certainly be faulted (but we hope also lauded) for extending the original findings from these separate areas beyond the range often intended for them.

To our knowledge, there are no studies that have simultaneously measured all the links in the chain we outline. One study that comes close is based on a multistage path analysis (LISREL) of cross-sectional data on 28-year-old Swedish males (Knox et al. 1985). They found that restricted learning opportunities at work were associated with increased adrenaline, which contributed in turn to high systolic blood pressure (independent of non-job factors). We hope to see more such multistage analyses in the future, particularly with longitudinal data that allow tracing of the time-related development of effects. The present state of research on these comprehensive pathways from environment to illness still has missing links in the evidence at several points. If, however, these catabolically accelerated, anabolically retarded pathways to CHD risk that we propose are confirmed, high-demand/low-control jobs are clearly a dangerous misfit to human physiological capabilities. Our review leads us to suspect that epidemiological studies of work-related physiological response and cardiological illness could provide us with some of the answers about the missing links in the chain, as well as an assessment of the validity of the chain as a whole.

4

Psychosocial Job Characteristics and Heart Disease

Medical science has developed a remarkable unanimity of opinion regarding the causes of heart disease, and in most countries job stress is *not* among the commonly accepted causes. The exceptions are Denmark, Norway, and Sweden, where the psychosocial risk factors at the workplace are receiving increasing recognition. In the United States, the accepted risk factors are often listed in both scientific journals and the mass media, as part of a well-intentioned campaign of preventive medicine via education about sources of heart disease. They include high serum cholesterol, high blood pressure, smoking, and lack of exercise, as well as Type A personality and heredity. Articles with titles like "Steps to Prevent a Heart Attack" appear in respected, high-circulation U.S. magazines, all citing major health scientists and U.S. government health administrators in harmonious agreement about steps people can take to reduce their own health risk.

This degree of conviction seems surprising, given the mixed success of many large-scale experiments aimed at reducing cardiovascular risk factors by changing personal behavior alone. Experiments focusing on reduced smoking, diet changes, or hypertension medication have been very successful (Hjermann et al. 1980; Multiple Risk Factor Intervention Trial Research Group 1982; Salonen, Puska, and Mustaniemi 1979; World Health Organization 1984), but in several of the studies it has been difficult to show a lowered incidence of coronary heart disease itself, which is of course the goal. The unanimity on risk factors also seems surprising in light of the many questions about what causes high blood pressure and serum cholesterol, by far the two most important risk factors. Both of these are in part measures of internal physiological regulatory mechanisms that mediate the successful adaptation of the individual to the environment, as we saw in the previous chapter. Yet we hear very little about these environmental challenges. In public education materials, almost all heart disease is attributed to personal life-style. But as we have noted, smokers smoke more in high-stress settings, and we have seen that even leisure behavior is affected by work circumstances.

A Research Tradition with Many Questions

Stressful emotional situations have long been known to affect cardiovascular function. At the beginning of the twentieth century, Sir William Osler (1910) concluded, in an often-cited set of lectures on angina pectoris, that such neurogenic factors could cause coronary heart disease. A current example of the importance of such stressors at the workplace for cardiac rhythms is taken from the medical practice of one of the authors. The patient, a 45-year-old sales clerk who was responsible for one small department in a department store, had suffered a myocardial infarction several months before. While he was being interviewed in the doctor's office, three potentially dangerous tachyarrhythmias were registered on an electrocardiogram (see figure 4–1). The first occurred during talk about the acute life-threatening onset of his heart disease. The other two episodes, however, occurred during discussion of a specific work matter. There had recently been some thefts, and it was suspected that someone in his department was responsible. The patient was under strong pressure to find the thief, but he had no way of controlling the situation or finding out what was going on—a high-strain setting. Discussions about other important matters, such as the death of his first wife and his present sex life, were not associated with dangerous arrhythmias in this case. Clearly, failing to review work-related psychosocial causes of heart disease could be an important oversight.

Research into these causes of heart disease was long hindered by several factors: a lack of clear understanding about what specific aspects of work activity are most relevant; a lack of data, since few health data bases had detailed job information; and uncertainties about the objectivity of reports about psychosocial environments. Two themes from social epidemiology of illness in general had an impact on the early course of such research: the life-stressor tradition in illness research and investigations of social-class differences in illness prevalence.

FIGURE 4–1
Electrocardiographic monitoring of subject
during discussion of stressful work events

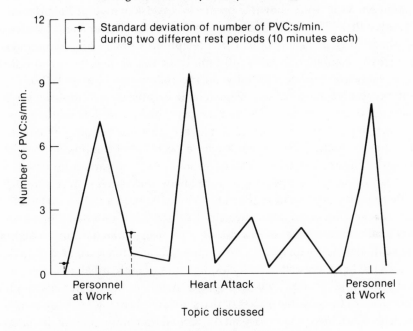

SOURCE: de Faire and Theorell 1984. Reprinted by permission of Warren H. Green.

Tabulations of stressful life events by Holmes and Rahe (see Rahe 1972), de Faire and Theorell (1984), and others showed correlations with many illnesses, leading many researchers to feel that demanding situations in the work environment could play a similar role for heart disease development. Indeed, middle-aged male heart disease victims more often reported long work hours, work dissatisfaction, or an unusual accumulation of life events at work during the period of or preceding myocardial infarction than did nonvictims (Blohmke, Schaefer, and Abel 1969; Buell and Breslow 1960; Sales and House 1971; Theorell and Rahe 1971, 1972; Wolf 1969). These studies were often criticized, however, because they were based on interviews of surviving victims of myocardial infarction, compared in retrospect with people who had not had a myocardial infarction. It was suspected that men who have recently suffered a myocardial infarction may search for the meaning of it and therefore exaggerate the psychosocial events or adverse life conditions that they had been exposed to during the period preceding illness. Medical experts were waiting for more causally conclusive "prospective incidence" or longitudinal change studies.

Soon several prospective studies were published, examining diverse measures of work-related stressors. In middle-aged Swedish building construction workers, reports of "any job difficulty or important job change within one year" were shown to predict excess risk of myocardial infarction (Relative Risk [RR] = 1.6) in a two-year follow-up (Theorell and Flodérus-Myrhed 1977). In a study of U.S. Bell Telephone workers, attending college at night in combination with full-time work was shown to be associated with excessive cardiac mortality during follow-up (Hinkle 1974). In a semiprospective study of two Belgian bank organizations, employees were followed during several years, and the psychosocial work conditions were characterized in retrospect by all employees. This study showed that one of the organizations, a private bank with a hectic work tempo and low employment security, had an elevated incidence of myocardial infarction in comparison with the other, a semipublic bank that was less hectic and had higher employment security (Kornitzer et al. 1982). In a follow-up study of American middle-aged men (Shekelle et al. 1979), self-reported job pressure was observed to predict excess risk of myocardial infarction, regardless of conventional risk factors. Thus, the studies indicated that excessive work demands might be associated with elevated rates of myocardial infarction, but there was little consistency on the specific nature of these demands and no discussion of the possible effects of decision latitude or low social support at work. In short, there was no overall conceptual framework, or gestalt, for understanding the impacts of the psychosocial work environment.

Another problem in the existing literature was that many studies of psychosocial job factors and coronary heart disease (CHD) had studied single occupations only. Such studies frequently appear to have been motivated by public concern about occupations suspected to be at risk, such as aircraft executives (Chadwick et al. 1979), air traffic controllers (Rose, Hurst, and Jenkins 1978), tax accountants (Friedman, Rosenman, and Carroll 1958), and auto assembly workers (Timio, Pede, and Gentili 1977). This method has the analytic advantage that such occupational groups could represent relatively homogeneous exposure to occupational conditions. The disadvantage is that the homogeneity of occupational conditions means there is little variance on job measures to associate with CHD outcomes. Instead, most of the variance is among individuals, on such measures as personality type.* No overall model of the work environment emerges, because a special segment of the workplace has been isolated.

Another historically important direction in cardiovascular epidemiology was plagued by other problems. Conventional social-class analysis certainly provided a broad gestalt for understanding the impacts of the occu-

---

*Also, risk factors were generally investigated rather than heart disease itself, because of the very large sample size needed for CHD analysis.

pational system, but it faltered because of lack of detailed insight into the job situation. Also, as we saw in our social-class discussions in chapter 2, the gestalt was probably the wrong one. The first rigorous social class analyses, from England after the Second World War (for a review, see Antonovsky 1968), seemed to provide clear evidence that coronary heart disease was a malady of the upper classes. This finding led physicians in the 1950s to search for causes of "executive stress," usually focusing the research on managers and professionals (Brady et al. 1958). The implications of a social-class gradient for heart disease began to change dramatically by the late 1960s. Studies of coronary heart disease incidence in North America, Great Britain, and Scandinavia (Antonovsky 1968; Hinkle et al. 1968; Koskenvuo et al. 1980; Marmot 1982; Pell and d'Alonzo 1963; Swedish Central Bureau of Statistics 1987) began to consistently show that men in the upper social strata had less heart disease than other people. These findings then led to new skepticism among the experts regarding the links between stress and heart disease, because most of them did not question the notion that executives and professionals have more damaging stress than others (Kasl 1979).

Obviously, a more detailed understanding of the nature of the work experience for each occupational group was going to be needed. One significant step forward was the finding in the late 1970s that high-status civil servants in Great Britain have lower rates of myocardial infarction than other civil servants (reported in Marmot 1982). This has been interpreted by Marmot both to confirm lower-class/CHD associations and, later, to confirm the associations between low task autonomy and CHD. In summary, the literature had provided much circumstantial evidence to link occupation to heart disease but little clear understanding of how the link might be forged. It was at this time, in the late 1970s, that Karasek, with a new set of Swedish findings (1976) suggesting an association between high-strain jobs and heart disease symptoms, teamed up with Theorell, with a background in clinical cardiology and life-stressor research, to test Karasek's demand/control hypothesis, using a set of data bases that could only be assembled in Sweden.

Finding the Data to Test the Demand/Control Model

It is not easy to get access to data sources that provide an opportunity to study the association between work conditions and heart disease. A very large sample (several thousand individuals) is needed, because myocardial infarction is not very common among working-age people, even though it is the most common cause of death in both the United States and Sweden. Furthermore, it is necessary to have information on conventional risk factors such as blood pressure and serum cholesterol, information that is available only on sophisticated data bases gathered by hospitals or national health statistical surveys. Most of the existing medical data bases did not gather detailed data on job conditions before 1980, although they have begun to collect such information more recently, particularly in Sweden, in part as a result of some of the research discussed below. On the other hand, data bases that contain detailed occupational information (such as those collected by the U.S. and Swedish Departments of Labor) rarely contain data on health status, particularly health status data that could be regarded as sufficiently precise. Thus we faced a dilemma that is common in occupational health research: there are no data bases that contain both useful job data and precise health data.

Our approach to this dilemma was a twofold strategy. First we explored the validity of self-report health data that did exist in several important Swedish data registers and demonstrated a strong correlation between self-reported cardiovascular symptoms and future cardiovascular mortality. In the United States, not even national survey samples of job situation and self-reported health existed. We therefore decided to employ a data linkage strategy, linking the job information for each occupation (shown in our occupational distribution maps in chapter 2) to job titles on major U.S. cardiovascular health studies. After testing the feasibility of this approach in the United States, we applied it to Sweden, using Swedish estimates of job characteristics for Swedish occupations and major Swedish health status data registries. More recently, we have been able to complete several studies in which we collected our own comprehensive data on both jobs and cardiovascular health. A number of other such studies are still in progress, utilizing major national health survey resources in the United States; an example is the Framingham offspring study (Kannel et al. 1979).

In the studies described below, we rely on either a subject's own description of his work (*self-reported*) or measures derived from groups of subjects working in an occupation (*aggregated data*). The latter method gives a less precise estimate of the true working conditions, because all subjects within an occupation are assumed to have the same job conditions, but it avoids the individually distorted descriptions of work that may be a source of error, as we have described.

Myocardial infarction—heart attack—is a very useful dependent variable in epidemiological studies and is the measure used most often in our studies. In epidemiological studies, the diagnosis is established by a combination of criteria that have been agreed upon by most epidemiologists. Because a myocardial infarction is usually a dramatic and potentially life-threatening disease, most subjects who suffer from it seek help. The number of false negatives—infarctions that are not reported—is therefore probably low in comparison with less stable measures, such as angina pectoris. One other advantage is that the onset of a myocardial infarction is clearly defined in time. There is one difficulty, however: the death rate in myocardial infarction is very high in the first minutes after the onset, and many victims—about one third—die before they even reach hospital. It is therefore a great advantage to include data from death registers that include nonhospitalized cases.

The First Test of the Demand/Control Model: Self-Reported Job Descriptions in Sweden

The first test of our hypotheses was based on a nationally representative data base called the Swedish Level of Living Survey. This comprised a random sample (1:1,000) of employed men below age 66 who were interviewed about job conditions and health in 1968 ($N = 1,915$) and 1974 ($N = 1,635$) (Karasek et al. 1981). All the data had been collected before our group started research on job conditions and heart disease, so we had to rely on questions formulated by other researchers, but by means of statistical procedures it was possible to construct psychosocial dimensions that were relevant to our exploration of demands and decision latitude. Our indicator of demands comprised two questions: Is your work hectic? Is your work psychologically demanding? Our indicator of skill discretion comprised questions about skill requirement and monotony. Unfortunately, no way of measuring authority over decisions was available, but one somewhat related index of "personal schedule" freedom was constructed, based on questions regarding freedom to have personal visitors, make personal telephone calls, and leave work for personal matters during working hours.

An indicator of increased heart disease risk had to be developed from the available answers to health questions. The index we decided to use, which we called *CHD symptom*, was made up of four questions concerning cardiovascular symptoms during the year preceding the interview: high blood pressure, trouble breathing, ache in the breast, and heart weakness. Men with CHD symptom in 1968 had markedly (four to five times) higher CHD mortality than other subjects during follow-up—a more effective predictor in this population than ECG measurements of heart disease. The frequency of reported CHD symptom was then related to the psychosocial job dimensions.

As we saw in chapter 2, skill discretion (or intellectual discretion) is one of the two main components of decision latitude. High demands and low skill discretion thus constitute an important aspect of job strain. The job situation in 1974 was first related to CHD symptoms the same year. Figure 4–2a shows the results of this analysis. In the most leisurely group (that is, no excess psychological demands and at the same time good skill discretion), no subject described CHD symptoms. The diagonal move from that group toward more and more strain is associated with higher and higher frequencies of CHD symptom. In the most extreme strain group, 20 percent of the men reported CHD symptom.

The next analysis was a prospective one (see figure 4–2b). In this analysis, none of the men who reported any of the four symptoms—even slight symptoms—in 1968 were included, to reduce the possibility that previous illness might cause subjects to select a particular type of job. For the remaining men who were asymptomatic in 1968 and were reinterviewed in 1974, the work situation in 1968 was related to the frequency of CHD

FIGURE 4–2 (a-b)
Job characteristics and prevalence and incidence
of coronary heart disease (CHD) indicator
(Swedish males: 1974, N = 1,621; 1968–74, N = 1,461)

Number on vertical bar is percentage in each job category with indicator
(two of four symptoms: ache in breast, trouble breathing, hypertension,
heart weakness)

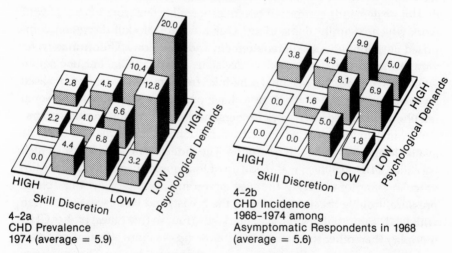

4–2a
CHD Prevalence
1974 (average = 5.9)

4–2b
CHD Incidence
1968–1974 among
Asymptomatic Respondents in 1968
(average = 5.6)

NOTE: Cell sizes, reading from right to left, are as follows, for 1974—high demands: 143, 222, 144, 20; medium demands: 93, 202, 287, 78; low demands: 40, 114, 205, 63; for 1968–74—high demands: 40, 111, 111, 155; medium demands: 116, 335, 123, 88; low demands: 57, 219, 70, 36.

SOURCE: Karasek et al. 1981. Reprinted by permission of the *American Journal of Public Health*.

symptom in 1974. Again, none of the men who reported low demand and high skill discretion reported CHD symptom in 1974. By itself this is a striking finding: we have located a population group on the basis of its job situation whose members develop no new heart disease ("Eternal Youth" jobs?). Of those in the most extreme high-demand/low-skill-discretion groups, 5 to 9 percent developed CHD symptoms. This diagram is less regular than the cross-sectional one, but it still shows the same tendency (the lowest-decision-latitude group also had the highest mortality, and not all were there to participate in the follow-up survey).

A second stage of our analyses involved simultaneous control of conventional CHD risk factors. It could very well be that men in the high-demand/low-skill-discretion groups were older, smoked more cigarettes, were more likely to be overweight, or had a lower educational level than others and that these factors could explain the association. We therefore made a multivariate logistic regression analysis that took into account all these variables at the same time and measured the relative contribution of each one to symptom risk. This analysis indicated that age, lack of intellectual discretion at work, and job demands were the only significant predictors of CHD symptom development, even after we adjusted for education, smoking, and overweight. Thus, our analysis showed that CHD symptom development was associated with work conditions in the way we had anticipated, although our indicator of personal schedule freedom (to make personal telephone calls, have visitors, or leave work) did not contribute to the prediction of symptom development between 1968 and 1974.

This data base allowed further analysis of disease development itself, providing information on heart disease during the follow-up period 1968–1978. The number of cardiovascular deaths in the part of the study population that had continued working after 1974 was small but sufficient to permit a case-control study. Our analyses showed that men who had reported high demands at work were more likely to be among those who had died. Men who had reported low personal schedule freedom at work were also more likely to be in this group. The combination of high demands and low personal schedule freedom was particularly associated with cerebrocardiovascular death risk in the subgroup with elementary education only (low skill discretion was not amenable to analysis because of the small numbers). Thus, the Swedish Level of Living Survey analysis provided support for our hypothesis in terms of both cardiovascular morbidity and mortality, even after adjustment for some of the conventional risk factors (Karasek et al. 1981).

Another, more recent study in Sweden (Theorell et al., Psychosocial work conditions, 1987) utilized similar job variables and provided us with data regarding job conditions and conventional risk factors. This was a retrospective study of nearly all (N = 85) the men below age 45 who survived myocardial infarction in greater Stockholm during a given period. They were compared with men without infarction who were strictly age-comparable but otherwise randomly selected from the greater Stockholm area. Job conditions, including demands and personal schedule freedom (defined as in the first study), were analyzed in a personal interview three to six months after the onset of the illness. In addition, two questions regarding lack of possibility to learn new things and lack of variety of work tasks, used as two separate indicators of low intellectual discretion, were analyzed. The results indicated that lack of variety of work tasks explained a significant part of the likelihood of belonging to the case group, even after controlling for blood lipids, smoking, alcohol, family history, educational level, hypertension, and Type A behavior."* The demand/control model was applied by calculating a ratio variable: demands divided by control. The new variables "demand divided by variety at work" and "demands divided by personal schedule freedom" both became significant explanatory factors in the multiple logistic regression. In this study of young men, lack of variety at work seemed to be the most important factor—almost as important, in fact, in discriminating infarction cases from healthy men as the tobacco-smoking variable. Demands per se added little to the prediction; it was only in interaction with low decision latitude that they made any difference.

Linking Job Data at the Occupation Level

Much of our work in relating heart disease to job conditions has been based on job characteristics that are estimated from occupational title. As we have noted, no direct job data is available in the sources with the best CHD health status information. To overcome this data deficit, we have developed, and used in hypothesis testing, two separate systems for estimating job characteristics, one for use in the United States and the other for use in Sweden. The U.S. estimates are the QES job characteristics for each occupation that we showed and discussed statistically in chapter 2, figures 2–2 to 2–6. This system gives us the advantage of being able to target high-risk populations for our analyses on the basis of occupational title and demographic information alone, reducing the susceptibility to self-report bias. A substantial disadvantage, of course, is that our measures are statistically weak because they miss the considerable variance in job situation that occurs within occupations (recall our discussion of bakers in chapter 2, p. 80).

*Measured by means of a Swedish version of the Jenkins activity survey.

U.S. STUDIES WITH MEN

The job information was linked with the U.S. HES (Health Examination Survey) and the U.S. HANES (Health and Nutrition Examination Survey). These clinical data bases, which represent the basis of U.S. national statistics on myocardial infarction prevalence,* had not been analyzed before with respect to job conditions. Our analysis is based upon 2,409 working men in the HES in the years 1960–1962 and 2,432 working men in the HANES in the years 1971–1973 (U.S. Department of Health, Education, and Welfare 1979a). (See Karasek et al. 1988 and Schwartz, Pieper, and Karasek 1988 for a discussion of linkages with U.S. QES data on job characteristics.)

First, we wanted to test whether men in occupations with a high degree of job strain, as defined in chapter 2, had a higher prevalence of myocardial infarction than men in other occupations. Our assumption was that the combined effect of high demands and low decision latitude is even worse than a simple addition of their effects. Therefore, high-strain jobs were identified in a simple way: each person's "psychological job demand" score was multiplied by his "lack of decision latitude" score (after adjustment for demographic characteristics). This would represent the lower right-hand corner of figure 2–1. Then the 20 percent with the highest combined scores were identified. The myocardial infarction prevalence among these men was compared with that of other men in HES and HANES; this comparison was made for each of six age groups. The results of this analysis are shown in figure 4–3.† With only one exception—the 45–54 age group in the HES—the prevalence in the strain group is two to three times higher than in the nonstrain group, and the overall relationships are significant in both data bases.

The next step was to test whether the associations between job characteristics and myocardial infarction prevalence were true even after adjustment for other relevant factors such as age, education, race, systolic blood pressure, cholesterol, and smoking habits. The multivariate logistic regressions showed that the coexistence of high demands and low decision latitude was associated with an elevated myocardial infarction prevalence. The order of magnitude of the association between job strain and myocardial infarction prevalence was smaller than the association between serum cholesterol and CHD risk, but higher than that between smoking and CHD risk in

*Prevalence in this context means the number of persons in a given group who have evidence of having suffered a myocardial infarction in the past (according to the criteria) divided by the total number of subjects in the group.

†The statistical strength of the overall difference in prevalence between strain and nonstrain was tested by means of the Mantel-Haenzel test.

FIGURE 4–3
Prevalence of myocardial infarction by age and job strain
(U.S. males: HES, 1960–62, N = 2,409; HANES, 1971–75, N = 2,424)

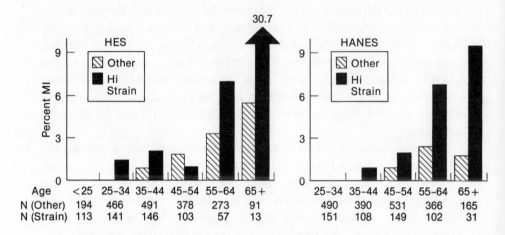

SOURCE: Karasek et al. 1988. Reprinted by permission of the *American Journal of Public Health.*

many other studies.* In both data bases, decision latitude and psychological demands as separate single factors were also statistically significantly associated with myocardial infarction prevalence in the predicted direction (see table 4–1). In both cases, a simple measure of degree of physical exertion in the job was negatively associated with myocardial infarction prevalence.

A second step in our U.S. occupational scoring strategy was to adjust each individual's occupation-based score for the effects of age, sex, education, and other demographic information that could distort estimates of health variable correlations in the HES and HANES surveys. For example, clergymen are generally older as a group than office boys and messengers and simultaneously have more job decision latitude. Without demographic adjustment, associations between age, decision latitude, and heart disease in multiple regressions may be biased (positively or negatively) because of age/occupation associations. To adjust scores, a covariance analysis was performed, which adjusts for disturbing effects of age, education, race, region, urban/nonurban residence, and self-employment (see Schwartz, Pieper, and Karasek 1988). The results after adjustment not only confirm the hypothesis but show greater consistency in magnitude of effects between the studies.

*Standardized odds ratios for job strain were 1.51 in the HES and 1.61 in the HANES.

TABLE 4–1.

Job characteristics and the prevalence of myocardial infarction among employed males in the U.S. HES and U.S. HANES surveys (multivariate logistic regression analysis with standardized odds ratios [S.O.R.s])

	HES 1960–62 (N = 2,409, 39 Cases)			HANES 1971–75 (N = 2,424, 30 Cases)	
Variable	S.O.R.	95% Significance (p≤)		S.O.R.	95% Significance (p≤)
Age	4.92	2.99 to 8.10 (.001)		7.26	3.78 to 13.90 (.001)
Race	−1.19	−.85 to −1.66 (.307)		1.24	.77 to 2.02 (.376)
Education	1.53	1.05 to 2.22 (.024)		−1.02	−.63 to −1.67 (.929)
Systolic blood pressure	−1.26	−.93 to −1.71 (.133)		−1.46	−.98 to −2.18 (.064)
Cholesterol	1.60	1.20 to 2.14 (.002)		1.20	.84 to 1.73 (.348)
Smoking	a	a		1.23	.87 to 1.75 (.241)
Job					
Decision latitude	−1.52	−1.02 to −2.25 (.038)		−2.00	−1.39 to −2.87 (.001)
Psychological demands	1.32	.91 to 1.90 (.144)		2.05	1.28 to 3.28 (.003)
Physical exertion	b	b		−1.47	−.96 to −2.24 (.072)

[a]Smoking not available in HES.

[b]Demographic and physiological variables forced into equation. Job variables eliminated if $p \geq .20$.

SOURCE: Karasek et al. 1988. Reprinted by permission of the *American Journal of Public Health*.

THE SELECTION ISSUE

The major weakness in the U.S. studies is the fact that these men were studied after they had suffered a myocardial infarction. While overestimation due to the search for meaning is not a problem as it was in the early research, which depended on self-reports, problems may arise because men have changed their occupations as a result of their myocardial infarction. We believe that this possibility is most likely to lead to an underestimation of the true association. It should be noted that the job-shift problem is usually interpreted to be an overestimation because of selection of high-risk individuals into high-risk jobs. The postulation is of a social Darwinian drift of the least fit into the least desirable jobs, because of lack of income or education or because of genetic weakness. Although conclusive research on the nature of these job drifts has not been undertaken for populations such as ours, we do not expect this classic "selection in" process to account for occupational shifts in these obviously unpleasant, stressful jobs. While selection into low-demand jobs is certainly plausible, we do not find higher levels of CHD in these occupations. Selection of higher-decision-latitude jobs is highly constrained in real work settings (it is equivalent to giving yourself a promotion). Selection into lower-decision-latitude jobs (a demotion) is unlikely unless accompanied by lower demands, and again such jobs do not show higher CHD prevalence. In any case, there is relatively little occupational shifting of any kind over age 30 in either the United States or Sweden.

Further support for our assumption that the observed associations are not due to selection is derived from three observations. First, in the HES and the three QES data bases, there are relatively fewer occupants of high-strain occupations among older age groups; for example, assembly line workers are predominantly young. Second, Karasek et al. (1981) found that the association between job conditions and heart disease symptoms was stronger among those who had not changed jobs during follow-up than in the total studied sample, which included a large group of job changers. Third, Theorell and Flodérus-Myrhed (1977) found that among building construction workers who had not had any serious heart disease symptoms previously there were stronger associations between psychological work load and prospective risk of developing myocardial infarction than in the total studied sample, which included workers who had had previous serious symptoms.

CASE-CONTROL STUDIES WITH SWEDISH MEN

To test our hypotheses on a larger scale, we utilized the Swedish national registers of health data and working conditions data. They made it possible to examine the causal associations prospectively: we could define subjects' occupations and follow them up over time to observe the development of new myocardial infarctions.

First it was necessary to create a Swedish occupational system similar to the American one.* There are two systems (Alfredsson, Karasek, and

---

*There are a number of differences between the Swedish and American occupation classification systems. The Swedish systems have less precision than the American one. They use single questions and make no effort to combine questions into dimensions. In the Swedish systems there is no way of adjusting the occupational scoring of a person to demographic characteristics. The only exception is age in the second version, in which there are two different systems for older and younger workers. On the other hand the Swedish systems, particularly the second one, are based upon larger samples of interviewed subjects.

Theorell 1982; Alfredsson, Spetz, and Theorell 1985), one simpler and one more elaborate. In both systems, occupations are classified on the basis of single questions, not dimensions composed of several questions, as in the American system. Demands are represented by the single question: Is your job hectic? Intellectual discretion is tested with two different questions: Is your job monotonous? Does your job give you the opportunity to learn new things? Decision authority is determined by the question: Can you influence work hours in your job? High-risk occupations, defined as those 50 percent of the occupations that had the highest percentage of workers reporting "hectic work," for example, were compared with occupations in which fewer reported "hectic work." For multivariate analysis, the occupations were divided into quartiles with regard to percentage distribution of responses.

The first occupation classification system was used in a case-control study made more rigorous by historical traditions of recording social data in Sweden. Since 1686 the clergy in Sweden have registered the population in parishes. This registration has now developed into a highly efficient civil registration system. The population within one part of the greater Stockholm area was followed up in the inpatient care registry in the medical information system of the Stockholm county council and in the death registry in order to find cases of myocardial infarction during the period 1974–1976. We studied 393 men aged 40–64 who had suffered a myocardial infarction during the study period, comparing them with 973 control persons, in five age ranges.

The main hypothesis—that job strain would be associated with increased incidence of myocardial infarction during the follow-up period from 1970 to 1974–1976—was tested with "strain" defined by means of three different combinations of questions, namely: "hectic and monotonous," "hectic and nonlearning," and "hectic and no influence over pacing." Occupations above the median for both variables in each one of these combinations were defined as "strain occupations" in three different tests. All of them showed significant associations with myocardial infarction risk (the third test was close to statistical significance), with relative age-adjusted risks between 1.3 and 1.5.* It is noteworthy that all these associations were much stronger in the younger segments of the studied groups. Under age 55, all three tests were statistically significant (Alfredsson, Karasek, and Theorell 1982), with relative age-adjusted risks between 2.0 and 2.3 (see table 4–2).

*As in the American studies, each one of the single variables was also tested. "Monotony" was the only variable that showed association with myocardial infarction when tested by itself, and that association was weak.

TABLE 4–2.
*Type of occupation and relative
age-adjusted risks of myocardial
infarction in Swedish males
(Stockholm case-control study,
5-year follow-up; cases, N = 334;
controls, N = 882)*

	40–64	40–54
Hectic and monotonous	1,3*	2,3†
Hectic and nonlearning	1,5†	2,3†
Hectic and uncontrollable (with regard to pacing)	1,4†	2,0†

*Almost significant statistically .05 < p < .10.
†Statistically significant $p < .05$. Two-tailed significance tests were used since this was the first study using this methodology.

A second series of tests was performed in order to explore the possibility that the observed associations may have been due to factors other than job strain. The frequency of heavy lifting, the proportion of subjects with minimum mandatory education only, the percentage of immigrants, and the percentage of cigarette smokers in each occupation were used as simultaneous control variables (one at a time). None of these factors could explain away the associations observed. In a final multivariate analysis (multiple logistic regression) taking account of all the studied variables, the combined multiplied interaction between "hectic" and "nonlearning" was observed to be significantly associated with infarction risk (Alfredsson and Theorell 1983). The combinations of hectic work and each one of a number of physical stressors—sweating, noise, heavy lifting, and vibrations—were also associated with increased risk. These observations are noteworthy in view of the fact that neither hectic work nor the physical stressors were significantly associated with risk when these factors were explored separately. Again we may be dealing with an interactive phenomenon, this time between a rushed tempo and physical risk factors.

STUDIES WITH WOMEN

Is job strain equally dangerous to men and women? This issue has been insufficiently addressed in research to date. A general discussion of men's and women's longevity and occupational conditions has been published by Waldron (1976) and a review of women's heart disease risk by Eaker,

Packard, and Wenger (1988). Frankenhaeuser and her associates (Frankenhaeuser and Johansson 1975) have examined men's and women's (as well as girls' and boys') psychoendocrinological responses to demands and challenges. Nevertheless, most of the studies of the association between job conditions and heart disease have been limited to men, mainly because the serious manifestations of coronary heart disease (myocardial infarction and sudden cardiac death) are much less common in women than in men, and therefore, much larger groups of women than men have to be examined in prospective studies.

In the Swedish Five County study described later in this chapter, heavy overtime work (at least ten hours per week) was associated with a lowered myocardial infarction hospitalization incidence in men but an elevated incidence in women. How can this gender difference be explained? First of all, to a great extent women and men work in different jobs. As we saw in chapter 2, women more frequently report low authority over decisions and low skill discretion in their jobs. Applying the demand/control model, we could speculate that those who are forced to do overtime work in uncontrollable and boring jobs—as is more often the case with women—will suffer more strain than those who do overtime work in stimulating, controllable jobs. Another possible explanation could be the difference in social roles: women have more responsibility for the care of home and children and may therefore find it more difficult to work overtime than men. The total burden of work—paid and unpaid—is greater for working women.

The most systematic large-scale study of women's job conditions in relation to heart disease is the Framingham study—a longitudinal cohort study of men and women in a city in Massachusetts. The prospective results from this study indicate that female clerical workers (whose jobs can often be high strain) with at least three children have a markedly elevated risk of developing coronary heart disease (Haynes, Feinleib, and Kannel 1980). These results may indicate that the double role of mother and worker may contribute to heart disease. Recently, the incidence of CHD was studied in relation to the demand/control job model in both men and women in the Framingham cohort. A fifteen-year follow-up using our U.S. occupation classification system showed that high-strain jobs had higher CHD risk than other occupations. The relative risk of myocardial infarction and angina pectoris was almost significant for men, 1.5 ($p \leq .10$), but not significant for women (relative risk of 1.4) (La Croix 1984). When self-reported job data were used, the findings confirmed the model for women but were less convincing for men.

In the Swedish Five County study, the excess risk associated with working in "strained" (hectic and monotonous) occupations was stronger for women than for men. Thus, despite the (possibly biologically determined) much lower incidence of coronary heart disease in working women, the findings indicate that job strain is associated with risks for women at least as strong as those for men.

FAMILY-WORK INTERACTIONS

One common counterargument regarding associations between job conditions and heart disease is that for many people family conditions are more important to general well-being than job conditions and that family conditions may influence job conditions to the degree that analyses that do not take family life into account are impossible to interpret. It is true that most of us spend more of our lives outside work than at work and that associations with excess risks of myocardial infarction development have been documented for major changes and difficulties in family life, such as an unsupporting spouse (Medalie et al. 1973), single marital status (Kraus and Lilienfeld 1959; Lynch 1977), bereavement (Parkes, Benjamin, and Fitzgerald 1969), and dissolving social networks (Bruhn and Wolf 1979; Marmot and Syme 1976) or lack of social participation on the whole (Welin et al. 1985). Nevertheless, family life is not strongly associated with the job variables that we have discussed.

In one large cross-sectional study of 8,700 full-time male and female white-collar workers in Sweden, work issues were more salient than family issues for both men and women (Karasek, Gardell, and Lindell 1987). While both work and family factors had significant associations with a set of thirteen health outcomes, the work variables explained substantially more variance in health status than the family variables. (For the heart disease indicator in that study, however, family problems were the strongest correlate of risk for men.) Work effects have been clearly shown to carry over to family life in one study of blue-collar workers in the United States (Piorkowski et al. 1981). Of course, adverse job conditions could be buffered by good family support as well. The effects of the working environment extend beyond working hours, as we saw in examining work/leisure associations in chapter 2. The unresolved strain arising during a hectic, boring, and uncontrollable work day may have carryover effects on leisure time. The release of psychological tensions from work could create conflicts in the family. Furthermore, the children in the family, who are greatly influenced by the behavior of their parents, may be taught to release tension at home rather than at work. These patterns might then be carried over to the next generation, perpetuating unhealthy solutions of problems arising in a bad working environment.

Results with the Expanded Model: Social Support and Physical Demands

SOCIAL SUPPORT

As we noted in our expanded psychosocial model at the end of chapter 2, the support of co-workers and supervisors may be one of the most important factors ameliorating stress in the working environment. In the work of Johnson (1986), the term "iso-strain" was introduced to describe a job with high psychological demands, low control, and low social support. In Johnson's studies, dimensions of "demands" and "decision latitude" (a combination of "authority over decisions" and "intellectual discretion") were constructed by means of factor analysis of the national surveys. The resulting dimensions are close to the U.S. QES measures described in chapter 2.

The findings from the expanded model including social support are consistent with the hypothesis in chapter 2. Using interviews and follow-up studies (1976–1982) in registries of a random sample of employed Swedes, Johnson found that workers who reported poor social support, excessive demands, and poor decision latitude consistently reported more heart disease, mental fatigue, digestive system diseases, and lower back pain than other subjects. Analyses of possible confounding factors clearly showed that this association was not due to nonwork social support, marital state, age, sex, immigrant status, socioeconomic status, rural versus urban residence, income, smoking, or physical job demands.

The same trends were observed for cardiovascular deaths. For mortality, the effect was found on the good side of the strain model: those with low-strain work conditions died later from cardiovascular disease than others. Figure 4–4a shows the relation between age and cardiovascular mortality in relation to degree of iso-strain (demands × lack of support × lack of control). The 20 percent with the highest scores, the 20 percent with the lowest scores, and the middle 60 percent are compared. When cardiovascular death rate was studied as a function of age in the three groups, it was seen that the low iso-strain group had a much slower progression of death risk with increasing age and that, on average, the men in this group died more than seven years later than the other men. Not only is death earlier, but disease takes its toll earlier in life, as is seen in figure 4–4b, which shows the relation between age and cardiovascular symptoms. In this case there is an even gradient: the higher the iso-strain the more prevalent and earlier the symptoms. Among blue-collar workers in the risk group (high iso-strain level), cardiovascular symptoms develop seven years earlier than among

FIGURE 4–4a
*The combined effects of job strain and social isolation
on cardiovascular mortality
(randomly selected Swedish working males, N = 7,219; nine-year follow-up)*

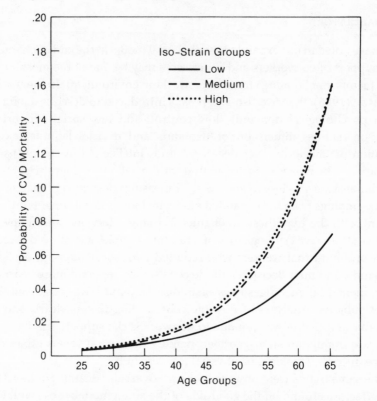

SOURCE: Johnson, J., Hall, E., and Theorell, T. in press. Reprinted by permission of the *Scandinavian Journal of Work, Environment, and Health*.

blue-collar workers in the low iso-strain group. The strain differential was much stronger in the blue-collar groups than in the white-collar groups (Johnson, Hall, and Theorell in press). Among the white-collar workers the statistical effect of iso-strain is later—visible only after age 45—and weaker.

Figure 4–5 shows the results of Johnson's analysis of heart disease prevalence using the expanded model from chapter 2, which now includes demand, control, and social support. The diagram shows the expected demand/control pattern in the high-support group: those who reported job strain had the highest heart disease prevalence. In the low-support group, on the other hand, it was the active subgroup that reported the highest prevalence of heart disease, although the high-strain group was highest for other illnesses. Regardless of job social support, the low-

FIGURE 4–4b

The combined effects of job strain and social isolation
on cardiovascular disease
(randomly selected Swedish working males, N = 7,219)

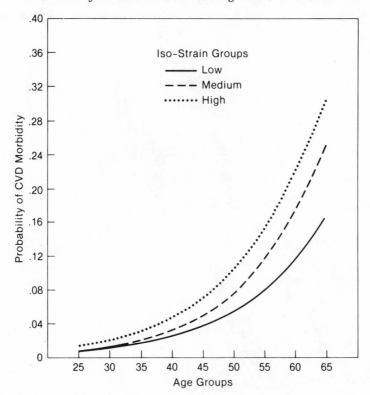

SOURCE: Johnson, J., Hall, E., and Theorell, T. in press. Reprinted by permission of the *Scandinavian Journal of Work, Environment, and Health.*

demand/high-control groups report the lowest heart disease prevalence (Johnson and Hall 1988).

PHYSICALLY DEMANDING BLUE-COLLAR WORK

As we noticed when reviewing the results of the demand/control/support studies of Swedish workers, the associations between job strain and illness were stronger for male blue-collar workers than for other groups. Why do male blue-collar workers appear to suffer more from adverse psychosocial work conditions? One possibility is that physical hazards are more common in these groups and that it is the combination of psychosocial and physical hazards that we observe. Another possibility is that psychosocial hazards among blue-collar workers might interact with

FIGURE 4–5 (a-b)
Social support, the demand/control model, and prevalence of CHD symptoms
(Swedish males and females, 1976–82, N = 13,779)

Number on vertical bar is age-adjusted CHD prevalence ratio for each job category
(1.00 reference group is high support, high decision latitude, low demands).

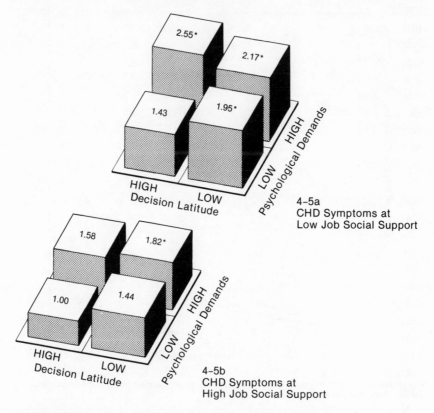

4–5a
CHD Symptoms at
Low Job Social Support

4–5b
CHD Symptoms at
High Job Social Support

*Statistically significant difference from reference group ($p \leq .05$).

NOTE: Males and females were combined since prevalence was similar: males, 5.66 percent; females, 6.03 percent. Symptoms were reported in interviews and evaluated by expert panels. Mid-levels on job scales were excluded.

SOURCE: Johnson and Hall 1988. Reprinted by permission of the *American Journal of Public Health*.

physical strains, that some of the excess risk associated with psychosocial factors is caused by concurrent unexplored physical factors. We have also seen the opposite: physical demands can mask the strength of associations between psychological demands and decision latitude (see chapter 2, p. 65n; and Johnson and Hall 1988). We do not have the answer to these questions; they will have to be addressed in future research.

Differing definitions of physical effort are the cause of some confusion in studies of heart disease and physical demands. That physical exertion in general is associated with a lowered prevalence of heart disease has been found in large-scale American studies (Paffenbarger et al. 1970). In our U.S. studies based on occupational titles, the question on which the physical exertion categorization is based deals with the amount of physical exertion required in the job.* In the Swedish studies, however, the main variable used is one specific kind of physical exertion, namely, repeated heavy lifting required in the job. As pointed out in several studies (reviewed by Kihlbom 1976), heavy lifting involves static physical demands that are associated with marked elevations in diastolic blood pressure, whereas physical exertion in general, especially if it involves varying dynamic components, is associated with less blood pressure elevation. It is interesting to note in the Swedish studies that heavy lifting by itself is not associated with myocardial infarction incidence; it is only in combination with hectic work that it is associated with increased risk. This may be an illustration of a psychosocial and a physical factor interacting to produce excess risk.

Shiftwork and its concomitant frequent rotation between day and night work—another condition that is more common in blue-collar jobs—is associated with a perceived decrease in decision latitude. Interestingly, both in the Stockholm case-control study and in the Five County Study described later in this chapter, typical shiftwork occupations had a significantly elevated incidence of myocardial infarction and several other illnesses. Recent studies have indicated that there may be an increased CHD risk in workers who work for several years in rotating day and night shifts (Knutsson et al. 1986; Åkerstedt et al. 1984). Søndergaard-Kristensen and Damsgaard, in their thorough analysis of the literature on job conditions and heart disease risk (1987), have concluded that shiftwork is one of the established risk factors for coronary heart disease. Part of this association may be caused by psychophysiological mechanisms: a favorable change of the shiftwork schedule has been shown to decrease catecholamine output (Orth-Gomér 1983). It has also been shown that the lipoprotein levels are less favorable in shift workers than in other comparable workers (Knutsson, Åkerstedt, and Jonsson 1987). It is possible that changes in eating habits because of the shiftwork may also contribute to these associations.

Job insecurity is one important issue that especially affects low-status, blue-collar workers. Is a bad job worse than having no job? There is no obvious answer to this question in the available literature. Longitudinal studies (Brenner and Levi 1987; Hall and Johnson 1988; Kasl, Cobb, and Brooks 1968) of workers who lose their jobs indicate that a large proportion experi-

---

*We must also remember that the subjects in the HES and HANES studies have already suffered myocardial infarction. This creates a source of error: those who are easily exhausted physically because of a past myocardial infarction with remaining cardiovascular symptoms will often try to get a less physically strenuous job.

ence long-lasting physiological effects and deterioration of the social network. Karasek (1976) found that people without significant social roles—unemployed and without family support—had higher levels of symptoms and pill consumption than workers with high-strain jobs, although the percentages of those with problems were surprisingly close in the Swedish Level of Living Survey (see table 10–1). It is possible that these consequences may increase the likelihood of developing a myocardial infarction. The macro-epidemiological studies by Brenner and others (Brenner and Mooney 1983) have indicated that a country's heart disease mortality may increase—usually with a delay of at least a year—after a period of increased unemployment. A recent study in Sweden partly verifies this finding (Starrin et al. 1988). In our studies we have not been able to explore these questions, simply because our methods do not allow proper analysis. As Brenner and Eyer pointed out in their detailed discussions of the unemployment problem on a societal level, increasing unemployment is not a problem only for those who become unemployed. It also creates problems for those who remain in jobs but are constantly threatened with losing them (Brenner and Mooney 1983; Eyer and Sterling 1977).

Adverse physical conditions and shiftwork schedules often exist together with adverse psychosocial conditions. In these cases, it may be difficult to know whether the physical or the psychosocial factors are the most important contributors to risk. In our opinion, the psychosocial factors should be the primary target for action. The exploration of psychosocial factors may uncover physical strain, whereas the very specifically focused data on physical hazards in the work environment often reveal little about psychosocial risks. More important, when a process is begun to change the physical hazards in the workplace, it is often crucial to modify psychosocial variables such as workers' decision latitude to ensure that workplace changes actually take place.

The Pathway to Heart Disease: Job Strain and Blood Pressure, Smoking, and Serum Cholesterol

Our goal of preventing illness by redesigning work leads to a quandary when we consider that the evidence we have been reviewing relates to the largely irreversible condition of death of a part of the heart muscle. Most people do change their activities after a heart attack, but by then the damage is done. And yet the present state of our research does not allow us to predict with certainty who will fall victim and thus to change just those jobs on a selective basis. What we need are measures of intermediate impairment that could trigger job changes and yet could still be reversed, so that the individual would be left unimpaired. For this purpose we can investigate cardiovascular illness risk factors—well-established, usually physiological measures of impairment that are highly predictive of eventual heart disease—as indeed we do in chapter 6, where such interventions are discussed. Changing the level of risk factors through job redesign would, of course, promote health in the same logical manner that changes in diet, smoking, and exercise are claimed to do.

However, there is no more agreement in the broad community of health professionals that CHD risk factors are related to job conditions than there is on the associations between job conditions and heart disease itself. One important reason why physicians have hesitated to accept stress as a cause of heart disease is that most medical experts do not think in terms of a multistage causal model to link job and heart disease via risk factors. Consider the following theoretical example. A habitual, moderate cigarette smoker is exposed to an excessively demanding job situation where he is given no real decision opportunity—a high-strain job. He increases his daily cigarette smoking to very high levels. After six months, his smoking has accelerated the onset of a myocardial infarction, which develops five years earlier than it would have without the excess burden of smoking during the six months of unmanageable, excessive demands. Most experts in this field would regard the heart attack as the likely result of the cigarette smoking, and the person would be labeled as "loaded with a risk factor," regardless of whether or not the smoking habit has been influenced by socially determined risks such as job factors. We would conclude, however, that even though increased smoking may be the *pathway,* job conditions contributed to the development of a premature myocardial infarction in this case. From our perspective, job conditions could be regarded as potential causes in a wide sense, regardless of whether they influence heart disease risk directly via psychophysiological mechanisms or indirectly via conventional risk factors. Since blood pressure and blood lipids (such as cholesterol) may also be influenced by job conditions, this reasoning may be applied to all conventional risk factors.

It is also possible that job conditions could affect heart disease risk via both mechanisms simultaneously and that the joint effect may be greater than their sum. The possible causal network underlying the analysis is thus quite complex. There may be interactions between conventional risk factors and direct psychophysiological mechanisms. For example, the cardiovascular effect of an adverse job condition may be much worse in a cigarette smoker than in another person (McDougall et al. 1983); a blood pressure elevation resulting from job strain may become aggravated in a person who eats a lot of salt (Obrist 1976).

Even when medical experts admit that job strain may play some role in the development of coronary heart disease they frequently say that the job factors should still be disregarded because the conventional factors are sufficient causes and also easier to change. We challenge these notions. Several recent large-scale studies have shown that it is difficult to change smoking and eating habits in large segments of the population (Puska et al. 1979; World Health Organization 1984). It is conceivable that the efforts to change conventional risk factors would be greatly facilitated if public and occupational health officers knew more about people's reasons for smoking and eating unhealthy diets, some of which may have to do with work conditions.

Job Strain and Blood Pressure

There is a substantial literature indicating that blood pressure levels increase in stressful situations on the job, but until recently associations to specific job characteristics had not been documented. There is evidence suggesting that increased demands, particularly in combination with low control, give rise to increased heart rate and blood pressure (Rissler and Elgerot 1978; Taggart and Carruthers 1971). There is also data on risk factor profiles (Holme et al. 1977) that may indicate that workers in typical high-strain occupations have higher average blood pressure than others. The study of blood pressure variations in air traffic controllers by Rose, Hurst, and Jenkins (1978) was received with considerable interest because of the stressful nature of air traffic control. Among the factors associated with increased blood pressure elevations during stressful work periods were high initial blood pressure, excess consumption of alcohol, and lack of marital resources and other sources of emotional support. Even more impressive than the levels of blood pressure was the degree to which blood pressure varied during the course of the day.

Many new data collection technologies have dramatically facilitated the ability to monitor blood pressure in the job and are rapidly augmenting our understanding of the environmental causes of blood pressure variations. In a recent study, almost 200 people from a wide range of occupations in New York City were monitored with 24-hour ambulatory blood pressure monitoring devices. Substantially higher levels of systolic blood pressure were found in the high-strain jobs than in other jobs (see figure 4–6), as well as enlargement of the left ventricle (associated with increased risk of myocardial infarction). The study (Schnall et al. 1989) was a case-control study

FIGURE 4–6
Job characteristics and systolic blood pressure at work
(Males in diverse occupations in New York City, N = 206)

Number on vertical bar is blood pressure measured by
ambulatory monitor every 15 minutes.

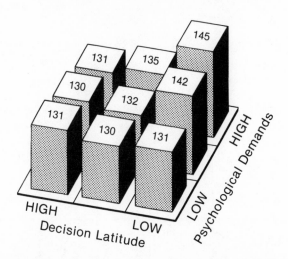

NOTE: Cell sizes, reading from left to right, are as follows—high demands: 28, 20, 12; medium demands: 23, 21, 13; low demands: 22, 30, 37.

SOURCE: Data from Schnall, Pickering, and Karasek 1988.

including both hypertensive and normal workers. Those classified as hypertensive were almost three times as likely to be in the high-psychological-demand/low-decision-latitude group as non-hypertensives. It is interesting to note that the classification of subjects as hypertensive was based on diastolic blood pressure differences, which in general have not been as strongly associated with the job strain model as systolic blood pressures. Another interesting finding was that the work strain dimension was as strongly correlated with blood pressure during leisure time as it was during work hours.

Figure 4–7 charts the blood pressure of four 28-year-old men with a history of hypertension (but not on medication), as self-measured once every hour. The first three men, in high-strain occupations, show very marked elevations and fluctuations, particularly of systolic blood pressure, during some of their work activities (shown in unbroken lines). The headwaiter (figure 4–7d) was resting before noon and started working during the late afternoon, continuing until midnight. His systolic blood pressure shows dramatic changes: it rises progressively during work and reaches its peak just before the restaurant closes at midnight. The taxi driver (figure 4–7c)

FIGURE 4-7 (a-d)
Blood pressure variations in a single working day

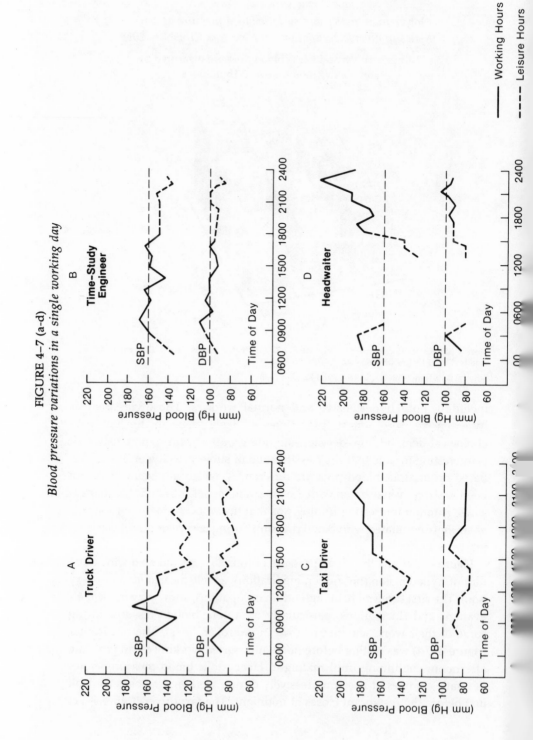

shows a clear drop in blood pressure during leisure hours in the middle of the day, when he was relaxing. During his work hours, he shows a high systolic blood pressure level with a moderate progressive rise culminating late in the evening. The diastolic blood pressure, on the other hand, shows small changes. The truck driver (figure 4–7a) was transporting loads of milk under constant pressure. During work hours his blood pressure is highly variable, swinging up to relatively high levels, whereas during leisure it remains stable at a low level. The last man, a time-study engineer (figure 4–7b), works in an active job—high psychological demands and high decision latitude. Despite the fact that he had documented high blood pressure at the age of 18, as did the other three men, he shows little change in blood pressure over the work day and little difference between leisure and work hours, although the time-study engineer shows a consistently rather high blood pressure level.

Often the associations between job strain and blood pressure are strongest in those with a propensity to react with blood pressure elevation, specifically those with a personal or family history of hypertension. The effect of family history is demonstrated in a study of six Swedish occupational groups whose job strain and blood pressure were monitored over a year's time (Theorell et al., Changes in job strain, 1988). The results are shown in figure 4–8; this study will be discussed in greater detail in chapter 6. Theorell et al. (Blood pressure variations, 1985) found in a sample of 28-year-old Swedish males that systolic blood pressure was more elevated during work activities in the high-strain occupations, although this was true only in subjects with high blood pressure at age 18. We must observe, however, that even repeated pronounced blood pressure elevations producing high average blood pressures may not lead to hypertension, even though they could be of importance to the development of cardiovascular illness. Specifically, recent research indicates that marked repeated blood pressure responses to regularly recurring stress may have significance to cardiac left ventricular hypertrophy (Devereux et al. 1983). Our uncertainty arises from the fact that no large-scale longitudinal studies of blood pressure changes related to psychosocial environmental stressors have been published from populations with substantial variance in job situation. Indeed, there are remarkably few reports about longitudinal changes in blood pressure at all, even as collateral findings in the major CHD epidemiology cohort studies (one such study was Gordon and Shurtleff 1973).

JOB STRAIN AND SMOKING

Again in the case of smoking, few studies have explicitly examined the effects of task structures, even though there are a number of studies that

FIGURE 4–8
*Systolic blood pressure during working hours
in relation to changes in job strain (longitudinal data)*

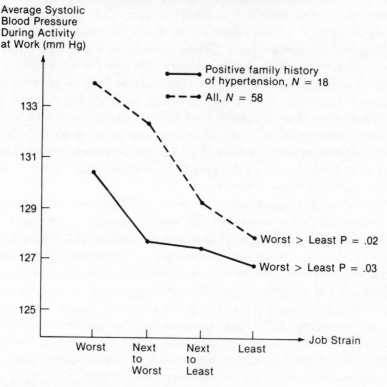

SOURCE: Theorell et al., Blood pressure variations, 1985. Reprinted with permission of Helen Dwight
Reid Educational Foundation © copyright 1985.

point to some association between job stress and smoking. Various studies
suggest that people smoke in stressful situations to lower feelings of stress
(Ikard and Tomkins 1973); to increase the capacity to cope with stress
(Nesbitt 1973); or to calm down during upsetting situations (Heimstra
1973). A number of other studies have shown a clear association between
occupation and smoking (for example, Sterling and Weinkam 1976) and
have attributed it to social class, but they have not simultaneously tested
hypotheses about job stressors that might co-vary by social class. More recently, the effects of job structure have been independently identified. In
the Stockholm case-control study described above, there were strong associations between a low level of intellectual discretion (boredom) and the
prevalence of cigarette smoking (Alfredsson 1983). Johnson and Johansson
(1988) analyzed the influence of physical as well as psychosocial job fac-

tors on smoking habits in a representative sample of the Swedish working population. In women, a low level of skill discretion was associated with increased smoking prevalence. Among men, shiftwork and piecework increased smoking. In women, a high degree of social interaction between colleagues at work was observed to increase smoking. This finding was contrary to expectations.

Several studies have examined the association between stress on the job and smoking within occupations. Caplan et al. (1975), studying administrators and engineers, found high job demands to be associated with difficulty in stopping smoking. Tagliacozzo and Vaughn (1982) found job-related dissatisfaction and stressors to be strong predictors of smoking behavior among nurses. Conway et al. (1981) found that job stressors and work load were the highest correlates of smoking behavior in a longitudinal study of naval basic training commanders. None of these studies examined the effects of low job control. Social support was found by Caplan (1971) to have a positive but interactive association with low smoking quit rates. As with the blood pressure associations, we still do not have conclusive longitudinal studies of job strain and smoking behavior, although changes in smoking behavior over time have been studied in a variety of settings, usually in connection with smoking cessation programs.

JOB STRAIN AND SERUM CHOLESTEROL

There is also ample evidence to show that serum cholesterol increases significantly in stressful situations, but again the role of specific job circumstances has not been clear. Dimsdale and Herd remark in their comprehensive review of the literature (1982) that most of this literature is based on studies on cholesterol and stressful situations done twenty years ago. The availability of new measurement techniques makes this a fertile area for renewed interest. The bulk of studies have examined the elevations in serum cholesterol that occur in medical students before their examination period, where typical elevations of 10 percent to 25 percent are found in seven out of seven of these studies (Dimsdale and Herd 1982). Wolf and his colleagues, in a five-month longitudinal study of patients in a research ward (with controlled diet and exercise), found strong associations, within individuals, between serum cholesterol levels and reports of stressful encounters with doctors and roommates (Cathey et al. 1962). In one study that clearly does examine work impacts, Friedman, Rosenman, and Carroll (1958) observed significant increases in serum cholesterol for income tax accountants before the April 15th income tax deadline, certainly a period of high job stress, and a drop thereafter.

Few studies have been published reporting long-term changes of serum cholesterol for groups of subjects. On the whole, there is evidence that the psychosocial job situation may influence serum cholesterol, but the influence of the job situation is still quite unclear. Serum total cholesterol is not the only relevant lipid measure; the influence of psychosocial factors on serum triglycerides, for example, is strong (Theorell et al. 1972), and Siegrist et al. (1988) have recently shown that adverse long-lasting job conditions may influence the ratio of low-density to high-density lipoproteins (LDL/HDL ratio), which is the strongest known indicator of CHD risk.

SUMMARY: ALL MAJOR RISK FACTORS

Pieper, La Croix, and Karasek (1989) have recently summarized relationships for all the major risk factors by using five different major U.S. data bases (U.S. HES, U.S. HANES, U.S. HANES II, the Exercise Heart Study, and the Western Collaborative Group Study) that could be linked to the job occupational system. In three of the data bases, there was a significant association between job strain and systolic blood pressure. In all four studies that contained the data, men in high-strain occupations smoked more than other working men. For diastolic blood pressure there were no strong associations. Serum cholesterol showed inconsistent associations—strongly positive in the EHS and WCGS but negative in the HANES and HANES II. In all the analyses, adjustment was made for age, race, education, body mass index, and—in the Exercise Heart Study and the Western Collaborative Group Study—also for Type A behavior.

For all the major risk factors, there is evidence to suggest association with environmentally induced psychological stress but almost no strongly conclusive evidence, such as would be provided in longitudinal studies of risk factor change as a result of job stress or of job demands and job control.* Indeed, the paucity of analysis of any sort on longitudinal changes in risk factors is remarkable, given the fact that a number of major data bases contain this information. We expect this to be an area of major research in the future, and in fact several studies of blood pressure changes are under way.

---

*Other CHD risk factors may also be associated with psychosocial job structure. Johnson and Johansson (1988) found that low skill discretion and low social interaction at work were associated with physical inactivity during leisure in men. Physical inactivity during leisure has been found to increase CHD risk in some studies (for instance, Elmfeldt et al. 1976). In women, high-strain jobs were associated with physical inactivity during leisure.

The Demand/Control Model and Multiple Illnesses:
The Swedish Five County Study

How much of the total risk of illness in modern society might be due to psychosocial job factors? Are other illnesses, beyond heart disease, affected by job stress? Mental health is very likely to be affected, as our depression findings in chapter 2 illustrate. Another very important pathway to disease could be the effect of stress on the immune system, which is reviewed by Kiecolt-Glaser (1985). The total magnitude of the impact of job stress is obviously difficult to assess at this stage of our understanding about such linkages. Our multiple factor analyses on national longitudinal data bases are bringing us closer to initial answers. One remaining hurdle affects all epidemiological research: the study never seems to be quite large enough to allow testing of some of the more sophisticated hypotheses or rarer illnesses. In Sweden, however, we were fortunate to have access to a data base much larger than is usually available in such research. It also allowed us to test our job stress hypotheses for job-related illness other than heart disease and formulate preliminary estimates of the total illness burden of psychosocial job conditions. It is a study of Swedish hospitalization for illness (morbidity) that investigates fully one-fourth of the entire Swedish working population: 958,096 working people living in five of the twenty-six Swedish political regions—"counties"—some urban and some rural. A register of hospitalizations was linked by occupation with job data in the Swedish national census from 1975. The same basic techniques as in the Stockholm case-control study described above were used, but in this study, the comparison groups were the total working population in the studied counties, the age spectrum was wider (20 to 64), and both men and women were studied.

Our first tests confirmed the associations between the job strain hypotheses and heart disease found in the studies described above. The most powerful psychosocial occupational predictor of myocardial infarction risk for men was the combination of hectic work and no learning (see table 4–3), with an age-standardized morbidity ratio of 1.6 for all working men below age 55 (1.3 below age 65). The most important predictor of myocardial infarction risk in women was hectic and monotonous work, with a relative age-adjusted risk of 1.6.* Although the Swedish data registers do not allow control for most conventional risk factors, these data bases are strong with

*The combination of hectic work with no influence over pacing was not a significant predictor for myocardial infarction either for men or for women, and hectic work with no learning was associated with risk in men but not in women.

TABLE 4–3.

Relative hospitalization rates for various illnesses in relation to occupational characteristics for males and females in the Swedish Five County Study

	Myocardial infarction		Suicide or suicide attempt		Alcohol-related illness		Psychiatric illness		Gastro-intestinal illness		Traffic accidents	
	Men below 55	Women	Men	Women	Men	Women	Men	Women	Men	Women	Men	Women
Few possibilities to learn new things	1.13	1.35	2.44	NS	2.55	NS	2.27	NS	1.65	NS	1.50	NS
Monotony	NS	1.43	1.98	1.51	2.34	1.90	2.10	1.54	1.59	1.56	1.51	NS
Hectic work	NS	NS	NS	1.44	.50	1.21	.56	NS	NS	NS	.70	NS
Hectic work and few possibilities to learn new things	1.28	1.57	2.15	NS	1.43	1.26	1.41	NS	1.48	NS		NS
Hectic and monotonous work	1.18	1.53	NS	2.34	NS	3.09	NS	1.58	NS	2.24	NS	NS

NOTE: Only associations that could not be explained away in the confounding analysis are presented. All standardized morbidity rates are age-adjusted (ages 20–64).

SOURCE: Data from Alfredsson, Spetz, and Theorell 1985.

regard to socioeconomic factors, and both studies indicate that the association between strain and illness risk is not simply due to socioeconomic factors. All tests were scrutinized for possible confounding associations due to type of county, type of community, marital status, cohabitation, nationality, full- or part-time work, type of employment, children in household, type of residence, and net income. Only associations that were still true after these tests are presented here.

Access to comprehensive hospital records in the Five County Study allowed us to observe associations with hospitalization during the year of follow-up for suicide attempt, alcohol-related illness, psychiatric illness, gastrointestinal illness, and traffic accidents (see table 4–3). Hospitalizations for all for these causes were more frequent in occupations with low levels of intellectual discretion, even after controlling for a number of socioeconomic and physical factors. In men, hectic work usually made little difference; in some cases, the relative risk was even lower when the combination of hectic work and low decision latitude was tested than when low decision latitude was tested alone. In women, however, hectic work often added substantially to the risk. For men, the strongest predictions were made for suicide, alcoholism, and psychiatric illness, where few opportunities to learn new things were associated with standardized morbidity ratios of 2.44, 2.55, and 2.27 respectively, and less strong predictions were made for gastrointestinal illness, myocardial infarction, and traffic accidents. The results of the study further confirm the importance of the interaction between demand and decision latitude to the development of myocardial infarction in both men and women as well as to the development of many other diseases in women (Alfredsson, Spetz, and Theorell 1985). Shaw and Riskind (1983) have made similar observations regarding several causes of death in an American study that utilized another American psychosocial occupational classification system linked to a mortality register.

A rough approximation is that the illnesses in table 4–3 account for about half of all hospitalizations associated with significant mortality risk (9 percent cardiovascular illness, 21 percent psychiatric illness, 2 percent suicide, 10 percent alcoholism, 4 percent gastrointestinal, and 3 percent traffic accidents).* The average excess risk shown to be related to low skill discretion (monotonous work and not learning new things), weighted by sex and frequency of illness, was a very large 78 percent (relative risk of 1.78). We must emphasize that these weightings and aggregations are preliminary and that there are several potential uncontrollable sources of error in such

---

*Major serious illnesses excluded in this tabulation are cancer, other accidents, diabetes, and gynecological illnesses (based on total Swedish hospital visits in Alfredsson, Spetz, and Theorell 1985, table 1).

calculations. For example, in the case of alcoholism, we may not be dealing with illness caused by job conditions; it could be the other way around, a "downward drift" phenomenon. Such a phenomenon could also partly explain the associations for psychiatric illness. On the other hand, the assumption that all workers in one occupation have the same conditions tends to give rise to spuriously *weak* associations. With these limitations in mind, it is interesting to note that such crude and simple questions, analyzed in this way, provide such powerful predictions.

To estimate the overall attributable risk of psychosomatic illness related to the demand/control model, we must have an estimate of the proportion of workers exposed to the adverse condition, as well as an estimate of the strength of the effect. As a starting point, we may calculate the proportion of cases of myocardial infarction among men and women in the working ages that could theoretically be prevented if we could decrease the level of job strain from the occupations with the worst demand/decision latitude combinations down to the average level in other occupations (which, of course, does not represent the optimal level and is certainly not the same as being "unexposed" to stress, as we shall discuss). This is called the *etiological fraction** (Olsen and Søndergaard-Kristensen 1988). Using the Five County Study and the Stockholm case-control study data for cardiovascular disease, this was estimated to be 9–13 percent for women. For men, the estimate was highly age-dependent. For working men below 55, the etiological fraction was 7–16 percent, and for all men below 65 it was 3–7 percent. In the Swedish studies, we estimated that 15 percent of the working men and 25 percent of the working women were exposed to job strain. In the United States, similar job strain calculations with demand and decision latitude resulted in etiological fractions of 25 percent and 33 percent respectively to the males in the HES and HANES above.† The Swedish and American data are not strictly comparable since the former is based upon incidence and the latter on prevalence. However, the low-skill-discretion measures, by themselves, in the Five County Study identify 50 percent of the population. Their 78 percent excess risk implies an etiological fraction of 28 percent for the illnesses mentioned above. Since these are 50 percent of serious hospitalizations, this implies that 16 percent of *total* serious ill-

*The formula for etiological fraction (EF): $EF = \dfrac{\text{Percent exposed} \times (\text{excess relative risk})}{(1 + \text{percent exposed}) \times (\text{excess relative risk})}$

†Olsen and Søndergaard-Kristensen (1988) estimate a standardized risk ratio (top half divided by bottom half of population) of 2.0 for the low-decision-latitude/high-psychological-demands combination, the highest for any work-related heart disease risk factor. They estimate the etiological fraction for low-control/high-demand heart disease to be 6 percent for females and 14 percent for males, using a very conservative definition of the stressed population. In addition to the 28 percent estimate for overall low-decision-latitude stress-related serious morbidity, we have 25 percent and 33 percent for low-control/high-demands heart disease in the United States.

ness in Sweden could be remedied by increasing just the skill component of decision latitude to that of the average of other occupations. How far could job redesign really take us? We make a very rough estimate in the next chapter by calculating the preventable attributed risk from job-related psychosocial illness, using an average strength-of-effect measure from a broad range of studies,* and a summary of the impacts of job redesign strategies from chapter 9.

New and Old Research Questions Still To Be Answered

Measuring psychosocial factors at work and their impact on cardiovascular disease involves a broad range of special problems that have not previously been encountered in cardiovascular epidemiology. First, the direct measures of job data in the studies performed to date have been very meager, in many cases only indirectly estimated by occupational title. The reason is, of course, the lack of resources to do more rigorous study of job situations, in an expensive research field. It is especially ironic that researchers have been constrained to use transitory, short-term reports of working conditions in studying an illness that obviously has a long developmental period (House et al. 1986).

Notwithstanding such weak data, our general job-strain hypothesis has been supported in ten studies at the time of this writing, and completely rejected in only one, the Honolulu Heart Study, described below. Support has come from both self-report and job classification data, from both the United States and Sweden, and from both prospective and cross-sectional studies. And yet there remain important exceptions. The risk factor associations are still not clear in the small number of epidemiological studies so far undertaken, although in small field studies and laboratory studies blood pressure evidence is consistently accumulating. Certainly, the studies described above have generated a new set of questions.

The strongest contradictory results for the job strain model so far were found in a ten-year follow-up of Japanese-American men in Honolulu. In a study using the classification system, no associations were found between job decision latitude, psychological demands, and heart disease (Reed et al. 1989). One explanation may be that the conventional high-strain occupations in manufacturing are almost absent in this population and that the high-strain population in general is small. The age factor may also be important. Recall that in the Swedish studies the associations between job

---

*As strength-of-effect estimates, we have the average standardized odds ratio (SOR) for skill discretion of 1.48 in five CHD studies from Karasek, Schwartz, and Pieper (1983).

strain and myocardial infarction risk were much stronger before age 55 than after. In the Honolulu Heart Study, the follow-up began at a median age of about 54, so part of the explanation may be that the Hawaiian men were too old for these associations. Furthermore, much of the occupational experience of these subjects would have been in a preindustrialized Honolulu, dating back to the 1930s. It may be that our conventional cardiovascular epidemiological study age boundaries are inappropriate for occupational epidemiology. The Honolulu findings certainly suggest that psychosocial factors beyond the demand/control model must be addressed. Perhaps the traditional society's occupational mix is more conducive to cardiovascular health, or the traditional cultural social support system protects the individual from the adverse effects of job strain (although several tests for these effects did not observe such an interaction). Other studies have certainly found differences in cultural patterns regarding psychosocial conditions (Orth-Gomér 1979).

In Scandinavia, further findings continue to confirm the demand/ control model. Recently, in a ten-year follow-up of a cohort of Finnish men representing a wide range of occupations, all the classical medical risk factors were studied (Hahn 1985). The job analyses were based on self-reports at the start of the study. The results indicated a significant twofold elevation of myocardial infarction risk during the follow-up among those men who had described job strain, even when all the classical risk factors had been accounted for. A small ($N = 343$) but very carefully followed longitudinal study of employees of a single plant, a sawmill in northern Sweden, also provides confirmation of a significant association between low decision latitude and poor workplace social support on the one hand and mortality on the other (Åstrand 1988).

The psychological demand dimension has been more difficult to measure than the other dimensions, for reasons discussed in chapter 2. The measures of decision authority and skill utilization are much more robust. In both the Swedish and American linkage studies, the indicator of demands ("hectic" in the Swedish systems) is statistically weak because so little of the scale variation is between occupations. In a recent study of eighty-eight 28-year-old working men representing all kinds of occupations, men in occupations classified as "hectic" reported only marginally more "rush and effort" than other men (Theorell et al., Final Report, 1984). The results also indicated, however, that men in the hectic occupations were more often forced to use unhealthy coping styles (to cover emotional feelings) than others, so the hectic factor probably does have significant meaning. Nevertheless, as in the American data, the hectic factor is also associated with desirable self-reported work satisfaction and is more common in upper-class jobs. These factors suggest unmeasured pathways that may partly explain why the dimensions in decision latitude in general show stronger associations with heart disease risk than does the demand dimension. As we noted in chapter 2, however, there are important unanswered questions about which component of the decision latitude measure—skill discretion or decision authority—is the more important determinant of stress-related illness. Most of the analyses above, using preexisting data sources, have had more robust data on skill discretion. Few have contained comprehensive measures of control (decision authority).

Another serious measurement problem is underreporting of work problems. It is a greater problem in prospective studies than in retrospective ones (where overreporting may be a problem) and is probably of greater importance for early asymptomatic hypertension and propensity to sudden cardiac death than for other cardiovascular illness. We know that young men with early stages of asymptomatic hypertension have low levels of verbal aggression, which may make them less likely to report work problems if there are any. Also, as we have previously noted, job strain may be underestimated because of denial. For sudden unexpected cardiac death, our knowledge is insufficient, but there is a hint that candidates of near-future unexpected cardiac deaths may underreport work problems (Nirkko et al. 1982). If this is true, it is a very serious methodological problem in studies of this kind.

Some of the associations between job strain and cardiovascular illness risk are very probably caused by the association between job strain and the risk factors: blood pressure, cholesterol, and smoking. Most of the cardiovascular epidemiological studies that have taken the psychosocial factors into account have used simple multivariate analyses. Unfortunately, when the accepted CHD risk factors have taken their variance out of the equations, very little has remained for the psychosocial factors to explain statistically. Thus the traditional structure of cardiovascular epidemiological research itself inhibits positive findings between job structures and heart disease, attributing them instead to risk factors that are themselves affected by job structure.

From a medical-biological standpoint, insufficient attention has been paid to the fact that different manifestations of coronary heart disease have very different physiological origins and thus could have different psychosocial correlates. The studies of job strain in relation to conventional risk factors are suggestive of some pathways, but this is still an area where much additional research is needed. The findings are least consistent for serum cholesterol, with strong associations in some studies and none in others. Cigarette smoking seems to be the risk factor most consistently as-

sociated with job strain, with some significant association apparent in almost all studies. Systolic blood pressure is also generally significantly associated with job strain, whereas the associations are much less clear for
diastolic blood pressure (Pieper, La Croix, and Karasek 1989).

Conclusion

Overall, the cross-sectional studies that have included medical risk indicators as well as job strain measurements indicate that job strain may contribute almost as much to the statistical risk of coronary heart disease as some
of the conventional risk factors. We have found that the psychosocial job
conditions are associated with the biomedical risk factors and also have an
independent association with heart disease risk. Our discussions in chapter
3 identified a number of relevant physiological stress mechanisms outside
the conventional risk factors—such as blood clotting, cardiac muscle metabolism, and cardiac arrhythmias—that can directly precipitate CHD. In
sum, there is evidence of adverse effects from the job structures we have inherited for the past two hundred years and for plausible mechanisms for
these effects, although we suspect we are only beginning to understand the
broad context of these associations.

Unresolved research questions of the type we have discussed will often
lead epidemiologists to label such findings "strongly suggestive, but still
not conclusive." The implication is that the area is a promising direction for
further research. We agree that it is. Another implication, however, is that
the findings are not sufficiently conclusive to warrant public policy action,
such as job redesign initiatives. Here we disagree. While we understand the
importance of the unresolved scientific questions, the toll of actions taken
by uninformed professionals, who at present have very little understanding of the mechanisms we describe, continues to mount. The second half of
this book is addressed to the job design professionals, who along with
workers, managers, and now—we hope—health professionals redesign
jobs daily with or without the information provided by occupational health
scientists.

Indeed, with the magnitude of effects we have seen, we might expect
broad societal consequences. In the United States, overall health costs have
been skyrocketing.* The United States has hardly been the home of the hu-

---

*Heart disease, by itself, has probably increased somewhat in Sweden and decreased in
the United States since the early 1970s, but the causes and magnitudes of these long-term
trends are the subject of much debate (see Havlik and Feinleib 1979), beyond the scope of this
book.

manistic work environment during the last decades, particularly since the air traffic controller conflict in 1981. Could changes in the labor relations and managerial climate of a country's management structure have had an impact on these costs? Changes in the delivery of services have probably had a greater effect on health costs, but given the magnitude of excess illness burdens we have computed above, this question cannot be dismissed as irrelevant. If management structures originally conceived to increase efficiency in mass production have contributed to such costs, we face a true irony: in many of the most technologically advanced manufacturing industries, labor costs now represent less than 10 percent of expenses, and yet the use of old management models, based on labor cost cutting, may be significantly increasing the health cost burden.

It is interesting to examine the implications of our findings for managers. If an employer increases the demands on employees while concomitantly decreasing their decision latitude, the employees will experience rising blood pressure levels. Only some of them will react, and they will probably be the best workers—highly motivated and cooperative. Certainly the toll of badly designed jobs is high: our evidence builds a strong case that the work environment can become a biological prison that the average human being cannot endure without adverse physiological effects in the long run. From the perspective of business, these extraordinary health costs represent only a part of the total cost of poorly structured work. We will investigate the other costs in chapter 5 as we examine the effect of the demand/control model on learning and motivation, which even more directly affect productivity.

PART II

HEALTH, PRODUCTIVITY, AND THE RECONSTRUCTION OF WORKING LIFE

5

Psychosocial Job Characteristics and Productivity

The costs of illness and distress described in the previous chapters should be enough by themselves to motivate new management policies. Yet these losses represent at most half the cost of poor psychosocial work design. Productivity losses through lost skills, lost motivation, and lost opportunities for development of new capabilities by both workers and firms are at least as important. Indeed, we believe that these costs are so severe that they justify a reconstruction of work design and management policy from the most basic beginnings: the nature of productivity and the goals of a firm. The next six chapters of the book focus on the feasibility and processes for the psychosocial redesign of work.

Worker well-being must be at least as important a goal for the future as profit. It can no longer be made an intermediate step on the pathway to profitability of the firm. This may strike many readers as an unrealistic hope, but only such a major reorientation of priorities is consistent with the maximum welfare of all members of industrial societies—who now, in both the United States and Sweden, are mostly employed men and women—which must be the ultimate justification of any economic system. We obviously cannot rely on Adam Smith's "invisible hand" of individual profit maximization to deliver the kind of well-being referred to in the last four chapters. Most of the above costs we have described have never been incorporated in the balance sheets that accountants prepare for economic policy makers, but these omissions affect many people. While firms must make a profit to survive, it is even more important that the population itself survive, and in a healthy state. New balance sheets and definitions of the bottom line will have to be developed, or individual well-being and firm profitability will fail to coincide in the future as neoclassical economists hypothesize they have coincided in the past (Samuelson 1980). This ambitious goal of reconceptualizing our economic system is already implied by a number of best-selling management theorists and recently by economists as well (Thurow 1984; Dumas 1986; Bowles and Gintis 1987).

The feasibility of such new directions has already been demonstrated. Decades of Quality of Work Life and Industrial Democracy projects have shown that it is possible to promote employee well-being and participatory decision making and at the same time enhance productivity. And yet the linkages between productive behavior and psychosocial job structure have remained unclear in the eyes of many observers. These experiments have certainly not had sufficient impact to reverse the still-dominant effects of conventional production management policies in areas such as short-term cost accounting, personnel selection and training policies, marketing forecasts, inventory scheduling models, or financial investment and acquisition strategies. Most management decisions are still following what we call "old methods." In spite of increasing numbers of programs in U.S. industry using participatory decision-making slogans, there is almost no evidence of major structural changes in the U.S. Fortune 1000: only slightly over 1 percent have majority self-management programs in place (Lawler, Ledford, and Mohrman 1989).

In some cases the Quality of Work Life projects have lacked influence because QWL-oriented scientists and practitioners (we are in this group) have not been able to meet the valid standards of the conventional approaches on their own terms. There has often been lack of scientific rigor in demonstrating results, and data quality has often been weak (see p. 182). This is not the primary problem, however. The primary problem seems to be that many positive results of the experiments have been obscured in the process of translating them into the old frames of reference and methodologies that the conventional approaches require. We will see in the next section, for example, the difficulty of assessing psychosocial costs in economic terms. The new experiments will require new criteria to show the strength of their findings. New definitions of productivity may also make it easier to reconcile the separate goals of firm effectiveness and employee well-being. We will present our own new definition of productivity later in this chapter. Thus, work-life policies are in a time of transition. New reality conflicts with old models, but the new realities have lacked the strength of a comprehensive explanatory framework. We believe such new paradigms are on the way.

Another problem, mainly for U.S. job redesign research, is simply political conservatism with respect to work life issues. This is ironic given the ultimate goals of worker well-being. The chosen topics of scientific inquiry often seem to avoid sensitive issues such as worker decision making, worker social collectivities, or occupational health liabilities in general— that might upset existing power positions of managers. Moreover, profit-oriented corporate goals have been accepted too readily as the final criteria of the success of "humanistic" job redesign efforts. Of course, it is the company that pays the bill for job redesign research in the United States, since few public funds are available for these projects, and their sponsorship of the research has led to distrust on the part of the very people—unions and employee groups—who stand to gain most and who could be the strongest supporters of these issues. Research that avoids politically sensitive issues may be financially expedient, but it is really neither in the workers' nor in management's long-term interests. It leads to distorted science and ultimately fails to provide much of the information needed to organize production effectively. As Hackman (1984) has noted for industrial psychology, the overall result has been that scientific inquiry in the United States has been handicapped in contrast to the major progress made over the last two decades by German, Scandinavian, and Japanese researchers. It is to these countries that we will often have to turn for both practical experiments and new scientific methods.

Estimating the Economic Costs of Work-Related Stress

In order to broaden understanding of our findings, we will attempt in this section to translate the losses due to the illnesses described in the previous chapter into economic costs for companies and for the country as a whole. While these costs will be staggering, our real point is that any simple translation of psychosocial costs into dollar figures to add to the conventional balance sheets will be an inadequate formulation of the problem. Such translations are a basic premise of modern (neoclassical) economics and the inheritance of Jeremy Bentham, the eighteenth-century Utilitarian philosopher (Harrison 1983) (see chapter 1). This well-known contemporary of Adam Smith and exponent of his ideas claimed that all pain and pleasure could be measured in economic quantities, and thus be incorporated within the mechanisms of individual choice in a free-market economy—free from the fetters of social decision process, as the neoclassically oriented entrepreneur would look at it. We think we have shown this to be a gross factual omission for our contemporary workplaces, but it also raises a moral question. Attempts to totally replace the collective social judgments that have determined what levels of well-being are acceptable for most of human history, by cost calculations based on murky market prices, is an abdication of unavoidable moral responsibilities. And yet we find this is what is happening in the mental health field in the United States (Kiesler and Morton 1988) and in many other areas of health. Indeed, the very methodology of Utilitarian cost analysis is problematic for the issues addressed in this book. Such analysis breaks down a system into its elemental components, attaches a price to each, and then adds them up. The value of the whole is no more than the sum of the prices of its parts. But in the systems theoretical models we discussed in chapter 3, we found that it was precisely the interactions between the system's components which were the primary determinants of strain and learning phenomena. Reduction of work organization problems to their elemental cost components is one step in problem solving, but for true problem analysis it must be superceded by an understanding of the system's function as a whole. We claim that there must be altogether new methods of assessing industrial output, in which health and developmental capabilities of the employee appear as goals in their own right. Having registered these objections, we will, nevertheless, briefly review the consequences of undesirable psychosocial work environments in terms of economic costs, which at least allows us to directly address the current health cost debate.

Health Costs

Estimation of the economic costs of stress-related illness is complicated by the fact that most of the true costs are never reflected in a dollar-measurable form. True economic costs are supposed to be reflected in the dollar prices established in an open market of buyers and sellers bidding for a good. One cannot put such a price on a worker's psychological distress or lost future growth potential. Who would buy it and what price would be agreed upon? Even the cost of treatment is an underestimate of distress. For example, the depression and exhaustion of workers in high-strain jobs (see figures 2–4 and 2–9) may lead to misery, but they are often not severe enough to result in a hospital visit or even a prescription. Yet depression and exhaustion, with frequencies of 27 percent and 15 percent of the U.S. population, and 15 percent and 32 percent of the Swedish population (Karasek 1979), are much more common than the symptoms of heart disease, which range from 2 percent to 5 percent in both countries.* The eco-

*There is a substantial literature, beyond the scope of this book (see Schwartz, Myers, and Astrachan 1973; American Psychiatric Association 1980), about the appropriate criteria for conditions such as depression, particularly for clinical diagnoses. Our criterion for most of the

nomic invisibility of these very prevalent costs is certainly one reason why they have not figured more prominently in public debates, particularly in the quantitatively oriented debates in the United States.

Other vocabularies could put these costs more clearly into focus, without trying to put a dollar price tag on them. We could review the benefits of healthy work environments. For example, a policy dialogue in the language of health risk assessment might begin with the observation that for an adult of your age and sex the average life expectancy is thirty more years, but for you, in your psychosocially desirable job, it is thirty-seven years (as we found for blue-collar Swedes in chapter 4). In addition, your job carries with it a 13 percent chance of depression and a 10 percent chance of exhaustion, versus the respective averages of 27 percent and 25 percent. Which would you prefer, disregard for work redesign or a life that is likely to be seven years longer and twice as free from psychological stress? Many people could join in such discussions without having to have the costs translated into dollars and cents.

It is difficult to develop reliable monetary estimates of stress-related losses. Three levels of error-prone estimates must be made: first, the job stress–related component of total health costs; second, the preventable component of these health costs; and third, the preventable costs of poor design that are reflected in productivity losses. But one fact is beyond dispute: the costs are very large. We can begin with the overall costs for health care in a U.S. national context. These are very high and rapidly growing: $511 billion in 1987, which was 11.4 percent of the gross national product, as opposed to 7.4 percent of the GNP in 1975 (Ginzberg 1987). At the company level, in 1985 average health care costs were 11.8 percent of the wage bill, or $2,560 per employee—up over 100 percent since 1977 (U.S. Chamber of Commerce 1986). Herzlinger and Calkins calculated in 1986 that 24 percent of company profits were spent on health insurance, and in 1985 Herzlinger and Schwartz noted that these costs were rising so rapidly that "if unchecked, in eight years they will eliminate all profits for the average Fortune 500 companies and the largest 250 non-industrials" (p. 69). For both General Motors and Chrysler, Blue Cross/Blue Shield, and not a steel company, is the largest supplier (Sloan, Grumman, and Allegrante 1987). In 1983, Chrysler had direct health care expenditures for employees, dependents, and retirees of $6,000 per active employee, $600 per car sold (Califano 1983).

---

depression tabulations in chapter 2 (figures 2–4a, 2–4b; 2–9) is generally more liberal and much less complex, as noted on p. 49 *n*: an average state of fair to poor on eight pairs of life descriptions. "Depression" in Karasek (1979) (used in figures 2–4d and 2–4e) and Karasek, Gardell, and Lindell (1987) corresponds to at least one moderately severe problem on one of the three measures roughly reflecting depression (with anxiety and sleeping problems). "Exhaustion" corresponds to unusual exhaustion at one of several times during the day.

Estimating the job stress–related component of the total health care bill is difficult. Approximately 50 percent of all U.S. deaths are attributable to cardiovascular disease (CVD), as we saw in chapter 4. We also saw substantial associations in Sweden between job characteristics and psychiatric disorders, suicide, alcoholism, gastrointestinal illness, and traffic accidents. Taken together with heart disease, these diseases cause about 54 percent of mortality. While it is not possible on the basis of our data to compute the exact number of hospitalizations for these diagnoses in the Swedish Five County study that were related to low skill discretion, we estimate that the above illnesses account for approximately 50 percent of the hospitalizations with high mortality (Alfredsson, Spetz, and Theorell 1985).

In 1984, estimates of the costs of cardiovascular illness alone in the United States were placed at $64.4 billion, including indirect costs (Herzlinger and Calkins 1986). One obvious difficulty in making such estimates is the inclusion of these huge indirect costs. Two hundred billion dollars of the $250 billion estimated total costs for mental illness were due to the indirect but documentable costs of social welfare programs, mental illness–related traffic accidents, and direct losses to victims of crimes linked to mental illness and drug abuse (Franklin 1986). The extraordinary imprecision in cause-specific monetary estimates is reflected in the variance in the estimates of two researchers for the cost of smoking (which we in turn associated with job stress in chapter 4): one puts the cost to a company at $366 to $601 per employee (Kristein 1983), the other at between $4,000 and $5,000 (Weis 1981). However imprecise the exact economic costs, the fact that they are escalating rapidly is clear. Workers' compensation, which has traditionally not been allowed for any but the most clearly demonstrable causes of disability or death, showed an increase in job stress–related claims from 5 percent in 1980 to 14 percent in 1986 (Grippa and Durbin 1986). In Sweden, the number of claims for workers' compensation grew from 190,000 in 1980 to 260,000 in 1988—a 37 percent increase (National Insurance Bureau 1989).

The true costs should probably be considered to be that portion of job stress–related illness that is preventable by feasible job redesign strategies. Since such illnesses have previously been seen as inevitable instead of preventable, their costs have often been considered to be zero. But as we will attempt to show in the remainder of this book, many of these problems are preventable—and often by strategies provided by decades of practical experience. Our review of attributable risks in chapter 4 found a range of etiological fractions from 3 to 16 percent for myocardial infarction from job strain and 28 percent for all serious stress-related illnesses from low skill discretion. These were the very rough estimates of the beneficial impacts that would be obtained by increasing the skill discretion in low-level jobs up to that in the remainder of the population.

We would actually prefer a more precise target: our goal would be jobs with the decision latitude of a craftsman, a nurse, a foreman, or an office supervisor. On the basis of strengths of association discussed in the previous chapter* the serious job redesigns of the type we will be discussing might eliminate about 23 percent of the risk for cardiovascular illness through changes in decision latitude and another 11 percent through changes in social support at work.† (Because of the lack of general associations with psychological demands, methodologically our weakest measure, no gains are noted there.) The percentages might be similar for other stress-related illness, as they appeared to be in table 4–3. Using the extremely rough estimates of total job stress–related morbidity and mortality calculated in chapter 4, we estimate that reductions of as much as 16 percent of the direct health care costs—$80 billion per year in the United States—might ultimately be feasible. This exercise in wild speculation at least leaves us with estimates that are roughly consistent, when indirect costs are added, with estimates recently appearing in the national news media placing costs of job stress at $150 billion per year (Freudenheim 1987; Miller 1988) and with the National Science Foundation Study finding of $100 billion total costs per year (Matteson and Ivancevich 1987).

Productivity Costs

Most experts would observe that the direct costs of job stress, large as they appear to be, are probably only a minor fraction of the true preventable costs of poor psychosocial job design. Although their illness may not lead to an economically measurable health care cost, exhausted or depressed employees are not energetic, accurate, or innovative at work. The losses that result loom larger than health care as preventable costs. To estimate their magnitude, Matteson and Ivancevich (1987), professors of busi-

---

*To calculate the final attributed risk from the calculations in chapter 4, we have used an average Standardized Odds Ratio (the relative risk associated with one standard deviation change of the risk factor) for skill discretion of 1.48 from Karasek, Schwartz, and Pieper (1983). This average risk ratio should be regarded as a crude estimate, based on a combination of both prevalence and incidence data (combined because of consistency) in five studies in the United States and Sweden. We use our analysis of possibilities to change decision latitude in chapter 9, which describes job redesigns for low-status workers, bringing their decision latitude to foreman levels. We summarize decision latitude impacts on illness risk reduction by quartiles of the population (lowest quartile: .25 x 2.0 standard deviations improvement = −13.6 percent; second lowest quartile: .25 x 1.0 standard deviations improvement = −8.1 percent; third quartile: no change; top quartile: .25 x .5 standard deviations reduction [see chapter 9] = −1.2 percent) for a total risk reduction of 22.9 percent. We estimate the independent contribution of social support to be roughly half as much, on the basis of prevalence of heart disease symptoms in Johnson and Hall (1988).

†This computation is more sensitive to those with the lowest levels of decision latitude—who also have the highest risk. Thus, the total effect is greater than in the calculations of etiological fraction in chapter 4.

ness administration, divided the U.S. economy in 1987 into fictitious firms of 1,000 employees each and looked at the costs of job stress. They addressed four types of costs: the costs of absenteeism, the costs of extra employees needed to do the job of the stress-impaired work force—these are the two largest costs—turnover, and sabotage. Given the national statistics on absenteeism and turnover, their calculations are not unreasonable. Of an 8 percent absenteeism rate, they estimated that 4 percent is preventable; of a 10 percent turnover rate, they assumed that 4 percent is preventable; and they added an additional 5 percent of the work force to cover preventable ineffectiveness on the job—the largest cost. For their typical (fictitious) company, the total cost turned out to be 7 percent of sales—$2,770 per year per employee. When they aggregated this figure for the whole U.S. economy of 108,000,000 employees, they arrived at a preventable cost figure of over $300 billion per year, not including the direct costs of preventable health care we have already discussed.

Whereas Matteson and Ivancevich assumed the costs of lost effectiveness to be 5 percent of wage costs, Hunter and Schmidt's (1982) estimates of the costs of skill mismatches on the job, when linked to our U.S. national statistics on the interoccupation variance in skill discretion, would imply losses of between 9 percent and 15 percent of the wage bill.* While these fractions are again hopelessly hard to estimate precisely, the losses can easily represent a significant fraction of the total wage bill. Clearly, misutilization of skill can result in huge losses for a firm. To understand the magnitude of skill-related losses and gains, we will first review theories of work motivation and skill utilization and then look at the results of the last several decades of Quality of Work Life and Industrial Democracy redesign practice. As we will see, the average improvements in productivity and employee well-being are approximately of the same order of magnitude as the rough estimates above would imply.

Productivity and Models of Motivation, Active Learning, and Skill Utilization

A central example of the problem of insufficient attention to worker well-being is reflected in the scientific model most commonly used in the United

*Hunter and Schmidt use supervisor estimates of the cost of mismatched skills to estimate that the costs are 40 percent to 70 percent of the wage bill times a factor that is the within-occupation variance of skills divided by its total variance. This fraction is about 55 percent for skill discretion in the U.S. economy in our data (see the appendix), times a factor relating skill and performance (.4 in their model).

States to link psychosocial work design to productivity and well-being. In this model, employee well-being is an intermediate step on the pathway to profitability: a happy worker is a productive worker. Well-being is a second priority. This lack of equal attention has led to the use of vague measurements of well-being, such as satisfaction questionnaires. It confuses scientific analyses of the dual goals of health and productive behavior and makes it difficult to separate the costs to worker, company, and society.

Thus, we believe there are problems with what are considered to be classic negative findings in the field. For example, Perrow's still popular work *Complex Organizations: A Critical Analysis* ([1972] 1986) concluded that psychological characteristics of the task (job design and human relations issues) are not important determinants of productivity. His conclusions were based on a model that introduced the crucial (perhaps very damaging) intermediate variable of job satisfaction to link job design and productivity. When little relation was found between job satisfaction and performance in a classic review by Brayfield and Crockett (1955) and another by Vroom (1964), the validity of the entire causal sequence, starting with any humane changes in psychosocial job characteristics and ending in productivity, was implicitly rejected (Aldag, Barr, and Brief 1981; Lawler 1986; Vroom 1964). But the use of this model, with its intermediate satisfaction variable, may have been the major error, for Vroom himself actually does find *direct* associations between decision making and productivity (1964, pp. 186–187). More precisely defined models, with separate mechanisms for predicting well-being and productivity (or motivation), could more successfully link job characteristics directly with performance. The demand/control model is, of course, one such model.

It is helpful at this point to look back at the work organizational theories introduced in chapter 1 and review Adam Smith's original rationale for limiting the breadth of a worker's task in order to increase productivity. The advantages he saw were greater depth of skill, leading to higher output; less wasted labor from physical shifting of a worker's weight between different tasks; and an easier interface to the machinery of his era. Over time, the switch from physical to mental work and the use of broad-based computer interfaces have weakened the last two advantages of specialized tasks for many jobs.

Recently many researchers have criticized Smith for his important omissions relating to the losses that result from divided tasks: not only stress but the huge costs of employing supervisors and planners to coordinate all the divided activities. The magnitude of coordination costs can be huge; in one modern aerospace company, only 13 percent of the labor costs are for the hands-on labor producing or assembling the aircraft components (Joe

Nardi, personal communication, October 1985). The remainder is the cost of administrators, clerical staff, and technicians to keep track of the parts, of workers, and of each other (plus engineering design costs). Similarly, Reichwald's study of an office setting (1983) found that the total cost of producing letters increased when a pool of highly specialized typists replaced general-purpose secretaries. Even though a simplistic measure of secretarial output—keystrokes per hour—increased for secretaries whose tasks were limited to keyboard punching instead of thinking about and organizing whole communication processes, the total cost of producing letters actually tripled because of the increased costs of coordinating the newly specialized jobs and easing friction between individuals.

The major test of Smith's formulation, however, has to do with the costs of learning and motivation. Smith reasoned that it was a waste of resources to teach every member of an organization how to do the organization's whole job; while an individual was mastering all the activities, that person's production would be less than optimal. This is obviously a valid concern for extremely complex processes, but not for much of the work that organizations do. Clearly there are limiting factors. Smith's costs must be balanced against the advantages of broader task assignments: flexibility to reorganize the whole job when employees know most of the component tasks, the ease of learning new activities from a broader skill base, and the motivation that is associated with the intellectual stimulation of learning. The most productive level of specialization thus varies from one task to another, depending on the relative importance of each of these factors (Boucher 1988). Nevertheless, at the level of the job as a whole, coordination costs and lost flexibility are powerful general arguments against specialization. For very long-term employees, learning costs—even start-up costs—tend toward zero. Thus we are left to conclude that, at the task level, one of the most important determinants of productivity in mental work for permanent employees has to do with motivational advantages of learning and enhanced capabilities, an issue we examine in detail below.

WORK MOTIVATION THEORIES AND THE ACTIVE LEARNING HYPOTHESIS

Our model of motivation, derived from the basic demand/control theory of chapters 2 and 3, has much in common with several other theoretical motivation models, but also some important differences from them. Our initial definition of motivation is that it is an environmentally facilitated, active approach toward learning new behavior patterns or solving new problems—the active learning hypothesis of chapter 2. Our original hypothesis was that effective learning occurs in situations that are challenging enough to be interesting but not so demanding that capacities are over-whelmed. In such situations, new skills and the motivation to tackle new challenges develop apace (Csikszentmihalyi 1975; Hebron 1966). We can relate two important intellectual traditions to our model. The first, from U.S. cognitive psychology, is the social learning theory work of Albert Bandura (1977), a very general learning theory, now often used to describe optimum strategies for individual health-enhancing behavioral changes, such as weight loss. Related theories, applied specifically to factors that managers can use to increase worker motivation, are the expectancy theory work of Hackman, Lawler, and Oldham (Hackman and Lawler 1971; Hackman and Oldham 1976, 1980) and the goal-setting work of Locke (Locke et al. 1986). An entirely separate theoretical tradition of learning known as *action theory*, which focuses on active planning of the worker's own behavior in the work environment, has come from the German psychologist Winnifred Hacker (1978), with related work by Volpert (1974) and Frese and Sabini (1985).

Bandura's work relates learning to a personal perception of control ("self-efficacy") as opposed to the environmental control we have discussed. Motivating situations are those in which one has a perception of controlling procedures that affect an important set of outcomes (Averill 1973) and of increasing one's capabilities; they are situations that provide feedback on the effectiveness of one's performance. Bandura and his colleagues have built an impressive array of empirical evidence for the importance of self-efficacy on effective learning procedures: in exercise testing (Ewart et al. 1983), in reduced catecholamine excretion (Bandura et al. 1985), and in weight reduction (Bernier and Avard 1986; Glynn and Ruderman 1986). These findings on the effects of control seem congruent with our less rigorously tested learning hypotheses of the demand/control model. One shortcoming of models derived from social learning theory, however, is that they collectively underemphasize the significance of situation-based stressors, or the impact of overtaxing situations on learning. To the extent that demands are included (as the "importance," in expectancy theory terms) or goals are set very high (in the work of Locke and colleagues), they are seen as challenges entirely initiated by the individual, not as requirements, as in a sweatshop work environment.

By contrast, German action regulation theory, in some of its recent empirical formulations (Volpert et al. 1983), explicitly focuses on the multiple levels of environmental restrictions on a worker's control. Action theory postulates that for truly satisfactory self-development—learning in the broadest sense—people must be able to control the use of their own skills on three levels simultaneously: intellectual strategy formulation, flexible action repertoires, and sensorimotor reactions. In the context of the work environment, this means that workers' intellectual capabilities will not develop fully and poor productivity will occur (Hacker 1978) if workers cannot, for example, plan their daily work routines, as factory workers under Taylor's principles cannot do. The same would be true for managers who are prevented from direct contact with production processes, as they are under conventional management strategies. Such problems are further exacerbated by poorly designed computer-based work, as we will see in chapter 8.

The theory has several important implications for the dynamic hypotheses relating stress and learning processes that we developed in chapter 3. According to action theory, learning the solution to a new problem requires the highest level of skill—intellectual strategy formulation—only when that situation is first confronted; after the situation has been mastered, the person can perform it using standardized actions that become automatic, like sensorimotor responses in well-practiced manual tasks. This substantially reduces the energy needed in the situation, but the standardized actions offer no possibility for further comprehensive intellectual development. New challenges must constantly be confronted—and offering them will be a significant challenge for work designers. We address this goal at the end of the chapter with a new definition of productivity.

An even more important dynamic implication of action theory is provided by Frese and Stewart (1984): under high-stress conditions, people favor highly automated actions over actions that require intellectual strategy formulation, and it is therefore difficult to replace previously learned and routinized responses with new patterns of action (Poulton 1971; Semmer and Pfafflin 1978). Classic early research showed learning difficulties in very demanding situations (Courts 1939; Stauffacher 1937). Watson and Henry (1977) found that learning experiences for animal subjects could not be consolidated into new behavior patterns if these experiences were followed by demanding instead of restful activities. Their finding is consistent with our explanations of stress and learning in terms of system equilibrium (chapter 3). Frese and Stewart have hypothesized that intellectual planning requires increased intellectual capacity that is not available in times of stress. Stressful situations therefore prevent the self-development idealized by action theory from occurring, because they allow only routine response (Frese and Stewart 1984).

Action theory's discussion of multiple levels of learning adds an important insight to our hypothesis that stress inhibits learning (see chapter 3). Our demand/control model's stress development hypotheses can be used to distinguish between job situations that lead to two levels of adaptive (learning) behavior. *Open-loop learning* occurs in active jobs where workers develop solutions in anticipation of future problems—in other words, engage in strategy formulation (Umbers 1979). Routinized, *closed-loop learning* is much more limited adaptive activity. It occurs in high-strain jobs where workers can perfect their automatic error-correction responses only after problems have happened; strain inhibits more creative responses. Inasmuch as action theory is formulated in general terms, its predictions may also apply to groups of workers and organizations. If so, rigid hierarchical management strategies that limit workers' responses in times of high job demands not only take a toll in terms of individual stress but also limit learning at the organizational level. The organization in a crisis mode may not have the capacity to make precisely those long-term plans that would reduce its risk of facing further catastrophes in the future, as we will show in chapter 7. This situation is analogous to the negative spiral of behavior that we predicted for individuals when stress inhibits learning (see chapter 3).

To predict worker productivity, however, we probably need a modification of the simple active-learning hypotheses described in chapters 2 and 3, because the effects of strain and fatigue could independently reduce productivity (Jamal 1985). We therefore predict that productivity will result from the combined effects of an active-learning submodel and a psychological-strain submodel (see Karasek 1981a). For computational purposes, in the study described in the next section we simply added these two effects, giving them equal weight, but more sophisticated assessment of their separate contributions is needed in the future.

This additive formulation raises an important question: is the passive job or the high-strain job the least productive? The expanded formulation above is consistent with observations on negative learning or motivational deficits: traumatically stressful situations, in conjunction with low control over the stressor, are the most destructive of skills. Seligman (1975) discovered that dogs who receive a few trials of inescapable shock begin to accept shock passively, without attempting to escape. One important finding of the learned helplessness literature is that prior learning of an active response can inhibit the induction of passive behavior that the uncontrollable stressors would otherwise induce. But once the passive response pattern has been learned, it is very hard to eradicate; only total retraining by an outside agent restores activity (Glass and Singer 1972; Hiroto 1974; Seligman 1975). In one study (Thornton and Jacobs 1971), human subjects repeatedly confronted with stressful situations in which they could exercise no control over the outcome stopped tackling the problem; 60 percent reported as their reason, "Since we have no control, . . . why should we try?" We suspect that in the long term, passive work is more closely related to productivity loss than high strain, consistent with the findings on passive leisure and political activity reported in chapter 2. For conventional short-term measures of productivity, however, where long-term learning is less relevant, stress-related losses of high-strain jobs could dominate. Moreover, traumatic shock–based decrements in capabilities could be most severe in high-strain jobs, as the learned helplessness literature suggests. In any case, this is clearly an area requiring more research.

The implication that motivation can be negative under some job circumstances suggests that one must worry about organizationally induced destruction of work capacity. Workers who begin their careers with significant skills from high school and college may lose them through a job-based process of learning-in-reverse: *learned helplessness*. There is a developing literature describing the manner in which employees' behavior patterns are molded by the job (Van Maanen and Schein 1979). Findings of job-induced passivity would be particularly significant, because they would suggest the possibility that poor motivation to work was also learned in poorly designed work situations. Comments like "That's not my department," "That's not in my job description," and "It's best not to rock the boat around here" may be learned responses to early job experiences in which taking initiative and using extra skills and judgment were severely penalized as overstepping the bounds of one's (unnecessarily restricted) authority. Such associations are consistent with findings on "used and unused" capacity in studies of adult socialization and aging. If skills are not used, they are lost (Denney 1982). Schleicher (1973) found that workers in repetitive jobs show lower intelligence levels at high ages, whereas workers with intellectually demanding jobs show no age-related decrements. Others have also found evidence that unused skills atrophy over the life span (Berkowitz 1965). Kohn and Schooler's classic work (1973, 1978) used longitudinal data to show that intellectually simplistic jobs are associated with decreasing intellectual flexibility in activities overall.

Using the Demand/Control Model for Productivity Analysis

The demand/control model was used to analyze productivity in a study of five firms from a range of industries in Michigan—a hospital, a printing company, a research and development firm, and two auto accessories manufacturing firms (Karasek 1981a). Demand and control were evaluated by means of questionnaires and scales similar to those described for the QES surveys in chapter 2, along with supervisor ratings of productivity ($N = 228$ in two waves).* Productivity measures were based on a supervisor's rating

*The study data was gathered as a validation study for the U.S. QES data (Quinn 1977, by the University of Michigan Survey Research Center) and is roughly representative of the U.S.

of employee effectiveness on a combined scale of quantity and quality ($r =$ .75). Skill underutilization was measured by asking respondents to estimate the years of education required to perform their jobs and comparing this estimate with actual respondent education—the same method used in the national assessments of skill routinization in figure 1–2.

When the effects of both the active learning and the psychological strain mechanisms of the demand/control model are added,* as discussed above, analyses of the associations in figure 5–1 confirm the significance ($p \leq .05$) of an interactive association between job characteristics and productivity. Productivity is associated with high job demands only if decision latitude is high. If decision latitude is low, then higher levels of job demands are associated with reduced productivity measures. In economists' terms, high decision latitude seems to be a *co-factor of production*—necessary to ensure that work demands are translated into useful output.

Intuitively, one would expect that productivity would increase as job demands increased. Why does this not happen at low decision latitude? Our model predicted that when decision latitude is low, the worker may not be able to transform the potential energy of the stress of heavy job demands into the desired action. Constrained by time-paced operations and arbitrary rules, the worker may repress this energy internally, where it may manifest itself as mental and physiological strain. Indeed, figure 5–1 shows the familiar strong associations between depression and high-demand/low-decision-latitude jobs. Furthermore, the figure shows that skill underutilization is highest in the low-status jobs (low decision authority and skill discretion) where jobholders with low levels of education are likely to predominate—with an average of three years of education wasted. By contrast, the average high-status worker has a job requiring skills beyond his or her formal educational training—a definite challenge to learn on the job. These associations confirm the findings shown in figure 1–2 on skill utilization from a random sample of the U.S. work force as a whole.

This study suggests that applying the theories of Smith and Taylor may lead to underutilized skills and, furthermore, that motivational energy that might otherwise be available to accomplish tasks is transformed into adverse stress reactions when workers are not free to exercise reasonable lev-

---

work force (with a slightly higher proportion of blacks and females). The response rate was initially low, but improved dramatically from the first to the second wave (19 percent to 55 percent) due to an improved method for locating subjects' supervisors. The findings do not differ between waves.

*Each strain and learning component is a multiplicative interaction term with the zero point one population standard deviation unit into the respective low-strain and passive-job quadrants of figure 2–1. These components are equally weighted, and the strain term is subtracted from the learning term. The interaction is much stronger using decision authority than using skill discretion, in spite of the fairly strong correlation between these two measures ($r = .53$) (Karasek 1981a, table 2).

FIGURE 5–1 (a–c)
*Job characteristics and depression,
skill underutilization, and productivity rating*
(Males and females in five U.S. companies in Michigan, 1977, N = 222)

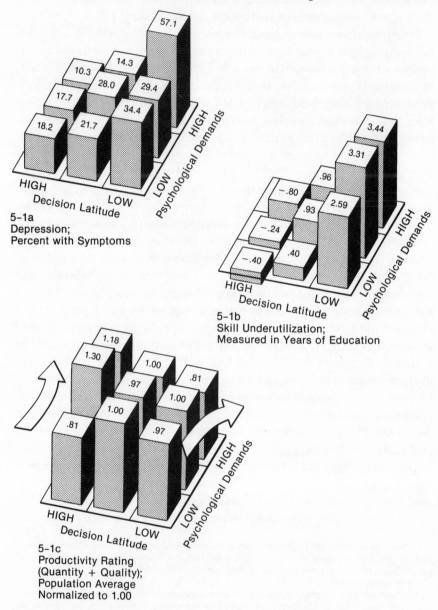

5–1a
Depression;
Percent with Symptoms

5–1b
Skill Underutilization;
Measured in Years of Education

5–1c
Productivity Rating
(Quantity + Quality);
Population Average
Normalized to 1.00

NOTE: Cell sizes, reading from left to right, are as follows—high demands: 30, 22, 28; medium demands, 23, 26, 17; low demands: 13, 24, 34.

SOURCE: Karasek 1981a.

els of decision making. For several reasons, however, the findings should be interpreted with caution: the study is correlational, not experimental; the sample size is small; the validity of supervisor reports has been criticized (Berg, Freedman, and Freeman 1978); and the implications of individual differences are not tested. Nevertheless, the job scales and the associations between job characteristics and mental strain symptoms closely parallel those from the nationally representative surveys discussed in chapter 2. And as we shall see in the next section, these productivity findings are consistent with a broad range of results from QWL practice in increasing skill variety and autonomy.

UNDERUTILIZATION OF SKILLS

The workers whose skills are underutilized are not in professional jobs, but in low-status jobs where the assumption has always been made that the worker was too poorly qualified to accomplish a skilled task. Clearly, the job design, not the skill of these workers, is limiting the productive potential of these jobs. Papstein and Frese (1988) have demonstrated the importance of decision latitude in the workplace to the use of newly acquired skills: computer programming skills acquired by workers were used in the work process only when workers had high decision latitude. Low-status workers, the group that we find with the highest levels of underutilized skills, have jobs in which skill requirements and decision opportunities have been kept low by inappropriate management techniques. The implication is that what we need is not a new educational emphasis for society but a way to design organizations to use the skills and develop the capabilities that people already have.

A review of the distribution of job decision authority suggests that the judgment capacities of the U.S. work force may also be underutilized (Karasek 1981b). For highly skilled blue-collar workers such as craftsmen and repairmen, relative authority lags substantially behind relative skill levels, particularly for younger workers. Low-skilled blue-collar workers suffer potential underutilization not only of the actual use of acquired skills but of their ability to use judgment with respect to the use of skills. For higher-status white-collar workers such as professionals, managers, and sales personnel, skill level and decision authority are high from early stages in their careers and they both remain high for older workers: that is, capabilities remain fully utilized.

If the old management policies are not productive, then why do hierarchical authority structures and narrowly restricted job boundaries persist so tenaciously? The highly specialized division of labor entails a burden for managers, the responsibility for coordinating all the specialized tasks and making comprehensive plans for the future. Yet many people find such planning burdens to be the positive kind of demand (the active situation of figure 2–1) which is intrinsically rewarding: the "plum" assignment or the career cornerstone. Perhaps managers have become overly accustomed to a monopoly on such rewarding psychosocial opportunities and are hesitant to yield their prerogatives (Hayes and Abernathy 1980). Radical critiques of management philosophy (Marglin 1974; Stone 1973) suggest that the real goal of labor specialization strategies today is to maintain management prerogatives to control workers and allocate productive surpluses. Berg, Freedman, and Freeman (1978) observed that whatever the reason for the policies, managers appear reluctant to engage in experiments that threaten their unilateral control over production processes.

Pessimistic views about this political resistance to change led to Braverman's (1974) predictions of long-term declines in the absolute level of skills required under capitalism, but this has been a highly controversial topic, with substantial evidence on both sides of the question (see Aronsson 1987 for a review of this literature). The U.S. Department of Commerce statistics show that the actual education level of the U.S. population has steadily increased over time but for the first time the skill level requirements of jobs in the U.S. economy declined between 1960 and 1970 (Berg, Freedman, and Freeman 1978; see also Dubnoff 1978; Rumberger 1980; Spenner 1979), in spite of the apparently increasing technological complexity of U.S. industry. A decade later, the quadrennial U.S. Quality of Employment Survey, based on detailed interviews of a random sample of U.S. workers, found that the percentage of workers who claimed they had significant skills they could not use increased from 27 percent in 1969 to 36 percent in 1977 (Quinn and Staines 1979). More recent figures from direct population survey data are not available, because the U.S. government, during the 1980s, stopped collection of direct questionnaire measures of work environment data—a striking omission in comparison to increasingly sophisticated Western European data of this type.

It is curious that there has been so little public concern about skill underutilization at a time when increased productivity is a national goal. But a common observation in the 1970s was that the U.S. work force had become "overeducated" for existing jobs; the implication was that Americans should seek less education.* The United States had invested too heavily in "human capital": the labor force was too skilled for existing jobs and had acquired a luxury taste for meaningful, challenging jobs, which were

*Ivar Berg noted the decreasing economic rewards to education in *Education and Jobs* (1970), and Richard Freeman (1976) observed a declining economic rate of return on higher education (8 percent in the early 1970s, down from 11–12 percent in the early 1960s). It must be noted that this observation conflicts with Kendrick's (1978) prediction that national productivity would increase over the last decade precisely because of higher skill levels.

unfortunately in increasingly short supply. The underlying model was that overeducation led to low satisfaction and ultimately to poor productivity. The implied solution at the time was to restrict education, to fit the work force (or the individual) to the low-skill jobs that were available.

These prescriptions are ironic in light of the very different current debate on U.S. educational policy, which now laments functional illiteracy and the fact that students seem to have lost the motivation to study fundamental subjects. Educators should not be mystified; the message only a few years ago was that industry did not have jobs for educated workers. The new call is—as it should be—for excellence in education, to provide the scientists and engineers that will be needed in the future. But what of those who will never be scientists or engineers? Marshall has noted that the educational skills of the lower half of the U.S. work force may soon be among the poorest in any of the industrialized countries (1988). Perhaps this is partly a response to perceived job opportunities. The jobs most commonly listed as likely to be available in the future are cashier, waiter and waitress, janitor, prison guard and custodian (Silvestri and Luckasiewics 1985; McMahon 1987), along with temporary jobs of various kinds. These promise no more than the underutilization of skills shown in the findings we have described (Härenstam, Palm, and Theorell 1988).

Jobs should be designed to match workers' potential skills: they should use all skills available and provide a platform for further skill development consistent with growth of self-esteem. The "overeducated" worker is also the underutilized factor of production, an underutilization that would hardly be permitted in the case of capital. It is surprising that many national economists emphasize development gains through technological development of physical resources and not through effective utilization, much less development, of the labor factor of production. An alternative policy to use human resources such as labor and skill as effectively as possible has indeed guided Japanese economic policy over the last decade (Rosen 1988). And the effective use and expansion of worker capabilities has been the cornerstone of a whole new generation of successful work organization policies to which we now turn our attention: the U.S. and Scandinavian Industrial Democracy and Quality of Work Life experiments.

Health and Productivity Outcomes of
Quality of Work Life Job Redesign Projects

The fundamental goals for the Quality of Work Life programs in the United States, the Industrial Democracy projects in Norway, and the Working Life projects in Sweden have much in common with the goals of this book: to achieve a dual increase in employee well-being and productivity. As a source of evidence on results of job change strategies that are often similar to those implicit in the expanded demand/control model from chapter 2, these experiences, which we will discuss together under the general rubric of Quality of Work Life (QWL), represent an important compendium of practice. The similarities between our job design dimensions and some of the Quality of Work Life job redesign changes are strong enough to allow us to assess the validity of our theory. Kopelman's (1985) review of two decades of QWL job change studies shows that our dimensions of skill discretion, decision authority, and social support have close parallels to some of the most important QWL interventions: job enrichment, job enlargement, responsibility for a complete product, and feedback or work group formation, respectively. Such changes represent over 80 percent of the QWL interventions reviewed by Kopelman from the last two decades of practice. These have much in common with Emery and Thorsrud's ([1964] 1969) list of work-related psychological needs, are also central components of Hackman and Oldham's (1976) often-used Motivating Potential Score, and are crucial elements in Lawler's (1986) formula for QWL effectiveness: increased knowledge for low-status workers, information flow (related to our measure of skill discretion), and power (our decision authority dimension). Lawler also includes financial reward equity.

There are also significant differences between our model and the QWL approaches (see table 5–1). The Quality of Work Life literature curiously omits measures of psychological (or even physical) job demands and of health outcomes. These omissions not only diminish potential research support from health professionals but make it impossible to differentiate problems of passivity and low motivation from stress problems, to analyze comprehensively the effects of new technologies, to understand the significance of physical health hazards, or even to understand the impact of the stress of job change processes themselves. A review of the QWL literature also makes clear some shortcomings of our own conceptual framework. We have still not included group- and organizational-level factors in our analytic preoccupation with the micro-level impacts of job structures (needed to explain a causal connection to heart disease). Even though we expanded our basic model to include work-group social support in chapter 2, further extensions will be needed. We have still overlooked Kopelman's fifth common QWL intervention, responsibility for a complete product and creation of new client-worker communication linkages—and have also omitted Emery and Thorsrud's ([1964] 1969) meaningful interface between work and the broader community. These last three issues have much in common,

TABLE 5–1
*Job dimensions in the demand/control model and
major QWL job redesign strategies*

Demand/Control Model	QWL Job Redesign Strategies
1. Increase in Skill Discretion	Job Enrichment
2. Increase in Skill Discretion	Responsibility for Complete Product
3. Increase in Decision Authority	Job Enlargement
4. Increase in Social Support	Feedback
5. Increase in Social Support	Work Groups
6. Increase in New Value	New Client Relationships
7. Increase in New Value	Meaningful Job Interface
8. Decrease in Psychological Demands	(not available)
9. Decrease in Physical Demands	(not available)
10. (not available)	Organizational Context: a. multilevel management support b. union support
11. Occupation Category Analysis	c. product type
12. (not available)*	Job Security

*Discussed in a macroeconomic context.

and are partly addressed in our new productivity definition later in this chapter. (Career security, also noted by Emery and Thorsrud, is held until the end of the book.) It will be clear in the following chapters that models of job redesign must look a good distance beyond individual-level task structure, to address organizational-level and even market-level phenomena, to ensure successful job redesign efforts.

A summary of the major QWL literature reviews will give us a more precise estimate of how common associations between QWL job redesign, productivity, and health really are. Katzell, Bienstock, and Faerstein's (1977) review of 108 U.S. worker productivity projects from 1971 to 1975 found that they were associated with cost reductions in nine out of nine cases and with quality increases in nine out of eleven cases. Pasmore et al. (1982) found that 134 sociotechnical work redesign projects undertaken in North America from 1950 to 1980 were successful in increasing productivity in 89 percent of the cases and quality in 97 percent of the cases. Metaanalyses of multiple studies by Miller and Monge (1986) show a correlation between participation and productivity of .15, and participation job satisfaction of .34 (although Wagner and Gooding [1987] have less optimistic assessments). In one of the best-documented reviews, Kopelman (1985) comprehensively examined 32 work redesign projects during the last two decades, primarily from the United States but including some from Scandinavia, that gathered data on both productivity and well-being. Our review of his data on projects with quantitative measures* found an average productivity increase of 17 percent for twenty-two projects and a quality increase of 42 percent in sixteen projects. Well-being also improved in these studies: studies with quantitative absenteeism data showed a 19 percent decline. Twenty out of twenty-four studies with job satisfaction data registered improvements. These improvements in broadly defined productivity measures are consistent and significant, and the quality improvements are quite large. The statistics certainly support some of our speculative estimates of the costs of lost productivity from work-related stress and underutilized skills, discussed earlier in this chapter.

In the studies Kopelman reviewed, positive evidence is clearly available for improvement of health and productivity when absenteeism and job satisfaction data are included as measures of employee well-being. As we will see in the next chapter, clinically rigorous health data is more readily available from the Scandinavian countries, while U.S. studies often have only health-related information such as absenteeism or job dissatisfaction data. While illness is the major cause of absenteeism, other factors, such as family responsibilities, are also associated (Karasek, Gardell, and Lindell 1987), and short-term absenteeism may even protect employees against long-term illness (Edgren and Ander 1982). In spite of these potential contaminations, in this section we will use absenteeism as an indicator of health status† (of course, absenteeism also measures productivity loss). Kopelman's review included twelve useful studies with both absenteeism and productivity data. Of these, two-thirds showed joint improvement. In the six studies with quantitative data, absenteeism dropped by an average of 23 percent and productivity increased by an average of 16 percent. In the studies with quantitative data for both absenteeism and quality, absenteeism dropped 18 percent on average and quality increased 29 percent on average—quite important improvements. Kopelman also observed in his review of these studies that the impact of the Quality of Work Life strategies

*Kopelman's published analysis is based on median statistics. We have reanalyzed his published data using mean value statistics where quantitative data was available to derive our estimates. We have also omitted one study with obsolete data from Volvo in 1973 (see instead Agurén et al. 1985). Another study of auto industry changes reporting both productivity improvement and positive well-being effects for employees involves Saab-Valmet in Finland (Kauppinen-Toropainen and Hanninen 1981).

†Scientific support for this somewhat questionable measure exists in the form of studies that show that absenteeism correlates much more highly to health indicators than to other work, family, or demographic factors. In a representative sample of 8,700 male and female full-time white-collar workers, absenteeism correlations for males with seven self-reported illnesses (including heart disease) are 2.17 times as high as they are for sex or marital status; 3.92 times as high as for other (mainly family) stressors; and 2.52 times as high as for psychosocial work characteristics. For females, the respective multiples are 1.75, 2.68, and 2.53 (see Karasek, Gardell, and Lindell 1987 for variable definitions).

is cumulative: that is, productivity increases more and absenteeism declines more in situations where more of the five QWL strategies he discusses are employed.

Kopelman's review also confirms the importance of moving beyond the individual-task level of the original demand/control model to the social level. Just as we found social support affecting stress symptoms in chapter 2, so too does the social context of the task affect productivity. The work group, the labor union, and the organization not only have an impact on the associations observed but are crucial in the process of participatory strategies to redesign work, which we will be discussing in the following chapters. The quality of social feedback from the surrounding organization is so significant that all the positive absenteeism findings in Kopelman's review occurred only when feedback was also present (in the four studies in which there was no feedback, absenteeism did not change at all). We will discuss the social context of health-oriented job redesign in more detail in chapter 6.

More precise evidence on the impact of changes in job decision latitude on long-term health status is available in a representative study of all Swedish white-collar workers (Karasek in press; Karasek, Gardell, and Lindell 1987; Lindell 1982; Wahlund and Nerell 1976). Data was collected in a large random ($N = 8,700$) survey of full-time male and female white-collar workers in Sweden's Federation of White-Collar Unions, TCO. Twelve indicators of physical illness, psychological distress, and health-related behavior, including heart disease, depression, pill consumption, and absenteeism, were developed. For roughly one-fourth of the sample, company-initiated job reorganizations (presumably to improve productivity) were undertaken during a two- to four-year period before the health status reports were recorded (Karasek in press). While the data is actually from a cross-sectional survey, because of the relationship in time between job changes and health status reports, the randomized and blind "interventions" (the job changes), and the large, randomly selected non-change population serving as a control group, this data can support substantial causal interpretation about the effects of control on health status.

The study examines the effects of two types of control at the job. Employees whose jobs had changed were asked to report (1) whether they had had influence over the change process and (2) whether the job change resulted in more or less decision latitude in terms of task variety, task decision authority, and possibilities for skill development. The two measures are combined in table 5–2. Our primary hypothesis, that increases in job control are associated with lower risk of illness, is confirmed by a comparison of the groups that reported increased task control and influence (column A)

TABLE 5-2

Illness rates after job reorganization under different levels of employee control
(Swedish white-collar workers)

| | Job Reorganization Population | | | | | No-Reorganization Population | | |
| | Levels of Control | | | Total Rates | Signif. Diff. Between Groups A,B, and C | Total Rates | Signif. Diff. Between Reorg. and No-Reorg. | Signif. Diff. Between Group A and No-Reorg. |
	A[1] Change: Increased Control	B[2] Change: Intermediate	C[3] Change: Decreased Control					
Men								
Depress.	13.7	18.4	27.8	20.6	***	13.3	***	·
Exhaust.	39.5	51.1	52.4	48.2	**	35.5	***	*(-)
Dissat.	8.7	23.8	45.3	27.7	***	18.1	***	***
Heart	3.4	7.4	8.6	6.8	*	4.6	*	·
Dizzy	2.2	7.1	10.0	6.9	***	4.5	***	·
Head	5.7	9.9	14.3	10.4	***	8.0	*	·
Stomach	16.9	21.7	24.4	22.2	*	15.4	***	·
Respir.	10.3	9.8	15.7	13.7	*	7.6	***	·
Aches	18.8	21.4	25.3	22.1	*	18.1	**	·
Pills	4.1	6.0	10.2	7.0	**	5.7	·	·
Absent	5.0	7.8	10.7	8.1	**	6.6	*	·
Smoke	17.8	16.1	14.3	15.9	·	14.8	·	·
Total N =	320	434	439	1,193		3,688		

(Physical Illness brace spans Heart through Aches.)

	Measure	(N=166)	(N=269)	(N=309)	(N=744)	sig	Total (N=2,879)	sig	sig
Women	Depress.	21.1	29.3	35.6	30.1	**	20.3	***	•
	Exhaust.	55.4	45.3	59.2	53.4	**	42.4	***	***(-)
	Dissat.	7.2	18.9	31.4	21.5	***	15.5	***	•
	Heart	6.6	7.5	7.4	7.3	•	4.0	***	•
	Dizzy	13.3	17.1	15.7	15.6	•	12.3	**	•
Physical	Head	22.8	23.4	25.5	24.2	•	18.9	***	•
Illness	Stomach	22.9	27.4	23.3	25.5	•	17.9	***	•
	Respir.	18.7	19.4	16.5	18.0	•	12.0	***	**(-)
	Aches	25.9	27.5	37.9	31.5	**	24.1	***	•
	Pills	9.7	9.8	13.3	11.9	•	6.7	***	•
	Absent	18.1	18.8	21.7	18.9	•	15.9	**	•
	Smoke	23.5	14.4	11.0	13.8	**(-)	11.6	**(-)	***(-)
Total	*N* =	166	269	309	744		2,879		

[1]Subjects had process influence and obtained more job decision latitude.

[2]Subjects had either influence or greater job decision latitude, but not both.

[3]Subjects had no influence and obtained similar or reduced job decision latitude.

NOTE: Significant differences in rates are calculated with simultaneous control for age.
***$p \leq .001$ **$p \leq .01$ *$p \leq .05$ •p = n.s.

SOURCE: Karasek in press. Reproduced by permission of John Wiley and Sons, Ltd.

with those that reported diminished task control and no influence (column C), controlling for age and sex. It is noteworthy that these findings show a significant relative reduction for eleven out of twelve illness indicators for males, especially the two more rigorously validated and practically important measures, heart disease risk and absenteeism (see Karasek in press), clearly related to increased influence and control on the job. Indeed, for men, increased control is significantly associated with reduced illness in all cases except exhaustion and smoking, controlling for age. For women the picture is positive but weaker, especially for young women (possibly because of unmeasured family responsibilities). For women, only depression, job dissatisfaction, and muscular aches show significant reductions (although positive trends exist in all cases except for heart disease in young women). The fact that these associations appear in a fairly homogeneous white-collar study contradicts the suggestion that associations with job decision latitude are primarily a reflection of social class or occur only in blue-collar groups (see chapter 2).

One surprising finding, based on the number of subjects in each category, is that most job changes even in Sweden, in the midst of one of the most active periods of workplace humanization, involved reduced, rather than increased, control—a situation especially pronounced for older workers and women. Another revelation is the fact that when employees do not have organizational-level influence over the job change process, changes in their individual jobs are much less likely to turn out favorably. On the other hand, employee involvement in participative processes that do not ultimately lead to desirable task changes appears to result in the disappointment of expectations. This is shown to be unhealthy for younger men.

This study also shows that, as expected, major job reorganizations in general are associated with increased symptom rates, presumably from the stress of change (see Reorganization vs No-reorganization Population 'Total' Columns). Of course, these short-term effects should not be taken as an argument against redesigning jobs to improve health consequences; these job changes are an inevitable part of the industrial development process and had been undertaken by management to improve productivity in any case, usually with little regard to improvement in health consequences. It is important to note that for all men, and often for women over 40, job changes involving more control were enough to offset the negative impact of the job change process itself, often to a significant degree. Thus, if an inevitable stressor in modern society is industrial change, then an effective antidote may be participation in decision making at the workplace.

In retrospect, we must observe that lack of data has hindered the analysis of joint effects of QWL experiments. Although we will present cases that do include such information (in chapters 6, 7, and 8), health or even safety data is usually missing altogether from QWL studies (see Pasmore et al. 1982). Managers, engineers, and even social scientists have so far had little understanding that the proposed job changes could affect aspects of health status as serious as coronary heart disease and therefore have not requested such data. Furthermore, companies are willing to allow only limited experimental manipulations of their operations by outside researchers. The result is that much of the data and methodology in QWL job change studies, including the productivity data, is poor in quality by standards set for experimental medical research, quantitative social science research, or engineering laboratory research. Feasible experimental methodologies (such as quasi-experimental retrospective designs) can be formulated for this context (Lawler, Nadler, and Cammann 1980), and certainly the work of researchers such as Seashore and Lawler demonstrate the possibility of high-quality research in this area (see Hanlon, Nadler, and Gladstein 1985; Goodman 1979; Lawler, Nadler, and Cammann 1980; Seashore et al. 1980), but such rigor is uncommon.* Of course, lack of financial resources to document what are essentially practical experiments is a major cause of such omissions. Negative findings often go unpublished and undiscussed. An even larger set of problems has to do with data, on both productivity and employee well-being, that is suppressed by the company. The reasons are company secrecy and—a disturbing new development—hesitancy to expose the company to legal liabilities for negligence by possessing knowledge of hazardous conditions under which their employees work.

New Skill-Oriented Measures of Productivity

Researchers analyzing the overall effectiveness of QWL often concede that while job redesign almost always increases the quality of output, it cannot reliably be expected to increase the quantity of output, in terms of dollars per hour (Frank and Hackman 1975; Hackman 1980; Katzell and Yankelovich 1975; Kopelman 1985; Lawler 1986). To begin with, these detractions seem unnecessarily self-deprecating in view of the fact that the clear majority of studies reported in the previous section do find an increase in quantity of output (and almost none find a decrease). These would be considered good results in drug trials in medical research or, for that matter, in

---

*Katzell, Bienstock, and Faerstein (1977) appended the comment "questionable methodology" or "unclear statistical significance of findings" to 68 percent of 272 hypotheses on work redesign, productivity, and job dissatisfaction in their review of 108 studies. Taylor's (1976) comprehensive analysis on 120 work redesign studies found large disparities in quality: 62 had some control group design and 50 had some longitudinal measurement, but almost none had randomly selected or systematically matched control groups.

Taylor's early experiments in classical job design (Kopelman 1985; but see Barnes 1980). Nor should the fact that quantity is a less predictable result than quality be grounds for dismissal of QWL in today's quality-conscious markets.

It is significant, however, that many of the job redesign studies that show evidence for improvement in both health status and productivity involve a broader definition of productivity than is traditionally used. Conventional output measures of quantity per hour can be constructed only in industries where the output consists of tangible objects produced in large repetitive sequences and where individual job contributions can be clearly isolated and quantified. In today's service economy, such measures are not even definable for perhaps 80 percent of the U.S. or Swedish work force. Their output is difficult to quantify in Utilitarian cost/benefit terms, yet it is the type of output that is produced in the most recently founded sectors of the economy, such as decentralized health care; in the most technically advanced sectors of the economy, such as computer software; and in those sectors that yield the most employment opportunities, the service industries. In short, alternative definitions of productivity are at the core of future industrial output.

The main problem, then, is not so much in the limited success of job design as in the limited usefulness of our conventional output measures, which overemphasize dollars per hour. This lack of an adequate output measure even prevents the introduction of "gain sharing" plans, in which employee bonuses are to be calculated on the basis of percentage productivity increases from baseline performance. While such programs work in manufacturing, they often cannot be used in the service industries because there is no way to *define* either base or improvement output levels (Lawler and Ledford 1982). What is clearly needed is conceptual elaboration of output measures that go beyond production quantities and labor costs. Such measures would serve as more rigorous yardsticks of the true effectiveness of Quality of Work Life projects.

Where shall we go to find such new definitions of output and their accompanying principles of successful production? One of the themes common to critics of modern industrial organizations in the United States and Sweden, such as Peters and Waterman (1981) and Swedish industrialists Carlzon (1987) and Gyllenhammar (1979), has been the underutilization of creative resources at all levels: in workers' skills that are unutilized or insufficiently developed and organizations that rigidly inhibit rather than facilitating creative adaptations to their environments. Indeed, the need to formulate new production output measures that reflect the creative capabilities of individuals and organizations is felt by researchers in many areas: sociologists, epidemiologists, psychologists, economists, and management theorists. In chapter 1 we summarized the manner in which major changes in the economy—changes that are having as important an impact as the industrial revolution—have reinforced the need for new measures of industrial output. We must have a value system that reflects human needs to grow creatively, to develop and use skills, as well as business needs for productive innovation. It must recognize the importance of social processes in, for example, the production of services to people. It must stimulate socially sanctioned and constructive challenges. Finally, it must go beyond object-based value (materialism) in a world where our physical resources are limited and our environment increasingly fragile.

At the present time, the output value of a firm is, of course, measured in monetary form, but the new kinds of production we have discussed permit a much broader definition of output value for the future. Dollars, kronor, and yen are measures of output based on the value of goods or services determined in a market among many buyers and sellers (an auction among strangers). The monetary, marketplace-determined value of production output usually applies to the physical objects produced or services delivered—things or services with clear boundaries, which can be distinctly and completely packaged and transferred from the producer to the consumer. Marx called this *alienable* or *exchange* value, because its value could be so easily removed from the laborer, and he called the resulting economic system *materialism,* because it commonly dealt with value in the form of material objects. Marx differentiated exchange value from a broader form of output value that occurs in more "natural" (precapitalistic) production, *use value,* which the worker shared even when producing for a customer. He claimed that use value was overlooked and underproduced by the conventional economic system.

A NEW OUTPUT MODEL: NEW VALUE

Our new definition of output value is one subcategory of use value, one that we believe is particularly well suited to developments in our emerging economy. The basic requirements for a definition of output value are not complex: we must simply identify something that can be produced by one party and is desired by another party—preferably desired through many cycles of trade, to ensure a robust economy. We believe that skills, when appropriately interpreted, can fulfill these conditions. Indeed, commerce in skills is already an important part of modern economic activity, both in the cooperative movement, on one hand, and in high technology transfers, on the other (Killing 1980). Pay-for-knowledge has been introduced as a compensation plan in a number of large companies (Jenkins and Gupta 1985). When skills are measured as production output, a very different set of production and trade structures is required than for conventional economic outputs. The active learning processes of our psychosocial model become even more important determinants of productivity. In the discussion below, we outline an alternative model of output value that could serve as a supplement to conventional market-based value—and that is more congruent with the dual goals of health and productivity.

One example of skill-based production is, of course, education. Providing a person with education enhances that person's capabilities and may even stimulate him or her to seek further education and capability development. How do we measure the value of what that person has acquired? Education, like much health care and most research and development activity, has value that is difficult to measure in conventional economic terms. We will elaborate on the traditional definition of skill in order to develop a new output measure, which we call New Value. How does this new conception of output compare to the conventional monetary measures of output? We see five major differences between New Value and conventional monetary output value: (1) New Value is non-zero-sum; (2) it stimulates needs; (3) it is process oriented; (4) it is long-term oriented; and (5) it resides in people, not objects. Let us examine each of these points in more detail.

1. *Unlike economic value, New Value is not "zero-sum."* Conventional (neoclassical) economics deals with desirable goods that are scarce; what one person gets, another cannot have. This conception is certainly appropriate for the most basic necessities such as food and shelter and of mass-produced objects of all kinds. However, the New Value properties of education cannot be described in this way. Lessons may be taught over and over to many individuals without diminishing in utility for any one of them, and the value of what is taught is not lost to its producer during the exchange. Contrast the value of the skill of cake baking to the value in the cake itself. The cake itself has conventional zero-sum economic value, which is reflected in the well-known adage that "you can't have your cake and eat it, too." But you can teach cake baking to many pupils and not lose your own cake baking skill in the process; indeed, your skill might be enhanced.

2. *New Value creates desirable new needs, rather than satisfying biological needs.* In conventional economic output, what one party produces is desired by the second party for its value in reducing tension by satisfying biologically driven needs (Scitovsky 1976). By contrast, a little education, rather than satiating desire to learn, may whet appetites to learn more and may lead to further growth of capabilities. This fulfills a human need of a different type which is not tension reducing: the need for stimulation (White 1959). In the case of conventional output value, creating biologically unnecessary needs is often looked on with disfavor; an example is

the design of cars with planned obsolescence. However, the new needs created by New Value arise out of new skills that have been learned, skills which need to be used. The use of skills leads, in turn, to the need to learn more. Such a growth-oriented process of creating needs is easy to see in a normatively positive light. This process of simultaneously creating and satisfying needs is the mechanism that keeps the New Value portion of the economy going (of course, supplementing the still-needed economy of biological necessity).

3. *New Value is process oriented, not product oriented.* It is created during an appropriate collaborative social process that occurs between user and producer. Feedback from the user allows the producer to utilize and then increase skills by satisfying the user's dynamically developing needs (New Value development for the producer). Feedback processes also provide the user with creatively evolved products that encourage their own further uses, fostering creative growth in the user's capabilities (New Value development for the user). Part of the output value is creation of an effective chain of production in which what is produced for one person or company is incorporated into the production process of other people or companies. In this manner, the user is often a producer as well. Goods or services that stimulate creativity or further skill development in their use are called *conducive* or, in our terminology, New Value–generating. In chains of production of conducive goods or services, each capability received from the previous producer leverages the next producer's capability to produce more effective products. The dynamic advantages of a product that stimulates capabilities in users at several stages are not captured by conventional economics, which focuses on the product itself (materialism), not on the processes mobilized by production. Such value is also poorly measured by short-term economic calculations because of its orientation to the future and the uniqueness of the product's fit to each customer.

Finally, New Value's focus on the interaction between individuals and components of the production process means that it is *system-oriented*. New Value is not easily summarized by simple addition of the contributions of separate components, like conventional economic products—it is the value that comes from a particularly desirable combination of components.

Computer software is an example of a New Value–generating product. If a piece of software is good, not only will it increase the user's ability to do the original job, but it may suggest whole new applications to its user and thus stimulate both new products and the need for a more sophisticated program. Bad software (low in New Value) is just the opposite: poor instructions or faulty operation may make learning to use it a frustrating experience, and the skills learned may be impossible to apply elsewhere. Motivation for related activity will be dampened, and an updated version of the product will not be sought.

4. *New Value reflects long-term, rather than short-term, value.* New Value production is inseparably linked to growth of capabilities or skills—of workers, of engineers, of companies, and fundamentally, of the customers who use New Value–generating goods or services. Because capabilities de-

velop over time and through many cycles of feedback, this analytic framework has a long-term focus. The conventional economic model is based on short-term, instantaneous market assessments, demonstrated in current stock and money market transactions.

5. *New Value resides in the person, not the object.* Producing New Value involves adding value to a person or to organizations, both entities that can grow in the form of skills or capabilities. By contrast, production output that can be evaluated by neoclassical economics (such as machining cast iron or assembling an electrical circuit) involves adding value to inanimate objects—the production of goods. More generally, New Value must reside in an entity that is capable of growth and that can apply the skill when it takes action in its own environment. A skill has no value without a user. The user's other capabilities determine the ultimate effectiveness of the skill; they are co-factors in production. Thus, the value of the skill to each user is unique, as opposed to the biological needs for food or shelter, which are universal. While New Value is nonphysical in nature, it may be facilitated in its production by physical goods (conducive products), which are tool-like.

These characteristics can be summarized in the form of a new definition of production output: the New Value component of output is the part *that can facilitate the development of new skills or capabilities in the user.* Because the new skills are associated with growth of capabilities by the user, they will usually lead to a new set of needs, stimulating the user to use even more sophisticated, tool-like (conducive) goods and services in the future, increasing economic output and stimulating still further skills in the producer.

What organizational forms are consistent with the New Value system outlined above? Small-scale, decentralized production entities such as the autonomous work groups of the Industrial Democracy and Quality of Work Life experiments are a beginning, because they facilitate skill development and provide a platform for diverse, horizontal communication. Breadth of skills is required for success, signaling a significant departure from Adam Smith's principles of work organization. Also needed to unlock creative opportunities are relatively horizontal communication linkages directly linking producers and consumers (some may be within the company). Such direct communications imply fewer intermediate distributors. These new communications structures provide the feedback channels that allow workers to utilize fully and then increase their skills by satisfying the dynamically developing needs of customers. These feedback channels also provide customers with the possibility for creative growth in their own capabilities, through the use of conducive goods and services. The duality of these productivity-related benefits underscores the importance of symmetrical analysis of the actions of both producers and customers. These communication requirements imply not only highly skilled and responsible workers but smart customers as well (Karasek 1987a, 1987b). We can see not only more responsible roles within companies for workers engaged in such production, but also more responsible roles for them outside, toward the community and other consumers. These micro-organizational structures suggest a more community-based economic system, in which the competition that drives new production innovation is supplemented by a spirit of cooperation to avoid the perils of overly stressful or insecure working conditions. Such ideas are hardly new: suggestions of similar alternative economic structures have grown with the development of the industrial revolution itself, from Proudhon ([1851] 1923) in the nineteenth century, to Schumacher (1973) and Piore and Sable (1984).

How well does the definition of New Value capture the concerns of psychosocial work environment researchers? New Value is, of course, highest in the active jobs of the demand/control model, when constructive social affiliation is also present. We believe that New Value provides a normative platform for an economic model that positively evaluates "active" participation, self-determination, and growth of skills—broad forms of decision authority and skill discretion. At its core, New Value is a rejection of Marx's concept of alienation, because it accrues in individuals and social groups learning new skills, not in material objects. It provides at least one set of definitions about the specific content of feedback, new customer relations—a meaningful linkage to the community environment that we discussed in terms of previous QWL job redesign strategies in table 5–1. The new customer/producer linkages can arguably be considered a foundation for development of a positive sense of self-esteem, or social identity. Moreover, community social networks could be stabilized through the reciprocal connections involved in New Value development, in contrast to free-market conditions, which can destabilize them. Psychological demands, however, may be only moderately diminished. This drop could be a major improvement over existing Taylorized jobs, but it may not yield the kind of work conditions that would be considered relaxed. Chronic illness risks associated with work stress, however, could be substantially reduced, for in both U.S. and Swedish research findings associating heart disease risk with low decision latitude in chapter 4, "learning" new things (in the Swedish study) and "creative work" are central factors in the decision-latitude measure. Other researchers have speculated that "passive withdrawal" is associated with reduced immune system effectiveness (Arnetz et al. 1987). Such a mechanism would imply significant health benefits from the active work producing New Value. In the two case studies that close this chapter, we will examine the impacts of this kind of output on the health of both consumers and workers.

This book does not allow for full discussion of Karasek's New Value perspective or of the necessary relationships that must exist between it and our conventional exchange value system. Even in a superficial discussion we can see that the process for assessment of value is very different from Bentham's utilitarianism (1789), where all behaviors and states of being can be assessed as discrete "commodities" in a broad, impersonal marketplace. Instead, synergistic combinations of capabilities, developing between specific producers and users over time, determine the level of value. (For other discussions of New Value, see Karasek 1981b, 1987b, 1989a. A theoretically consistent discussion of the shortcomings of conventional economic models is provided by Lundvall [1985]). A brief comparison would show that the New Value system would always be secondary to our conventional economic system, because New Value is always a second priority in times of true adversity, when biologically driven needs for scarce goods such as food and shelter predominate. On the other hand, New Value's emphasis on socially creative productive relations, along with the fact that it subsumes material value into the lesser category of "tools" (evaluated as skill facilitators), make it logically the more general value system and thus more useful than conventional materialism as a primary framework under the conditions of an increasingly populated and educated world.

Conventional economic value will continue to exist, and it is obviously quite effective to describe transactions with the truly scarce goods that make up most of our past and much of our present economic life. But we do not think that the conventional economic value system, by itself, can work for the future industrial life we have described. It must be supplemented by a new frame of reference—such as New Value—that can deal with the development of human capabilities and social processes and that can make it easier to organize work environments that are both healthful and effective. In the case studies below, we show how the New Value frame of reference, together with conventional output models, provides a much clearer basis for understanding how work can be organized to produce both health and productivity.

CASE STUDY 1: THE ENSKEDEDALEN ELDERLY HOME

Our first case study comes from the Swedish service sector. It was an attempt by medical researchers Bengt Arnetz and Tores Theorell to document with physiological sophistication the medical impacts of a new patient care system for the elderly in a nursing home in Stockholm. The study also demonstrates the possibility of sophisticated scientific measurement in job change studies.

The primary goal of the job redesign was to increase the social competence and active coping ability of the nursing home customers: the elderly. Much literature reviewed by Arnetz (1983) had shown the importance of preventing passivity in the elderly in the preservation of health; indeed, Rodin (1986) had shown a 50 percent drop in mortality over an eighteen-month period resulting from increased decision making by nursing home patients. Arnetz and Theorell's experiment was designed to test the demand/control model prediction about activation strategies described in chapter 3: that increased control and challenge would increase anabolic hormones in relation to catabolic hormones, diminishing risk of illness in the long term. Inasmuch as the health of the patient was the product of the nursing home, this particular health outcome would also serve as a productivity measure.

The experiment involved two floors of a nursing home, one the experiment and the other the control (13 workers and approximately 60 patients on each). The experimental group experienced four months of new work routines involving more direct social contact between patients and health care workers, increased worker participation in scheduling health care activities, and activities based around patients' interest areas. After the health care workers received appropriate training in need assessment skills, they assessed the interests of each patient and stimulated activities for subgroups of patients based upon the patients' own interests. No extra working hours were expended in the experimental group. The study monitored carefully the physiological impacts of such programs on psychoendocrine hormones over a six-month period (Arnetz, Eyre, and Theorell 1982).

In at least one respect, this experiment has dramatic importance: it measured the effectiveness of health service delivery by looking at the impact on client's health, as opposed to conventional, easily quantified pseudo-output measures such as revenue per patient or patient visits per week. Those pseudo-output measures, styled after the conventional economic criteria that work for mass-produced goods, are increasingly often being used to measure output in the health care industries—wrongly, we feel. While they may reflect production costs, including labor input, they usually have very little relation to the true output: patient health; they may even have an inverse relation to patient health (von Otter 1985). The person who has received the service cannot be priced at the marketplace to determine the value added in the health care production process. Application of such models derived from neoclassical economics is often viewed by clients as an appalling decline in the humanity and quality of care in many industries (Koepp 1987). The important innovation in this case study was to measure, as output, the increased production value in terms of the person's capabilities, a measure of New Value at the level of the individual customer. The researchers went beyond measuring the psychophysiology of the patient (in itself a major step forward) to assess directly their patients' increased capabilities in terms of accomplished activities. This is finally a true measure of output value applicable to the service industries.

What were the productivity results in this new format? Social activities reported on the experimental floor did indeed increase for the experimental intervention group in relation to the control group (at the start, the activity differences between the groups was not significant [as desired]: at three months $p < .05$, and at six months $p < .008$). The nursing home patients themselves were often found to be taking over organization of the activities, not just participating in them. Significantly, the physiological measures also confirmed the predictions of the demand/control model from chapter 3: under more active conditions, patients had significantly increased levels of rehabilitative anabolic hormones, while catabolic hormone levels stayed relatively constant in spite of probable increases in metabolic demands associated with the greater activity levels. The personnel rated the patients on the experimental floor as increasingly ready to speak out (Arnetz 1983).

What about the health of the workers themselves, the primary theme of our book? The health of the caregivers for the experimental group improved. Figure 5–2 shows the rates of absenteeism (per person) taken by health care assistants in the experimental and control groups. It shows a clear trend of lower absenteeism in the job redesign group after the first three months. Official sick days per person over the ten-month follow-up period were 9.3 in the job redesign group versus 18.5 in the control group (Arnetz, personal communication, June 1984). According to the experi-

FIGURE 5–2
Worker absences in the Enskededalen Elderly Home

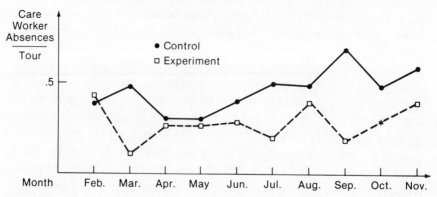

*Missing Data

SOURCE: Data from B.B. Arnetz, personal communication, June 1984.

menters, the most significant change experienced by the health care workers in the job redesign group was a dramatic and positive change in their self-image. Rather than just dispensing medicines prescribed by their superiors, the health care workers were now performing a true service for their patients, interacting with them and also stimulating their own social skills. The crucial change was that for the first time many of the health care workers felt that their skills were being utilized. This major increase in self-esteem for workers in such redesigned jobs is an effect we will find again and again in our case studies. A five-year follow-up confirmed the long duration of the higher levels of social orientation in the experimental ward personnel (Arnetz and Theorell 1987). We believe that this model provides evidence for the dynamic form of the demand/control hypothesis: increased learning leads to increased self-confidence and reduced risk of stress-related illness. It also provides an example of the active worker–active customer characteristic of production in a New Value frame of reference in which both health and productivity can be obtained.

CASE STUDY 2: MARTLAND HOSPITAL DIABETES CLINIC

Lazes (1978; Lazes, Wasilewski, and Redd 1977) described an analogous U.S. job redesign experiment undertaken in a diabetes-control outpatient clinic in New Jersey. In this case, patients were not nursing home patients facing death from disinterest and disengagement, but adults of all ages, otherwise healthy, with the chronic disease *diabetes mellitus*. This disease, while serious, can usually be treated through outpatient care. The ultimate goal of service delivery is again activation: the diabetic patient must be taught the skills to manage his or her own illness, through the resources of the outpatient clinic and its staff. And since the output goal involves enhancement of the capabilities of the customer, a New Value frame of reference is again appropriate.

The job design intervention in this case initially focused on very conventional management goals: correcting the health care assistants' clerical errors, reducing their dissatisfaction and absenteeism, and thus relieving the overloading of doctors' schedules. The clinic structure was a conventional hierarchy: doctors at the top, served by a broad range of semiprofessionals, most of whom performed bureaucratically organized clerical tasks. The solution chosen, however, was not the conventional panacea of increased supervision for the low-status employees but the progressive idea of giving employees a major new area of responsibility involving professional-level customer contact. The previously underutilized health care workers, many with public health training, were assigned to teach classes to patients on diabetes control procedures such as self-administration of insulin, diet main-

tenance, and exercise. This responsibility not only allowed much more personally engaging social contacts for these employees but also provided a
much more engaging set of teaching experiences for the patients and reduced loads on the previously overworked physicians, who now mainly
saw patients only when needs were critical. The case illustrates the danger
of preoccupation with an old-fashioned version of productivity improvement based on the conventional economic model: before the experiment
was undertaken, the suggestion of such high-contact teaching activities
had been rejected by the clinic as not affordable because staffing was already insufficient even to maintain accurate patient records. Relying on
that conventional approach could have led to actual restriction of overall
output.

The result of this redesign was a clearly demonstrated increase in productivity in terms of increased client engagement in the program: the kept-
appointment rate went from 52 percent to 71 percent; many more patients
were actively inquiring about medication and treatment methods; and patients became more aggressive in demanding their rights. The patients'
capabilities—New Value—clearly increased as a result. More conventional
measures of productivity, concentrating on intermediate outcomes, also
showed significant improvement: loss of records and incomplete record
keeping declined. No direct assessments of the effects on clinic workers'
health are available, but a combination of decreased stress-related illness
and increased job satisfaction is probably reflected in the fact that absenteeism dropped by 50 percent. In a corroborating finding based on longitudinal data from twenty-two patient wards, Holland et al. (1981), studied
the decentralization of a rigidly hierarchical mental hospital environment.
They found that increasing the participatory decision-making responsibilities of lower-level staff workers increased their morale substantially and
promoted more individualized patterns of patient care which, again, increased the patients' own capabilities to manage their illness. We would
recommend changes like this as a strategy to reduce the conventional economic costs of health care—a strategy that could both improve output (patient health) and improve the well-being of health care professionals.

Conclusion

We have now seen evidence that the demand/control model affects both
productivity and health, but through separate mechanisms. The separation
of the mechanisms for active learning and motivation from those associated with job stress means that job designs can conceivably be developed

to achieve both goals or neither one. We have seen that this imposes a double reason for managers, engineers, and job designers to consider carefully that low levels of decision latitude carry the double penalty of high stress and loss of innovative potential. The good news is that, for many jobs across a broad range of contemporary industrial settings, the increases in autonomy and skill utilization that could reduce stress are often congruent with new forms of job design and new conceptions of output value that enhance the quality, often the quantity, and almost always the humanity of the output.

In the remainder of the book, we take up the elements needed to form a feasible strategy for job redesign and review case studies from a variety of industrial sectors. In chapter 6, we review job redesign processes that emphasize health promotion in the context of groups at the workplace. In the final four chapters, we examine the impact of factors that transcend individual task structure in all settings. Chapter 7 addresses linkages between organizational structure and dynamics and job redesign. Chapter 8 addresses the effects of technology on socio-technical redesign processes. Chapter 9 examines the potential for interoccupational and political conflicts related to psychosocial job redesign. Finally, chapter 10 examines the macro-level social and economic effects of the market economy relevant to job stress and looks at the future of psychosocial job redesign in the light of changes in our overall industrial structure.

6

Integrating Worker Health Analysis and Job Redesign

As we pointed out in the previous chapter, Quality of Work Life research has often been inadequate from the health practitioner's perspective, either because the well-being measures used were too vague—job satisfaction, for example—or because the research focused completely on productivity. Health outcomes were rarely examined. Similarly, most medical professionals could be faulted because they rarely monitored the psychosocial job situation. The goal of this chapter is to integrate the contributions of medical care practice with the lessons of QWL job redesign. We shall describe processes of job change that are induced when the focus is on employee health. These changes must involve groups of employees, rather than the isolated individuals who are the focus of current medical practice, including most Employee Assistance Plans. Our main point is that increased employee awareness of the interplay between psychosocial work environment and health may start processes with a broad range of constructive and humane impacts on that environment. There are two points on which job redesign theorists agree. First, the process of job change cannot be predetermined in advance but must evolve out of a well-organized but organically developing process. Second—and almost in contradiction—the process must be initiated with a few clear, concrete steps: what could we do tomorrow? Such steps are discussed in this chapter. Health problems, which are very tangible for many employees, may be an important starting point for an organized effort to engage the employees in a search for new job design solutions.

Conventional Medicine and Knowledge of the Workplace

The most common interface between medical professionals and the design of work is, unfortunately, no interface at all. Employees contact the medical care system only after they have a severe health problem, and then their contact is with the doctors and nurses who are outsiders to the administrative structures that organize production. This distant relationship must be changed if our goal of ensuring the optimal combination of improved health and productivity is to be met. Physicians, nurses, and other medical care workers will have to assume new roles as joint design consultants and researchers along with their traditional role of care providers to the already infirm.

Before we examine these new responsibilities, let us consider an example of a typical worker/physician relationship. One of the authors was consulted by a 55-year-old man who reported attacks of severe pain in the upper part of the abdomen. Several times, he had fainted during these attacks. An electrocardiogram taken during exercise testing showed sequences of very irregular heartbeats (ventricular tachycardia), a potentially serious cardiac arrhythmia that may trigger pain and fainting if prolonged. The first attack associated with fainting had occurred one morning after he had had a sleepless night thinking about his work situation. That morning, he had had a violent argument with his boss and then had begun a task that involved lifting very heavy loads. The attack started immediately after the heavy lifting. It is likely that the sleepless night had brought his adrenaline and other catecholamines up (Theorell and Åkerstedt 1976), and that the argument further increased his catecholamine level. The heavy lifting, inducing dramatic increases in the demands on the heart muscle, was the last straw. Any one of the above factors could have triggered a serious arrhythmia in a vulnerable person, as we saw in chapter 3. But why was this man's heart vulnerable? He did not have seriously occluded coronary arteries (coronary atherosclerosis), and there was no indication that he had been born with a deficient electrical conduction system in his heart.

A traditional medical examination might have gone no further, ending with a diagnosis of arrhythmia and a warning that serious and progressively deteriorating ischemic heart disease was under way. The physician would have recommended the avoidance of traditional risk factors such as a high sodium intake and, to reduce the patient's psychological reactivity to the environment, would have prescribed psychoactive medications (which can have significant side effects, of course). Finally, the physician would have delivered the usually gratuitous homily that "difficult job and family problems should be avoided, if possible."

In this case, however, the physician was trained in psychosocial medicine, so he went on to ask further questions. Was there anything in the patient's job situation that could have made his heart more vulnerable? The description of the sleepless night and the argument with his boss gave some indication that there was. Further exploration revealed that the man had been appointed one year before as the supervising clerk in a supply department. After several months, the other employees in the supply department complained that the man was angry and unfriendly and quarreled with everybody. What nobody in the department knew, however, was that the company had decided to close down this supply department. When they laid off several employees, the supervisor, unaware of the company plans, felt increasing frustration: "I'm going to have to manage all these things with fewer personnel." Meanwhile, much of the developing dissatisfaction on the part of the remaining employees was directed toward him. The sleepless nights and the attacks started soon after.

Something drastic had to be done, because the symptoms that this man had developed were serious. After a period of sick leave, he was offered another job in the same company. The new job created less frustration, the man and the company were satisfied, and all the symptoms disappeared during a two-year period of follow-up.

The strategy selected was thus oriented to the individual. The supervisor was moved to a job that was much less strain-filled. Of course, he was fortunate: another job was available. But who would replace this man, and what health effects might that person suffer? It is of no use to the health of the work force as a whole if workers are merely shuffled between bad jobs. The solution, of course, as we saw in the previous chapter, is to redesign the job—a solution oriented to the environment.

Consider how much more might have been done, given our new understanding of the importance of psychosocial job conditions. The most important problems in this case were the lack of information given to the employees and the fact that a major change was being made without any opportunity for the employees to influence the decisions. The results were a tense atmosphere and a sense of insecurity. These—and the serious heart problems that ensued—might have been avoided if several steps had been taken:

1. If the occupational health department had had routines for monitoring the psychosocial climate in the supply department, it could have taken preventive action before serious symptoms had developed. It would have reported the problems to the managers, who would have realized that the health as well as the productivity of the employees was threatened.
2. The personnel department and managers should have informed the supervisor and all the employees about the future plans for the supply de-

partment. A forum might have been established in which everyone involved could make constructive suggestions to the company. This step would have allayed anxiety by allowing people to make realistic plans about their own futures.

3. Strategic human resource planning could have been undertaken to shift personnel gradually from this department to other locations in the company. The necessary training might have led to intellectual stimulation and positive motivation by all the employees to close the department more effectively.

A Health-Oriented Job Design Process

The first step in designing a health-oriented work environment is viewing health data not as a measure of individual well-being but as a measure of the environment's health conduciveness. It is the health- or illness-inducing properties of the work setting as a whole, not idiosyncratic individual responses, that are relevant for job redesign. To fix a faulty workplace, environment doctors—multiple professionals, including physicians—are needed to gather health data and use it in a collective form. The average health of a particular work group or department—its mean, age-corrected job satisfaction or blood pressure, for example—must be compared with that of other groups or viewed over time as job changes unfold. Methods for handling the health data must be set up to protect the confidentiality of individual health status information, which is not needed in the job design process and must not be accessible in it (obviously, such data can still be used in the context of normal, conventional contacts between patient and health worker). This approach to using health data in aggregate form to detect environmental problems is, of course, the standard perspective of the public health professional—often employed in a community service role. We are saying that this orientation must now be adopted by a much broader range of health professionals who deal with illness that may arise in the work environment.

INTEGRATING PROFESSIONAL ROLES: THE JOB
DESIGN/HEALTH PROMOTION TEAM

How do we collect and use such data? In the conventional occupational health care setting, even in a company medical department, the physician, the nurse, the social worker, the psychologist, the technician, and the physiotherapist have had clearly defined and distinct roles. The structure has often been designed to serve the physician, who has had unquestioned authority over all health-related functions. Activity has usually focused on individual consultations, work compensation cases, and inspections of work sites for physical environmental conditions and compliance with safety regulations. With the new focus on psychosocial job conditions as a source of illness, however, the contributions of each of these professionals must change substantially. Their fragmented roles must be reintegrated into psychosocial health and work design teams dedicated to detecting and resolving psychosocial work hazards. Such teams were crucial to the success of the Volvo job redesign efforts described by Wallin and Wright (1986). This engagement of a broad range of employees, rather than outside consultants or a single staff expert, to define the nature of workplace problems is consistent with the tradition of participatory job redesign research called "action research" (Lewin 1946).

Each member of the team has an important function in monitoring the organization, detecting early signs of malfunctioning, and collaborating on design decisions. The new role of the occupational physician involves wide medical knowledge and more use of knowledge in epidemiology, psychiatry, and physiology in planning surveys and evaluating interventions. The physician becomes a key analyst in determining to what extent health problems are job-related. The new physician no longer has a monopoly on wisdom, however, and must accept other professionals as equals. The nurse in this new team can detect early signals of malfunction and ensure that monitoring processes occur on a continuing basis. Another important function for the nurse is teaching employees to take various self-measurements, such as blood pressure, and to recognize psychological symptoms. In many countries the training of occupational physicians and nurses in these areas has improved.* The organizational consultant, the social worker, and the psychologist may be trained to guide group hearings and problem-solving groups. The physiotherapist, who often has an intensive therapeutic relationship with employees in long-term therapy (very often in groups), may also be trained to discover early signs of malfunctioning. The industrial engineer, ergonomist, or human factors specialist has special training in work design and is instrumental in the work redesign process. It is very important that the psychosocial health and work design group receive education from the three latter groups of professionals concerning health consequences of various alternative technical work redesign solutions. This group can also take the lead in extended collection of data (for

*In Sweden, such courses are formalized training procedures for occupational physicians and nurses, organized by the National Board of Occupational Safety and Health. These include psychosocial epidemiology and mechanisms. Special training courses in psychosocial occupational factors are organized at regular intervals for psychotherapists. As we saw earlier, the large occupational health team organizations have special training procedures in psychosocial factors.

example, from blood pressure monitoring, new job measurement instruments, and 24-hour ECG recordings), which will give the industrial engineer, ergonomist, and human factors specialist more objective information regarding the physiological strain induced by various work structures.

Clearly, one of the key elements in psychosocial work design is education. Traditionally, the role of work designer has not dealt with education. Indeed, in Taylor's conception of work design, the engineer was the intellectual master, and the worker was a passive recipient, taught only enough to carry out the assigned task. With the expanded role of education and increased employee awareness of problems, the employee no longer has a passive role but becomes an active information provider and a participant in the decision making of the design process. High-status occupations such as physicians and engineers will need to accept a new educational role themselves, as they teach both employees and health care professionals what health and productivity data to look for, and what solutions are physiologically, psychologically, technically, and economically feasible.

The Four Stages of Psychosocial Work Design

Improving the psychosocial work environment requires a well-planned collaboration between the employees, the occupational health team, and the job designers in a multistage occupational health promotion process. Figure 6–1 shows a theoretical model of a successful process. There are four stages: *engagement, search, change,* and *diffusion.* The first phase, engagement, is characterized by enthusiasm and energy. This energy is of course a necessary resource in overcoming the obstacles in the redesign process. The phase involves open group hearings in which the employees try to identify the problems together. An initial collection of limited job information and

FIGURE 6–1

Theoretical model of the successful health-oriented job redesign process

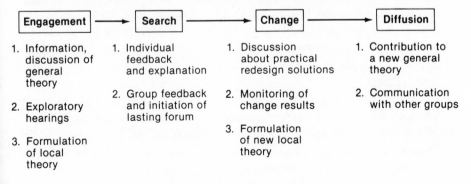

Engagement	Search	Change	Diffusion
1. Information, discussion of general theory	1. Individual feedback and explanation	1. Discussion about practical redesign solutions	1. Contribution to a new general theory
2. Exploratory hearings	2. Group feedback and initiation of lasting forum	2. Monitoring of change results	2. Communication with other groups
3. Formulation of local theory		3. Formulation of new local theory	

physiological and psychosocial data at this time helps to define the extent of the problem (see p. 208); if possible, employees will participate as research assistants. Contacts with all involved parties—union, supervisors, management, safety committee—should be established.

When the data have been collected, the inevitable question is, how is the information to be interpreted? as a loss to company profits, or a work environment inhumane for employees? At this point, a general conceptual model, such as the demand/control/support model, that accords at least equal concern to employee well-being as to productivity is essential. Such models also focus attention on the importance of organizational factors affecting decision processes and skill use. Without such a framework, management's much stronger and more easily articulated concerns for the company's bottom line will dominate the process that follows. After an initial understanding of the issues has been reached, however, with workers and company on an equal footing, further progress will require moving beyond general models to a local theory that grows out of the salient issues as defined by the members of the work situation itself (Elden 1983; Gustavsen 1987).

The search phase is an inevitable component of changes in the work environment. During this phase there is feedback both to the individual and the group. Employees exchange many different points of view on the problem and its solution. Feedback of health status data to group members can stimulate discussion of precisely what problems are associated with risk to health (see discussion, p. 210). A forum for discussion is initiated. Effective search processes are a well-documented part of the job redesign literature, and often rely on group problem-solving techniques (Lerner 1985). As employees develop a more articulated picture of their own work setting they will quickly find that the general models of the engagement phase will not provide the needed solutions. At this point the group may feel it is left without a structure, which can be a source of anxiety and of group conflict in itself. However, Elden (1983) describes the process of developing locally applicable "mental models" of the work situation which can serve as a link to practical solutions. The conflicts and discussions induced by the health-oriented psychosocial exploration constitute a developmental phase, toward a more sophisticated level of organization. In this search phase there is realistic appraisal of difficulties, and there may also be conflict and disappointment.

During the change phase, concrete proposals for change made by many groups with opposing interests have to be reconciled into a common definition of the problem and its solution—a politically viable local theory. Many promising change processes might stop at this stage, and that must not be allowed to happen. The employees should be informed that conflicts may arise, and management and supervisors should be prepared to allow such conflicts and to facilitate their resolution during a relatively long transitional phase (for a more comprehensive discussion of handling stress and conflict during organizational change processes, see chapter 7). For instance, in the primary care (public general practice) of the Stockholm region, personnel teams were recently instituted after long discussions. Such teams mostly consist of a physician, two district nurses, and two nurses' aides who meet at regular intervals to make decisions regarding the care of individual patients. A study (Doncevic, Theorell, and Scalia-Tomba 1988) has shown that this change, although it was generally regarded as desirable, induced long-lasting psychosocial problems for the district nurses. These human costs of the transition process were largely neglected by the administration: instead such problems should be anticipated and resources allocated toward their resolution.

The search and change phases are both difficult. If the process is to survive, both should be based on group consensus building from the start. If most employees feel there is an important collective health problem related to their work, they are more willing to endure disappointments during the search and change phases (Svensson 1986b).

Throughout the risky search and change phases, support is very important. The joint team should not abandon the work site after the search-oriented exploratory phase. Resources should be allocated so that employees know there is a real chance of changes resulting from the search phase. The support should be well organized so that it can be relied upon; regular meetings should be held to discuss changes being made and to allow the employees to ask questions and propose solutions. An occupational health care team must be available to take care of health problems discovered during the search phase (Wallin and Wright 1986).

It is also important that any new solutions to organizational problems be oriented to long-term development. The employees should be prepared to learn new roles that will pay off in the future, if not in the present. The change phase is ideally characterized not only by realistic solutions but by the development of a dynamic process for meeting new organizational challenges in the future.

During the last phase, diffusion, there is monitoring of the results of the changes and communication of solutions to other groups. Questions will immediately arise from outside—from management, other departments, or other researchers—about what was done and how it worked. Much of the process that occurred in the search and change phases, which made sense in terms of the evolved local theory, will not be understandable to workers outside the department immediately affected who are not familiar with the history, dynamics, and specific complexities of that situation. What general language should be used to communicate the findings? We believe that the language should be anchored in the management models used over the last several centuries to design the jobs in the first place—that is, a model like the expanded demand/control model described in chapter 3 (see also figure 6–2). Furthermore, parallels to well-known models of the labor relations process, such as the Scandinavian Industrial Democracy paradigms (Gustavsen and Hunnius 1981), will also need to be drawn. Such approaches can serve as generally understandable reference standards. Deviations observed from site to site serve as basis for discussion of the implications of the job change process in a more general social and political context.

A Study Using Job-Related Health Monitoring Feedback

The impact of health information feedback can be clearly seen in the Health Monitoring Feedback study performed in Stockholm. Six occupational groups were involved: physicians, symphony orchestra musicians, air traffic controllers, airplane mechanics, waiters, and freight handlers, a total of 181 individuals, 129 men and 52 women.

FEEDBACK AT THE INDIVIDUAL LEVEL

Four times over the course of one year, the workers measured their own blood pressure, both at work and during leisure. They also rated their emotional states and made notes of their work activities, with particular emphasis on the effects of decision latitude, psychological demands, and social support. Blood samples were drawn for the analysis of blood lipids and liver enzymes. During this year, group interviews with participants were conducted at the work sites in order to clarify collective processes that might not have been uncovered by the informants individually. After each data collection, written feedback was sent to each individual worker concerning both job and health status.

After a year we sent each individual worker some of the data from all four occasions. The workers' awareness of associations between the work environment and medical-physiological data increased as the extent to which health changes were related to simultaneous changes in the work environment became clear. Table 6–1 shows the information that was given to two participants in the study, both freight handlers. The first man is a foreman who reported high job demands during one period (February

TABLE 6–1
Individual examples of psychosocial and medical feedback
after one year of data collection

	Case 1: Freight Handler (Foreman)				Case 2: Freight Handler			
	Oct. 1984	Feb. 1985	May 1985	Sept. 1985	Oct. 1984	Feb. 1985	May 1985	Sept. 1985
Demands index (5–20)	12	18	12	11	11	12	12	11
Decision latitude index (6–24)	17	16	16	19	11	10	9	9
Systolic blood pressure* at work (mm/Hg)	126	142	129	133	145	149	144	150
Diastolic blood pressure* at work (mm/Hg)	93	96	90	90	95	106	96	108
Frequency of joy (%)	57	23	0	10	35	20	0	0
Frequency of sadness (%)	0	0	0	0	0	0	6	92
Frequency of rush and worry (%)	35	53	0	0	12	0	6	50
Frequency of irritation (%)	0	0	0	0	0	0	6	0
Sleep disturbance index (0–30)	8	12	11	11	17	17	17	17

*Mean blood pressure at work is based upon self-measurements once an hour (for detailed method de-scription, see Theorell et al., Changes in job strain, 1988).

1985) when his decision latitude was relatively low. These data coincided with a high systolic and diastolic blood pressure during working hours. During this period he also reported a high anxiety level and a relatively high level of sleep disturbance. The other man is a subordinate freight handler who reported a low level of decision latitude and very little variety in his work environment. He had constant sleep disturbances. At the end of the data collection period, he reported very high levels of sadness and anxiety, which coincided with his highest blood pressure readings. (Most of the problems were outside the work sphere and for reasons of confidentiality were not part of the inquiry.) The association between rising levels of job strain and a rising blood pressure during activity was not confined to the foreman in the table; such an association was observed in the group as a whole (Theorell et al., Changes in job strain, 1988) and reported as group average information to the whole group.

Increasing the individual's conscious understanding of these effects of the work environment through this process of health-oriented job redesign helps to make the person more aware of all kinds of work-related reactions (Levi 1972b). In the United States and among many Swedes, the person who experiences depression, anxiety, or sleeplessness feels personally deficient. As work conditions (as well as other objective causes) are reported to employers not by individuals but rather by groups of individuals, people lose their fear of self-deficiency and begin to develop a vocabulary to articulate the causes of their work-related problems. Often a great deal of emotion is expressed when this happens. Strain that has been repressed in the form of anxiety and depression is transformed into open anger, which, when properly focused and supported, can become the energy needed in the engagement phase of the constructive change process.

GROUP FEEDBACK AND THE EVOLVING AWARENESS OF A NEW JOB STRUCTURE

Feedback of information regarding joint variations in psychosocial conditions and medical-physiological variables to the work group sets in motion an inevitable process of job reanalysis and change. This group feedback process almost always has more dramatic results than individual feedback, but it can go very well or quite poorly. To ensure that it goes well, an appropriate social communication structure must be developed. The basic idea underlying the group forum method is that employees and supervisors can help one another formulate the important problems and find their solutions. Group forums can be organized at regular intervals to monitor the psychosocial environment and explore coping strategies.

In the second part of the Stockholm Health Monitoring Feedback study, group feedback sessions were held, at which a summary of the data collected from the individual workers was reported to each work site and compared with the findings from the other groups. Supervisors and union representatives were also informed of the results, both individually and in the company safety committee.

Table 6–2 shows the results from the psychosocial work environment questionnaires for the total group, reported over time, on the four occasions of data collection and after one year. The authority over decisions indices remained fairly constant, although intellectual discretion rose at the end of the period. Conflicts in the workplace and complaints about bosses increased during the whole process. The psychological demand index stayed constant during data collection, however, and decreased after one year. Thus, after one year of feedback procedures, the participants reported a less psychologically demanding job situation. One way of summarizing these findings would be to say that increased awareness of psychosocial work problems and increased conflicts due to this awareness may have been a consequence of the relatively extensive exploration of both personal

TABLE 6–2
Changes in self-reported psychosocial job characteristics
(Total group of men and women, including only those who participated in the
follow-up after feedback, N = 114–135, differs between questions.)

	First Obs. Oct. 1984	Second Obs. Feb. 1985	Third Obs. May 1985	Fourth Obs. Sept. 1985	After Feedback
Role conflict* ("In order to satisfy one . . . has to disappoint another.") (1–4)	1.44	1.46	1.53	1.65	1.73
High turnover of personnel* (1–4)	1.70	1.72	1.77	1.79	1.90
Boss cannot supervise and distribute job* (1–4)	1.72	1.63	1.70	1.75	1.99
Frequent conflicts with supervisors* (1–4)	1.16	1.20	1.24	1.33	1.41
Frequent conflicts in job* (1–4)	1.75	1.63	1.67	1.73	1.87
Demand index* (5–20)	13.7	13.6	13.6	13.1	12.7
Intellectual discretion index* (4–16)	11.8	11.9	11.8	11.7	13.3
Authority over decisions index† (2–8)	5.2	4.8	5.1	5.1	5.1

*Significant trend ($p < .05$), analysis of variance.
†No significant trend ($p > .05$), analysis of variance.
SOURCE: Theorell et al., The worker's own exploration, 1988.

physiological-psychological reactions and the work situation but that the employees found this process stimulating and therefore perceived the psychological demands as being lower (Theorell et al., The worker's own exploration, 1988). Medical follow-up showed that systolic and diastolic blood pressure levels during work hours decreased steadily during the year of study.*

Did the medical-psychosocial exploration have any effects on the discussions concerning the psychosocial work environment? Table 6–3 shows that discussion took place in the work sites during the final phase of data collection but also that the individual and group feedback processes increased the level of discussion dramatically; in two groups, more than 60 percent of the participants reported that such discussions took place. There were substantial differences between the groups, with physicians being much less likely (and having fewer opportunities) to engage in discussions in general. Some of these differences could be due to the way in which the researcher group approached the employees (later in this chapter, we will discuss several different frameworks within which a health-oriented job change process might be initiated).

TABLE 6–3
*Percentage of participants reporting discussions of the
psychosocial work environment*

	At the End of Data Collection (N = 133)	After Feedback (N = 139)
Symphony orchestra musicians	32	61
Air traffic controllers	33	61
Physicians	14	28
Freight handlers	35	41
Waiters	27	44
Airplane mechanics	21	29

NOTE: Percentages are based on two-thirds of the total number of participants. The remaining subjects were lost in the follow-up.

SOURCE: Theorell et al., The worker's own exploration, 1988.

*These results are not scientifically conclusive, because no control group was available. No corresponding decrease in blood pressure levels took place during leisure, however, so a likely interpretation of the results is that the arousal level during working hours may have decreased during the course of the project (Theorell et al., The worker's own exploration, 1988). At the same time, the blood concentration of liver enzymes decreased successively, a likely sign of decreased alcohol consumption in the group. In one group, tobacco consumption decreased. Thus, it is likely that the process induced by the medical-psychosocial exploration has had beneficial effects on the health of the average employee.

Table 6–4 shows the average systolic blood pressure at work and during leisure time in relation to self-reported decision latitude for the six different occupational groups. The average self-reported decision latitude (intellectual discretion and authority over decisions) differed highly significantly between the groups, in the manner expected according to the occupational plots presented in chapter 2. The highest scores were reported by physicians and the lowest by freight handlers. Systolic blood pressure during work hours as well as during leisure also differs markedly between these two groups, in a manner consistent with the demand/control hypothesis, whereas there are no striking differences among the other groups, which had mean systolic blood pressure in intermediate ranges. The percentage increase in systolic blood pressure during work hours in comparison to leisure time is much smaller among physicians than among other groups.

These findings were discussed during the group meetings, causing great concern among the freight handlers over the blood pressure findings and triggering discussions about the length of work cycles and ways of increasing the freight handlers' ability to control overload. Although less striking, the blood pressure levels among the symphony orchestra musicians were also high. This group has very little authority over decisions: the conductor

TABLE 6–4

Group means of self-reported decision latitude and mean systolic blood pressure during leisure and at work

	Number of subjects	Mean decision latitude	Age-adjusted mean systolic blood pressure during leisure*	Age-adjusted mean systolic blood pressure at work*
Physicians	19	19.5	120.6 ± 2.5	122.6 ± 2.6
Airplane mechanics	24	19.0	123.1 ± 2.2	130.0 ± 2.3
Air traffic controllers	20	17.0	122.1 ± 2.5	126.1 ± 2.6
Waiters	12	16.3	122.1 ± 3.1	126.7 ± 3.3
Symphony orchestra musicians	26	15.7	125.5 ± 2.1	130.1 ± 2.2
Freight handlers	27	14.8	127.9 ± 2.1	132.0 ± 2.2

*Mean blood pressure levels at work and during leisure have been based upon self-measurements of blood pressure approximately once an hour during one to four work days.

NOTE: Men only, $N = 128$.

SOURCE: Theorell et al. 1987.

of the orchestra makes practically all decisions. Whereas the high blood pressure levels among freight handlers may be due in part to heavy lifting under rushed and uncontrollable conditions, the high blood pressure levels among musicians may be due in part to very high demands for attention and very little opportunity to influence decisions. In the case of the musicians, the observations induced a number of proposals regarding the planning of rehearsals and the creation of small discussion groups to consider practical work problems. All these proposals had to do with ways of increasing either the collective influence over decisions or social support.

With the air traffic controllers, group hearings were used as a source of information in addition to biological and psychosocial individual monitoring. It soon became evident that group coping is extremely important in this occupation. With many aircraft coming in and going out of the airport, the individual controller must know his or her own precise capacity. If that capacity is exceeded, the passengers and crews in the air may be in danger. Colleagues must therefore be prepared to take over aircrafts from each other. Interestingly, this group coping process has become easier since a significant number of women have become controllers; women have had less tendency to try to show their strength, and the whole climate has been less focused on achievement, but no less effective. Information concerning this kind of group coping is hard to achieve when individuals alone are used as informants.

Among physicians, feelings of rush and worry as well as anger and sadness were reported more often than among other groups. High morning plasma cortisol levels in this group made it likely that these emotions did correspond to physiological reactions. Epidemiological studies have shown that physicians have a relatively high incidence of suicide (Arnetz et al. 1987). On the other hand, as expected from their high decision latitude and consistent with the low blood pressure levels among physicians in the study, the incidence of coronary heart disease in this group has been shown to be low. Discussion in the study group focused on ways of collectively coping with emotional feelings aroused by the confrontation with human suffering. There are several practical ways of helping physicians to cope collectively with this problem, such as the formation of so-called Balint groups, for structured social support (Balint 1964).

Waiters have been observed in our previous epidemiological studies to report high demands and low decision latitude (see chapter 2). Of the six occupational groups, the waiters reported the highest psychological demand levels. Decision latitude was reported to be rather low, and social support was reported to be much less available than in the other groups. Consistent with these observations, the mean total index of coronary heart disease risk was higher among waiters than in the other groups (corroborating findings of short life spans for hotel and restaurant workers in Norway by Karlsen and Naess [1978]). In particular, cigarette smoking was extremely common. Anger was reported to be felt frequently during the average working day. These observations sparked a discussion concerning monetary reward systems. The system in use in most restaurants was unfortunately extremely competitive and had a destructive effect on collaborative efforts. The discussion supported abandoning such systems.

The observations that induced intense group discussions among the airplane mechanics were the large differences—greater than in other groups—between blood pressure during leisure hours and blood pressure during work hours and the high serum cholesterol levels, which were also higher than in other groups. There were also a high frequency of "rush and worry" and a higher consumption of coffee than in other groups. The mechanics discussed the high demands on alertness and the constant conflict between tight schedules and safety. There was agreement among the participants that schedules had become tighter during recent years and were creating problems. Proposals were formulated for training new mechanics and making other job changes.

OTHER EVIDENCE ON THE EFFECTIVENESS OF GROUP FEEDBACK PROCESSES

Participatory job change, as we saw in chapters 2 and 5, means a reversal of conventional management policy through a combined strategy of increased participation in decision making and increased social interaction among workers. Methodologically sophisticated research has shown the beneficial effects on employee well-being of such joint strategies to strengthen decision-making processes in work groups. Jackson (1983) tested a causal model of participatory decision making in a hospital outpatient facility, using randomly assigned experimental and control groups with a pretest and a six-month follow-up period and involving several intermediate variables relating to perceived changes in the individual's role within the group. The job change intervention involved training all employees in participatory group problem solving techniques (Jackson 1983) and a doubling or tripling of the number of scheduled staff meetings to two per month. Jackson's analysis of the six-month postintervention data showed a significant drop in two job stressors related to decision making: role conflict and role ambiguity. As a result, employees in the experimental group experienced significantly reduced emotional strain, job dissatisfaction, absenteeism, and intentions to leave the job.

Increased control and social interaction also occur with the organization of autonomous work groups. In a rigorous longitudinal study of the effects of restructuring work groups for 90 workers in English industry, Wall and Clegg (1981) showed that a broad range of symptoms of psychological strain declined significantly in comparison with a control group when higher levels of group autonomy and more horizontal communication between group members were encouraged—that is, when workers began to make decisions formerly made by supervisors. In addition to increased effectiveness in production, increased motivation to work was expressed in workers' desires for more job-related information.

The complexity of the linkages between control and social interaction must not be understated, however. In addition to the causal mechanism we encountered in chapter 1—the division of labor ultimately restricts interactions between workers as well as between producers and consumers—other linkages could exist. Social support might facilitate the exercise of control in the work setting, as Johnson (1986) has suggested. Certainly the primary political dynamic of the labor movement in both the United States and Sweden emphasizes that workers will gain strength in relation to the company only through social solidarity. Gryzb (1981) argues that control may give workers the opportunity to develop jointly useful skills enhancing their social bonds and that restricted freedom may limit the potential rewards of social interaction. The possibility that work groups might limit decision latitude is raised by Homans' (1950) classic study of the behavior-controlling properties of cohesive work groups, but such a negative correlation is not observed in our national data. Finally, social cohesiveness in the group may tighten as a consequence of extremely adverse job conditions (a negative correlation with a different causal ordering). Models that can simultaneously incorporate all these diverse possibilities will have to be substantially more complex than our original demand/control model. Also, such future models must predict active behavior, not just stress-related illness.

One important example of using job change–related group feedback processes organized by health-care professionals is the use of occupational stress groups by Michael Lerner and the staff of the Institute for Labor and Mental Health in the San Francisco Bay area. In this case, the feedback has been psychological data. The groups, founded at the work sites, consist of about ten people who meet weekly for two to three months. Measurements of perceptions of and attitudes to the work, including demands and decision latitude, are the starting point of their discussions. Drops in absenteeism and improvements in psychological well-being in comparison to control groups were observed after use of these techniques (Lerner 1985).

The occupational health care team may also use group activities that have been organized for other purposes for constructive discussions about the psychosocial climate at work. For example, several occupational health care units have started stress management groups, programs that aim at improving the individual's capacity to handle stressful situations at work. Other programs at the work site started by the occupational health care team have been more directly focused on solving conflicts between workers (Wright 1985). In all these instances, the prime target is initially an individual problem, but changes in work organization may arise as a consequence of the therapy. When the workers start discussing stress reduction during work hours, their talk automatically leads to discussions about tensions, loads, constraints, and conflicts at the work site. For example, Chandra Patel's group teaching in industry utilizes a mixture of biofeedback and yoga combined with discussion of the work environment (Patel, Marmot, and Terry 1981; Patel et al. 1985). Another example is the teaching of Herbert Benson's relaxation response technique at the New York Telephone Company (Collings 1985). Striking effects in lowering blood pressure were seen in another stress management program for groups in industry (Charlesworth, Williams, and Baer 1984).

Thus, group teaching of stress management techniques could have organizational impacts quite beyond strengthening the individual's stress management potential. The most important issue is whether the workers are members of the same work setting. If so, and if the teaching takes place in a group at the work site, it is probable that discussions about the work organization and workplace problems will come up unless they are specifically prohibited (as they are in more shortsighted approaches). Workers can cross-check each other, and their joint observations will carry considerable force. These groups represent a natural basis for work environment change, formal or informal. It is possible that these consequences may have more durable effects on the health of the workers than the individually focused stress management program itself.

Practical Issues in the Monitoring and Feedback of Health Data

Gathering information about psychosocial factors of the work site is not always an easy task. The use of questionnaires, self-monitoring techniques, and feedback sets in motion inevitable psychosocial processes and introduces systematic sources of error. Several important considerations should be kept in mind.

Establishing the Ground Rules

The work redesign process must begin with some sort of contract or understanding among all responsible parties about the kinds of changes in the work environment that are likely to be made if they are found to be necessary. Great disappointment—and refusal to engage in further processes in the future—can result if a set of important problems is identified but management refuses to permit the necessary changes. Similarly, all participants in the process must understand how the data gathered will be used. The most important condition for a meaningful discussion is that key persons be informed in advance. For example, when a supervisor has been named by many workers as responsible for a poor social climate, these views should be discussed with the supervisor personally before the group feedback starts.

The Potential for Misuse of Information

In many work sites, employees are afraid of being laid off or punished if they complain about psychosocial conditions and may therefore consciously deny any difficulties. In some cases, personality questionnaires and psychological consultations actually have resulted in layoffs, justified by the claim that psychological testing showed that the employees did not have the appropriate qualities for the work. Employees often fear that personal information, particularly about health status and personality, may be used against them—even to fire them when they are in no way hindered from performing their duties. Swedish unions, fearing discriminatory selection of workers, have so far successfully fought against collection of personality inventory information in the job recruiting process, although job profiles have been used to achieve a fit between employee and environment in many work sites. In the United States, the Equal Opportunity Act has provisions against such discrimination, although there are no guidelines for or against the use of personality instruments, despite the fact that most of them are questionable predictors of performance. Indeed, "discriminatory protection," as it is called (Severo 1980), has been used in the United States to exclude pregnant women and blacks with sickle cell anemia because their future health risks may prove to be a liability to the company. We believe that not only are such tactics immoral but the mere suspicion that they could occur could mean that any data collection of the type described above would be strongly resisted—in our view, properly—by employees.

Thus, potential misuse of data must be clearly ruled out, to the employees' satisfaction, by job design teams. The employees can be protected by the use of anonymous questionnaires from neutral consultants who are not part of the local work process and precautions to avoid feedback of sensitive information that can be traced to individual workers. Employers are also vulnerable. In the United States, employers become legally responsible for employee well-being when they have knowledge of employee health status gained through the data collection processes we have described above. Ironically, distortions in U.S. legal practice (huge awards for some hazards, no attention whatever for most problems, and large fees for legal representation) have increasingly meant that employers avoid gathering job-related health information at all, a situation that should be redressed by legislative changes. In our opinion, the sad possibility that psychosocial job analyses will lead to lawsuits is an unavoidable result of the overly individualistic approach to rights in the workplace—particularly in the United States where labor union power has declined. The alternative to individual lawsuits are collective good-faith efforts to redesign a humane workplace, jointly supported by management and labor (see below). The presence of such job change programs—not avoidance of necessary data about working conditions—should be the employer's defense against unreasonable lawsuits.

Over- and Underreporting

As German industrial psychologists have pointed out (Frese 1982), employees are frequently not trained to analyze their own work situations. Their responses to questionnaires may therefore be misleading. This may be particularly true of jobs with low decision latitude, where there is a great likelihood of underreporting of some psychosocial problems. Of course, employees could also try to obtain benefits by complaining excessively, but in our experience this is a much less common problem with the use of self-administered questionnaires than underreporting.

Health and Other Priorities

How important is health? The health-oriented job redesign process we have described makes the assumption that the employees give health a high priority. This is not always the case; young workers in particular are often not interested in health issues, reasoning that they can accept dangerous work conditions in return for high pay. In these cases, the employees often have to consider the total picture before they are ready to accept changes intended to improve health.

Practical experiences with changes of shiftwork schedules for policemen provide a case in point. Two experiments, one in Stockholm and one in western Sweden, were performed with groups of policemen who were constantly changing their working hours between day and night work. In both cases, the policemen initially had a shiftwork schedule that was extremely condensed; as many work shifts as possible were gathered during a short period, to allow the policemen to have long periods of leisure between the work periods. The hypothesis was that a more spread-out shift cycle would be less harmful to their health. In the new schedule, the employees worked the same number of hours but on a schedule that was biologically more adapted to human needs.* In both cases, both the psychological information (quality and quantity of sleeping) and the physiological data indicated improvement (Fredén et al. 1986; Orth-Gomér 1983). The authorities in both cities were convinced that the improved shiftwork schedules should be tried. In Stockholm, however, the employees felt that while the new schedule meant a great improvement to health, other factors—mainly the long leisure periods—were more important than health, and consequently the change was not instituted. In the city in western Sweden, on the other hand, the policemen permanently switched over to the improved schedule. Thus, although health information can be a very important element in work redesign, workers may not be prepared to sacrifice other aspects to gain improved health.

INDIVIDUAL VERSUS COLLECTIVE APPROACHES TO JOB CHANGE

One serious objection that many Quality of Work Life professionals make to the health focus of job redesign efforts is that it places too much focus on the individual, leaving the worker's collective functions and Industrial Democracy behind. We agree this could be a problem to the extent that social and organizational linkages to health risks are overlooked, as indeed they have been in much occupational health practice. When these issues are included, however, our experience is that they raise awareness of employees and start dialogues that soon bring up overlooked issues of overall organizational function and structure. Often these issues have lain dormant in the company, seemingly harmless, but actually giving rise to unresolved conflicts that have prevented both the company and the workers from effectively mobilizing their resources. Occupational health and Industrial Democracy are complementary issues when the institutional support structures for job change have been established.

*Information gathered concerned blood pressure, blood lipids, and sleeping patterns. A group that did not switch over to the improved schedule served as a comparison group.

Institutional Support for the Redesign Process

The most critical difficulty that the job-design/health-care team may encounter is lack of real power. Psychosocial evaluations and group discussions will be of little use if the team lacks sufficient influence on the decision-making processes of the company. In chapter 7, we discuss the organizational contexts that are needed to support the team's role. Even with management and union support, however, the job redesign team may need additional assistance in surmounting the many hurdles. Fortunately, because the need for health promotion is recognized, external resources and authority frameworks are more available for health-oriented job redesign than for other types of employee-oriented industrial restructuring. The labor relations structures that always mediate politically contested issues between labor and management can establish an appropriate context for use of these macro-level resources, following models established by the Industrial Democracy experiments of the last several decades (these are discussed in Gustavsen and Hunnius 1981 and in the chapters that follow). In both the United States and Sweden, several types of administrative frameworks are available to support such teams, with both resources and formal authority. They may be organized in different ways, however, because of differences between countries in labor relations frameworks.

THE PUBLIC-SECTOR OCCUPATIONAL HEALTH TEAM

This is the kind of occupational health care that is offered to most employees by trained professionals working for the community, county, or state. The occupational health care team may be headed by an occupational health and safety representative who is an employee of the company but who has official government responsibilities. In that case, the policy and procedures of the team are influenced by local or national political processes, and proposed changes may be reinforced politically via labor/management negotiations. The Scandinavian countries have made substantial progress in regulating psychosocially hazardous work. In Sweden, special safety committees made up of representatives of the union, the employer, and the occupational health care team discuss such issues. Denmark has personnel especially trained in psychosocial hazard detection and correction. Paragraph 12 of Norway's landmark occupational health and safety act recommends avoidance of repetitive, unvarying, machine-paced, uninformed, or socially isolated work (Lov om arbeitervaern og arbeidsmiljø 1977).* According to several safety inspectors (Hans Hvenegaard, personal communication, October 1983), securing compliance with these kinds of advisory standards poses no more difficulty than enforcement of more conventionally regulated work hazards such as noise. In the United States, local National Institute of Occupational Safety and Health representatives are legally empowered to discuss the full range of workplace health issues with both employees and employers in nonpunitive consultation. They could fill a role similar to Norway's safety inspectors in pressing for changes in psychosocial work conditions. The Occupational Safety and Health Administration inspection officers can cite violations, but they do not often address psychosocial issues and are not authorized to provide design consultation services.

THE INDEPENDENT OCCUPATIONAL HEALTH TEAM

Companies may also buy the services of a health care team provided by a third party. In Sweden, payments to these teams are shared by the company and the union. For certain occupations, organizations such as the nationwide Bygghalsan (for building construction workers) and the Motorhalsan (for all automobile salespersons in Stockholm) have worked out detailed strategies for psychosocial job redesign using group feedback as well as some biological data relevant to heart disease risk (Axelsson et al. 1987; Lenke and Barklöf 1988; Lindell 1984; Wallin and Wright 1986). In these cases the union and the employers together decide on the policy and procedures of the occupational health team. The team, however, does not usually have decision-making power and may have difficulty influencing the company's personnel policy and work organization.

In Sweden, several of the large occupational health organizations have developed long-term educational strategies for combating psychosocial problems among employees (Axelsson et al. 1987; Lenke and Barklöf 1988; Lindell 1984). The most outstanding example is the Statshalsan, the occupational health organization for all state employees in Sweden, which has developed special educational packages in such areas as the social psychology of work, stress physiology, and problem-solving strategies (Axelsson et al. 1987). For instance, in special courses, usually of about thirty hours' duration, personnel consultants (mostly social workers) who are sent by the personnel departments in government agencies in different parts of Sweden are trained in the use of the packages, which include brochures and slides for lecturing. At the same time the organization has developed a

*In late 1974, preliminary versions of the Swedish findings in figure 2–4 were used to help confirm the need for such legislation.

standardized psychosocial questionnaire that can be used for all state employees. When the decision is made to examine the psychosocial environment in a work site, these questionnaires are distributed anonymously.

THE COMPANY-EMPLOYED OCCUPATIONAL HEALTH TEAM

A team composed entirely of company staff members may be better informed than an independent team about the organization, the problems, and the way in which decisions are made. On the other hand, such a team may have little influence over decisions and may have to accept changes that the team members feel endanger the health of the employees. This problem may be difficult to solve. One way to strengthen the influence of the health care team is to make it a separate department of the company and not, as is often done, place it under the personnel department, which may have difficulty coping with this new style of independently guided, employee-centered activity. Volvo's occupational health team distributes questionnaires on psychosocial factors in various work sites (Wallin and Wright 1986) and gives workers statistical summaries of the responses from their own work sites and from all the work sites taken together, for comparison. When changes have resulted from this process, a follow-up is done by means of the same questionnaire.

The Status of the Expanded Demand/Control Model: Multiple-Level Process Linking the Psychosocial Work Environment, Health, and Productivity

In preparation for examination of the large-scale determinants of job design—organization, technology, and interoccupational differences—in chapters 7, 8, and 9, it is appropriate to review the status of the original demand/control model we have been expanding since chapter 2. We have seen in this chapter that any general model of work design would ultimately have to be discarded in the intense exploration periods of the redesign process itself. Articulations of a new language relevant for the specific job circumstance would ultimately have to emerge. Such situation-specific models have been called *local theories* (see discussions in Elden 1983 and Gustavsen 1987). These differ from the general models of the work environment applied by Smith and Taylor and even from our own general models of chapters 2, 3, and 5. We can readily see, however, that both local and general theories play an essential role; each is important at a different stage of the process. The general model is important at the beginning and at the end of the process (see figure 6–1) when a description of what could happen or has happened must be translated into themes common to the outside world, so that the processes may be facilitated or duplicated. To assess success of the redesign effort, one is likely to focus on simple job dimensions, and on simple, short-term indicators of psychological or physiological strain or active learning that can be compared across work sites. Of course, it is actual measures of chronic disease and productivity change that are of final importance. Prediction of these outcomes requires more detailed attention to the many other factors described at the level of the individual and at the level of the organization and its technology, motivating the more complex final model we display in figure 6–2b.

We can compare our expanded model to the most commonly used multistage model of psychosocial illness causation in the workplace: the Michigan model in figure 6–2a. Our critique of that model in chapter 2 was that its complex web of multiple reciprocal relationships did not provide the basis for the simple mental models that could in turn serve as a platform of communication between the diverse range of job design participants. Nor did it provide a specific list of job dimensions to investigate, leading in practical terms to research with long lists of job, personality, and organizational variables that varied totally from study to study and from site to site. We claimed that our simpler model, evolved out of the management theories in chapter 1 that were applied (for better or worse) across the vast majority of work sites in the Western world, would form a more common reference point for dialogues. We further argued that a sequence of smaller models with rarely more than three or four variables considered at a time— each one specifically defined in terms of dimensions and mechanisms— would be more comprehensible for professionals of diverse viewpoints. This parsimony would be effective even if dimensions that were important in some specialized settings were omitted (if, of course, the chosen set of dimensions was indeed broadly useful).

Nevertheless, the Michigan model has influenced almost every step of our expansion of the original demand/control model. It is responsible directly or indirectly, through the related contributions of a generation of other researchers, for our inclusion of measures of social interactions, of individual personality, of coping behaviors, of physiological responses, and even the emphasis on multifactor hypotheses.

The result of our multistage expansion of the original demand/control model is shown in figure 6–2b. The original task-level demand/control model served as a reference point for model expansions in two directions. It fit intellectually in between the individually oriented processes affecting

FIGURE 6–2 (a-b)

Theoretical frameworks for research on the effects of work role on health

6–2a The University of Michigan Model of Work Environment and Health

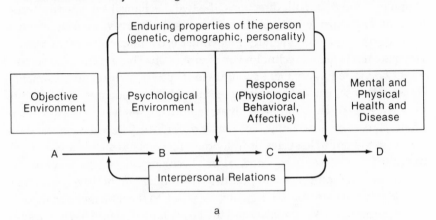

a

SOURCE: Katz and Kahn 1966, p. 584. Reproduced by permission of John Wiley and Sons, Inc., N.Y.

6–2b Social Organization of Work, Health, Productivity, and Management Model Feedback

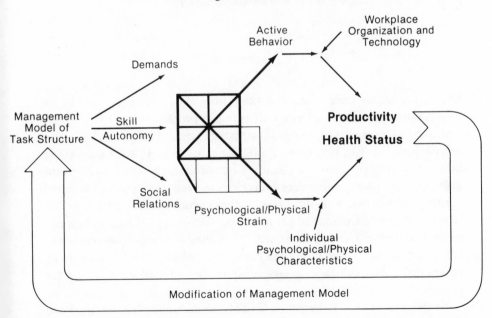

b

psychological well-being, physiological response, and health discussed in chapters 3 and 4, and the organizational-level phenomena which form the social context of the job change process discussed in this chapter and in chapters 7 and 8. In both directions, the two mechanisms of stress-affects-learning and learning-affects-stress serve as the bridges between levels.

We also examine productivity, involving the contingent factors of organizational structure and technology in figure 6–2b. These contingent factors might be viewed as analogous to individual physiological and personality information, which are important as individual-based contingent factors for the development of physical illness in both our model and the Michigan model. But there is an important policy difference. The Michigan model's focus on the multiple stages of individual response to stress implies clear pathways of intervention—medical or psychological—at the level of the individual. Our joint focus on productivity and health, however, allows us to go the further step of linking outcomes back to the management models that determine work organization—the larger loop in figure 6–2b. We suggest a more concrete set of analytic steps to affect environmental situations. Although individual interventions are also still necessary, we can see that such environmental intervention could lead to more far-reaching change. This environmentally based intervention, with its twin anchors of more rigorous health and well-being data and a more skill-oriented productivity conception, is what we label "work reconstruction."

Conclusion

In this chapter, we have found that monitoring of health status could be an important anchor for employee well-being in processes of work redesign and that the presence of health information actually helps to clarify the mechanics of at least one type of job change process. In both the United States and Sweden, there are already pioneering occupational health care units that are giving employees individual as well as group feedback regarding links between medical status and psychosocial job structure. We consider the combinations of previous approaches (individual and group, medical and psychosocial) to be crucial to starting the modification process. Ultimately these combinations will have to be linked to the labor-relations structures at the workplace, to ensure equity and a broad support base for change.

To the extent that it becomes broadly understood that, as we have claimed, future costs for health care in such important areas such as cardiovascular disease (and possibly alcoholism, psychiatric illness, and gastrointestinal problems) are associated with correctable changes in job structure, powerful institutional alliances for job redesign may be forged in the future. In the United States, 12 percent of company profits are spent on health care. In the United States overall in 1987, over $360 billion in third-party health premiums were paid by employers, unions, states, and national health insurance programs (U.S. Department of Health and Human Services 1988). In Sweden, where the national medical service is paid for by tax revenues, the Swedish government could have a greater interest in promoting positive psychosocial job design.

In the following chapters, we will face the real world of constraints on task- and group-level redesign processes that arise from political organizational conflicts, from market-based determinacies, and from the impacts of new technologies. We need not be immediately overcome by pessimism about the number of issues that must be addressed, however: our review will help to remind us how common major job restructuring processes actually are. All we need do is steer these mammoth forces in more humane directions, and as we will see, this has been done.

7

The Organizational Context of Job Redesign for Health and Productivity

In this chapter, we will begin to examine the broad context of job design processes that can increase productivity as well as improve health. Our task-level demand/control model must clearly be supplemented by an understanding of the organizational, technological, and political context of work design—the focus of this and the following two chapters. Indeed, at the organizational level it might appear that we must finally discard our task-based demand/control model altogether, go beyond even social support, and investigate the organizational structure and dynamics that shape the process. We will find, however, that even at this level there are some organizational counterparts to our task-level measures, and we can see some associated psychosocial mechanisms in operation.

Our goal in this chapter, as it was in chapter 3, will be to show these linkages. This time the linkages involve the organizational realities that are the main focus of both management and union policy making. We will focus on three major organizational processes associated with task-level psychological demands, decision authority, skill discretion, social support, and our mechanisms linking stress and learning. First, we will examine the importance of support for job change processes from the organization (or the society) as a whole, in order to diffuse resistance to and build foundations for the necessary new authority and specialization of labor patterns. Second, we will examine the impact of the stress of the change process itself on the nature of the organizational structures needed to ensure effective organizational-level learning. This process is analogous to the stress-inhibits-learning and confidence-building mechanisms we discussed for individuals in chapter 3. Third, we will examine how active jobs and New Value learning dynamics require new market interfaces with the customer. This step will bring us up one more level toward the larger social and economic context of job redesign.

The Importance of Support for New Distributions of Authority and Skill

We will begin by examining a case study from the manufacturing industries—the auto industry, the prototypical example of mass production.

Job Redesign at Volvo

Automobiles are typically mass-produced, physical goods that have provided the classic success stories for the models of work organization proposed by Adam Smith, Frederick Taylor, and Henry Ford discussed in chapter 1. It is perhaps surprising, therefore, that a new set of psychosocial job redesign policies that in many ways are the antitheses of those older approaches could have the success in improving effectiveness at Volvo in Sweden that Wallin and Wright (1986) have reported. Volvo's initial attempts at psychosocial job redesign began in the early 1970s with construction of such new-design factories as the Kalmar plant (see reviews in Agurén et al. [1984] 1985 and Plate, Gall, and Schütz 1985). Management's original goals were to provide more appealing jobs than traditional assembly line work for young workers in the tight Swedish labor market of the 1970s. The company's innovations in socio-technical design such as the introduction of autonomous work groups (further discussed in chapter 8, p. 256) achieved world-wide recognition, however, and in the 1980s, Volvo increasingly viewed similar changes as pathways toward improving not only employee health but also product quality and production process flexibility.

At Volvo, the main responsibility of the company health service is preventive medicine. Prevention activities originally focused on physical hazards, but more recently, under corporate medical director Leif Wallin, the effects of psychosocial job change processes have been monitored in an attempt to assess their effectiveness in reducing illness. These redesign efforts were stimulated by recent findings at Volvo (in part stimulated by our own research in Sweden) that low decision latitude was associated with more medical symptoms, more psychological stress, less interest in going to work, and lower job satisfaction. A general program of company-wide job redesign, paralleling the earlier changes, was instituted. Workers' range of skills was broadened through job rotation, task redesign, and increased training, and more work teams were set up, with higher levels of autonomy.

The specific changes in a range of white-collar jobs at another Volvo plant in Gothenberg, Sweden, illustrate the nature of these efforts and their results. The psychosocial changes did not occur in isolation but were accompanied by physical and technical changes congruent with the new psychosocial job redesign. A total of eight changes were instituted (Wallin and Wright 1986): offices and workshops were rebuilt in a new layout; the supervisor role was replaced by that of a more facilitative supervisor; management style was changed to a less authoritarian form; the attitude of the trade unions toward members and managers was changed to a less confrontational position; computer aids were introduced to improve work efficiency; work was reorganized to promote personal contact between customers and employees; teamwork was introduced; and antismoking campaigns were conducted (Plate, Gall, and Schütz 1985). Two years after the implementation of these changes, studies showed that psychosomatic symptoms such as depression and tiredness had dropped substantially (26 and 23 percent, respectively). Gastrointestinal symptoms and psychological problems were also reduced, smoking had dropped dramatically, and work stress had decreased. On the productivity side, there were also major improvements: customer demands were handled more effectively, overall motivation improved, the work load handled by employees increased moderately (in spite of decreased stress reports, as predicted in chapter 5), and profits from the section increased.

The psychosocial job changes described above were all oriented toward eliminating unnecessary organizational restrictions in employee decision latitude, increasing intellectually challenging tasks such as customer contacts, and building social cohesion in the work unit. These changes occurred at both the level of the task and at the level of organizational policy, in a mutually reinforcing manner. In addition, these changes had the strong support of both high-level management at Volvo and the labor unions at several levels. This was of course an unusually favorable set of conditions, and the results were accordingly impressive.

RESTRUCTURING HOME CARE FOR THE ELDERLY

Another redesign example occurred in the city of Örebro in north-central Sweden, with a population of roughly 120,000. The redesign was undertaken in the context of a decentralization of local public services to provide clients with a better integrated, customer-adapted service package (Gough and Vuonokari 1988). Municipal government strongly supported the changes as an attempt to increase "democracy in the workplace." The specific service challenge was the increasing size of the over-65 population of the city, which had led to heavier work loads for service workers providing home care for the elderly. The primary job redesign intervention was the transformation of a hierarchically organized, rigidly scheduled, two-tiered service structure of professionals and part-timers into a set of autonomous work teams with rotating leadership roles and group determination of service schedules. Here the challenge was to maintain quality of output and quality of working life in the context of adverse environmental pressures.

This customer-oriented package of services had to maintain the quality of care, the level of perceived work loads (which was high), and the existing high levels of employee satisfaction,* at a time when much of the personnel had to be replaced by younger, inexperienced workers because of retirements. The successful attempt to maintain productivity as well as employee well-being in this context of increasing demands was attributed to the increased control, independence, and responsibility that the workers were given in the autonomous groups. Only the loosening of organizational constraints, which permitted the necessary coping, relaxation, and experimentation with new solutions, made these transformations bearable and even positive. Job transformations can take a serious toll of illness when workers have little possibility of influencing the process, as discussed in chapter 6. The study of the home care for the elderly in Örebro further illustrates the importance of cooperative activity in the work group. The most important components of job satisfaction for the care workers were the experiences of "competence within the group" and "effectiveness in delegating work as part of group process." In this case, as in the Volvo factory, there was a broad organizational context that was supportive all the way up to city hall. Increased employee decision making was an explicit goal of local government, and the concomitant decentralization of the production structure made a broader range of independent decision making theoretically feasible.

*The workers' instrumental attitude response of "Only do it for the money" was only 5 percent. This is very low compared with Swedish male industrial workers (50 percent) or female industrial workers (> 50 percent).

The initial results indicated significant success in providing a more flexible organization of services within the home service worker section (Svensson 1986a) and in maintaining high worker satisfaction. Increased commitment of the municipal authorities was required, however, when opposition grew stronger from entrenched interests, such as mid-level managers protecting positions of authority and unions securing traditional occupational prerogatives (chapter 9, p. 296). The broad base of decentralization, the flexible work structures with their flexible occupational boundaries and resulting customer-adapted service packages, take continued support both from the service workers directly involved in the job change and long-term support from upper levels of the city administration.

OBTAINING THE "CRITICAL ORGANIZATIONAL MASS"

Recent discussions of work-life change programs in the United States and Scandinavia differ significantly on one important dimension: the degree of support at the organizational and societal level: not only support from company management and labor unions but overall political support for the changes in industrial organization. In Sweden, in Norway, indeed in Western Europe in general, the work force is much more highly unionized (roughly 85 percent in Sweden), and programs addressing labor's natural interest in conditions of work have therefore had an institutionally broader base of support there than in the United States, with its lower level of unionization (down to 18 percent in a survival-oriented labor relations climate). During the 1970s and 1980s, furthermore, national political themes of the labor-oriented political parties that are often in power in Western Europe occasionally gave substantial momentum to participatory and democratic decision making in Norway, Sweden, and other Western European countries. Important milestones were Norway's Work Health Law (Lov om arbeitervaern og arbeidsmiljö 1977) and Sweden's Work Environment Law (Arbetsmiljölag 1976), Participatory Management Law (Lag om medbestämmande 1980), and Social Service Law (Lag om socialtjänst 1980), as well as an important political debate on wage-earner funds (Meidner 1981). The West German Humanization of Working Life Program, started in the 1970s, has been the largest and longest lasting program in terms of total funding. In the United States, the Department of Health, Education and Welfare report *Work in America* (U.S. Department of Health, Education and Welfare 1973) certainly raised public awareness, but no political party strongly adopted its positions. Because high-level support is not automatic, QWL experimenters in the United States place greater emphasis on the importance of support within the organization, especially from top management, for the survival and expansion of job change programs. All major reviewers of U.S. programs have stressed this point (Katzell and Yankelovich 1975; Lawler 1986).

Perhaps the central variable for a comprehensive review of job redesign efforts is the degree of restructuring involved. Lawler defines the goal of redesign programs as "moving rewards, power, information and knowledge to lower levels [of the organization]" (1986, p. 4). He then ranks different redesign strategies in order of the comprehensiveness of organizational change, the likelihood that the work restructuring will endure, and the difficulty of achieving success. At the low end of Lawler's comprehensive change ranking are quality circles; in fact, no job structures are really changed by quality circles. The ranking proceeds through limited QWL approaches such as "job enrichment" and "job enlargement," in which changes in decision latitude are made at the task level, to development of work teams and different types of profit sharing, which is an economic, not psychosocial, change at the organizational level. The review then moves on to organizationally "well-supported" QWL programs such as union/management cooperation plus job enrichment programs, and finally to total plant redesign of technical and social systems (see chapter 8).

Lawler's critique makes clear that if a job redesign program is to last, it cannot depend on the goodwill of a sole executive sponsor (who may be promoted to another plant) or an outside consulting team. A short life span has been the fate of many of even the most highly publicized QWL experiments in the United States, especially those where only a small part of the work location was reorganized, such as the Rushton mine experiment (Goodman 1979). A similar experience has been described by Hanlon, Nadler, and Gladstein (1985). While acceptance of participatory management structures is increasing, a majority of company managements, in both the United States and Sweden, are still accustomed to hierarchical power structures and centralized control of information. In this context, job redesign programs of limited scope lack the strength to survive the reorganizations that constantly recur in industry. This is not an indication of infeasibility, but a reminder that innovative organizational changes need long-term support.

The problem of the short life cycle for limited job redesign forms is clearly illustrated by quality circles (Lawler 1986). Plant activity begins with a limited number of circles. Interest spreads quickly, and other groups are formed. In the meantime, the circles begin to develop suggestions for improvement that impinge on the traditional decision-making prerogatives of other organizational entities, perhaps even of those in top management who were initially most supportive of the idea. This natural desire for growth-oriented groups to seek ever-expanding authority soon comes up against some unmovable organizational obstacle that reacts and finally restricts or eliminates the program. Employees then may conclude that the quality circle program was really instituted only to elicit higher employee output and that there is little interest in the growth of employee skills. As a result of such scenarios, quality circle programs rarely last more than a few years, according to Lawler and Mohrman (1985). The problem of limited support is particularly evident in quality circle programs in the United States, because the quality circle approach is often sold to management by consultants as a "limited" job change that will not seriously "challenge" the existing decision and authority structures. Job enrichment programs that go beyond quality circles and actually make significant task-level changes in skill discretion and decision authority encounter opposition for similar reasons.

Many reviewers believe that such terminations of QWL experiments in the United States are the result of lost power struggles (Berg, Freedman, and Freeman 1978). Later in this chapter we discuss both support and resistance from management and unions. It is indeed true that improvements in the job situation of low-status workers are likely to meet with strong resistance from a full range of middle-level managers and first-line supervisors, who feel that their traditional decision responsibilities have been delegated downward to the shop floor. In view of the fact that job redesigners have rarely come up with attractive alternatives for these people, their resistance is not surprising. The vague suggestion that they start to function in the far less authoritarian role of a "support person" can lead to fears of redundancy. Yet, increased influence for low-status employees does not have to be seen as a zero-sum, win-or-lose threat to supervisory personnel. Many forms of decision making involve mutual influence in which one person's responsible contribution does not automatically restrict another's decision-making prerogatives, particularly in the areas of new-product development, introduction of new technology, and rapid response to new customer needs. Tannenbaum and his colleagues found in a cross-cultural study that high overall levels of control are characteristic of successful organizations (Tannenbaum 1962; Tannenbaum et al. 1974). These higher overall levels of control may promote health and productivity solutions by simultaneously ensuring increased employee responsibility and allowing management useful administrative information.

More optimistically, we must note that comprehensive job changes are very hard to kill when they are well rooted in many organizational levels, as full-plant reorganizations are. One of the most successful examples built on labor and management cooperation is Shell Canada's Sarnia petrochemical processing plant. This plant has successfully maintained its new organization form since 1979, utilizing a platform of multiskilled self-regulating teams, worker participation in the design process, and a supportive collective bargaining agreement emphasizing flexibility and support from both central labor and management. Other evidence for durability is a growing number of installations of this type in the United States and Western Europe (we will discuss these in more detail in chapter 8). The widely discussed Gaines Pet Food plant in Topeka, Kansas, had such capacity for endurance that the job redesign changes persisted when the initially supportive management was replaced by a new management specifically appointed to reverse the unconventional style of this General Foods installation (Lawler 1986, p. 224). Thus, once a new supportive organizational culture has been established to reinforce micro-level job redesign, the transformations may be able to resist substantial outside shocks, even hostile absentee management.

SOURCES OF SUPPORT: UNIONS AND OTHER EMPLOYEE INTEREST GROUPS

A major step in guaranteeing comprehensive multilevel support is the development of a cooperative union/management structure, as Lawler (1986) observes for the United States. The union is, of course, explicitly constituted to promote employee well-being, and union demands can balance management's traditionally greater interest in productivity outcomes. Indeed, as our brief historical comments in chapter 1 suggested, without unions neither the U.S. nor the Swedish occupational health and safety programs would have come into existence, and much of the research that has motivated this book would probably never have been done. Worker health programs are almost always stronger in companies where unions are strong. In Sweden, Norway, and much of Western Europe, joint labor/management approaches to job restructuring are almost unavoidable because of the high levels of unionization (although the unions are not automatically cooperative). The union/management cooperative agreements have the crucial ingredient of multilevel support: joint committees exist at several levels of the hierarchy. The committees range from central committees close in constitution to collective bargaining committees (although these are not collective bargaining units, and indeed these topics are not always legal collective bargaining topics in the United States, as they usually are in Scandinavia) all the way down to the shop floor committees, where job redesign modifies each employee's work-planning activity. Both Lawler (1986) in the United States and Gardell (1982) in Sweden have observed that the most comprehensive psychosocial job redesign programs have begun with acceptance of the job redesign agenda by the unions. Furthermore, commentators in both the United States and Scandinavia have observed that union/managerial arrangements have strengthened the participating unions (Gardell 1982; Macy 1979).

The evidence of expanded union participation is significant, because many unions in both countries continue to harbor well-grounded suspicions that QWL job redesign programs are management attempts to weaken members' reliance on the union. Unions observe QWL's capacity to transform advocacy of good working conditions into a management issue, often explicitly for the purpose of "busting" unions (Rosen 1988). The debate in the United States became particularly heated in the mid-1980s, when for the first time these redesigns were being undertaken on a large scale and when declining membership and opposition from the Reagan administration left labor feeling politically weak. Even though the United Auto Workers enthusiastically supported joint labor/management job design efforts, in several important cases strong opposition emerged from rank and file groups (Mann 1988), particularly for limited change efforts such as quality circles (Parker and Slaughter 1988). Parker and Slaughter (1988) have also criticized U.S. attempts to emulate Japanese auto production systems as "management-by-stress," claiming that they replace conventional union-based protections with a superficial form of participation and teamwork (see chapter 8, p. 266). (Others have praised it, however, as an excellent example of U.S. union/management cooperation.) Rosen (1988) observed that the limited task-modification-only focus of these kinds of changes refocuses the unions toward a company-oriented (often company-dominated) form of the Japanese type. The result is the loss of labor unions' traditional collective strength to advocate at the political level for worker interests such as day care for working mothers or a national commitment to occupational health and safety research.

Such concerns exist particularly in the skilled metal-working unions in both the United States and Sweden (the International Organization of Machinists and Aerospace Workers in the United States and Metall in Sweden), in spite of the unions' historic dedication to skill preservation and skill enhancement. These unions represent the core of strength of traditional unionism in industries where output is clearly conventional economic value, and hard-fought battles have been won to ensure the union share of the zero-sum benefits. Anything that could possibly jeopardize these gains is viewed with suspicion. Particularly in the United States, however, this traditional concern with wage rewards only can pose almost as much of a problem for psychosocial job redesign efforts as management's costs-only concerns. Centralized bargaining by the central union rather than by local unions may make sense for wage negotiations, but for psychosocial work redesign, a much more facilitative, technical-support-oriented, decentralized approach is probably needed. Union protection of rigid occupational classification systems can also pose a major hurdle for large-scale redesign efforts (Svensson 1986a), as we will see in chapter 9. As Sweden moves into the forefront of job redesign transformations, some labor unions (as in the United States) are leading the advocacy of job redesign and have articulated these goals with major policy statements, such as the report from the Central Union of Metal Workers on "Rewarding Work" (Metall 1987). Other, historically powerful unions have been apathetic about the new "job quality" bargaining situations, however, and pose a significant potential hurdle. But these views are changing, particularly in the Swedish Central Federation of Unions (LO), as we will see in chapter 9. We believe this is a fortunate development, for unions stand to lose much if they cannot represent their members' concerns about stress-related illness and new psychosocial structures for work. Health issues are inseparably linked to worker well-being.

THE LONG-TERM COSTS OF SHORT-TERM MANAGEMENT STRATEGIES

A management immersed in a hierarchical culture may perceive an ideological threat that can cause serious problems for job redesign solutions. Several projects to redesign the ever more highly automated and monitored jobs of telephone operators have led short lives for this reason. In a particularly ironic recent case, telephone operators were given such substantial autonomy that supervisors were not necessary. Although the program was running successfully, it was terminated without clear reason by AT&T (Howard 1985a). AT&T sponsors an active QWL experimentation effort, yet company executives have admitted that the ability to achieve lasting QWL job changes has been limited by the rigidity of AT&T's structures, embodied in many layers of supervision that restrict decision possibilities at all levels (Lawler 1986, p. 97). These job redesigns have not had sufficient "critical mass" to survive on the strength of their demonstrated effectiveness alone.

QWL experiences teach us that the mere fact that job redesign has double advantages in improving both health and productivity is often not enough to prevail against the hostile ideological environment of centralized decision making. The conflict is most severe when hierarchical management policies are reinforced with a zero-sum, short-term cost analysis. In that case, management's goals are almost always seen to be in direct conflict with workers' goals of well-being as these are reflected in psychosocial job redesign. Of course, our New Value perspective avoids this zero-sum conflict through collaborative processes, but little creative innovation is likely to arise in centrally controlled structures. This conflict is the clear message of the failure of a QWL program in a hospital in New York City (Hanlon, Nadler, and Gladstein 1985). During the startup period of the project, management's attitude was strongly positive toward job redesign. Then there was a turnover of management, and policies shifted to the point where they came into direct conflict with the fundamental prerequisites of psychosocial job redesign. Ultimately, the new management's policies led to a formulation of the problem as a trade-off between short-term, cost-based productivity and health:

> The QWL project was intended to decentralize decision making, while [management] was attempting to centralize control. The project focused on patient care, while [management] refocused the organization in the direction of better financial performance. The project attempted to foster collaboration across departmental boundaries; [management] sought to strengthen boundaries in order to [define control structures]. The project strove for union-management cooperation, while [management's] financial strategy demanded an "arms-length" and often highly adversarial stance toward the unions. In sum [management] was creating an environment that was hostile to the aims of the [QWL] project (Hanlon, Nadler, and Gladstein 1985, p. 224).

Often decisions such as these are ostensibly made to ensure economic profitability, even survival. However, the cost computations justifying production reorganization on the basis of short-term cost savings that form the basis of both "engineering economics" (Fleischer 1984) and standard accounting practices fail to measure long-term success, human capital development, and worker well-being issues of concern in this book. The goal of reducing short-term economic costs is probably the single most widely used justification for actions—increased demands, personnel cuts, and threats of layoffs—that increase workers' stress. Furthermore, as Kristensen documented in the case of the Danish meat-cutting industry (Søndergaard-Kristensen and Lønnberg-Christensen 1983), cutting labor costs is the reason used to justify instituting rigid, Taylor-oriented work procedures that further exacerbate stress-related problems that may already be associated with physically difficult and hazardous jobs (Parker and Slaughter 1988). But short-term, Fleischeristic, computations of what is necessary for economic survival may differ dramatically from what will be needed to survive in the long term, and responding to short-term economic pressure may lead a company to take actions that will be detrimental to its long-term success. For example, one of the largest manufacturers of sophisticated aircraft turbine engines in the United States in the mid-1980s was forced into the "disciplined" economic strategy of maintaining high profit margins each and every quarter of the fiscal year. (Many U.S. companies, it might be noted, have been forced to adopt such policies to avoid hostile takeovers, to which an organization is more vulnerable if its stock prices are low because of recently announced low quarterly profits.) This new financial approach meant that to fill some orders for which the company would be paid within a potentially low-profit quarter, workers had to disassemble completed turbine engines meant for other future orders to obtain one critical part that might otherwise have taken a week to produce. Because turbine engines consist of thousands of parts and take hundreds of hours to assemble and test, disassembling a completed engine to scavenge for a part was enormously costly. Such policies hardly helped the company toward its stated long-term goal of rational planning of production processes in preparation for computer-automated manufacturing technology. Instead, responsible employees concerned for the health of the company saw what appeared to be arbitrary actions being taken without good reason and suspected that their own efforts might be just as precipitously sabotaged.

Such examples of short-term thinking are common in recent critiques of U.S. management. They differ significantly from the decision practices widely utilized in other industrialized countries. The Japanese ringi method (Ouchi 1980) devotes much energy to developing a consensus about long-term plans, as do the joint labor/management discussions in Sweden for selecting new technologies (Oscarsson et al. 1988). These processes involve a broad range of employees, increasing employee decision latitude, at least to some degree. While the planning processes are time-consuming, the involvement of so many participants in the learning that goes into making the decision means that the employees are prepared to implement the plan much more quickly.

Organizational Learning and the Impact of Change Stress

The job change process has impacts both on the individual and the organization. We believe that past discussions of organizational change processes that emphasize the importance of learning have tended to overlook the impact of stress on these learning processes, even when the stress originates in the learning process itself—that is, when learning involves a restructured organization. A recent case study of a health-oriented organizational change process (Golembiewski, Hilles, and Daly 1987) has contributed to our understanding of the anatomy of the stress mechanisms in the change process. In the human resource department of a successful, growing pharmaceuticals company, an organizational development (OD) process was instituted to solve problems connected with the company's overly rapid expansion. The expansion had led to the recruitment of many new employees, which meant increased demands on the human resource staff and had ultimately resulted in severe turnover (37 percent per year) and a major morale problem. This study of a small department (31 employees) is outstandingly well documented, especially in illuminating how the process of job redesign itself resulted in stress reduction. Five separate sets of questionnaires on job situation, well-being, and motivation were administered over a two-year period to both the job redesign group and a near-control group. The consultants analyzed the situation as a burnout problem—the classic designation for what we have called a psychological strain problem among white-collar professionals. In such cases, low levels of task-based responsibility and skill usage are usually not the initially identified problem; in this case, a work environment diagnostic test showed satisfaction with professional development but heavy psychological demands and a lack of social support.

The job redesign intervention strengthened the workers' social network for participatory change through problem confrontation, group consolidation around problems, building consensus for change, and announcement of a new career progression plan. Golembiewski described the intervention as a classic United States–style organizational development case, where positive social process is established first and social structure is changed later, but we feel that structural change at the task level was applied from the very beginning. If we liberally relabel some of the constructs and work environment measures (Moos 1981), we find that what the researchers measured as results of the interventions were reduced psychological job demands and increased control by employees over their own actions—both stress-reducing changes, according to our model.

The changes worked successfully, reducing burnout by 50 percent (emotional exhaustion was the central measure used) by the end of the third measurement period. A major drop in turnover rates was also observed, from 37 percent to 20 percent after the first year and 17 percent by the end of the second year (overall company turnover rates were 13 percent). In addition, very significant increases in "innovativeness" occurred, as well as marginal increases in task orientation and work involvement, showing that employee productivity motivation also increased; more objective measures of output are difficult to record in the human resource context. In short, the study provides evidence that the redesign was successful in improving both health and productivity.

THE ORGANIZATIONAL CONTEXT OF INDIVIDUAL LEARNING

Golembiewski postulates an important requisite for the success of job redesign processes when a major goal is to reduce stress: the participants must be "active" people, not "passive" and socially withdrawn. The classic OD intervention is a strong stimulus, requiring confrontation and the additional stresses of change. For passive people such processes might represent overload.

We believe that Golembiewski has identified an important limitation for stress-oriented job redesigns, but we have a different interpretation of "active": we think it is a measure of the job situation, not of the personality. Golembiewski's measure of active orientation actually measured the employees' work environment, not their personality orientation. Twenty-nine of 31 reported higher-than-normal job autonomy and job involvement. Thus, these human resource employees had good jobs in comparison with other groups we have investigated. We believe that the true conclusion of this study is that a high-stimulus job redesign process worked well with those who already had a good job structure. The implication is that job structure that allows responsible decision making and stimulation by all participants is the true prerequisite for even more successful change. Golembiewski implies that positive structural factors facilitate reduced stress by concluding that task structural changes are "leading indicators" of burnout reductions.

What, then, is to be done for the workers who need these changes the most because they are already in passive (or high-strain) jobs? The implication of our observations is that organizational redesign approaches that put good social process ahead of structural change might not work in high-stress settings. The task structure may be generating so much strain that open communication and problem solving are not possible. Golembiewski and his colleagues pointed out that the confrontational OD processes can be too stimulating for already-stressed workers (Golembiewski, Hilles, and Daly 1987). For strained workers, it may be folly to set up good talking processes before appropriate structures have been created.

Golembiewski prescribes several first steps for "time-bomb" organizations or highly stressed employees, such as time off, vacation, and flextime. A process of incremental structural change can then be undertaken in the context of a structurally supportive and democratic process. We suggest role rotation and gradual lifting (or nonenforcement) of a broad range of bureaucratic constraints. We also believe that, early on, skills that employees have already mastered but have been officially forbidden to use should be searched out and utilized. For lower-status employees, the use of these skills will begin the process of building self-esteem. Of course, it may take longer to develop more sophisticated skills, such as effective participation in large-scale decision-making processes.

Collective discussion of mutual problems will also build the feeling of social support among workers. Peer support for expressing criticism of structurally based problems can also begin immediately, with appropriate safeguards against managerial reprisal. This process not only provides a very important vent for strain but in our experience actually serves to convert internally destructive depression into the energy for action that will eventually be needed to complete a change process. It is important that channels for creative change be available to focus these new energies. Inasmuch as constructive formulation of the problem and the search for solutions provide such channels, problem confrontation can begin quickly, but one must go slowly enough to see that energies do not outpace realistic change possibilities, or the result will be disillusionment (Karasek in press). Of course, it is the role of the job-redesign/health-improvement team, in cooperation with management and the union, to ensure that unnecessary obstacles to the processes are removed and that creative options are supported with needed resources whenever possible. Such teams were crucial to the success of the Volvo redesign efforts described earlier in this chapter.

ORGANIZATIONAL LEARNING IN TIMES OF STRESS

Our review of motivation theories in chapter 5 provided support for our hypothesis that stressful job situations could inhibit learning for individual workers. Does an analogous process occur at the organizational level? Crozier's (1964) examination of the French postal system facing the Christmas rush provides a classic example of a negative spiral in which job stress leads to increased organizational rigidity rather than to change. As the pressures for production increased, the organization's leadership resorted to ever more rigid mechanisms for controlling employee behavior instead of more flexible regulations that might have allowed individual employees to cope successfully with the stress of the increased output demands. The result was that employee behavior became ever more aberrant, bureaucratic processes became almost totally inflexible, stifling all innovative solutions, and finally the organization fell below even its normal levels of performance. Similar behavior is described by the "threat-rigidity" hypothesis of Staw, Sandelands, and Dutton (1981), in Gouldner's classic discussion of how managerial restriction of mine workers led to a wildcat strike (1954a, 1954b), and in Pasmore and Friedlander's (1982) description of stress and injuries in manufacturing processes. Bourgeois, McAllister, and Mitchell (1978) pointed out the increased centralization of authority that occurs in turbulent environments, and Gladstein and Reilly (1985) observed similarly dysfunctional long-term behavior stimulated by time pressure.

Let us illustrate this process by means of a hypothetical example of a company that troubleshoots computer system software for accounting procedures for its client companies. As a relatively young company, it wants to build its client base, and its policy is therefore to respond immediately to all customer requests, which come with great frequency around corporate income tax filing dates. Unfortunately, the company has not yet been able to train or allocate its personnel optimally. It typically operates in a fire-fighting mode, in which all long-term plans must be dropped in response to crisis situations. For example, Ms. X is assigned to a software development project that the company expects will become an important part of its future business. When an emergency comes along, however, it always seems that Ms. X is the only one with sufficient skills to handle the customer's problem, so she must be taken off the long-term project and sent off to the customer. Meanwhile, Mr. Y must be shifted temporarily into this long-term project; he has nothing else to do, and because he has less skill, he cannot be sent to the customer. Of course, he will be shifted out again as soon as Ms. X returns, with the result that he contributes little to that project and retains little from it, while Ms. X must take the time to familiarize herself with the present status of the software development. Ms. X and Mr. Y have not increased their individual skill levels, nor has the company as a whole advanced toward its long-range goal of developing new software.

This hypothetical case description corresponds disturbingly closely to the experiences that many fully employed engineering graduate students working in large aerospace firms in Southern California have reported to one of the authors. These graduate engineers often feel that whenever the company faces a crisis, they are in danger of being removed arbitrarily from projects that will promote not only their own long-term careers but, in their view, the company's long-term interests. In many cases, they feel that other personnel could have been reassigned, if the company had given any thought to the development of long-term growth in skills. These engineers perceive the company's actions under stress as devastating moves for the company. The impact on the engineers is a sense of powerlessness and disengagement from the work process that is hard to imagine for such highly trained and intelligent professionals. We will discuss in later chapters the way in which the stressful periods of corporate reorganizations due to mergers and acquisitions have similar demotivating effects on employees at all levels of the organization.

Building the Learning-Based Organization

One of the most important topics in the last two decades of organizational change research is taken up in the U.S. and Scandinavian literature on organizational restructuring to build "learning-based" organizations—that is, organizations that replace fixed-form, hierarchical bureaucracies with flexible structures which can adapt to changing external conditions and changing employee capabilities (Argyris and Schön 1978; Elden 1983; Gustavsen 1976, 1985, 1987). From our observations above and in chapter 5, we can add to this discussion by specifying an additional requirement for learning in stressful contexts: truly adaptive learning situations require the organization to be in a state of challenge, but not out of control—that is, it must not be in a state of strain. In these views, we may be in conflict with advocates of "crisis learning" (sink-or-swim learning situations). We believe that while crises may indeed precipitate the multiple organizational tensions that lead to necessary and revolutionary change, most often crisis learning results in adoption of equally rigid alternatives, as we saw above and in chapter 5. The new organization has not had the opportunity to act as a true learning structure, because it has not been allowed to search for solutions and to fail without the fear that the new structures will be swept away (see chapter 6, p. 206). According to our model, learning occurs more easily under circumstances in which decision latitude is commensurate with the challenge, not overwhelmed by it. Otherwise, simple preexisting programmed responses are invoked to defend against the continued threats. Of course, it is usually the established order that puts up sufficient resistance to generate the continuing threat for the changes. Many political revolutions with initially democratic goals—the French Revolution, for example—have been forced into rigid, combative structures because the forces of counterrevolution have strongly resisted any change at all. The pro-change groups are provoked into even more focused attacks against the old order and energy is deflected from the constructive changes that could secure the foundations of the new system.

One of the most important new perspectives emerging from the U.S. and Scandinavian organizational change literature is that of *change-process democracy,* the empowerment of lower-level employees, in which the process of learning is as important as the final organizational solution (Elden 1983; Gustavsen 1976; Sandberg 1976). In this perspective, consultants and managers must not act as elites, guiding the process toward predetermined ends, but must facilitate the process of participants finding their own solutions through problem analysis and trial-and-error. Employees develop their own mental models of the work process—a local theory, as we described in chapter 6—instead of uncritically adopting cookbook prescriptions from outside sources.

If we combine the lessons of this approach to the organization as a learning structure with the insights earlier in this section on the processes of change in stressful job settings, it becomes clear that autocratically instituted, top-down job change processes are not likely to reduce stress, because of the new demands generated by complex change processes. In such a situation, appropriate social supports are not likely to be constructed, and there are many constraints on employees' ways of coping. The organizational structure is rigid (Golembiewski, Hilles, and Daly 1987), and the stresses of the change process will overpower the limited coping capacities of the workers. The alternative is change that starts with support from the bottom. Especially for low-status workers, the process of empowerment that will ultimately generate favorable structures must begin with slow but steady learning-based building of self-esteem. Change must be generated from the bottom up, unless the structure is already sufficiently favorable to permit effective coping with stress and unhindered promotion of new solutions. Research on practical examples of complex job change involving new technologies indeed shows that change is more effective when it begins wtih grass-roots initiatives (Oscarsson et al. 1988; Gough and Vuonokari 1988; Westcott and Eisenhart 1986).

Our investigation of organizational processes thus shows the utility of an organizational-level elaboration of the dynamic form of the demand/control model from chapter 3; the limitations on learning in the face of strain have their sources not only in the past experiences of the individual but also in the present environmental circumstances of the organization. Our findings and case studies have both shown that the job change process can be especially difficult in organizations where the level of psychological strain is already high. One lesson from chapter 6 was that worker participation was an important precursor to developing task-based control to alleviate health problems. The second lesson was that stress is induced by the change process itself, so that the short-term cost of change must be balanced against long-term gains (although there were often net gains from participatory change within a year, and large losses when no participation was permitted).

The final question is, should change start from the top and move downward or from the bottom and move upward? The answer appears to be both. We have just seen that job changes to cope with stress must be grounded in new learning of skills and development of social structures directly involving all the personnel involved—a bottom-up process. Although this is a necessary condition, it is not a sufficient basis for success in most organizations. Earlier in the chapter we also saw that the organization as a whole—its multiple levels of management and union decision makers—must provide organizational support for the job change process, to overcome the forces of inertia against change. Thus, a full vertical slice of support, from bottom to top, is needed for long-term success in job redesign.

Room to Grow: New Linkages to the Market

Surprisingly, one of the most common reasons why QWL job redesign projects fail is success. As all major reviewers of QWL experience have noted (Hackman 1980; Katzell and Yankelovich 1975; Kopelman 1985; Lawler 1986), the growth of capabilities and self-confidence on the part of employees involved in any job enrichment activity is dynamic in quality. As they develop more skill, they want and expect still more participation, as we will see in the Almex case study in chapter 8. This dynamic relationship between responsibility and skill growth is congruent with the motivational component for active jobs in the demand/control model discussed in chapter 5 and with the evidence we saw in chapter 2 that work experience can socialize behavior patterns (Karasek 1976, 1978; Kohn and Schooler 1973, 1982). But the employees' desire for more decision authority and skill discretion often conflicts with organizational rigidity. When that happens, the project begins to stagnate and eventually dies; there is lack of dynamic space in which to grow.

The major issue in dynamic growth is not the absolute level of employee participation permissible or feasible but the space allowed for expansion of skills and responsibilities, wherever the starting point. Thus, in a company with little history of participatory management, quality circles might actually be a useful start. Using them as a first stage to build employees' skills, knowledge, and confidence in their ability to participate, management must then be willing to engage in a second stage, further organizational restructuring in line with the task structures that evolve. Management decision prerogatives cannot be arbitrarily invoked as a limitation. A labor/management power struggle can be avoided by means of decision structures that allow more influence for everyone. Control, unlike cost and revenue, need not be viewed as a zero-sum commodity.

Such expanding levels of overall control are perhaps easiest to imagine in the case of expanding product and service offerings, where employees' skill and responsibility growth are needed to fulfill the "smarter" job, which in turn is needed to serve demanding new customers. In these companies, the challenge is to design "smart products" and educate consumers to use them—important elements of New Value production (see chapter 5). In industrial settings where product development is limited, there may be less possibility for employee responsibilities to grow.

The possibilities for product or service development would appear to be especially limited where large-scale mass market and distribution programs are based on product uniformity. Companies that describe their success in terms of market share are often dealing in enormous volumes of mass-produced products. Brand recognition, depending on absolute product uniformity (such as in McDonald's hamburger or its counter sales job), is a major element in market control and expansion plans. There would appear to be little space for employee growth in producing such products.*

Adam Smith's dictum, as we saw in chapter 1, was that the scale of the market determines the amount of division of labor that may occur. The implication is that increased specialization of labor (or at least repetitive tasks) will occur as the scale of the market increases. Business strategies involving major increase in market share have obviously been especially popular in the last decade for U.S. companies (in the financial news, mergers and their impacts on market share are dominant topics). One unfortunate consequence may be reductions in employee decision authority and the expansion of repetitive, monotonous job experiences as large companies in market-dominant positions expand in what are becoming global markets. Sioukas and Karasek (1990) have found that increasing market scale is empirically associated with decreasing decision latitude in concentrated industries (those in which the top four companies have over 40 percent of the market). Thus, processes connected with increased market share and world markets may, more clearly than organizational policies, force a choice between company profitability and employee health: your money or your life.

It is noteworthy, however, that not even this threat has discouraged QWL programs. Indeed, psychosocial job change programs are much more common among large corporations and corporations with market-determined uniformity of product or service. Of course, this is only to say that QWL is more common in the jobs that probably need QWL the most. One of the major QWL strategies employed in these cases is to attack the problem by changing the producer/consumer relationship. In Kopelman's (1985) review of the last two decades of QWL programs in the United States, we would classify 23 of the 26 companies in programs with classifiable data as having just such orientation to mass-undifferentiated products. These in-

*Taylor's (1976) review of 120 work redesign projects from many countries concluded that the majority are undertaken in small-scale settings (fewer than 100 employees), such as a single department.

cluded AT&T, Philips, auto manufacturers, large insurance companies, and large government agencies. Significantly, 15 of these 23 programs attempted to establish new client relationships. Thus, an extraordinarily high number of companies were willing to experiment with changing the most basic element of its production organization, the nature of the customer's ability to influence the type of product (not just its quantity or price).

One such "hopeless" job design case involved stock transfer clerks in a very monotonous, highly specialized behind-the-scenes job at Bankers Trust in New York City in the 1970s. Very high rates of expensive errors, high turnover, and very low decision latitude were the primary problems. The solution involved changing the link between producer and customer. The stock transfer clerks were organized into small groups, each of which was assigned to an industry-based subdivision of the stock market (Dettleback and Kraft 1971; Frank and Hackman 1975; Hackman and Oldham 1980). Groups were given substantial autonomy over their internal work organization and growth space for taking on new responsibilities and learning new skills.* Stock clerks could ultimately become familiar with the nature of the major stocks traded and the requirements of the company's major customers within the industry subunit. After a period of such directed exposure, they would be encouraged to learn new skills and possibly even to enroll in appropriate classes. Such job redesign changes could result in much more satisfactory service for the customer, such as automatically anticipated information on particular stock performance, as well as better health for a worker who is allowed to work to his or her full potential.

An experiment that has proved highly successful in combining new organization of production and a new market interface was undertaken at a truck factory in Finland in the early 1980s. The factory produces heavy-duty trucks for the Finnish market, where stiff competition is provided by international truck producers such as SAAB, Volvo, and Mercedes. This company totally reorganized its truck assembly production facility from line production to decentralized, group-based assembly in order to accommodate production of a new truck design based on modular components.† The change process represents the ideal of organizational support: all members of the firm collaborated equally to attain a common, complex goal. During the five-week reorganization period, all 250 assembly employees, together with the engineering staff, management, and an organi-

---

*The final result is hard to determine in this case, because there were several changes of management, several waves of consultants, and a change of technology in the stock transfer process in the mid-1980s that significantly affected these jobs.

†Matti Pöyhönen and Juha Venho, personal communication at the truck factory site, October 1983.

zational development consultant, met continuously to redesign the production layout cooperatively, working with a large Lego-block scale model to convey information. To restart production, the company simply moved all production equipment out of the building and moved it back, in a new production configuration, a month later—with the assistance of over 250 newly knowledgeable worker-consultants. This redesign epitomized a new integration of engineering, management, and employee viewpoints. It also involved minimal new capital expenditures. The redesign process served as the necessary training and orientation activity for all factory employees, who in the future would have to have a thorough understanding of production based on a new, more flexible truck body design. The new product design involved modular truck body components, to facilitate adapting each truck to the customer's needs.

The truck plant reorganization process was successful in productivity terms and has facilitated a new interface with customers that increases sales. The customization of the truck allows the company to set market prices: its competitors are forced to price their mass-produced product under its price. As each truck body passes through assembly, the customer's company name is affixed to it, giving the workers, who may personally know the customers in this region of Finland, a motivating feeling of accomplishment. Customers are also invited to watch the assembly of truck modules in progress when they pick up their own vehicles and leave stimulated with thoughts of how they might be able to use new modules or components to expand the use of their own trucks. The result has been requests for new modules to fulfill special needs, modules that often later become the company standard offerings. In short, this flexible decentralized production lays the foundation for future additional sales, an important ingredient for this company's success in the face of international competition. We can see the self-sustaining aspect of New Value–oriented production of new-use, conducive products—a clear example of linkage between the psychosocial job structure and the new producer/customer associations discussed in chapter 5. Although we have no data on direct health outcomes for employees, absenteeism is very low, and high employee morale attests to high levels of employee well-being.

This new kind of worker-consumer connection necessarily implies much more direct worker-consumer communication and quite possibly a smaller scale of market (in Adam Smith's terminology). This allows relevant product information to be transferred between producer and product user— much more complex information than traditional price/quantity information. Such communication could allow both workers and consumers to have greater influence over and a more creative contribution to both the production and the distribution processes. The social processes involved could increase the overall stability of economic relationships, as we will see when we contrast them to processes involved in world market competition in chapter 10. While such new forms may seem very different from our present industrial organizations, their benefits could be irresistible.

Conclusion

In the next chapter, our attention will switch from the forces of organizational inertia that we discussed above to a set of almost unstoppable forces for organizational change: new technologies. These new computer-based technologies have been associated by many researchers (Edwards 1979; Gordon, Edwards, and Reich 1982; Howard 1985a; Noble 1984; Shaiken 1984) with increased workplace stress; the question, then, is whether these new technologies inevitably force us to trade health for productivity or whether there are alternatives. We will find that the search for health- *and* productivity-oriented alternatives leads us first to an appreciation of how much the impact of new technologies is dependent on social and organizational choices that have been made inside the firm. This connection has led job redesigners of the last three decades to label their large-scale redesign attempts as *socio-technical* job redesign.

8

The Technological Context of Job Redesign

So far, we have discussed the health and productivity consequences of job redesign as though they resulted from changes in the social structure of work alone. Of course, technological and economic aspects of job redesign also have had major impacts on both productivity and health in these cases. Indeed, one clear message of this chapter should be that the technical and social systems of work must be reorganized together, in an integrated *socio-technical design*. There are tight linkages between technological change and changes in the psychosocial job structure in the areas of decision processes, skill allocations, psychological demands, social interaction, and communication patterns. Technology often serves as a lever magnifying the impacts of the division of labor—for better and for worse.

To determine the nature of effective socio-technical job design solutions, we must examine separately two different generations of technology: the conventional automation technologies of the post–Second World War era, exemplified by the automobile assembly plants of Detroit, and the rapidly growing computer and communications technologies. For the former, we now have a well-developed set of jointly optimal social and technical solutions, but for the latter, we do not yet have clear solutions, possibly because the technologies are still new. The introduction of computer systems is probably the major factor that is currently bringing about the redesign of job structures in both the United States and Sweden. An optimistic view is that these computer-based changes could offer new opportunities for humanistic change of the psychosocial structures of work. A more pessimistic view observes that in the United States (although not in Sweden), psychosocial considerations are presently running a distant third place behind economic goals and technological design requirements in influencing the direction of these changes.

Turner's study (1980) of 1,400 mortgage loan processing clerks and financial investment officers showed how computerization can force a choice between productivity and health, the central dilemma of our book. In the late 1970s, batch-processing computer systems, in which all work orders are processed together at the end of the day according to the computer's schedule, increased productivity but at the same time left bank clerical workers with little control over the process. These systems were associated with higher levels of worker psychological strain (Turner 1980). An alternative interactive computer system, which allowed the clerk to begin computer processing at his or her discretion, was associated with lower job stress but also with lower productivity, as measured by percentage of successfully performing loans processed. The choice was productivity *or* health.

Fortunately, such a forced choice can be avoided. The dilemma posed by the use of large central-processing computers has now been significantly modified by the introduction of personal computer work stations, which can provide workers as much computational power as the old mainframes yet give the operator almost total control over processing times for many types of tasks. This second-generation technological innovation has thus removed a major technical constraint to more decentralized and democratically structured work environments. Solutions that can achieve positive health *and* productivity consequences are now feasible. It is up to the organization to decide how to use this new technology, however; the old work methods and old system of computer interfaces can be used to restrict worker control, just as before. There is now a social choice to be applied to the technological systems.

The usual consequence of technological systems that have been planned unilaterally by managers and engineers, without employee involvement, is a forced trade-off between productivity and health. Such situations are very common in the United States, but fortunately they are now disappearing in Scandinavia, through processes of participative technological choice. Such processes often occur in the context of joint union/management technology review teams (Oscarsson et al. 1988; Lund and Hansen 1986). The problem with unilateral planning is that considerations of human well-being are often left out of the decision calculus altogether. System planners follow their natural instincts to increase their control over the system, or simply acquiesce in the inertia of the existing institutional hierarchy, as Zuboff (1988) clearly describes, often at the expense of worker control. Workers' roles become residual to the function of the machine. Alternatively, the computer-based system can be designed to serve as a *tool* to leverage the workers' existing skills. In this chapter we will note many existing examples of this positive alternative to the status quo, as well as a very complex set of challenges for the future.

Socio-Technical Design in Manufacturing Automation

Almex AB is a medium-sized manufacturing firm in Sweden that dominates the world market for mass-transit bus ticketing machines, a product that must be customized to the requirements of each city transit system. Almex is a member of the Wallenberg Group's Incentive Investment division; that is, it belongs to Sweden's largest capital-owning network of companies.

The job change process at Almex began with separate initiatives coming from the local labor union's interest in shop floor democracy (Gardell and Svensson 1981) and management's interest in an engineering redesigning of the product lines to reduce component inventories and to increase design flexibility (Sandell et al. 1976). The convergent impacts of these two initiatives yielded a truly socio-technical change in the new production and organization. The cornerstone of the new job design was the institution of autonomous work groups, which in turn were integrated into the overall organizational structure by union policies and by liaison strategies between work groups and management. The flexibility and adaptability of the new group-oriented production assembly was made technically feasible through the simplification of the product's design by the engineering staff.

The Almex product is a small, customized fare-ticket printing machine. On the old assembly lines, many hundreds of parts, in ad hoc combinations, were required to make the roughly one thousand product variants that were produced to order—often in quantities of under five. In spite of the product diversity, the specialized workers could perform only a small range of tasks; they were not trained to solve problems arising out of customized production. With the assistance of the Institute for Manufacturing Technology (headed by Gunnar Sohlenius), at one of Sweden's major engineering universities, the manufacturing engineers consolidated the many parts into a much smaller number of component "modules," which then could be assembled into roughly ten basic product types (Sandell et al. 1976). This simplification of the production design improved not only the efficiency of orders from suppliers, but made it easier for workers to grasp the complexity of assembling the final machine. The work groups could easily adjust to customized variations in the product and developed a sense of responsibility toward the customer. In some cases the work groups facilitated the redesign of a ticketing machine to fill an unusual customer order (Åhlström 1980). This ability to respond rapidly to customer demand was a vital component of Almex's successful international competitive strategy.

One of the most important aspects of the Almex job redesign, well documented by Gardell and Svensson (1981), was the multilevel organizational support generated for the job redesign strategies. Organized labor *initiated* the work reorganization in 1975 and management cooperated in bringing the majority of the assembly workers into autonomous groups. There was also substantial cooperation between the employee groups and their local labor union. Members of the autonomous work groups had higher levels of union interest than other workers (36 percent with a high level of interest versus 11 percent, respectively). Not only were supportive structures for the job redesign implemented at the organizational level by both labor and management, but there was horizontal support as well. Gardell (1982) has highlighted the importance of white-collar support for job changes that primarily affected blue-collar (direct assembly) employees. Just as crucial was another type of cooperation, between the engineers in product design and the organizational redesign process.

The new assembly work groups, consisting of five to fifteen workers, were given responsibility for determining all aspects of coordinating the assembly of the complex ticketing apparatus. The workers' use of their skills thereby increased, necessitating new training for workers (often crosstraining between workers) as well as increased task-level decision authority. The workers assumed many of the responsibilities of supervision, and the supervisor thereafter became a liaison/resource person. Of course, the work groups increased the employees' instrumental social support through work structure that allowed mutual assistance on tasks, and that support in turn led to positive personal reactions of group members toward each other, or emotional social support.

The generally positive productivity effects of the Almex job and product redesign are confirmed by the trend in the company's profitability at the time that work groups were introduced in 1976: the return on investment for 1974 was 8 percent, for 1975 12 percent, for 1976 19 percent, for 1977 14 percent, for 1978 16 percent. Management comments indicated that the job reorganization resulted in fewer customer complaints and increased flexibility (Gardell 1982). Reduction in health risk was attested to by questionnaire measurements: psychological stress was experienced "very often" or "rather often" by only 7 percent of the employees in the autonomous work groups but by 18 percent among the workers remaining in conventional (low-control, low-social-support) assembly situations. Only 2 percent of the autonomous-group workers reported that they were "too tired at night to pursue hobbies or meet friends," while 22 percent of other employees reported such problems. These lower reports of psychological strain and higher levels of job satisfaction* existed in spite of the fact that the autonomous work group gave employees "more work." Group employees reported greater responsibility for coordinating and planning their own activity, in the context of highly variable customer demands. Indeed, group-based employees admitted higher levels of psychological demands (16 percent responded that they often had too much to do, as opposed to only 10 percent of other employees). But these increased demands did not lead to higher levels of psychological strain, health risk, or even tiredness. The redesign led to lower levels of reported stress, in our opinion because the work groups gave the workers substantially greater control and freedom to organize their work life on the micro level, as well as significant input into macro-level decisions.

The interviews conducted by Gardell and Swensson (1981) indicate an important mechanism by which more control at work may reduce job stress: increased worker self-confidence and self-esteem. Our model in chapter 3 predicts that growth of competence occurs as a positive spiral of results, involving an increased feeling of mastery and starting with expanded opportunity to use skills. Increased environmental control leads to more skills and to increased self-esteem, which in turn allows people to master challenges with less residual tension. Employee interviews suggest that just this process occurred at Almex (Åhlström 1980). The increased opportunities for making decisions afforded by the autonomous groups and the more readily grasped production technology led to increased possibilities to make successful decisions and to the desire for still further growth of responsibility (Svensson 1986b).

The desirability of multi-focus, organizationally comprehensive approaches to job redesign has actually been evident from the beginning of the Quality of Work Life experiments. Interestingly, the psychosocial job design principles from the 1950s in England, investigated by Trist and Bamforth (1951) and Melman (1958), evolved from observation of the negative impacts that Smith's and Taylor's principles of the division of labor were having upon old craft groups that were just being exposed to what was then considered modernization. Many of the early examples of job

---

*Levels of satisfaction in Sweden are often measured by levels of instrumental attitude toward the job ("I only do it for the money" versus "I do it because I'm interested"). Fifty percent of all Swedish industrial workers report that they only do it for the money, and exactly the same finding was true of the *non*–group-organized Almex workers. Of the group workers, however, only 20 percent reported that they only do it for the money.

redesign from England and Scandinavia in the 1950s and the 1960s, such as the British coal mining redesign experiences (Trist and Bamforth 1951) and the redesign efforts at Norsk Hydro by Emery and Thorsrud, attempted to reverse these changes. Autonomous work groups became the central theme in many of these projects. Their more comprehensive approach was labeled *socio-technical design,* because production technology had to be reorganized as well as new psychological and social structures found for work organization.

More recently, such projects have been discussed from an organizational structure perspective as "new design plants" in the United States (Lawler 1986) and reviewed as "new factories" in terms of new production engineering implications by the Swedish Employers Confederation (Agurén and Edgren 1980). Many of the most publicized and most successful socio-technical designs are completely new plants. These examples include the new Volvo auto assembly plants in Sweden, the Gaines Pet Food plant (General Foods) in the United States, and the Shell petrochemical plant in Sarnia, Canada. Currently the best publicized example is the unfinished but highly touted General Motors Saturn plant in Tennessee, a $3.5 billion investment. Redesign strategies that address many levels of the organization and include redesigning production clearly appear to constitute the formula with the greatest promise. Although the new production technologies at GM and at Volvo represent expensive investments, Volvo's new technologies have generally been no more costly than conventional production technologies (Edgren 1981). While start-up at a new factory location with a new labor force avoids the stress of job reorganization, it obviously adds to the threat of job insecurity. Many other plants, including Trist and Bamforth's (1951) ground-breaking experiments, represent comprehensive but successful transformations of existing structures. The NUMMI GM–Toyota joint-venture auto plant in California has been very successful with a redesign that used much of the existing machinery and labor (Parker and Slaughter 1988). The Almex work redesign and the Finnish truck factory redesign, described in chapter 7, also demonstrate that it is economically feasible to reorganize an existing plant according to socio-technical principles.

An important characteristic of socio-technical redesign is, of course, the engineering changes that are made in the design of production technology in almost all the major examples. Most of the socio-technical experiments, however, are still primarily social innovations; only 16 percent involve a major change of the production technology itself (Pasmore et al. 1982). It is primarily the technology of production organization, not the machines, that has been modified: the configuration of machines and the contact of humans with them; the proportions, timing, and scheduling of labor, machinery, and material inputs; and data flows for customer modification, inventory control, and so forth. In the United States, mastery of this aspect of technology has traditionally been the province of industrial engineers, while in Western Europe, which is just starting to establish industrial engineering departments, mechanical engineering departments often address these topics. In the Volvo plant in Kalmar, Sweden, and the forthcoming GM Saturn plant in Tennessee, the new machinery and its configuration differ so dramatically from old automobile assembly line equipment that it might initially appear to be extremely difficult to transform an old plant into a new one, but the Finnish truck factory example shows that such changes are possible.

A prime example of the new interface between human workers and technology is the auto chassis carrier at the Kalmar Volvo factory, which has been designed with both social understanding and engineering skill. The heavy automobile chassis is carried on an individual mobile carrier that can be freely moved about under its own power and can tilt the auto chassis into different positions to allow the assemblers to work comfortably. This technology stands in dramatic contrast to chassis transport in Detroit plants, where an overhead assembly chain, with an auto chassis rigidly attached, is moved at a fixed, inexorable speed through each work station, determining the worker's pace and forcing the worker to bend and reach uncomfortably to perform the task. The primary achievement of the Volvo auto chassis carriers is the freedom they provide: the social organization of work is no longer rigidly tied to the technology in a manner that forces workers and management into a struggle for control over conveyor speeds (a concern in Detroit assembly lines). The worker is no longer obliged to work at an externally fixed pace on a rigidly delimited task. The work is now self-paced or group-paced and is performed in an ergonomically comfortable and healthful physical position. At the same time, technically optimal production rates and part inventories can still be ensured, with cooperation from the work teams. In short, both the technical and the social components of this production process can operate in an optimal manner; it is a design much more likely to yield both health and productivity results. Of course, the work group must now coordinate the team's contributions with plant production while maintaining overall levels of output and quality. Management liaison and inputs from engineering staff are still required to organize production at this level. Most significantly, a new breed of engineers who can deal knowledgeably with the social organizational issues of work is required, not only in design of the new production technology at start-up but more than ever in facilitating later modifications in the flexible production processes.

What do these new socio-technical jobs actually look like from a psychosocial perspective? The jobs of production workers (that is, direct value–adding workers such as assemblers and cutters; police officers and nurses would also qualify) differ from those in other companies in their respective industries in a manner consistent with our model in chapter 2 and the QWL job redesign experiments discussed in chapter 5. Work teams are the core design element, particularly when the task is too complex to be handled routinely by one person. The groups have substantial decision authority to schedule their tasks and to allocate tasks within the group, in coordination with overall factory production plans. The routine coordinating functions of supervision become group decisions. The result is more nearly equal roles and more emotionally supportive social relationships. Although the supervisor or group leader still performs liaison activity with higher management and other groups, he or she becomes a resource person, as do personnel and engineering staff members, providing more task assistance (instrumental social support) for group members.

Furthermore, in socio-technical job redesigns the organizational structure as a whole is changed, with fewer levels of managerial hierarchy and thus fewer limits on decision latitude as well as greater equality of status. Often management adopts explicit new organizational philosophy statements that emphasize the basic human worth of employees, their need for career growth, and their rights and that recognize employee development as the best pathway to profitability. Rarely has health been explicitly measured, but obviously the organizational structure makes this a supportive context for health improvements, as the Almex case illustrates. Organizational support from labor unions has often been crucial in initiating and maintaining vitality in these new plant solutions. Staff support functions such as production engineering and personnel also change to fit these new philosophies, serving to support work teams and not just higher management. (Unfortunately, economic reward structures have not always changed in this same egalitarian manner [Lawler 1986]; Bernstein [1974, 1976] sees a solution in worker-owned cooperatives.) The organization-wide acceptance of the need for continual organizational evolution ensures that employees have room to grow on the job. Actually, achieving continued change has been difficult even for these new-design plants (Lawler 1986), but even the limitations implied by a uniform, mass-produced product can be modified in such a plant, because the decentralized work groups give a natural communication base in which consumer and producer can discuss product changes, as the truck factory case study showed. Taken together, these changes also assure that a critical mass of the organization is supportive of new, basic changes in the individual's employee job structure.

How successful have the comprehensive socio-technical designs been, particularly in terms of our dual criteria of health and productivity? The success of Trist and Bamforth's first socio-technical design is well documented (Trist et al. 1963). Of two work organizations with the same coal-mining machinery, the one with the socio-technical redesign had a 95 percent capacity utilization, versus 78 percent for the original system. Absenteeism was 8.2 percent in the new system (4.6 percent for sickness and 3.2 percent for accidents); in the original system it was 20 percent (8.9 percent for sickness and 6.8 percent for accidents). Specific data have been difficult to obtain for later socio-technical redesign projects, with the exception of the Gaines Pet Food plant in Kansas, where productivity increased dramatically and accidents were significantly reduced. In 1973, two years after redesign, the plant had 4.4 injuries per 100 full-time employees versus 19.3 for the U.S. food products industry as a whole and 7.2 for all U.S. General Foods plants (Clack 1974). After several years of operation, the Volvo plant in Kalmar, Sweden, recorded productivity successes and absenteeism reductions (Edgren 1981). There is consistent, albeit indirect, evidence for overall productivity success, although the health consequences have usually been poorly documented. Even the indirect evidence of productivity is compelling: such designs are being built in ever-greater numbers. As Lawler (1986) states, "The list of companies with new-design plants reads like a who's who of the [U.S.] Fortune 500. They include AT&T, General Foods, PPG Industries, Procter and Gamble, Sherwin-Williams, TRW, H. J. Heinz, Rockwell, Johnson and Johnson, General Motors, Mead and Cummins Engine. . . . a good guess would be that at least forty large corporations have one or more, and that overall two hundred or more are in operation" (p. 170). In the United States in the early 1970s, there were fewer than five such plants, and now the investment in them has reached the level of General Motors' multi-billion-dollar commitment. In Europe there is also a growing number of successes such as Volvo which, soon after its success at Kalmar, established six more new-design plants in Sweden and one in Holland (Jönsson 1980).

Computer-Based Technological Change and Job Design

If there were no more to socio-technical redesign than is illustrated by the examples we have just given, we might be seeing a lot of humane job redesign efforts now, but a whole new generation of technological changes currently in process is altering the very core of the job and organizational structure. For example, manufacturing companies involved in the production of agricultural machinery (Shaiken, Kuhn, and Herzenberg 1983c) are implementing major computer-based automation of their production systems to realize several advantages: lower production costs, particularly for direct labor; better integrated and more comprehensive data over all company operations; flexible, rapid response to customer demands; better accountability by employees; and improved long-range planning. Equally comprehensive changes have occurred in service industries such as insurance and banking.

How do these computerized production systems and automation affect health and productivity? In our view, the primary factor determining the computer's effect on the job is the manner in which its introduction changes the task structure and the communication procedures of the work process. Turner and Karasek (1984) use the title "Software Ergonomics" to emphasize that it is not the physical computer characteristics, such as video display glare or processor speed, that have the most profound impact, in spite of the unequivocal evidence for musculoskeletal and eye strain problems from uninterrupted video-display terminal (VDT) use. It is the manner in which control over software and computer hardware are related to the worker's control over his or her own multiple tasks that make the major difference. To understand these linkages at the task level, Turner and Karasek identified four elements of computer software systems that affect the task-structure elements that we discussed in chapter 2: work flow (human/computer division of labor), dialogue quality, system reliability, and system complexity.

But the major socio-technical problems and potentials manifest themselves at the level of the organization as a whole, as computer-based systems transform communications between the components of the organization. These impacts can be best analyzed by means of the basic themes of work organization that we have emphasized since chapter 1: changes in authority structures and high or low status in the company; changes in skill allocation; changes in the psychological demands of work; effects on social interaction patterns; and effects on job security.

Authority, Skill Allocation, and the Impact of Computer-Based Technologies

The computer is nominally designed to aid the employee, to serve as a flexible extension to his or her capabilities. Its use as a tool implies that the human is in control, and that the computer, not the human, is to bear the main burden of adaptation. It is with this idea that computer vendors sell management on the computerized office or factory of the future; each executive and professional is to have a work station, like a genie-in-a-bottle, to do that person's bidding, handling routine reports, production scheduling, and correspondence with "user-friendliness."

This pitch, of course, is only for management; it is not given to all employees. There is an invisible boundary line in the corporation: above the line, the computer is advertised as the employee's tool and servant, but below the line, the employee must follow the dictates and requirements of the computer system. The use of the computer system and the method of operation are not up to the discretion of employees but mandated by organizational policy. The computer may diminish skill levels and autonomy for low-status workers while increasing them for high-status workers. It seems to work as a lever, amplifying the effects of the existing organizational structure's division of labor.

The results of this strategy in a number of studies of VDT use among low-status workers suggest that it leads to substantial health and morale problems. The effects of computer use on health are clearly more negative for lower-status workers. This conclusion is supported by several recent studies of diverse Swedish administrative and technical workers (Aronsson 1984), diverse U.S. clerical workers (Smith et al. 1984), bank clerical workers (Turner and Karasek 1984), and a national sample of clerical women (The 9 to 5 Survey on Women and Stress 1984). While the survey of clerical workers showed that fully 68 percent of respondents found that working with the computer had made their jobs "more interesting and enjoyable" and 54 percent had found it "less stressful and easier to do," the job changes that were most strongly associated with computer use involved increased time pressure and reduced possibilities for control over the task, precisely those job characteristics found to create health risks in chapters 3 and 4. When further analyses were performed with respondents subdivided by occupation, rates of frequent health problems were significantly higher for the clerical workers who used computer systems. For that subgroup (17 percent of the total sample), the association between computer use and increased illness were highly significant for nine out of nine health indicators. Haynes and La Croix (reviewed in Schnorr, Thun, and Halperin 1987) compared female office telecommunications workers who used VDTs with office workers who were not using VDTs. The study showed that the prevalence of angina pectoris–like symptoms was significantly higher among the VDT users. In general, VDT users reported a lower level of decision latitude, and an interaction of VDT use and decision latitude was found for angina pectoris. Together with the computer monitoring studies that we will discuss below, these findings suggest that the computer will have negative impacts on health to the degree that it is used by management to restrict employees' control over their work. It is not hard to understand why workers and managers can have substantially different perspectives on the efficiency and desirability of computer-based systems; the computer can strongly amplify their control—or lack of it—in the work process.

Even worse consequences for workers' well-being occur when the workers themselves are the subject of the data collection. The U.S. Office of Technology Assessment (1987) has estimated that in 1986 roughly 6 million workers were monitored by computer systems; for some occupations, such as technicians, the figure was 20 percent of the work force and growing. The monitoring possibilities that computer systems offer can lead to some of the most disturbing restrictions in employee decision latitude. The invasion of personal boundaries leave workers angry and resentful that their personality integrity has been undermined: where does their lifespace stop and the computer's begin? Such possibilities for control are inherent in the computer's ability to collect information about all aspects of employees' activities involving computer use and then to centralize the information for review by higher management. Monitoring illustrates a particularly perverse form of linkage between control and demand in the computer context: computer systems may be introduced as a method of ensuring high output rate by making it impossible for employees to vary their pace or take occasional rest breaks. In one medium-sized machining firm outside of Stockholm, skilled machinists were asked whether their performance rate on computerized machine tools was monitored. They replied that Swedish computer-aided machine tools did not have such circuitry, but when they found it in foreign machines, they disconnected it. Unfortunately, for office-based computer systems this is not easy to do; monitoring routines are often inseparably linked to the software of basic system operations, so that their existence is hard to find (not to mention disconnect) without examining the detailed program code. Limitation of computer monitoring is clearly an area where bargains between employees and management will have to be pursued in the future with a substantial measure of trust, to safeguard employee health and self-esteem.

The computer system can also dramatically affect the nature of communication patterns on the job and, thus, social relations on the job. Turner's study (1980) found that lower-status mortgage loan clerks experienced increased psychological strain with computer use, because of the higher demands created by new dependencies that arose when the computer system was introduced. Before the job was computerized, the clerk might have been able to check out special cases or exceptions with a co-worker. With the computer system, new forms of malfunctioning could force the clerk to depend on software technicians who might be less helpful and sympathetic than co-workers. The technicians were in a different location and had higher status, different goals, and probably less concrete knowledge of mortgage loan irregularities. New job demands might mean they were simply too busy to assist. These complex new dependencies raise another perspective on the implications of social interactions at work: social interactions in this context are certainly not always positive or socially supportive, reducing psychological strain. They may have a negative effect when the social relationships are forced, particularly when one person is in an inferior position with respect to the other, introducing social insecurity via new patterns of reliance and dependency.

The impact of computer technologies on skill levels has been the subject of much debate (Howard 1985a; Noble 1984; Shaiken 1984). Of course, many new jobs created by the introduction of computer-based technologies bring substantial intellectual challenges—in maintenance, in programming and system analysis, and in production of the computer hardware and software itself (although unfortunately such systems result in an overall loss of jobs [see U.S. Office of Technology Assessment 1986]). Because of the positive health effects of intellectual discretion and skill growth, discussed in chapter 4, giving employees the opportunity to learn new skills at work could be considered a health promotion strategy. Because of the social context of some of the new technically skilled jobs, however, there can also be problems with these jobs as well. Even managers report being overwhelmed by the power of centralized data collection procedures and often feel powerless to intervene to alter them (Zuboff 1988). Majchrzak et al. (1987) found in a study of the use of new computer-assisted design (CAD) systems among engineers and draftsmen that in the first system implementation, workers carried out more routine and more formalized tasks than before, in spite of the fact that the CAD system had the potential to free technicians from routine tasks and allow them to be creative. Overall, draftsmen's feelings of satisfaction dropped. They speculate that this occurred both because routine operations were easier to run, and because management, eager to see numerical proof of increased effectiveness with the new system, ran more routine operations in order to provide such evidence.

Maintenance workers in computer-integrated manufacturing systems unquestionably have intellectual challenges in their new tasks, and this job is in the low-strain quadrant of our occupational maps in figure 2–2. But the responsibilities of keeping the system running when downtime is very expensive, or when one problem can quickly lead to a full production stop in domino fashion, or when there is risk of damaging equipment far more expensive than before, can remove any leisurely quality from the job, as happened for many maintenance workers, in the agricultural equipment plant described by Shaiken, Kuhn, and Herzenberg (1983c).

In spite of the increased skill and education requirements for the work force as a whole, it appears that the majority of blue- or white-collar operators are indeed deskilled and beset by a combination of boredom and stress—or threatened by job loss—by the introduction of present computer production systems. Edosomwan (1986) reported on experiments with such a job design for workers who use a computer-automated system for inserting computer chips into circuit boards. The computer was programmed to move the circuit board into the appropriate position and shine a light on the insertion location; the operator had only to pick up the chip and insert it into that exact board location. In comparison with the previous manually guided production process (already a dismally repetitive job), the new system substantially increased productivity but even further reduced employee control and skill usage. The result was decreased job satisfaction and a rise in employee health complaints. We believe that job redesign strategies for computer-based jobs can help to avoid such problems. The employee who uses the system can also be the employee who writes the design specifications for the new computer-based version of the job, in cooperation with a technical professional. A skilled and motivated operator can identify those elements that a human being can do better than the automated system: spotting irregularities, setting up for new products, changing quality levels, and suggesting solutions for quality problems, for example.

New Forms of Constraint and Psychological Job Demands

There are two very different sets of possible implications of computer- and communication-based changes at the organizational level. One is positive, related to the flexible, decentralized production systems that new technologies make economically feasible; a second, negative scenario is related to centralized management strategies in which information control is a primary strategy, used by the company to reduce uncertainty within its environment.

In our strategies for designing desirable jobs, to be described in chapters 9 and 10, flexible, computer-based technologies are an essential building block of humane and productive work organization. Computer-assisted, reprogrammable machine tools could give individual workers and work groups the potential for a much broader range of output and make possible a dialogue with customers never open to the assembly line worker. The enormous computational capability of even small computer work stations could give one person the capability of coordinating production processes that before required the powerful central computers of a large organization's central staff, making possible the creation of social networks of small-scale, equally powerful producers, who would operate cooperatively and quasi-independently. Adam Smith's coordination costs would be dramatically reduced, and the work structure would promote, rather than limit, skill development. These possibilities are further encouraged by the most recent developments in telecommunications, utilizing computers and digital information processing to make network connections between many independent work stations technically feasible. Research on electronic mail systems has found equalization of status differences as the computer promotes equal access to all network members (Bikson and Eveland 1989).

The negative psychosocial implications of computers and communication technology are rooted in some of the primary themes of influential management theories from the last several decades. March and Simon's (1958) classic model of organizational process based on information theory first makes some important concessions about the reality of life in an "information society": information is expensive to gather, so decisions must be made on less than perfect information ("bounded rationality"). March and Simon's next proposition is more disturbing. They observe that a major operational goal of organizations is to minimize uncertainty, both inside and outside the firm. This perspective legitimates exercise of control by managers facing decision making in more and more turbulent environments, but for workers this perspective can present problems. To ensure that employees do what they are told, managers may exert "unobtrusive" control over subordinate behavior by selectively withholding access to information. This is a potentially even more comprehensive form of control than exercise of personal authority. In order to illustrate the potential of the computer-controlled work environment to control behavior, several recent writers (Foucault 1979; Zuboff 1988) have pointed to our Utilitarian economist Jeremy Bentham's (see chapter 1) manuscript (1794) about a new form of prison: *Panopticon, or the Inspection House: Containing the Idea of a New Principle of Construction Applicable to Any Sort of Establishment, in which Persons of Any Description Are to be Kept Under Inspection.* In the Panopticon Prison, every aspect of a prisoner's life could be minutely scrutinized by observation at a distance. Even more pernicious, while the warden would need to expend little energy actually observing them, the prisoners would never know when they were being observed, so they could never relax. Zuboff's study of the utilization of computer systems in eight U.S. companies (1988) has indeed shown that management's path of least resistance is to use computer systems to reinforce preexisting hierarchical control patterns.

THE COMPUTER-MEDIATED SOCIAL INTEGRATION OF THE WORKPLACE

In many installations the impact of the computer is not overt restriction of employee behavior, but a newly magnified form of constraint that derives from the increased independence of the system as a whole. Indeed, probably the most significant impact of large-scale computer systems is the interdependence they introduce in the work process. The new configuration that results from computer-based integration of functions operates differently from its components: it is an interdependent system, with both human and technical elements. The emphasis on interdependent systems has resulted not from the computer alone but from the new (since the mid-1970s) management policy of producing products just when customers need them, to reduce inventory holding costs. The Japanese have made famous the "just-in-time" production system, often used for auto assembly, in which a component is produced only when it is needed for assembly into a completed unit, instead of being produced for inventory. The Japanese worker is given substantial authority over decisions about how and when to switch production from one machine to another and even whether to stop the entire production process. In Japanese literature, this system is therefore also known by the joint title "just-in-time and respect-for-worker" system (Sugimori et al. 1977; Japanese Management Association 1983, p. 25). In the United States, however, both translations of the term and implementations of the approach have dropped the "worker respect" half of the title. If the worker does not determine the mediation between customer-driven demands and machine capabilities, the job can simply become uncontrollable for the employee.

Parker and Slaughter's (1988) "management-by-stress" critique of the very productive, and often discussed, General Motors–Toyota NUMMI joint-venture auto plant in California claims that this U.S. version of just-in-time assembly production is not really a participative, team approach, but a system of maximum rigidity with highly integrated operations that put stress on employees. All parts of the system are pushed to peak performance in order to identify weak points in need of further design improvement—they appear with dramatic clarity as the entire, tightly integrated line stops immediately. While workers are given a wide variety of tasks and have power to alter work routines in cooperative conferences, they must adhere to these adopted procedures rigidly. This critique highlights an important issue for the demand/control model: while these jobs would appear to be enriched and "active," they are instead reported as stressful. This corresponds to Kern and Schuman's (1984) critique of new job designs where tasks have been packed in, with no opportunity for rest breaks.

The unresolved question is the amount of control really afforded in the U.S. context. Parker and Slaughter claim these jobs represent an even more rigid implementation of Taylorism in which the worker's informal powers via union-enforced seniority—their limited but secure job boundaries, their minor slowdowns, and most important of all, their "buffer stocks"—have now been eliminated. The highly integrated production system has no place at all for the buffer stock which would allow machine-paced workers to work ahead and then relax at their own discretion. In an example taken from another computer-automated auto production facility (Shaiken, Kuhn, and Herzenberg 1983b), a union steward noted: "Now if [the assembly workers] could put something up for a little bank [i.e., buffer], it would be very, very good to those guys . . . they could basically get their time back. A worker added: "At least you'd have something to look forward to . . . there's nothing to look forward to anymore" (p. 42).*

When comprehensive computer-based integration is added to large-scale manufacturing systems, both the advantages and disadvantages are magnified. In the ideal new automated office or factory, all work processes are linked together in an unbroken chain of communication. No information is lost, no information is distorted because of human error, and management has easy access to overviews of the system. Another major advantage of such systems is that they allow the product to be changed to a customer's specifications by simply changing the computer program—customized production made economically feasible. Ideally, such computer-integrated systems could be easily decentralized. Unfortunately, when these new production technologies are simply added into old-fashioned, hierarchically controlled production organizations, the advantages of flexible production can fail to materialize, and a whole host of new stress-related disadvantages can arise. Under the conditions of centralized system control, management's new goals of fast response to customer orders regardless of their timing forces employees to take up the slack in the system, yielding a very uneven work flow and no power to modify their own work procedures. "Respect-for-workers" can easily be overshadowed by reverence for "good data." Pre-formatted machine-based communication processes are likely to be unforgiving—unlike human communications structures—and even minor formatting errors can stop all data from being transmitted. If all production processes are tightly linked together in a chain, one malfunction can stop all others in a domino effect. Systems become so integrated that one can speak of "system failures"; no part of the system is broken, but the system as a whole fails to handle a particularly heavy load.

*The director of manufacturing engineering felt differently about the reduction of buffer inventory: "The pressure we're putting on ourselves for more uptime [is probably] what we should have been doing anyway. . . . The urgency of getting [a breakdown] fixed is done with more speed because of the urgency" (p. 32).

Shaiken, Kuhn, and Herzenberg (1983b) describe the resulting paradoxical combination of the monotony of routine monitoring and the unpredictable, overwhelming demands that occur in such interdependent systems: intense stress when things are not going well and boredom when they are. It is precisely the dilemma predicted by Simone Weil in the 1940s ([1949] 1952):

> The continual possibility of accidents . . . [deprives monotony] . . . of the very remedy it usually carries within itself, namely the power of hushing and lulling the mind to a point where it becomes insensitive to pain. Anxiety thwarts this lulling effect and obliges one to the awareness of monotony, though it is intolerable to be aware of it. Nothing is worse than the mixture of monotony and accident (pp. 52–56).

To operators in customer-driven factories, unpredictable alterations make the system appear to be without plan, because workers have not been given a sufficient mental model of the process. Indeed, no one but a few programmers in the entire factory may have a clear understanding of the operation sequence or why errors occur.

It is not always the lowest-status workers who feel the most pressure in computer automated installations. In the welding repair department in the U.S. auto factory described by Shaiken, Kuhn, and Herzenberg (1983b), the repairmen on the automated fixtures loved their new job's intellectual challenges and breadth. Their supervisors, however, had the full responsibility for keeping the extremely complex assembly line moving, and the costs of delays approached $1,000 per minute. In thirty-three months, nineteen first-line supervisors had changed to different jobs: turnover was running at 150 percent per year. "This has been the hardest three years of my life," one supervisor commented. "There isn't any relaxation. . . . I've walked out of here and sat in my car unable to move getting myself together." Another noted, "[The pressure] takes its toll, on the good people, smart people. No babies. There is no one who [wants to be promoted to supervisor] anymore in this department" (Shaiken, Kuhn, and Herzenberg 1983b, pp. 26, 27).

There are solutions to these problems of computer-aggravated interdependency: one can use the computer's computational capabilities to divide complex processes into parallel, decentralized units. Computer-controlled, flexible, decentralized production systems—operating in parallel, rather than in a single sequential system like the assembly line—can route customer demands for specialized products directly to the production workers in charge, rather than transporting this huge information volume through the organization as a whole (see Agurén and Edgren 1980 for a description). Another alternative is to design computer-based "smart systems" that can adjust to minor malfunctions, or comprehensive overall trouble-shooting functions. All these solutions should augment, not replace, the skilled and motivated operator capable of taking significant decision-making responsibility. But the planners of new computer systems often have as their goal the replacement of these very human capabilities, placing system operators in a passive role which is often error prone.

Another solution is to build into the design of the integrated system the interpersonal and human/machine interfaces that will buffer the mistakes and exceptional conditions that integrated systems inevitably confront. The tight spots and locations of pressure buildups must be accurately predicted and the operators at those points provided with sufficient resources to alleviate the problems, including discretion over temporary modifications of production. Manual overrides to automated systems must be available so that when there is a system problem, well-motivated workers can get production back in operation. Otherwise workers are left idle, unable to solve problems that are well within their actual capabilities: "If the system doesn't work, nothing gets done. We sit there all day and smoke—there is nothing you can do. Everything is at a standstill" (Zuboff 1988).

DATA ABSTRACTION: THE LATEST STAGE IN THE DIVISION OF LABOR

In earlier historical eras, when products were produced for direct barter, the worker received direct feedback on quality from the customer. In later stages of increasing specialization, the direct-production worker successively lost important aspects of control to other professions: first, the customer connection was lost to the entrepreneur; second, the control over tools was lost to the factory owner; and third, the control over work processes was lost to Taylor's new managers. Now two additional separations have occurred in computer-mediated work: the worker in a highly automated process may be disconnected from necessary feedback about the performance of the equipment being used and may also lose control over the format in which he or she communicates. Communication between the worker and the production environment is now structured by the computer's software.

A major recent theme in the literature on what Zuboff (1982) calls "computer-mediated work" involves tasks in which information is highly abstracted from real production-related objects (the widget, the customer). That is, the computer's model of the widget or the person is based on a limited number of rigidly defined parameters in a data base (Gregory 1987). While this clearly structured model has the advantage of being very effectively processed by the computer, it can fail to capture some qualities that make the widget or the person unique and thus create a systematically in-complete model of work activities (Kubicek 1983) and limit both creativity and control over the process.

Computerized mail and filing systems represent data in a much more structured form than it exists in the mind of a secretary going about the tasks of secretarial work, such as writing office memos, sorting piles or files of notes on a subject, organizing personal conferences, and communicating instructions (Adler 1985). Well-structured systems for handling such com-plex data are necessary for development of effective office work proce-dures in an "information society," and progress is being made in developing more "human-structured," natural-language software tools.

The field of artificial intelligence and expert systems development is one in which progress is being made dealing with unstructured data. Progress is being made slowly, however, and there are differences of opinion on the ul-timate effects of such systems (Östberg, Whitaker, and Amick 1988). Expert systems have often been conceived of as devices for extracting knowledge from workers and transferring it, like any other commodity, to the company—a process which met with much resistance from craftsmen at the beginning of the twentieth century. The commodity definition of "knowledge" which fits this approach (Gregory 1987) is illuminating: it re-quires that knowledge be separable from the people who do the "knowing," and that knowledge be subdividable into small elements that can be recombined by predetermined sets of rules (like atoms within molecules). This definition differs dramatically from our New Value conception of knowledge as an element in a skill-building process where growth occurs through synergistic social interaction processes.

Different roles in the organizational hierarchy can lead to very obvious differences in viewpoints about the desirability and accuracy of such highly structured, centrally gathered information. Ultimately these differ-ences are rooted in the distinctions, enforced by Frederick Taylor, between those who plan and those who do. Managers want centrally collected data on systems performance and costs, in order to make future plans for the systems. They like to have the overview of the system's functioning that is available in the computer-based systems, and they like not having to rely on "error-prone workers" for production of status data.

Dealing with aggregated and abstracted production data can also cause costly errors, however. The problem with the abstraction necessary for present computer models is that the resulting data may not accurately de-scribe reality. For example, the computer may provide dollar amounts that are valid measures of financial performance, accurately reflecting the real world of bank balances and stock market quotations. But for "hands-on" workers, the computer may not be as trustworthy in reflecting the "dirty," complex physical world with which they must deal. One group of maintenance workers at a newly automated French chemical refinery refused to believe the readouts of computerized control equipment designed to show what valves were operating correctly. After experiencing several failures of the sensor system, they insisted on making costly trips out to the field to put their ears against the valves, to hear whether fluid was really flowing (Alain Wisner, personal communication, January 1984). The computer control system had been designed by engineers to measure flows at various key valves, allowing a single plant operator to observe a panel light to see if a particular valve was functioning properly. But these workers had already experienced several faulty readings due to computer errors, and for them (as well as for the public) bad data is much worse than no data at all.

Workers deal with objects or people as physical or social entities that are only imprecisely summarized by the rigid data formats of the computer. The problem with data abstraction is that it fails to provide what the worker feels is complete and accurate feedback about the state of his or her world; the result is a feeling of loss of control in that real world. Examples of mistrust of highly abstracted data, in situations where the worker no longer has direct physical connection to the work process, abound. Zuboff (1988) cited workers at an automated paper pulp mill: "[Before], when you put your hands on things," one worker commented, "you knew what you were doing" (p. 152). Mistrust of the computer system's data may also relate to workers' safety: unexplainable occurrences need happen no more than once to foster suspicions that the system's operation is beyond the workers' control. Shaiken, Kuhn, and Herzenberg (1983c) quoted a worker saying of his robot co-worker, "I've seen the thing move and nobody touched the button" (p. 51).

Ehn (1988) has written of new approaches to the design of computer hardware and software that could reduce these problems. Such new technologies can be configured as tools to leverage the further development of existing worker capabilities, as we saw with our skill-based output (New Value) in chapter 5. Ehn describes how conventional systems thinking, in spite of its extraordinary payoffs in terms of effectiveness, usually involves design processes guided by outside experts and hierarchical, rigidly procedural central computing departments that lock users out and are not concerned with enhancing users' skills. As an alternative, Ehn proposes that software be designed by the workers themselves, in a process assisted by experts who are willing to learn about the workers' jobs in detail. Ehn cites a number of examples, including some in which he has participated directly, such as the design of publishing software for typographers in Scan-

dinavia, as well as U.S. examples by Winograd and others at the Xerox Palo
Alto Research Center, the birthplace of many of the software systems that
inspired the development of Apple's Macintosh computer.

Ehn builds these new design approaches on a platform of worker empowerment and upon two philosophical traditions that emerged in the
mid-twentieth century. From the existentialist phenomenologist Martin
Heidegger, Ehn and colleagues draw an understanding of the "everyday-
ness" of work activity which illuminates workers' own practical processes
of building skills through environmental interaction. These concepts help
break down the barrier between the practical work activity and the expert's
design process. From Ludwig Wittgenstein, Ehn and colleagues evolve a
framework for understanding interactions between users and tools and between different groups of users. Language itself embodies socially determined understandings that cannot always be reproduced by computer software structures. Since these socially communicated understandings are the
foundation for our own sense of identity, computer systems have the ability
to alter significantly our conception of ourselves in the eyes of others (what
G. H. Mead [1934] called the "looking glass self"). Here we can glimpse a
set of fundamental impacts of the computer on human interaction that are
beyond the span of our original job characteristic model, or the stress or
skill development processes—a challenge for future research.

The possibilities for such technological design processes are not just
utopian hopes; they are close to the core of precepts that have been most
successful in bringing into the workplace new technologies that really
work. One of the general conclusions of the Swedish Work Environment
Fund's five-year study of the fifty most significant installations of new
technology in Swedish industry (Oscarsson et al. 1988) was that the introduction process is most effective when it is worker driven. As new production demands emerge, the firm creates the infrastructure in which
new technologies can be adopted and provides information about new
production tools, but it is the workers (including those at professional levels) who evolve the new work process that brings in the new technology
and determine its detailed specifications. The employees recognize that
they must have the new technology to get the job done and are motivated
to make it work as effectively as possible. This perspective is not inconsistent with the Japanese Management Association's (1983) description of
the technology implementation of Toyota's "just-in-time/respect-for-
worker" auto production: first, the social organization of the work process
must be made to function effectively and humanely, usually as a result of
joint worker/management consultations, and then the needed hardware
and software can be ordered.

Could such participation directly affect the well-being of the participants, as well as their skills and social relations? Macy, Peterson, and
Norton (1989) undertook a methodologically sophisticated longitudinal
study of a work restructuring process in the nuclear power engineering department at the Tennessee Valley Authority directly involving employees in
the redesign of their work procedures—that is, advocating a new procedure, participating in joint discussions, or actively implementing new
plans, and evaluating the results. In comparison to a control group of similar employees without participation opportunities, the employee who
could affect the decision-making process had significantly improved well-
being—measured in terms of job satisfaction—over the duration of the
change process. This general improvement in well-being occurred in combination with higher reported work efforts and a 20 percent improvement
in quality—hallmarks of an active, highly motivating job setting. These
findings of associations between participation in the process of design and
improved well-being over a two-year follow-up period are, of course, consistent with our findings described in chapter 5 for the health of Swedish
white-collar workers across the full industrial spectrum (Karasek in press).

COMPUTER AUTOMATION AND JOB INSECURITY

A major source of stress with respect to computer-based technologies is
job insecurity; we will be taking it up in greater detail in the last chapter.
Here again the effects of technology differ dramatically for high- and low-
status workers (U.S. Office of Technology Assessment 1984). Clearly, low-
skill jobs are being lost in manufacturing, and the new jobs created by these
new technologies are for the highly educated and the young. Worker concern is justified, given the fact that most computerization programs have as
a goal the reduction of direct labor costs, even when these costs may represent less than 10 percent of manufacturing costs. In most cases, the questions of job loss have to do with company decisions on which workers to retain and retrain and which ones to replace (U.S. Office of Technology
Assessment 1985, 1986, 1987). The issue thus is skills: those required versus those that workers have or can acquire. Companies actually have significant policy latitude in this area, for the division of labor—the allocation of
tasks to workers—can in the long run be affected by management decisions
about technology acquisition, about products to be made, and about career
structures. Long-term planning for technological changes makes it much
more feasible to retrain existing workers. When workers perceive that no
such planning has taken place, they are justified in being anxious about
and resisting the introduction of new technologies.

Conclusion

The clear message is that the computer, like any other tool, may be deployed to leverage substantial job changes that can be either positive or negative. Its effects will depend primarily on social choices. It is disturbing that we do not see more joint social and technical experimentation on these issues. Few social scientists and medical professionals are signing up for technical courses that would allow them to understand the impact of computer systems on the work environment, and the technologists who drive system development seem not to be comfortable incorporating the complexities of social processes into their designs. The technologists' solution to the factory of the future is often the "workerless factory"—a goal that will be of limited benefit for most of us. What about the effect of new technologies when health care itself is the product? The subject is beyond the scope of this book, but it is noteworthy that we can clearly see here both strongly desirable effects, and the opposite. Of course, we have used advanced computer-based technologies in this book's research—for health status monitoring, in statistical analysis, etc. However, we note critics who see the increased technological complexity of health care in countries such as the United States as primarily a reflection of profit motivation, which on balance increases health risks (Illich 1977), and which has been a major contributor to the increased cost of health care. In the positive case we have Ehn's "tool" conception of health care technology of use to both the patient and the health care practitioner. On the other hand, we may have complex monitoring technologies that alienate patients, reduce the possibilities for constructive social interaction between professional and patient, and are the antithesis of our New Value conception of "conducive" aid to the provision of health care.

Our case studies have shown how computer systems can be designed to leverage increased acquisition of skills. Most of our negative examples were found in large organizational structures, where, as Zuboff (1988) has described, the computer is used by insecure managers to maintain and reproduce their familiar hierarchical authority patterns rather than as a lever to increase either productivity or worker well-being. The clearest correlate of the negative, stress-related effects of computer and automation systems is the lack of involvement of employees, both before the design for a new technology is implemented and when decisions are being made about how it is to be operated. Worker input certainly need not diminish the degree to which an optimal technical solution is attained, although engineers and managers often act as though that were the case.

On the contrary, workers have essential information about the actual operation of the system that may never be reflected in the aggregated and structured data bases reviewed by management. This information is vital to productivity. Of course, the employees are the only useful monitors of the health effects of the system, particularly in the sphere of stress-related disorders.

9

Job Design Strategies for Different Occupational Groups

The political/organizational conflicts, market-based issues, and impacts of new technologies that we have examined in the last two chapters result in major differences in the job redesign process from one situation to another, even when the job redesign is viewed from the perspective of worker health. In this chapter, we will try to bring some order to the enormous number of potential differences in situations and strategies by referring back to the occupational structures we first investigated in chapter 2. We will use these structures to define a small number of occupational groups, which in turn can be used to illuminate what we feel are some of the major political conflicts that are likely to occur, both within and between occupations, as job redesign strategies are undertaken. We use only nine groups to differentiate all occupations in the work force, and we examine only five major sources of conflict over job change, but we feel that these at least constitute a more realistic description than past approaches, which had only one best set of principles to design a job—Taylor's and Smith's—and even one best way to undo the job designer's damage.

Although these occupational groups are derived from our analysis of the U.S. national work force in chapter 2, we claim these groups will be relevant to understanding conflicts within the firm as well. In some respects individual firms are microcosms of the society as a whole: they contain both managers and workers, both blue- and white-collar workers, both clerical workers and technicians. Certainly different types of firms have different mixes of occupations—service industries have more service professionals and manufacturing industries have more machine operatives—but most major firms contain a broad range of occupations with fundamentally different conditions of work. Our second point is that the new political perspectives needed to understand our changing industrial world are most likely to be grounded in differences in conditions between different occupational groups. For example, differences in the society's rewards to firm owner/managers and blue-collar workers and in their conditions of work have been the primary themes of political conflict in the modern political world (capitalism and its Marxist critique). As our industries and working situations evolve, constructive political solutions must be built upon an understanding of how emerging occupational groups fare by comparison to others in the change process. Many of the occupational groups we will discuss have been paid little attention by today's politicians, creating a vacuum in political discourse. A greater understanding among politicians of the political implications of psychosocial job conditions will be important in alleviating this problem.

The practical necessity of understanding the circumstances of multiple occupational groups is shown by a brief review of the labor union structures that have recently emerged in the United States and Sweden. In the United States, with the slow shrinkage of organized labor during the 1980s to under 18 percent of the work force, little progress has been made in developing new structures. The organization of white-collar and service workers has proceeded slowly, but within the umbrella of the existing AFL-CIO. In Sweden, however, the evolution of labor market structures has proceeded at a dramatic pace since the late 1960s. Gradually disappearing is the simple labor market structure, in which a strong and centrally organized confederation of labor unions (LO, similar to the AFL-CIO of the 1950s in the United States) negotiated with a strong and equally centrally organized confederation of owners (SAF). Since then, white-collar and service workers have developed their own labor confederation—TCO, the union of salaried employees, and later SACO, the corresponding union for the university educated. These became very strong by the late 1970s and have now subdivided into half a dozen smaller, independent confederations of unions. Administrative and technical workers are most likely to be members of SALF, the union of supervisors, SIF, the union of industry clerks, or SACO; public service workers are likely to be members of ST, the union of state-employed clerks, or of SKTF, the union of community-employed clerks; and private service workers are likely to be members of HTF, the union of workers in privately owned shops. There is also a union of workers employed by communities: SKAF. We think that the present assembly of smaller labor confederations is the natural result of the major differentiation in occupational conditions that we have discussed in this book. A simple division into two classes, owners and workers, does not reflect the present complex occupational reality. Our analysis also provides evidence of the major differences in job circumstances that still remain within unions. For example, Metall, the metal workers union in Sweden, still represents both machine-paced assembly line workers and skilled craftsmen, groups for which we have recommended major differences in job redesign strategies.

Occupational Categories Relevant to Job Redesign Strategies

As we saw in chapter 5, the old organizational structures are tightly linked to the conventional definitions of output value. Bringing about widespread psychosocial change of work environments requires a new measure of production output. To create our set of nine occupational classes, we return to the new definition of productivity developed at the end of chapter 5. We saw there that a type of creative skill or capability development could be used as a new output measure for the organization and thus for society as a whole. This measure, called New Value, is not only an important measure of the organization's development of capabilities but also a reflection of the individual's development of skills, self-esteem, and active behavior pattern. Of course, such new measures of production output do not entirely replace the existing measures of materialistic economic output but supplement them. Our set of occupational categories and job redesign strategies will thus be built on both systems.

We think that the different conditions of work which have contributed to the multiplicity of unions in Sweden (as discussed above) can be graphically illustrated by examining major occupational groups on our plots of psychosocial job characteristics. But which occupational groups shall we discuss? Examination of all 150 occupations used in our linkage research in chapter 4 presents the reader with an impossibly complicated picture (appendix, figures A-1 and A-2). Therefore, we have arrived at the small set of nine major occupational groups, illustrated by the list of 38 selected occupations from chapter 2, using the sociological method of "ideal types." Ideal types are simply descriptive examples selected to illustrate as clearly as possible a set of theoretical relationships, while still accurately representative of the full range of real situations (if not of all the non-conforming details).*

In developing our set of ideal types, the first decision (Karasek 1989b) was to select occupations that could represent the conventional status system's (our A-system) high- and low-status groups (manager/owners, physical laborers), with an intermediate group in traditional economies also included (craftsmen and independent farmers). These occupational types could hardly be overlooked. Second, we wanted to illustrate the same range of "have and have-not" status in our New Value system (the B-system). Professionals clearly had many New Value elements in their jobs and assembly line workers had few, and an intermediate category of administrators and technicians could also be identified. When we matched the categories with the empirical evidence of the plots, however, it was clear that three separate groups would be needed to illustrate low levels of New Value, so several groups of service workers were added. The plots also revealed a set of workers marginal to production processes in general, who were low on both status scales, so a final category was created. The complete set of categories is shown in table 9–1. Obviously, partitionings of occupations other than the one we present here for illustrative purposes would be possible. However, some sense of the empirical validity of the groups can be gained by observing their actual homogeneity in terms of the dispersion of the separate occupations in each group (the small roman numerals represent the occupation's actual job scores) in the three lettered sections of figure 9–1 (and by review of the 100-plus omitted occupations in the appendix). We feel that the plots do indicate some coherence within these nine sets of occupations in terms of our psychosocial conditions of work, which was our goal.

The nine groups are presented below with 38 illustrative occupations which have been empirically located on plots using the U.S. nationally representative QES data from 1969, 1978, and 1977 (for both men and women, $N = 4,495$). These plots represent, from left to right: the conventional social class model, using decision latitude and physical demands

*The 38 occupations were selected to be illustrative of the full range of 150-plus occupations in the U.S. Census 1970 occupation classification system (the 1980 Census categories would not have led to significant differences in occupations selected at this level of aggregation, and there is no more recent U.S. national job characteristic data than that we are using, unfortunately). The selections were made on several criteria: clarity of differentiation on the four psychosocial job dimensions; representation of men and women; representation of strain, active learning, and economic well-being differences; and representation of both traditional and emerging industrial technologies. However, no system that selects only one out of four detailed occupations can be perfectly representative (they actually include 33 percent of the work force). We have probably erred on the side of homogeneity of the categories to clarify our ideal types.

TABLE 9–1
Nine typical occupational groups

1. Managers (IA)	5. Bureaucratized service workers (IIIB1)
Manager (Trade)	Dispatcher
Public official	Deliveryman
Bank officer	Fireman
2. Professionals (IB)	6. Commercialized service workers (IIIB2)
Architect	Sales clerk
Physician	Nurses' aide
Electrical engineer	Waiter
High school teacher	
Natural scientist	7. Routinized workers (IIIB3)
	Assembler, electrical/transport
3. Craftsmen (IIA)	industry
Carpenter	Cutting operative
Farmer	Garment stitcher
Machinist	Billing clerk
Lineman	Keypuncher
Repairman	Telephone operator (future
	low-status information
4. Technicians/administrators (IIB)	operative)
Clerk supervisor	Office computer operator
Nurse	
Foreman	8. Laborers (IIIA)
Programmer	Miner
Health technician	Construction worker
Stationary engineer	Freight handler
(future computerized process	
operator)	9. Marginal workers (IV)
	Janitor
	Watchman
	Gas station attendant
	Temporary worker*

*Not assessable in QES data base

NOTE: Representative occupations are empirically grouped according to data in the U.S. Quality of Employment Surveys for 1969, 1973, and 1977 for both men and women. $N = 4,495$.

SOURCE: Karasek 1989a. Reprinted by permission of Baywood Publishing Co.

(figure 9–1a), then our primary demand/control model (figure 9–1b), and finally the expanded psychosocial model, using decision latitude and social support (figure 9–1c).

The occupations have been ranked roughly in terms of status (levels I, II, III, and IV): the "haves and have-nots" on the conventional and the New Value scales of the rewards to workers in each occupation. These rankings are questionable since we did not empirically measure these rewards; we have only inferred them from the occupational titles themselves (manager

FIGURE 9-1 (a-c)

The occupational distribution of psychosocial job characteristics
(U.S. males and females, N = 4,495)

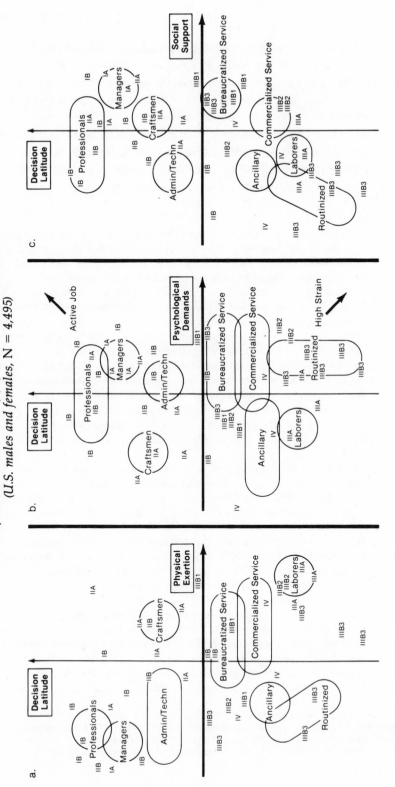

SOURCE: Data from Quality of Employment Surveys 1969, 1972, 1977.

versus assembler). Occupations should actually be ranked in both systems, and occupations that are high in conventional economic status need not necessarily be low in New Value; indeed there is probably a substantial correlation between their rankings.* But the differences are enough to confirm the value of identifying two separate status systems. While managers are high in financial rewards of work, they are not the highest in job characteristics associated with New Value, as can be seen in figure 9–1b. Professionals are the highest here, but professionals' economic rewards (while high) are lower than those of occupations in the manager group.

1. *Managers (IA).* The label "managers" refers here to high-economic-status occupations in charge of production and distribution of conventional economic value, even in the public sector. As representative occupations we have chosen manager (trade), public official, and bank officer.
2. *Professionals (IB).* Here we have selected a set of occupations characterized by high levels of creative opportunity and skill development. Some of these occupations are also high in economic status. These occupations control the flow of knowledge in an "information society," either creating it, managing its use, or controlling its communication. In some ways these professions deal with one "invested" form of New Value: skills transformed into knowledge. High New Value–status occupations include such professionals and sophisticated knowledge workers as architect, physician, electrical engineer, high school teacher, and natural scientist. Clearly, not all white-collar employees fit this description, nor even all professional workers in the conventional U.S. Census classification systems.
3. *Craftsmen (IIA).* These are mid-level occupations in terms of economic rewards, often working with physical objects but always working with relatively high levels of skills and independence: craftsmen and tradesmen. Many of the occupations in this group, although once common, are now threatened with extinction in both the United States and Sweden. We have selected carpenter, farmer, machinist, lineman, and repairman. The fact that these jobs are held mainly by males perhaps reflects their earlier origins and may explain their recently poor employment trends. We will have much to say about their potential for future growth.
4. *Technicians/Administrators (IIB).* These are the mid-level occupations in terms of New Value: mid-level professionals and administrators, mid-level knowledge workers, and technicians. People in these occupations have moderate levels of skill and opportunities for creative development. They have some decision authority, but are never totally in control of their work. This occupational group has grown enormously in recent years, in both the United States and Sweden; it actually contains a preponderance

*We are empirically restricted from utilizing New Value *outputs* as an empirical measure, since little measurement progress in this direction has been made. Of course we have claimed in the previous sections that the *inputs* of psychosocial work experience (below) are relevant for development of illness risk, active learning orientation, and social affiliation at work.

of females (and usually represents a fairly high female career aspiration). In this group we have selected clerk supervisor, nurse, foreman, programmer, health technician, and stationary engineer (future computerized process operator).

5. *Bureaucratized Service Workers (IIIB1).* This is the first of three groups of occupations low in New Value. These are little-discussed nonprofessional service production workers, without direct client contact, who make the wheels of society go around, sight unseen. These workers are often employed in large-scale service bureaucracies, with little freedom to make decisions in spite of their crucial social functions. Their services are delivered by such large-scale organizations (often in the public sector) that the output becomes mass-produced according to fixed rules, and the services become commodity-like. Workers have little chance to receive feedback from customers on their own contributions, and little chance to influence the service in any case. The nature of the service they provide is often implicitly public in that it is available to the society as a whole or serves broad social purposes, although these workers are not always in the public sector, particularly in the United States. For this group we have selected dispatcher, deliveryman, and fireman. The jobs are most commonly held by males.

6. *Commercialized Service Workers (IIIB2).* The second of three occupations low in New Value also provides services, but with more direct personal contact than workers in the above group. This name is also slightly misleading; these workers' jobs are often quite similar when they are employed by the public sector (which is quite common in Sweden). Their services have often been commercialized—that is, turned into routine, mass-produced commodities, privately oriented toward particular customers. Private service workers are beset by a commercial denigration of the service function, because the impersonal marketplace transforms their work into impersonal actions. This characteristic is unfortunate, for jobs such as food delivery and preparation and health care might otherwise bring significant respect and require significant skill and could be high in New Value. The low levels of authority at work plus the commercialization often lead to poor treatment of workers by customers, as well as by higher-status co-workers.

    The job demands on both private and public service workers are often very high, physically and psychologically; they often include the professional obligation to serve effectively in important, even life-threatening situations. It is interesting to note that while males predominate in public service occupations, the private service occupations are largely female dominated. (An analogous sex difference is observable between craftsmen, generally male, and administrative/technical workers, who are more often female.) The private sector occupations have been growing in the economy for decades. For this group we have selected sales clerk, nurse's aide, waiter (and waitress).

7. *Routinized Workers (IIIB3).* This is the third and most commonly referred-to group of occupations low in New Value. They have routinized tasks, often machine-paced on the assembly line, without customer contact. While they have traditionally been assumed to be most common in

mass-production settings, many new white-collar (and "pink-collar" and office automation) jobs have very similar characteristics. The entire value of their labor has been transformed into wages, because few skills are learned. While these occupations themselves have not always grown rapidly, their characteristics seem to be replicated in a growing number of other jobs. To represent these occupations we have chosen assembler in the electrical/transport industry, cutting operative, garment stitcher, billing clerk, keypuncher, telephone operator (future low-status information operative), and office computer operator.

8. *Laborers (IIIA)*. These are the low-status occupations in terms of conventional economic rewards: the physical laborers in physical goods production. Their crucial struggle has classically been to gain their fair share of the production profits (a goal that has probably been better attained through organized labor unions in Sweden than in any other country). Whatever their wages, they remain exposed to the hazards of physical labor. To represent these occupations we have selected miner, construction laborer, and freight handler.

9. *Marginal Workers (IV)*. These are occupations which are ancillary or incidental to the main goods or service production tasks of the firm. They are also usually among the lowest in rewards in both the New Value and in economic compensation. They include temporary workers ("secondary" labor market jobs) who can often be hired and fired at will and who receive very low wages and few benefits, in addition to learning no skills. This is, disturbingly, the fastest-growing occupational category in the U.S. economy. The temporary office or factory worker is the classic occupation here, but it could not be measured in our sample. We have selected janitor, watchman, and gas station attendant.

Before considering the strategies that can be used in job redesign to improve the psychosocial job characteristics of these occupational groups, it will be interesting to note some examples that demonstrate the degree to which job redesign can affect these characteristics. Consider the job situation of production welders, previously closely supervised in a fabricating plant at General Electric, who were reorganized into fairly autonomous teams of twelve welders (*Business Week* 1972). The welders in this redesigned system are given responsibility for scheduling and planning their work loads and can also determine how much time it will take to meet specifications on any items requiring special techniques, a task formerly done by methods-and-standards engineers. The welders, routinized workers who formerly held a position toward the bottom of the decision-latitude axis on the occupational map in figure 9–1b, now have decision authority equal to that of foremen in manufacturing, who are administrative/ technical workers (above the center of figure 9–1b). This shift represents an increase of over one-half of the occupational variance in decision authority in the U.S. work force (1.5 standard deviations). Because these welders now do technical planning of subtasks for custom jobs as well, they have even acquired some of the skill discretion of industrial engineers, who are classed as professional workers. This change represents an increase of almost 2.0 standard deviations in skill discretion, a shift from the bottom quintile to the top quintile of the U.S. work force in this one skill area. Similar increases in decision latitude have probably occurred for the assemblers in the Almex case study described in chapter 7, along with increases in social support that move them from the lower left-hand quadrant of figure 9–1c to the center of that plot. The health care workers in the Swedish nursing home study and the U.S. diabetes clinic have assumed many of the responsibilities of registered nurses and some of the pedagogical responsibilities of teachers. These latter occupations are higher in decision latitude by roughly half of the full U.S. occupational variation on that dimension (1.25 and 1.5 standard deviations higher than nurse's aides, respectively). Of course, these estimates are inferred by us from occupational titles and not directly measured. In spite of their roughness, such estimates still represent useful new information, because almost none of the job change experiments in our literature or case studies have yet used nationally standardized scales to assess interoccupational job change directly, although some recent studies using our nationally standardized scales discussed in the appendix are under way. Nevertheless, these examples make it clear that even the limited job changes already being undertaken are large enough to have a major impact on the national distributions of job characteristics, if they were to be applied on a large scale.

Job Redesign Strategies:
An Interoccupational Perspective

The different occupational groups above have different conditions of work and therefore require different strategies for job redesign. Furthermore, many of the barriers to broadly conceived job redesign—that is, our work reconstruction—involve conflicting claims between occupational groups that must be resolved before progress can be made: claims for economic rewards, claims for New Value benefits, or claims for social standings. In the sections below, we consider five different approaches to job design, some within one of our nine groups, others involving multiple groups.

We begin with the most common theme regarding conflicting job design strategies for different occupational groups. This obviously has to do with the distribution of income. Although the economic rewards of the job—

wages to the laborers and profits to owners and managers—have been specifically omitted in this book's focus on the psychosocial side of work, these issues can hardly be totally overlooked. A feeling by workers that there is fairness and equity in their share of economic rewards has been one essential foundation for every long-term, large-scale experiment toward progress in worker well-being of which we know (Lawler 1986). In both Sweden and Norway, strong unions and equitable wage policies have provided the base of occupational security upon which humane work reorganization and Industrial Democracy projects have taken place. Japan has company-dominated unions but gives much attention to job security, along with respect for workers and allowance for their participation in decisions. It has been in times of relative economic prosperity, in the early 1970s in the United States and in the last two decades in Sweden, that psychosocial advances have moved most rapidly (although such advances did not accompany the high-income prosperity of the 1980s in the United States).

On the other hand, strategies that weaken workers' support networks and unions are likely to lead to conflict and mistrust of management, which would certainly undermine the potential effectiveness of autonomous groups, new customer linkages, or joint-participation structures. Such policies in the hands of some unscrupulous managements have been one recent problem with QWL programs in the United States (see Parker and Slaughter 1988). Since unions have often been the employees' only protection against "give-backs" and other recent wage-cutting tactics, union-busting threats undermine employees' belief in the basic equity of workplace change and ultimately in the QWL program itself. Feelings of insecurity about income can be a significant source of stress in itself (Karasek, Gardell, and Lindell 1987). No institutional structures are perfect, however. Unions that have been most successful in providing their members with ample wages and political efficacy have been among the most resistant to progress in psychosocial job change, as we saw in chapter 7.

Once basic economic equity has been guaranteed, attention must turn to elimination of the physical risks of conventional production technologies that afflict primarily laborers: hazardous machinery, noise, vibration, dust, and exposure to proven toxic and carcinogenic chemicals, such as vinyl chloride monomer and asbestos. The institutional structures that have administered the occupational health and safety laws in both the United States and Sweden were originally dominated by professionals such as physicians, chemists, and industrial engineers, who were trained to detect and combat hazards in such industries and who had academic backgrounds anchored in the quantitative "hard sciences." When psychosocial hazards have been addressed (for routinized workers and occasionally for service workers), different professional support groups and administrative approaches have been involved, as we saw in chapters 5 and 7. A potential linkage that could promote cooperation between these support groups is the focus on the process of hazard elimination (that is, of engineering design in classical occupational safety terms). Increased participation in multiparty decision processes about how to make workplaces safer has been shown to be the most effective strategy in removing physical hazards permanently (Åstrand and Lagerlöf 1980). Occupational hazards, as well as the psychosocial costs and benefits of work, have usually been considered to be outside the realm of cost analysis, and perhaps that is why economists have so studiously overlooked their distribution, and even their existence. We can no longer use the same economically based quantitative framework for the analysis of the remaining conflicting strategies for work reconstruction.

The discrepancy between figures 9–1a and 9–1b provides insight into the specific shortcomings that hinder attempts to understand all occupational conflicts in terms of the conventional economic have/have-not (right/left) analysis. It fails to address the main issues of exploitation for many modern occupations. Figure 9–1a illustrates an "historical" conflict between laborers and owner/managers because it emphasizes the physical demands of work important in earlier industrial eras. The conventionally exploited—the low-status, poorly paid physical laborers in figure 9–1a, lower right—may be partially included in the New Value–exploited— figure 9–1b, lower right. Thus, there are some low-wage physical laborers who have high-strain, socially isolating jobs, and there are some who have passive jobs, low in psychological demands. But the passive jobs are decreasing in the U.S. work force. The three major occupational groups mentioned above—routinized white- and blue-collar jobs, bureaucratized service professionals, and commercialized service professionals—which have grown dramatically since Marx's time, are overlooked in the conventional political conflict depicted in 9–1a. While they often have low wages, they are most clearly deprived in terms of New Value benefits. These New Value–dispossessed constituencies have been overlooked until recently even by labor unions in the United States (most such workers are still unorganized), and no political parties in any Western industrial democracy or socialist country have made their working conditions a political issue in any significant way. These are large occupational groups, and among women they probably represent a majority of workers. Addressing their needs constructively could have significant political implications.

THE NEW CRAFTSMAN'S JOB

As we saw above, three of the nine occupational subgroups have deprivations that are most clearly understood in terms of their lack of New

Value. Routinized workers, with low levels of both control and normal social relationships on the job, are among the clearest losers in the bargain struck to create a mass-consumption industrial society. Machine operatives, assembly workers, and clerical workers doing discrete, repetitive, often machine-related tasks have lost almost all opportunity for creative skill development. These occupations often limit social interactions as well, not only because the use of machines enforces physical separations but because Taylor's theories explicitly discouraging group work have been applied.

The jobs in mass production of goods and mass clerical functions that can be easily Taylorized are probably the jobs most in need of redesign both from the health perspective and from our new productivity perspectives. Unfortunately, redesign may be harder to achieve in these occupations than in any others, because of the mass-market character of the output for many of these jobs, as we saw in chapter 7. In spite of such potential difficulties, however, these occupations are the ones that have most often been the focus of QWL job change efforts, which resulted in enriched and enlarged jobs and autonomous work groups; 40 percent of QWL changes through 1976 were specifically for assembly jobs (Taylor 1976). The most successful strategy for routinized jobs appears to be comprehensive change of the production structure, transforming production for large consumer products such as automobiles and appliances from the traditional assembly line into group assembly operations. These new job redesigns also restore social relations, often in the context of work groups, to these goods-producing occupations.

A New Value perspective can offer further insights for these groups. The job redesign solutions just described have seldom included changes in customer relations involving redesign of the service or product. This has placed an upper limit on the potential for New Value growth in these jobs. New market structures linking consumer and producer in a series of interactive product or service customizations should make further New Value increases possible. Such linkages have been observed even with goods that had previously been mass-produced, such as trucks, as we saw in chapter 7. When customers have been brought into direct contact with workers, they have generated demand for more customized products. Workers' skills then return to skill and responsibility levels characteristic of the craftsmen occupations—a major improvement.

Clearly, in searching for a new general solution to the problem of New Value exploitation we may want to take a new look at craftsmen's jobs. Craftsmen are also involved in the production of physical objects, but the objects are not mass-produced; the output is often adapted to each client.

In this category we find, for example, automobile repairmen, who have tasks that vary for each automobile. These tasks could never be as tightly standardized as the assembly line tasks of routinized workers. The same is even more true of craftsmen such as plumbers and tool and die workers. What could be measured and standardized for these workers? Only if the customer agreed to forgo individually adapted output could these jobs be Taylorized—an impossibility in most cases.

Short-sighted economic pressures, however, ostensibly to improve market competitiveness at the company level, are pushing for the adoption of more Scientific Management for remaining craftsmen's jobs, just as these philosophies were used in the early twentieth century to transform old craft occupations into the disciplined, routinized factory worker. Many skilled craft tasks have already been clumsily forced into the Taylor mold, including construction jobs, repair tasks, and skilled machining (Shaiken 1984). From the perspective of stress-related illness, such changes are in exactly the wrong direction, changing low-risk into high-risk jobs. While short-term measures of economic productivity may increase (as they did for routinized jobs), leaving shortages of skilled craftsmen, long-term productivity of these workers individually, and even more in groups, often declines.

Piore and Sable, in *The Second Industrial Divide* (1984), provide an entirely different view of craftsmen's jobs. They suggest that these jobs represent part of a model for a future pattern of industrial growth, a pattern that is more conducive to the development of worker skills and to flexibility in organizational output. They call this pattern "flexible specialization." In this view, craftsmen's jobs are not historical relics that should "realistically" be treated to Taylor's discipline. With appropriate modifications of organization and market structure, they are highly relevant models for the future. From our perspective, these jobs could produce high levels of New Value and be supportive of new forms of social integration in the community.

Up to this point, the interest in such customized-production jobs has focused on strategies for increasing their economic effectiveness, but they can have significant New Value advantages as well. New technologies are now available, based on easily reprogrammable computerized machinery controls, that allow an operator to set up a job to meet customized client requirements in much less time than it would have taken with conventional equipment such as manually operated lathes, milling machines, and typesetting equipment. Since the new computerized automation is better adapted to producing variety than to mass-production output (indeed, conventional machinery yields lower costs for mass production), flexible specialization can justify an increasing amount of direct contact with the customer. Such a design could increase the demand for, not eliminate, skilled workers. In this perspective, productivity increases are gained in the form of increased product adaptability and quality, not increased quantity of output (which could indeed eliminate labor).

Examples of such high-technology, customized production processes are increasingly common in many locations in the industrialized world and represent important new areas of technological advance, such as custom computer chip production (Roy 1987) in the United States. Examples of successful new manufacturing networks of highly skilled craftsmen in northern Italy (Hatch 1987) and northern Denmark and of customer-directed production in central Sweden (Sandell et al. 1976; Wendeberg 1982; Rehnström 1987) undermine the claim of economic determinacy for mass production and specialization of labor. Some of these companies are examples of the socio-technical design solutions discussed in earlier chapters (Almex and the Finnish truck factory). These examples imply that craftsmen's jobs, if developed in the context of new organizational structure and appropriately combined with new computer-based technologies, might serve as a new general model for the production of "service-like" goods: goods that develop dynamically and interactively in response to customer needs, just as human service must. Because this type of production utilizes employee skill and decision capabilities, this new model could both maintain low risk of illness and yield high productivity. In fact, such skilled groups are often instrumental in the development of their own health and safety programs. The best news is that such production yields a new type of "customer-friendly" output that may be increasingly important in the economies of post-industrial countries.

JOB REDESIGN STRATEGIES FOR THE NEW VALUE-DISADVANTAGED IN THE SERVICES

Two other groups, bureaucratized and commercialized service workers, have jobs where the New Value output that characterizes other service jobs is distorted by production and management policies that are holdovers from old economic-value production policies. As a result, the New Value that might be derived from the direct personal contact with the public is lost. These two groups differ in the degree to which they have direct public contact. Bureaucratized service workers are impersonal service workers such as deliverymen and dispatchers, who have less direct customer contact than commercialized service workers such as waiters and health care aides. Nevertheless, recent accounts in the popular press document the general public's dissatisfaction with the decline of both kinds of services in the United States. For example, an article titled "Pul-eeze Will Somebody Help Me" details the particularly poor record of large-scale producers in such areas as banking, retail sales, and air travel. In contrast to commerce in the small town, where buyers and sellers would anticipate a long-term relationship in the interests of both, "the seller acts as though the customer's gain is his or her loss and not mutually beneficial" (Paul Schervish of Boston College, quoted in Koepp 1987, p. 51). The reason given is that businesses overwork service workers to cut labor costs and keep prices low. This is certainly true, but it is just the manifestation of an even more fundamental reason: services are being turned into commodities, to be packaged and transferred to the customer like barrels of oil or electronic wrist watches, where profit alone motivates the producer. The value of every action is translated into a stranger's dollar evaluation in a classic case of Bentham's Utilitarian assessment of value gone awry. Many nonmaterial aspects of service disappear altogether: humor, empathy, exchange of personal information, social network building, along with the potential for mutual long-term growth.

Such distorted customer relationships are rarely the choice of the service employees. Both groups of workers are often employees of large organizations and have less decision latitude than other service workers with higher professional credentials. Organizations dominated by a concern for cutting short-term costs have started to apply Taylor's job design principles to these relatively powerless lower and mid-level professional workers (in hospitals, for example). Zuboff (1988) noted that as early as 1970 some Taylor-oriented work measurement experts were reporting that 75 percent of their consulting was for clerical jobs. Such developments have led to criticism of "assembly line health care" in Sweden from the perspective of both the service worker and the patient (Gardell and Gustafsson 1979) and health care for profit only in the United States (Hirschorn 1988). It must be admitted that some of these workers, particularly the public service workers, often can do their jobs without much information about the specific client. For example, ambulance drivers operate quite similarly for all patients. But this impersonality is not usually necessary, and may be replaced if the worker is empowered to make some significant decisions about how to serve the customer. Again, the presumed economic necessity of these policies for service industries rests on false arguments, in our view. Human service outputs must be measured differently, as we saw in chapter 5. Moreover, service markets are more often than not local markets, and they cannot support the elaborate specialization of labor that mass production of goods has involved, even according to Adam Smith.

What are the appropriate job design strategies for such lower-level professionals? For both groups, we feel that customer contacts in which specially tailored services are transferred to responsive customers would increase New Value. This strategy reintroduces the personal element of service through the process of direct feedback, which we discussed in chapter 5. And because service workers' skills are often underutilized, even when personnel are overworked, such changes could increase productivity (in a quality sense) and potentially reduce risk of stress-related illness as well. In several cases in chapter 7, we saw that New Value–oriented strategies that provided the patients of health care institutions with skills to take control of their own lives led not only to more active patients (who were also healthier) but also to more satisfied and creatively stimulated workers in the institutions (Arnetz and Theorell 1987; Lazes 1978; Holland et al. 1981). This increase in both customer satisfaction and positive social identity for workers stands in stark contrast to the overbureaucratization and commercialization of the assembly line health care production structures noted earlier.

Collective actions, such as strikes, by bureaucratized service workers (for example, in large transport bureaucracies) can have a major impact on the operation of a complex society. One hypothetical problem of redesigning jobs for this group, discussed in Sweden, is that giving broad-based decision power to the service workers could lead to crippling miscoordinations and work stoppages for the society's infrastructure. How can the people who keep the trains running on time be given wide decision latitude? In reality, this may not be such a problem (Elvander 1982; Svensson 1986a). The example of just such a job redesign solution—for many municipal service workers in Örebro, Sweden—indicates that redesign is practical for many such jobs. The increased decision latitude must be accompanied by a well-coordinated process of decentralization of the service structure as a whole, which not only facilitates multiactor decision making but reduces the dependence of the society on the actions of a single small group of employees. Such a decentralized structure can still be quite effective in service provision, as the Örebro case study shows clearly.

REDISTRIBUTING CREATIVE OPPORTUNITIES BEYOND THE NEW VALUE ELITE

Inequitable distribution can be a problem even if rewards are skill development opportunities, rather than income. As we saw in chapter 5, New Value actually lends itself to development of new forms of non-zero-sum organizational structures, in which a full range of occupations might experience increases in creative opportunities under the appropriate conditions. Within the conventional bureaucratic hierarchy of occupations, however, the creative output of some occupations—for example, medical professionals—seems to come at the expense of other occupations, such as nurse's aides and other health care assistants in group IIIB2. Since, as McGregor reasons in Theory Y (1960), creative potentials are broadly distributed throughout the population and not limited to isolated geniuses, this zero-sum structure leads to a waste of human resources. One source of problems is the very large scale of today's organizations and market structures. In a bureaucratic organization of professional engineers, for example, one senior design architect or engineer is placed in charge of very large-scale architectural or engineering projects, while others working on the project have their creative freedom restricted. Of course, the same scale-related restrictions in creative decision making can be observed when a single large multinational corporation replaces a number of smaller operations: many fewer people are making what they consider to be important decisions, even among managers and professionals.*

The inequitable distribution of creative opportunities and decision-making opportunities can partially be resolved by alternative decision structures within existing institutions, by changing responsibilities between occupational groups. The jobs of the professional and the manager do not need job enrichment, job enlargement, or additional social interaction. Indeed, some of our analyses in chapter 2 showed that our basic demand/control hypotheses may fail to hold for this group, precisely because increasing decision opportunities may increase rather than reduce psychological strain for these occupations, as we saw on p. 50. Skill requirements are already so high that additional requirements to learn skills may become a psychological demand rather than a coping opportunity. For those managers at the very highest levels of the organization, the primary job demand is to make decisions, so additional decision opportunities are not likely to diminish stress. Nor are most managerial and professional workers eager to have more meetings and other social contacts at work; they already spend much time in such meetings and some have social contacts as a main source of job demands.

Clearly, many of these jobs are already so high on our job design scales that the appropriate health intervention might be to diminish their demands by reducing their decision latitude and social interactions rather than increasing them. This strategy would off-load some of the ever-increasing decision responsibilities and qualification requirements of those at the top of public and private bureaucracies to lower-level occupations such as our bureaucratized and commercialized service workers, and even the technicians and administrators. Such a policy could diminish the enor-

*Another form of the problem of restricted decision opportunities due to large-scale market distribution occurs when a single musician's records are sold around the world, displacing many creative local singers, who lose their audience and have less opportunity to sing professionally as a result.

mous disparities in decision-making opportunity between blue-collar and professional workers from both ends of the occupational spectrum, reducing overload decision demands at the top of the hierarchy and increasing decision opportunities and skill utilization at the bottom end. The result might be a health-promoting double attack on psychosocial health risk at work. Some other redistributions, however, may require a different approach, as we will see below and in the next section.

One subgroup of professionals stands out from the others in figure 9-1b (and gives the group its oblong shape): engineers, scientists, architects, and artists involved in creative efforts with high decision latitude but low social support. It is remarkable that more attention has not been paid to effective job design for these "designer" jobs (Nadler 1981). Certainly such jobs could not be designed by Taylor's principles: such conventional job design results in lost productivity for these occupations. Productivity of the organization as a whole would profit by closer integration of these isolated professionals with other occupations, for creative contributions that are truly isolated may ultimately be irrelevant. We believe that the custom-production model involving more interactive contact with clients through product innovations—the strategy that we describe above for craftsmen—may represent an element of the solution, because it will force these professionals into more intimate contact with other occupational groups.

Some of these professionals have developed personal attitudes that limit social engagement (Nadler et al. 1989), so increased social integration is likely to meet with substantial resistance. These workers are reminiscent of Ayn Rand's (1950) description of the isolated genius and often seem unwilling to spend time doing undesirable tasks with lower-status technical/ administrative or routinized personnel. Many of these professionals feel that clerical functions, meetings, and other social interactions also dissipate their energy for more creative duties. A major complaint of engineers is that they are required to do too much clerical work, which diminishes their opportunities to deal with state-of-the-art technologies (Ritti 1971; Guterl 1984).

Such objections would seem to make it difficult to improve the job of the engineer without worsening the clerical job. Often, however, professionals are really suffering from administrative procedures that may have become excessive because of overly rigid and formalized organizational structures. In both the United States and Sweden, with private and public health care systems respectively, physicians are making similar complaints of increased paperwork, restricted freedom to use professional judgment, and arbitrary cost controls imposed by accountants, as they come under the control of ever-larger organizational structures (Arnetz et al. 1988). These complaints of low decision latitude are really related to the overall structure of the work process for professionals: lack of skill utilization; transformation of creative and service-like activities into commodities, just as for lower-status workers; and lack of nonhierarchical communication structures.

MODERATING THE IMPACTS OF NEW TECHNOLOGIES

One of the most important, but least predictable, challenges for job redesigners in the future will be the unequal occupational impacts of new technologies. While production planners and accountants have often found their job capabilities substantially enhanced by data processing technologies, other occupations, usually lower in status, have lost skills, lost jobs, and experienced significantly increased stress, as we described for some computerized manufacturing automation jobs in chapter 8. The occupational groups probably at greatest risk for such undesirable impacts are our administrative and technical workers and our routinized workers, because they are infrequently given decision authority over the selection of new technologies and because information handling and communication are central to their tasks. In the past, office equipment operation, order processing, production planning and expediting, drafting, and process monitoring have involved information processing in a relatively unstructured format. With the advent of computer-based systems, however, workers in these areas are compelled to deal with much more structured data, which substantially affects task structures and often reduces decision latitude, as we saw in chapter 8. The major threat perceived by many of these workers is, of course, that their jobs may disappear altogether, as has already happened for manual type layout and manual data entry. Even the threat of job reductions may weaken the bargaining power of these groups to command more humane job conditions. (In the United States, most such jobs are not unionized; they are unionized in Sweden.)

Management is almost always in control of both the technological resources to design and the capital resources to purchase new technology. As a result, computers have sometimes been used to increase management's leverage in labor/management relationships. A negative example of failure to collaborate appears to have been the U.S. FAA's development of air traffic control software systems, without collaboration between the FAA and the union of air traffic controllers, in part to replace the controllers because of their confrontational stance in labor relations negotiations. In effect, the computer was placed in the role of strikebreaker, as Shaiken discusses (1984). A new computer system that could handle air traffic with a dramatic work-force reduction appears to have been in preparation well before the widely publicized strike and lockout in 1981, without the detailed knowledge of the air traffic controllers; its existence of course weakened their bargaining position. Unfortunately, the computer system was not able to take over the load of air traffic controllers, and this truly nonparticipatory example has been associated with clear declines in the quality of service and safety of airline travel in the United States.

Zuboff's (1988) discussion of technological change documents other ways in which management in eight major U.S. companies uses its power over the design of computer-based technologies to enhance its control over workers. A major difficulty is that if managers use computerized systems to augment their own power and not to maximize the learning and understanding capabilities of workers ("informating," as Zuboff calls it), then a major vacuum of effective functioning in such systems is likely to occur. Managements do not receive sufficient understanding of the production process through their abstracted data, and workers have less motivation to participate in what they consider to be intellectually repressive jobs.

In the future, more democratic dialogues will be needed. The importance of worker participation in these decisions is not only implied by our empirical findings on stress-related illnesses, but a fundamental component of the learning-process model. Such participation is an essential political and ethical component of the Industrial Democracy movements in Western Europe, which are having significant influence in the United States as well. The Utopia project, undertaken to write occupation-oriented software for the Scandinavian typographers' unions, was a very ambitious attempt to give unions a role in designing technology. The software for typesetting under development for the union by 1982 was designed to take advantage of, maintain, and further develop the sophisticated, existing craft skills of workers in the Scandinavian typographers' unions (Ehn 1988; Howard 1985b). We cannot claim that the Utopia project led the way to "desktop publishing," but it was certainly moving in the direction of computer-enhanced craft skills in the early 1980s, before commercial software publishers took up the idea.

The Rigidity of Occupational Boundaries

Sharing the decision-making opportunities of higher-status managers and professionals could provide more New Value in other jobs but, not surprisingly, such changes in occupational prerogatives are often resisted because they involve crossing boundaries created by professional education and training. As we saw in the case of the health care workers in Örebro (chapter 7), some of the higher-status professionals were unwilling to share responsibilities with fully competent lower-level professionals because they had made a larger previous investment in educational training and wanted both economic and career development rewards from that investment. In another example, a group of older bus drivers in Gothenberg resisted an improved overall bus schedule, because their new routes would actually be worse than the ones they had earned by seniority under the old plan (Barklöf 1988).

In such cases, flexibility might be increased if the higher-status group did not fear it would lose, but had only to share prerogatives with others, or if intellectual stimulation increased for all groups as a result of the change.

Resistance to yielding these jealously guarded prerogatives is perhaps the major obstacle to job redesign solutions that dramatically reallocate role responsibilities. But it must be remembered that this hurdle is grounded in social traditions, not optimal current productivity (or health) policies, and therefore is subject to change in the long run. Removing it will mean establishing more broadly defined career boundaries, boundaries that can ultimately be crossed as a reward for professionally meritorious work experience (Svensson 1986b). In some cases, one-time "buy-outs" of professionals with rigid prerogatives—New Value golden parachutes—may be needed to place the organizational structure on a better foundation for the future.

Another occupational boundary problem arises in the redesign of marginal workers' jobs. Many of these positions are held by minority or foreign immigrant workers, victims of discrimination in both the United States and Sweden. Low wages may be the predominant problem for these jobs, because psychological and physical job demands are only moderate, and while there is no decision authority, there is often significant personal freedom on the job (Karasek 1976). Redesigning tasks is probably too limited a strategy for dealing with the problems of these jobs. A task-based solution is to eliminate such undesirable jobs altogether by distributing the tasks, through job rotation, to other occupations. It is in fact the result of many redesigns creating autonomous work groups, in which tasks such as restocking parts, maintenance, and cleanup are shared by all the higher-status production workers. These extra tasks do expand the labor demand for multi-task production workers, which could theoretically be filled by the displaced marginal production workers; but for these often-underprivileged groups, the loss of their jobs, however deficient, would almost always be considered a personal disaster. There must, therefore, be a major societal commitment to community-sponsored training and career development programs if such jobs are absorbed through job enlargement. This is an issue for equal-opportunity legislation or other political policies that can ensure equality of opportunity.

Ultimately, all the solutions above represent a reunification of previously specialized skills, or despecialization. However, there are still strong trends toward specialization, due to increasing market scale, computerization, and the classic argument that specialized workers do better jobs because of their greater depth of skill. But the productivity penalties are probably increasing faster: inability of specialists to coordinate effectively in rigid organizational structures and the inability to formulate solutions to new problems that transcend old occupational boundaries. The implication is that the duties of higher- and lower-status New Value occupations and even of laborers and craftsmen may have to be recombined, at least to some degree, in order to maximize the well-being of each group.

Still, the suggestion of despecialization for the society as a whole seems almost heretical. Isn't it a rejection of what has heretofore been considered an almost unchallengeable basis for social cohesion in a civilized society: the ever-increasing interdependence of roles as a result of ever-increasing market specialization? Of course, we are not suggesting a total rejection of specialization; what we are advocating is a limited return from the current extreme levels of role fragmentation. These make it impossible now to develop consensus among the experts discussed in chapter 1 on a definition of the job stress problem. In fact, there are important examples of despecialization processes now under way, including an increasing emphasis by U.S. organizational development specialists on the need for liaison skills that cross occupational boundaries. Technology is already forcing many of these occupational boundary changes, particularly for clerical and technical jobs; Zuboff (1988) has noted that successful computerization presupposes flexibility and ability of individuals to constantly readjust themselves to new developments and trends. Other pathways to improvement may be found by examining work roles in Japan. There is a striking contrast between the very narrow roles of workers in American companies and the broad roles of those in Japan (Ouchi 1980). The Japanese emphasize lifetime rotation through many roles, nonspecialized career paths, holistic instead of segmented problem analysis and consensus-building among divergent perspectives—in short, all the processes necessary to move from extreme specialization toward greater integration of roles. Few American businessmen would now argue against the success of Japanese management in general; the importance of despecialization is especially evident in the many examples of successful Japanese product development. The hidden costs of extreme role specialization may well have been larger than previously supposed, and they promise to increase substantially in the near future unless alternative strategies are adopted. Ultimately, there can be little progress in reducing the barriers of role specialization without significant change in educational systems, particularly at the level of graduate and professional education at the universities. University faculties, ironically, can be very reluctant to broaden their horizons to communicate outside their disciplines. Students, in turn, are left with few integrative skills to combine their newly acquired specialized capabilities into broadly practical strategies. We will expand our discussion to the broad implications of global specialization in the next chapter.

Industrial Relations Strategies in Transition

New strategies for conflict resolution will be needed to bring the new work redesign solutions to reality. The once-clear differentiation of workers and manager/owners lent itself to a straightforward left-versus-right model for occupational conflict resolution. It involved a set of clearly related political parties and labor relations processes that were legally mandated in both the United States and Sweden. But these existing strategies were developed to resolve the classic conflicts of economic distribution—a power conflict best illustrated by our "historical" map (figure 9–1a). Not only has the clarity of worker/owner role conflict disappeared, as the tendency among labor unions and employers to play their roles in the old class conflict has weakened, but a whole new set of potential conflicts has emerged that has no clear reflection within political parties or within the labor relations law presently in place. While unions have begun to address some of these issues in both the United States and Scandinavia, no new political combination immediately suggests itself that is closely related to existing labor union structures and that might form the basis of a comprehensive new conflict-resolving structure. Neither does the old concept of ownership of the means of production clearly demark power relationships in information and service economies as clearly as it did in a manufacturing economy. Perhaps the analysis of our nine occupational groups could play some role in developing these structures.

Where shall we turn for further insight? The Industrial Democracy movement is an obvious potential source of understanding about what political structures might provide the right context for the job changes involving control in the workplace; it has served precisely that purpose for the last three decades. The Industrial Democracy movement was born in Norway in the early 1960s out of an attempt to broaden the possibilities for participation in company decision making by workers at all levels, and at the behest of Norwegian politicians who saw it as an avenue to both a new dynamism in industrial development and a natural extension of political democracy (Emery and Thorsrud [1964] 1969; Gustavsen and Hunnius

1981). It was the enthusiasm engendered by this broad democratic moral perspective, not just the possibility of improving work's psychological effects, that inspired the early Norwegian projects and the many later developments in the United States and Western Europe we have labeled Quality of Work Life programs, even when the changes were at the small scale of redesigning a single job. Because of the breadth of their political implications, Industrial Democracy programs have developed uniquely in each country in conjunction with the country's labor relations framework and are still enjoying outstanding successes in countries where the labor relations climate is favorable, such as the cooperative labor/management programs for industrial development in Sweden and Australia (Gustavsen 1987). But as national labor relations frameworks are slow to adjust to new industrial realities, Industrial Democracy programs can be caught in those weaknesses. Given this difficulty we shall offer some speculative thoughts about the future development of the Industrial Democracy movement.

If democratic and humane work environments are to exist in the future, the Industrial Democracy movement will have to expand to encompass issues it has not addressed in the past. The Industrial Democracy movement has up to now accepted without question the basic macroeconomic forces that determine the conditions of employment in the labor market, true to its role as a participant in existing labor relations institutions. It has never attempted to replace labor unions, the union/management dialogue, or affect the labor market, choosing instead to deal only "with those issues of task performance that emerge when people have passed through the factory gate or office door" (Fred Emery, personal communication, March 1989). This used to be sufficient—one could improve job structures wholly within the existing context of a country's labor relations system—but it is not sufficient in the present economy. Now the Industrial Democracy movement is left with little to say about the most important new macroeconomic issue that affects job conditions: the global market. And this movement has not been effective in situations where labor unions were weak; it had little effect on the United States in the 1980s or on many countries in the process of industrialization. In the future there will have to be a macro-level expansion of Industrial Democracy's purview to include "humane" economic strategies (the New Value example in chapter 5 is one suggestion) to countervail locally the strength of global economic power. At the same time it will not be possible to develop such new strengths through centralization of existing labor relations institutions: the critique against bureaucratic powers in labor relations are already too strong (for example the Swedish experience of an overbureaucratized "participation" law [Gustavsen 1987]). Instead decentralization, matching decentralization of firms and unions, is needed.

A new link to worker well-being, for example through health issues, will be needed, perhaps along lines suggested by Gustavsen and Hunnius (1981) or along the lines of the conflict issues outlined above. The movement has not yet developed a strong focus on health, although health and environment have become major social issues in both the United States and Western Europe.

Industrial Democracy projects have focused primarily on improving the work situation for blue-collar workers in large manufacturing industries with mass markets. Rather than a one-sided commitment to increase productivity in heavy, export-oriented industries, new strategies for productivity relevant to service industries must be found. Few of these projects have focused on the service workers or the direct worker/customer connections we began to discuss in this chapter. Eric Trist, one of the movement's founding contributors, observed that most of socio-technical demonstration projects were focused on improving the "interfaces between the nonhuman and the human system" relevant to the production of goods, but were little adapted to organizations where human interfaces were the product, as in the service industries (1981, p. 12). The new linkages to the customer, relevant in both goods and service production, could be developed on the Industrial Democracy movement's existing base of labor/management dialogues. If the call for democracy is not, by itself, enough to bring about working life change, then new links between the worker and the customer may be needed as the basis for a new economy.

Conclusion

We will not be able to overlook another set of job-related political issues, social stability in the economy as a whole. A book on job stress cannot totally overlook the issue of job insecurity, whether the source of that insecurity is the community economy, the national economy, or the world economy. We have devoted no attention to this issue so far because the problem of job insecurity rarely seems to be resolved by redesign of the job, the work group, or often even the organization as a whole. It is at the level of the marketplace, and thus the level of the economy as a whole, that the job design principles of Adam Smith and Frederick Taylor manifest this effect as a concomitant to labor specialization. The possible solutions are therefore also of a very broad political and economic nature. Job insecurity, a major source of instability and worry to workers in many countries of the world economy—not the least to workers in the United States—will be discussed in the next and final chapter.

10

Jobs of the Future and the Global Economy

Although this book has been broad in scope, many readers will be justifiably concerned about the important issues that we have omitted. We have said little about the relationship between job stress and family responsibilities. We have also said little about the community economy and stress; about cures for stress that are targeted on the individual; about job insecurity and stress; about changes in the competitive position of countries in the new global marketplace and their impact on economic security and the pressures of work life.

There is much to say in these areas. For example, in the United States, two quite conventional, nonpsychosocial problems could have contributed to increased feelings of job-related stress over the last decade: working hours have increased—from 40.6 hours per week in 1973 to 48.8 hours per week in 1988, according to a recent Harris Poll (Hechinger 1987)—and real income has dropped. Incomes for American families with children dropped 7 percent in real terms between 1973 and 1985, in spite of the large increase in two-income families (Danziger and Gottschalk 1987). In the lower two-fifths of the U.S. income distribution, real income dropped 25 percent (Sweden has not experienced such changes). In short, we have excluded many areas that both laymen and experts relate to stress and have instead concentrated almost exclusively on the micro-level, psychosocial world of work and its impacts.

Actually, many of these issues can be connected to broad underlying themes relating to the organization of economic structures that we discussed in chapter 1. A brief examination of some of these linkages can put our suggested solutions in a broader context. The problem with linkages, of course, is that when all the above factors are connected, they could implicate the whole gestalt of Western industrialization as the cause of stress-related illness. When such a large problem is defined, no practical solutions may appear to be feasible. We cannot turn back the clock to an earlier economic structure, and if everything must be changed, it may appear that, realistically, nothing can be changed. But we feel more optimistic: we think our discussions are identifying several themes that are central levers for change—regardless of the magnitude of the transformation—and with implications broad enough to affect multiple facets of modern life.

The Macro-Level Costs of Modern Production Organization

Our starting point is the division of labor in society, the specialization in work tasks that leads to reduced decision latitude and the market relationship between buyer and seller which is used to reap its benefits. It may seem that we have merely chosen the easiest issue for our explanation of stress and learning phenomena: the micro-level social relations in the typical industrial work task. However, this is the same starting point that Adam Smith chose for his *Wealth of Nations* in 1776, the book that probably more than any other drew up the blueprint for modern global, free-market capitalism. Adam Smith so firmly believed in the central importance of the division of labor that he constructed his logical discourse precisely upon this cornerstone: the title of the first chapter of his book was "On the Division of Labor." Indeed, Smith was not alone in his assessment of the importance of this issue. The founder of modern sociology, Émile Durkheim, as early as the late nineteenth century attributed the basic cohesion of industrial society to the "organic solidarity" that occurred when each specialized production worker had a role complementary to that of fellow production workers ([1893] 1964). Thus, we feel that in our book we are addressing a full range of issues relevant to modern industrialization, using the same central concept its creators used. And while Smith touted the clear advantages of his approach for increasing productivity, even in 1776 he could clearly see the possibility of undesirable side effects; toward the end of the *Wealth of Nations* he observed:

> In the progress of the division of labor... the great body of people comes to be confined to a very few simple operations, frequently to one or two. But the understandings of the greater part of men are necessarily formed by their ordinary employments. The man's whole life is spent in performing a few simple operations... [and he] naturally loses, therefore, the habit [of solving problems] and generally becomes as stupid and ignorant as it is possible for a human creature to become. The torpor of his mind renders him not only inca-

pable . . . of rational conversation . . . generous, noble or tender sentiment. . . .
[or judgments about] the great and extensive interests of his country . . . [but]
equally incapable of defending his country in war. . . . But in every improved
and civilized society this is the state into which the laboring poor, that is the
great body of the people, must necessarily fall, *unless government takes some
pains to prevent it* [emphasis added] (Volume 2, Book V, p. 302).

Industrialization and Heart Disease

A number of researchers have reviewed macro-level problems related to
Smith's description of the economic system as a whole. In general, we believe that the implications of many of these studies are not inconsistent
with the more micro-level analysis in this book. Several epidemiological
studies of cardiovascular illness across communities have tested the effects
of different levels of Western industrialization and urban development.
One of the first such studies examined the transition of the small, healthy
town (1,500 population) of Roseto in northwestern Pennsylvania. During
the 1950s and 1960s a local doctor noted very few new cases of myocardial
infarction of 40- to 50-year-olds (our stress-risk age) over the course of sev-
enteen years. The stable, ethnically coherent, tradition-supporting community was hypothesized to be evidence of a protective social climate that reduced the risk of heart disease. This hypothesis was supported as Roseto
changed character over the following decades to match the mobile,
tradition-disrupted and competitive free-market environment of its surrounding region. As predicted, its heart disease rate went up correspondingly (Bruhn and Wolf 1979).

Various aspects of the socially fragmented, culturally weakened, and
competitive character of Western industrial society have been described by
Marmot and Syme (1976), Sterling and Eyer (1981), Haynes, Feinleib, and
Kannel (1980), and Henry and Cassel (1969) in relation to mortality and
morbidity. Marmot and Syme studied Japanese-Americans in different
stages of acculturation to Western values and social structures in northern
California. They found that the more Westernized the communities were in
terms of broken traditions and consequently the more disrupted and
conflict-ridden the social networks, the higher the prevalence of heart disease. Waldron (1979), in a cross-cultural study covering over a dozen societies, showed that the rise of blood pressure with age was greater in societies
that had greater involvement with a monetary economy, more economic
competition, more contact with people of different cultures, and more un-
fulfilled aspirations.

JOB INSECURITY IN THE MARKET ECONOMY

A second set of macro-level social costs associated with modern economic Western systems is job insecurity. We have postponed this topic until now because its explanation involves a different aspect of Smith's model—market linkages—which have a broader social character and imply a different set of solutions. As we recall from chapter 1, the beneficial effects of Adam Smith's division of labor could be reaped only through broad-based free-market trade in goods and, symmetrically, free-market trade in labor. One major disadvantage of this labor trade is that any worker can be replaced at any time in the name of economic efficiency, for a price. This is certainly a much less stable basis for determining a person's major social role than was found in primitive societies or precapitalist production (in craft guilds, for example). What are the effects of job insecurity on stress-related illness? It might be supposed that the effects would be slight, that having nothing to do might be preferable to some of the jobs we have described, or that the variety of a job change might be salubrious. In fact, there is little support for such suppositions in the research on job insecurity. One of the most memorable case studies of mass community unemployment (Jahoda, Lazarsfeld, and Zeisel 1971) describes life in an industrial working-class town in Austria during the mid-1930s. Unemployment related to the Great Depression in this rather isolated community led first to a diminution of expectations and activity, then to a disrupted and extended sense of time, and finally to a steady decline into apathy for the community as a whole. Illness increased, except for families with children below the age of 6.

Data from the nationally representative Swedish Level of Living Studies in 1968 (Johansson 1971) revealed similar findings: inadequate participation in adult life's most important spheres—"unemployment" in both work and family life—is associated with increased use of tranquilizers and sleeping pills, and psychological strain symptoms (see table 10–1). The 6 percent of the men in the age group 35–59 who did not have full-time employment had much higher symptom rates than other men in the same age group. This was particularly true of the men in this group who did not have children. On almost every indicator, the low-employment men without children had triple the incidence of psychological problems as the societal average. If we compare the men of low employment and those with normal employment, both without children at home, the difference is even more striking: the prevalence of psychological problems is 5 to 1. It seems that it is not the burdens of work and family that are associated with the highest

TABLE 10-1

Unemployment and family life in relation to mental strain symptoms in Sweden

Percent of Total Population With Symptoms		Men Age 35-49				Women Age 35-49			
		Low Employment		High Employment		Low Employment		High Employment	
		No Children	With Children	No Children	With Children	No Children	With Children	No Children	With Children
		%	%	%	%	%	%	%	%
1) Use of Tranquilizers	10.9	36.7	15.8	5.8	5.2	21.0	14.3	10.3	10.0
2) Use of Sleeping Pills	6.5	22.7	10.3	2.7	3.1	7.0	3.5	5.9	5.8
3) Nervousness, Anxiety, Worry	23.4	60.5	47.1	15.1	9.1	43.6	28.3	25.5	11.6
Number of subjects	5,852	29	18	263	430	155	388	144	52

SOURCE: Karasek R.A.: Unpublished analyses of Level of Living Survey (Levnadsnivåundersökningen), Institute for Social Research, University of Stockholm, Stockholm, 1975. The data base is discussed in Johansson 1971. The analysis excludes the institutionalized population.

levels of psychological distress but lack of them. Some of the subgroups are small, however, and it is always very difficult to draw causal interpretations from cross-sectional data of this kind (the study covered only the nonhospitalized population, but ill subjects can be an important component of our low-employment groups). Still, we can see that there is a very strong association between unemployment in life's most important social roles—work and family—and strain symptoms. These observations about the psychological need for meaningful social role participation should give food for thought to technologists whose view of a future utopia is a world of totally automated production, without labor, where people are "free for higher pursuits."

Unemployment may have dramatic effects not only on those who become unemployed but also on those who remain working. Brenner (1987) has observed that rising unemployment is usually followed by increased cardiovascular mortality, often with a time lag of three years. A Swedish group has recently made a similar study (Starrin et al. 1988), finding that the association between unemployment and mortality occurred within one year. Dramatic effects of unemployment on mental health (Starrin et al. 1988), cortisol levels (Brenner and Levi 1988), and immune function (Arnetz et al. 1987) have been observed. The effects are probably particularly damaging for young unemployed people, who may develop problems of excessive alcohol consumption as well as psychosomatic symptoms normally found only in middle-aged people (Hammarstrom, Janlert, and Theorell 1988).

A common argument against improvements in the psychosocial work environment is that they will be so expensive that they will necessitate laying off employees. The adverse job conditions discussed in this book, however, partly derive from the same causes as unemployment, as we shall see in the next section. Harvey Brenner (1987) has discussed the relationship between unemployment and mortality. He believes that it is instability rather than unemployment that causes high mortality. A company that goes through a lean period, with few orders, will have to lay off many employees. Because of the unstable market, the same company may soon face a boom period, forcing the few remaining employees to work extremely hard, but in the face of uncertainty (Kerckhoff and Back 1968). The threat of becoming unemployed may cause psychiatric problems by itself (Brenner and Levi 1988). We might add that increasing unemployment may also mean that the remaining employees become competitors: who will be fired next? In the end, of course, all these phenomena contribute to a broad-based, decreasing sense of control.

THE EFFECTS OF THE GLOBAL MARKETPLACE

It is commonly accepted that the economies of the world are rapidly being linked into an integrated global market. Adam Smith's hypothesis about market scale offers an illuminating perspective from which to speculate on the consequences of this integration. In his theory, the extent to which the specialization of labor would be economically profitable was limited only by the extent of the market: a small market implied little division of labor, while a global market implied profitability for an almost unlimited specialization of labor (and thus negligible decision latitude). With a global market, a large producer could achieve economies of scale and undercut the competition from other countries. One huge factory might produce all the videocassette recorders for the world, with each of its many employees engaged in a very minute aspect of that product's manufacture. This example is extreme, but often one reads in financial news comments to the effect that the world will soon only be able to support ten to fifteen producers of a major product, such as computer chips (Dobrzynski 1988).

Smith's prediction that division of labor would increase productivity for mass-distributed goods appears, at least in the long run and at the most general levels, to have been supported beyond anyone's wildest hopes. Although public and humanitarian goods are consistently underproduced, and although many formerly stable indigenous economies are now unstable, the internationalization of trade has minimized regional shortages and increased the range of products available to many people. Indeed, there is actually now a severe world overcapacity of production in many major industries: ships, steel, automobiles, petrochemicals, home electronics, and textiles, according to the *Wall Street Journal* (1987).

But global interdependence and production overcapacity are leading to a new set of job insecurities for workers around the world as the workers of one country compete for jobs with those of another country. This modern form of economic warfare inflicts subtle psychosocial wounds. Smith's market transactions were most efficient at allocating resources when they were impersonal (money-based), as frequent as possible, and based on simple price and quantity information—almost the antithesis of the new product design communication processes we discussed in connection with New Value in chapter 5. The possibilities for just such market transactions have grown steadily over the last century, but with the advent of computer-based international market transactions systems this activity has exploded (Miller and Winkler 1988). Now the instantaneous communication of price and quantity information around the world by rapidly expanding computer and satellite technologies means that the customer—or the competitor—is only a phone call or a keystroke away (Keller 1988).

Ironically, the eighteenth-century Utilitarian theory of market-measurable value for all human welfare that underlies these transactions (Bentham 1789) was initially designed as an individually-based social-choice alternative to monarchical institutions; now it has fostered a new tyranny of the international market. The almost unlimited competition may contribute to the lowered feeling of job security right down to the task level, for everyone from stockbroker to corporate manager to manufacturing worker. We could imagine comments of the following sort: "Now I have to compete with all these low-paid people in Malaysia, and with some guy in Germany. Some smart guy in Venezuela may eradicate my business by simply touching a button on his computer." This macro-level competition represents an extremely abstract force for most of the participants that is very different from normal biological competition and can create a profound feeling of insecurity—and equally strong feelings of powerlessness—at all levels of operation.

This market information is also making possible the continuing growth of company mergers and acquisition, and what is being bought and sold—and often broken up in a matter of months—are decades-old company employment structures (Lawrence 1986). The psychosocial costs of such wholesale disruptions of job and management structures are the subject of many journalistic reports; for example, Noble (1988) reported that after Texas Air's takeover of Eastern Airlines, psychological strain symptoms among pilots increased from 21 percent to 44 percent in one year, compared with a change of 8 percent to 14 percent in the rest of the industry. Yet the human costs of these changes still do not appear on the balance sheets of the decision makers in these processes.

The fact that trade markets are now computerized in the international arena makes it possible for market fluctuation in one country to be amplified into economic instabilities that disturb the normal exchange of goods and services with another country, actually undermining the point of the international trade system in the first place. The interdependence of markets and the apparently destabilizing effects of rapid transactions (which have facilitated the growth of transaction-based speculation) were claimed by many experts to have exacerbated the market instabilities that led to the stock market crash of October 19, 1987 (Peterson 1987). Such speculative monetary transactions take on a life of their own. While the value of world trade in goods and services was $4 trillion in 1987, the volume of transactions in foreign currencies was $65 trillion. That means that every dollar of trade in material goods inspired, directly or indirectly, $16 in speculative transactions (Hiltzik 1987). These sources of instability plus the technologically augmented levels of interdependence have led authorities to feel that without social and political interventions, stock or money markets could get out of control (Sanger 1987). For companies regarded as takeover targets, future employment stability is increasingly dependent on such marketplace conditions. It would not be surprising if these recent developments in the international economy were contributing to general feelings of increased personal powerlessness by many employees, in all occupational groups, in working environments all over the world.

The logic that justifies the aggregation of economic units and the search for increased markets has traditionally been the reasoning, derived from Smith, that large-scale producers enjoy operating economies; we hope we have clearly restricted this argument. But now we believe that new nationalistically based rationales may be dominating. The belief that the countries with the biggest companies have the strongest warriors in global economic competition may justify collaborative policies by government and private industry to favor industrial aggregation, in spite of the fact that workers, the economic foot soldiers in every country, have much to lose in terms of psychosocial well-being from such policies.

Specific evidence to support the existence of some of these associations comes from recent research testing Adam Smith's widely believed (but rarely empirically tested) thesis about market scale and increased specialization (decreased decision latitude) for workers (Karasek and Sioukas 1990). Our U.S. QES national survey data on decision latitude, described in chapter 2, was linked via detailed industry code to U.S. Department of Commerce data for manufacturing industries on firm scale, value added per firm, and concentration ratio (the degree to which trade in the industry is monopolized by the top four firms in the country). Just as we predicted, the larger the scale of the market (really the relative size of the firm in the industry), the lower the average worker latitude to make decisions, especially in concentrated industries. In a broad defense of the beneficial political implications of capitalism, Milton Friedman in *Capitalism and Freedom* (1962) discussed the "inevitable" freedom associated with free trade in open markets. To the extent that the social relations affected by our economic structures are market relations between small businessmen, outside the firm, Friedman's claims have a foundation. But he has clearly omitted the areas of freedom that we discuss inside the workplace. Here we see that increased scale of markets, accompanied by increased dominance of large-scale firms, is associated with restricted freedom during the working day for the vast majority of workers.

A second test using the same data base showed that increased scale of operation was also associated with increased job insecurity at the detailed industry level (Karasek and Sioukas 1990). We further anticipated that increased scale would be associated with increased psychological stress, but that was not the case, except for selected groups of women. Instead, the more general pattern was that job demands decreased with increasing scale at the industry level, especially for workers directly engaged in the industry's central production tasks; a big company seems to involve less hard work than a smaller one. This finding is confirmed by cross-company survey data which find lower levels of worker engagement and satisfaction in larger companies (Hartman and Pearlstein 1987). Together with increased insecurity, this finding left psychological strain levels rather constant across market scale.

The disturbing news for world economies, of course, is that this combination of low demands and low decision latitude is associated with passivity in workers, on the job and off, as we saw in chapter 2. Passive workers do not innovate, nor do they engage in the active leisure-time pursuits that consume the goods and services of others. Have we gotten more material productivity at the cost of pushing workers to become socially and economically inert, just as Smith speculated two hundred years ago? Such passivity probably represents a greater potential danger to future societies than even the stress problems, for it implies long-term insufficient economic demand as well as reduced participatory democracy. The global economy may be not only sociobiologically dangerous but economically unstable and politically undemocratic.

The primary conflict between the current thrust of economic development and the approaches advocated by this book should now be clear. The shape of our industrial future may be formed in the choices between two directions of development. On the one hand, we have the global market and its pressures for applying Adam Smith's model of division of labor on a world scale. On the other, we have the major benefits to be gained in future productivity and health through alternative models of management and economic organization. Our arguments against the former direction and for the latter can now be formulated in more comprehensive terms.

While the conventional economic structures have certainly been productive in terms of mass-produced material goods, lifting portions of the world's populations into great material affluence, they have created two major problems. First, production overcapacity has resulted in job insecurity for many workers in the industrial world. Too much productivity has led to the problem of too little secure work in economies that are increasingly oriented toward export production instead of to local commerce. The zero-sum nature of this mass-produced output has lent itself to major inequalities of reward, leaving many workers and countries in extreme poverty to support the overall affluence. And many goods that are socially useful and could be produced but have less potential for generating market profits are hardly produced at all, as Cooley and others (see Wainwright and Elliott 1982) have clearly demonstrated in England. The second major problem with Smith's model is, of course, our book's primary theme of reduced worker decision latitude and decreased social support, leading to stress and reduced intellectual stimulation and growth. Smith's principles of work organization now seem to be a liability for the very reasons that were previously considered to be their strengths: they can reduce productivity and skill utilization—a weak position for any theory.

Furthermore, the psychophysiological costs of Smith's model may be even harder to pay than we have already indicated. Perhaps human beings are simply not physiologically adapted to the stresses produced by the new socioeconomic institutions that we have evolved so quickly—quickly, that is, from the time perspective of evolutionary change of human physiology. We may be genetically and cerebrally "hard-wired" to perform best in a different set of social structures. We still have roughly the same physiological response mechanisms as our hunter-gatherer ancestors, and therefore the ungraspable aspects of modern work create a biologically very abnormal situation. For animals, demands are always associated with unescapable biological needs and social affiliation; an animal tries to meet demands only when others with whom it has a close social affiliation are being threatened or when biological needs are to be fulfilled. In the present working world, goals are obscure and abstract for many workers, and social affiliation is generally considered unimportant, indeed has been officially discouraged in the work environment. These biologically unnatural approaches certainly contribute to an increasingly common feeling of being stressed. Similarly, we have lost the patterns of learning by apprenticeship in socially reinforcing group situations that supported our hunter-gatherer ancestors. Now, as for many Swedish workers discussed in chapter 2, the workplace is the primary teaching forum, but what kind of forum, when social relations are competitive rather than socially reinforcing?

Our basic conclusion is the gut feeling—which no feasible research could easily verify—that continued unfettered industrial development of the type we have criticized in this book, leveraged by the rapidly escalating change to a global economy, is inconsistent with a healthy future for the human race. Too many of the problems we have discussed in this book will become too extreme for too many people.

If present industrialization is increasingly unhealthy, a return to the past is unthinkable. We would like to hear many more debates about a broad range of new, comprehensive models for economic development, models that augment the health and capabilities of our populations and at the same time preserve the physical health of the planet. A crucial question is what new calculus of human well-being or what political decision-making structures could be developed to balance the psychosocial advantages of more decentralized, smaller-scale production against the obvious appeals—and less obvious costs—of large-scale enterprise and global economic integration. How could one argue for limiting specialization of roles, and mobility for people and capital? Yet some such limitations would seem to be inescapable. What would new social systems look like? Karasek's New Value definition might represent the beginnings of one such alternative, but requires elaboration that is beyond our present focus. On a more limited scale, numerous pragmatic examples of alternative patterns of work organization have already become a major focus of even U.S. management planning, although they still lack the power of intellectual generality that Smith's original forms possessed. In the sections that follow, we take the next step by reviewing the desirable and undesirable jobs implied by our psychosocial perspective and briefly extrapolating these to a few glimpses of the socioeconomic structures that may be consistent with them.

Worker-Friendly Jobs in the Future Psychosocial Work Environment

In spite of our dire predictions, the major thrust of the second half of this book has been the positive message that alternative, humane work environments are entirely feasible and indeed already exist in many locations. Before we try to summarize these directions, however, it is worth commenting further on what we think the solutions will *not* look like. We do not believe that future work environments should be modeled on the existing pattern of a single country—not, at least, the United States or Sweden. The U.S. model of management served as a glittering example of successful work organization for several decades after the Second World War, and yet we have criticized strongly what we feel are psychosocially inhumane job conditions that currently prevail in this country. Sweden, on the other hand, has been a source of many good examples, a major supporter of the research we have undertaken, and in a short period of time has become one of the most materially successful economies in the world. While we recognize that Sweden has succeeded in reducing many of the unnecessary anxieties of modern working life, however, our feeling (also not supported by research) is that Sweden has not yet discovered the key to facilitating the new types of creative engagement in work environments that the New Value model describes, although Sweden is perhaps the country closest to tackling such challenges. The problem may have to do with the large scale of economic enterprise. Both the United States and Sweden are dominated by relatively large-scale economic institutions in both the public and private sectors (notwithstanding Sweden's small population).

Another place we would not look for solutions is in the easy-to-quantify, Utilitarian measures of classical economics and the hard, classical physical sciences. Of course, the United States and even Sweden (Sundbom 1971) continue to have many jobs that are both good and bad because of clearly quantifiable deficiencies, such as low wages and hazardous physical conditions (and both low-wage and hazardous-exposure jobs are an increasing problem in the United States). Nevertheless, since the early twentieth century, the major trend has been a decline in the numbers of workers with bad jobs of this type and an increasing importance of the psychosocial issues we have identified above for six of our nine occupational groups: professionals, craftsmen, administrators and technicians, routinized workers, bureauratized service workers, and commercialized service workers.

Table 10–2 summarizes the features that in our view will characterize the bad jobs and the good jobs of the future.

Consider the difficulty of applying hard-science measurement criteria—dollars, physical environment, physiological threats—to distinguish between the good and bad job situations. The bad job in the future industrialized world, although it pays well and has decent physical working conditions, is still a horror of modern debilitation: no opportunity to learn, computer monitoring, boredom interspersed with crises, unexpected layoffs, no rights, social isolation, interworker competition, and loss of contact with the real world of customers, data, touch, conviviality. The good jobs are good because they offer the potential for human development: learning, user-friendly tools, responsibility, negotiable demands, stimulating challenges, co-workers as teachers, pride of accomplishment in creative achievement, customers whose growth restimulates the worker's. We cannot transform the bad jobs into good jobs by increasing wages, decreasing working hours, or removing physical hazards. The criteria that distinguish between the good and the bad jobs transcend our old, neoclassical economic or physical-science-based models of the workplace and will require a new science of work design based on psychosocial criteria.

While there have always been bad jobs and good jobs, their nature has changed dramatically in the twentieth century. Our conceptual understanding of work has lagged behind our practical examples. In the remainder of this section, we will revisit some of the positive examples of work design to help suggest where these new models for the work environment are to come from. As we pointed out in chapter 4, the beneficial effects on mortality of healthy work can be even more substantial than the ill effects of a bad job.

HUMANE JOBS FOR AIR TRAFFIC CONTROLLERS

We may begin by noting that many of the psychosocial problems in modern work environments can be eliminated through application of simple common sense, based on respect for workers rather than ideologically based subjugation of workers to managerial authority. To illustrate, we can find a remarkable variety of good and bad psychosocial work environments even within the modern working world of air traffic controllers. To most Americans, reducing stress in the air traffic controller's job must seem almost hopeless; productivity has presumably already been pushed to the breaking point. During the mid-1970s, disturbing reports describing the work situation of the air traffic controllers in North America were published, showing high prevalence of diabetes and hypertension (Rose, Hurst, and Jenkins 1978). These reports came out at a time when air traffic controllers were complaining about supervisory policies and unmanageable work loads and were used as one of the arguments for job improvements. The ironic result of this protracted and hostile dialogue between the air traffic controllers and the FAA was a strike action in 1981 in association with contract negotiation and then a lockout (Shaiken 1984). Over half of the civil traffic controllers were then fired. Since that time, the system has been operating with the remaining controllers, supervisors, and new recruits but is still below required strength, and there is no effective union. At times, national complaint sessions have been organized, only to be canceled, and tension continues to grow among the present controllers in the United States.*

By comparison, the jobs of the Swedish air traffic controllers, using similar (or newer) technology, with the same safety requirements, and handling the same airplanes, sounds like a job design from another planet. Recently the well-being of civil air traffic controllers in Stockholm (the fourth largest airport in Europe) was studied by means of instruments to measure emotional states, repeated blood pressure measurements during working hours and during leisure time, and blood analyses of carbohydrate metabolism and serum lipids (Theorell et al., Arbetsmiljö, levnadsvanor, 1987). The results indicated that the air traffic controllers did not have high blood pressure (it was among the lowest of the diverse occupations studied) either during working hours or during leisure time. Nor was there any evidence of

---

*Personal communication by the staff of the Committee on Public Works and Transportation. Hearings on FAA HR-98-83, 98th Congress, March 27, 1984.

TABLE 10–2
The new bad and good jobs: beyond the material rewards of work

New Bad Jobs	New Good Jobs
1. Decision Latitude: Skill Discretion	
Nothing is being learned, nothing is known of the product's destination. There is no hint of future development on the job. New technologies are difficult to understand, and knowledge is limited by secrecy requirements.	The job offers possibilities to make the maximum use of one's skill and provides further opportunities to increase skills on the job. New technologies are created to be effective tools in the workers' hands, extending their powers of production.
2. Decision Latitude: Autonomy	
The worker's minutest actions are prescribed and monitored by machine or by supervisors. There is no freedom to independently perform even the most basic tasks. New technologies restrict workers to rigid, unmodifiable information formats.	There is freedom from rigid worker-as-child factory discipline. Machine interfaces allow workers to assume control. Workers have influence over selection of work routines and work colleagues and can participate in long-term planning. It may be possible to work at home during flexible hours.
3. Psychological Demands	
There are long periods under intense time pressures, with the threat of unemployment at the end. Or there are long periods of boredom, but with the constant threat of crisis requiring huge efforts. There is great disorganization of work processes, with no resources to facilitate order.	The job has routine demands mixed with a liberal element of new learning challenges, in a predictable manner. The magnitude of demands is mediated by interpersonal decision making between parties of relatively equal status.

4. **Social Relations**

Workers are socially isolated from their colleagues. Random switching of positions prevents development of lasting relationships. Competition sets worker against worker.

Social contacts are encouraged as a basis for new learning and are augmented by new telecommunications technologies that allow contact when isolation was previously a necessity. New contacts multiply the possibilities for self-realization through collaboration.

5. **Social Rights**

The implied level of trust in the worker is nil. Management is a remote "Big Brother," the worker a second-class citizen with no rights or true responsibilities.

There are democratic procedures in the workplace. A bill of rights protects workers from arbitrary authority. Workers are represented by a grievance council or union, which reviews common worker problems periodically.

6. **Meaningfulness: Customer/Social Feedback**

There is no feeling of social value to the job: the worker either has no understanding about what customers might really need or is doing something that lowers personal pride (producing poor-quality goods, misleading customers, producing war materials in peacetime).

Workers gain direct feedback from customers, because they can complete enough of a product or service that the customer can evaluate their contribution. The power of new production technologies, placed in workers' hands, enables customers and workers to work together, customizing the product to meet customers' needs and providing new challenges to workers.

7. **Family/Work Interface**

Work roles are separated from community and family roles. Unrestrained job competition, for both men and women, forces family disintegration. Sex-role conflicts worsen.

Work-load sharing between sexes promotes sharing of family responsibilities and allows more energy for family activities.

impaired carbohydrate metabolism, which would indicate early stages of diabetes. Significantly less "rush" and "irritation" were reported than in any other group studied. When the participating air traffic controllers were asked to explain these results themselves, most of them said, "Our job is so dangerous that the work environment has to be organized in such a way that we are not exposed to situations in which we become irritated; an angry or anxious traffic controller is dangerous" (oral statement made during group feedback, Arlanda airport, Stockholm, June 1987). Another interesting theme in their descriptions had to do with ways of sharing excessive loads. Each individual air traffic controller has to know the limits of his or her own capacity to handle several simultaneous flights and also must recognize when the demands exceed this capacity. Colleagues must be prepared to take over without protesting (the introduction of women controllers facilitated this requirement). This overall result can be obtained only after proper education (at a civilian training institute, as opposed to U.S. military-based training) and when a supportive, trusting atmosphere has been created. The employer, the Swedish government, has also realized the importance of maintaining a sufficient number of air traffic controllers to create flexibility in crisis situations. The present U.S. trend in air traffic controlling is toward increased computerized monitoring of the controllers themselves and drug testing. U.S. air traffic controllers live in fear of computer-monitored "near-miss events"; the third error and you're out forever, and the computer *does* make mistakes (personal communication, see p. 315n). There is no evidence that the Swedish air traffic controllers are less diligent or cause more aircraft collisions. There is at present no computerized monitoring of their performance.

There are several possible explanations of the differences in the findings of the U.S. and Swedish studies. The physiological studies were done about ten years apart, and there have been important international changes in the practice of traffic control in that time. Ten years ago in Sweden, the pilots were in command of all the important decisions; today the air traffic controllers enjoy shared command. There may also be differences in recruitment procedures (the Swedish civilian as opposed to the U.S. military focus), education, employment procedures, and the way in which regular health check-ups are conducted. We have no comparative national data that would explain the U.S./Swedish health differences scientifically. The Swedish air traffic controllers themselves believe that the creation of a flexible, safe environment is the most crucial factor. If this is true, we are comparing two different solutions, both of which provide good air traffic security. The U.S. solution, however, takes place at the expense of the health of the air traffic controllers, while there is no such cost in the Swedish example. The financial cost of Sweden's employing a "sufficient" number of air traffic controllers could be higher (we have no data), but the future total expenses for impaired health in the American controllers may ultimately extend to disastrous safety implications in the United States; there have already been huge costs in terms of flight delays. This concern is clearly reflected in U.S. journalistic coverage and congressional investigations.

The Swedish example looks effortless and self-evident. Actually, their psychosocial work environment had been the focus of major design changes. This example of the air traffic controllers shows that job design for health and productivity does not require development of new theories but simply the application of common sense, without the ideological intention to subordinate the worker. The primary elements of the Swedish redesign were a little respect for the dignity and responsibility of technicians, a willingness to permit the controllers' assumption of collective responsibility for traffic coordination (handing off planes), and humane staffing patterns that avoided unrealistic psychological burdens. Some of our examples below, however, required more elaborate changes in the conventional model of work organization outlined in chapter 1.

CREATIVE JOBS FOR HIGH-TECHNOLOGY CRAFTSMEN IN A MANUFACTURING NETWORK

The air traffic controller could be considered representative of administrative and technical workers, one of our six remaining occupational groups. Two other groups, craftsmen and routinized workers, can be illustrated to examine the "inevitability" of large-scale enterprise and undiluted global competition.

In chapter 9, we noted that the traditional, autonomously functioning craftsman in the small-scale enterprise may not be a relic of the past but may, with appropriate supporting changes, be a model for future manufacturing activity (Hatch 1987; Piore and Sable 1984). Flexible, computer-based technologies allow more rapid set-up, even of custom-designed parts, eliminating a major previous cost of customer-adapted production. New social organizational models involving networks of small-scale producers organized in a community of mutual interest, in which cooperation coexists with competitive spirit, have been successful models of industrial development in several countries, such as in the northern Italian example discussed below. Ultimately, we believe that the new craftsman's job involves another element, one that has not often entered into the descriptions of this new job prototype: the active, as opposed to the passive, customer, the smart customer who is willing to accept the challenge of learning how to formulate needs and communicate them efficiently to the craftsman. These jobs occur in goods production, but they represent a dramatic contrast to the dismal descriptions of life for the routinized worker on the old-style automobile assembly line (Kornhauser 1965; Walker and Guest 1952). These new craftsmen's jobs involve increased intellectual stimulation, limits on psychological demands through personal relationships, and social interactions based on pride of accomplishment by the worker and stimulating new possibilities for the customer. All these are characteristics of effective New Value production and are also consistent with the model of psychosocial health promotion that we have outlined.

In the Emilia-Romagna region of northern Italy there are 90,000 manufacturing firms in an area with a population of 4 million (Hatch 1987). The vast majority of these firms have been founded during the last two decades and are owned by former factory workers. These small firms (one firm for every five workers in the city of Modena) network themselves together to get business that would be beyond their capabilities in isolation. While they compete intensely among themselves to develop the most innovative products, cooperation allows them to succeed in the world marketplace in technologically complex areas such as textile equipment and robotic manufacturing installations. Small firms jointly fund a trade association which in turn provides each of them with administrative and market information services. Public/private partnerships in the region provide advanced technical support in several industrial sectors. Small cities such as Modena have provided low-cost industrial space to 500 small businesses employing 7,000 workers. In this network model, firms alternate partners, and quickly learn that delivering each other conducive products and being each other's "smart" customers leads to strengthening of the network as a whole.

The workers in these very small, tightly interlocked new manufacturing companies are often highly skilled to begin with, but they are also constantly using new technologies and solving new customer problems that further stimulate their skill development. The high motivation of these workers, their mechanical skills, their sense of pride in craftsmanship, and their entrepreneurial sophistication have been described by a variety of researchers (Hatch 1987; Piore and Sable 1984). The Emilia-Romagna region had the strongest economic performance of any region of Italy between 1970 and 1987, moving from an average wage rate of 90 percent of the national average to 125 percent of the national average and moving into second place from seventeenth in regional per capita income.*

A more precise analysis of these work situations is beyond the scope of this book, but it is clear that these managerial principles differ dramatically

*Richard Hatch, personal communication, June 1987, Aalborg, Denmark, Conference Lecture.

from those proposed by Smith and Taylor. Advantages come from small-, not large-scale enterprise; from skills that are broadly based, not narrowly restricted; from workers who plan their own work instead of relying on management to do all; and from workers who may establish direct communication with customers directly (and often ultimately go into business for themselves) instead of allowing a distant management to corner all knowledge of customers' needs. Instead of focusing on economic profits alone, workers and managers together strive for a combination of economic success and collective well-being. It is a modern antithesis of Henry Ford's automobile factory at River Rouge in Detroit in the 1920s, but it is an economically successful model for the 1990s. This combination of emphasis on the collective well-being of the network of producers and competition on the basis of innovation instead of cost cutting has also been a vital element of the current success of Japanese industry (Dore 1983; Piore and Sable 1984). As yet we have little research on the psychosocial health of workers in such settings, but if their reported levels of intellectual stimulation are any indication, they have some very important components of a healthy work environment.

The New/Old Health Service Worker with Reestablished Client Interactions

Finally, we will review jobs in the service sector, where the bulk of employment in the future is likely to come from, as it has in the last several decades. In the area of health care, the principles of service-like goods production such as we have described for the new craftsman may ironically be needed to rescue the service industries themselves from increasing use of old mass-production–like models to reorganize health care. Following the principles of Adam Smith's model, the modern solution to efficient hospital care reached its peak in the early 1980s in both the United States and Sweden: the larger in scale the hospital complex, the more specialized the functions, and therefore the more efficiently the consumer's needs could be met. Typically, the specialization of labor reached its highest levels with the professional workers—physicians with many extra years of training beyond medical school. Specialized physicians were aggregated into specialized treatment wards, where in combination with some of the most expensive new medical technologies, state-of-the-art care was administered and research undertaken. Extreme specialization of roles also developed at very low status levels, for bureaucratized service workers, in ancillary services such as ward cleanup and moving beds between wards.

One example, Huddinge Hospital, in a suburb south of Stockholm, is well known in Sweden because of its enormous size and because it became the subject of a novel critical of large-scale impersonal medical care (Jersild 1978). Impersonality is apparent as soon as one enters the five-block-long Huddinge Hospital. Upon walking in the door, the patient must engage in an intimidating act of self-diagnosis. Before seeing any human being, the patient is required to stand in front of a huge wall filled from floor to ceiling with a daunting array of "take-a-ticket" machines and select the specific disease he or she wishes to be treated for. The patient is then placed on a list (of totally unknown length) to await treatment by one of over fifty different departments, each relating to a different illness. One's impression, upon visiting the hospital, is that if you are not already a good doctor yourself you are soon likely to enter an administrative-technical-bureaucratic maze that could make anyone sick. This Kafkaesque hospital entrance is certainly no place for any of the many patients that Dr. Hans Selye, the pioneer of modern stress research, referred to when he said that most of his patients had symptoms of general malaise not clearly connected to a specific organ problem. Whatever malaise the patient entered with, it is likely only to be increased by this hospital interface. Illich's (1977) critique of such large-scale, impersonal hospital systems as creating illness ("iatrogenic illness") comes to mind.

But think how much money this approach saves the hospital: the ticket-number system means that the doctor, like the modern bank teller, is unlikely ever to have a wasted (that is, spare) moment due to logistical failures in shuttling patients among sections of the huge institution. It is health care by an efficient assembly line of experts. In addition, hundreds of generalist physicians are relieved of routine diagnostic activities and "hand-holding" and instead can be engaged in development of cutting-edge treatment techniques for very specifically defined problems.

Of course, personal care implies an element of hand-holding by its very nature. Such social support is one of the care elements that has gotten lost in the mission statement for Huddinge Hospital. Not all these personal care encounters would have to be seen as scientifically trivial: they are an important learning experience for patients in gaining information on managing their own health problems (this is a learning process that develops over a number of visits with the same doctor). Nor would such interactions be seen as trivial for the new kinds of physicians we discussed in chapter 6, to whom understanding the patterns of disequilibrium between several physiological systems is an important medical question and teaching patients how to analyze and treat their stress-related problems (from work or elsewhere) is the most important skill to be developed. Of course, many wards in the big Huddinge Hospital do provide a warm, humane environment for many patients—we are not saying that good care is impossible in a big hospital—but the large scale and the philosophy behind it create difficulties in providing humane warmth.

Ironically, the personal, comprehensive care that we advocate was more likely to have been given in the smaller, more old-fashioned hospitals that Huddinge was supposed to replace. For example, Serafimer Lasarettet, a much smaller and older hospital in the center of the city, had a management policy that encouraged broad interactions between patients and doctors and among the doctors and other professionals. This participatory context was manifest in a broad sharing of responsibilities between doctors and nurses in intensive care units, for example, where this hospital was one of the first in the world to allow qualified nurses to give patients certain types of injections and to run defibrillating equipment without direct doctor supervision. In the opinion of one of the authors who did his residency there, the hospital's role as a teaching hospital was much facilitated by this cross-disciplinary exchange and the close contacts with patients.

More current positive examples of jobs that promote health and productivity for new public and private service workers were presented in chapter 5 in the descriptions of the Martland Clinic in New Jersey and the Enskededalen Clinic in Stockholm. In each of these small health care units, the staff was reorganized to treat the patient as an equal partner in the process of creating a joint patient/institution care strategy. It involved an active customer who was willing to learn how to manage his or her own diabetes or to organize his or her own activity in the elderly care center (but with assistance, not alone and intimidated, as at Huddinge). Lower-level staff members were not locked into limited bureaucratic routines but had the major responsibility of teaching smart, intellectually aggressive patients who actively wanted to know what they could do to improve their condition. These workers had to facilitate a broad range of activities in patients with unknown needs. This approach may have been feasible only within small-scale nonbureaucratic units, where close communication could mediate unrealistic demands and summon uncatalogued resources. These were new job demands, to be sure, but the challenges made these medical workers feel alive and purposeful. Such healthy feelings arise out of active experiences shared with patients whose best interests are also to confront a similar set of challenges and mastery opportunities in the process of becoming healthier and more capable.

The models we have described are more relevant for chronic illnesses than for acute, life-threatening situations, but such treatment represents an increasingly large portion of medical care and is the absolute core of preventive medicine and thus should be of rapidly increasing importance in the future. It is noteworthy that since the mid-1980s, guidelines for the future of care in both countries have illustrated a change away from large-scale care strategies. In the United States, some new trends involve smaller-scale clinics associated with private health care plans, and many neighborhood-scale health clinics are opening (although these have no direct public funding and therefore are hard to use by many of the low-income people who have been the clients of the large, but often defended, public hospitals). Sweden has also emphasized the need to reverse these large-scale trends and to decentralize care provision, but evidence from ongoing studies, for example, Bejeroth (1989), suggests that the old hierarchical behavior patterns described by Gardell and Gustafsson (1979) are so far being altered only superficially. It may be a long time before the changes are completely realized. But at least a new set of patterns has been established. These new kinds of roles follow a different set of intellectual models from those Adam Smith provided, but we believe they are consistent with the psychosocially humanistic goals we have presented in this book and even with the brief guidelines we provided for New Value productivity in chapter 5. They are also consistent with the many suggestions for decentralized, smaller-scale, and flexible organizational structures of the many contemporary management theorists cited in earlier chapters.

Conclusion: Future Choice and Political Challenge in a Time of Transition

In this book we have tried to create a link, via our research findings on health, between new work design practice and a large body of medical and social science research. We have suggested one set of conceptual models that could serve as a platform for joint action for otherwise diverse professionals without compromising scientific validity. We also hope to bridge the gap between those who wield technical and administrative expertise and the workers, managers, and medical professionals who are having to deal with the problems our present industrial structures have helped to create. So far the models have substantial empirical support, piece by piece, but as an integrated strategy they need further validation. More investigation of pathways for practical implementation is also needed, and hopefully would encourage debate about alternative approaches toward combining the issues we address. In the sections below, however, we will assume that we are correct so far and go on to engage in some pure speculation about the broader consequences that follow from our thinking.

The changes in organizational structure suggested in chapters 7 and 8 may be sufficient to ensure the survival of good jobs. But perhaps there are macro-level social factors—embedded in and even logical extrapolations of the social settings that created the new air traffic controller, the new crafts-man, and the new hospital worker—that could magnify the beneficial ef-fects of these settings. Could we find social contexts for good jobs favorable enough to yield new forms of social harmony? What, for example, is the genesis of the jobs described in chapter 4 that had no strain or heart disease symptoms, consistently deviating from the industrial dilemma?

Let us imagine an economy based on an alternative social organization of work. We are looking for a social framework that, while maintaining mate-rial well-being, can provide active jobs for all: jobs where decision possibil-ities match responsibilities and everyone can elevate his or her skill to the level of an art, whatever the job. Such a society will not be overrun with clinics and hospitals, since some freedom from illness has presumably been attained (the challenge is to keep it that way). New Value economic behav-ior, based on producing the kinds of goods and services that develop skills in the user as well as in the producer, should move us in the right direction, supplementing conventional free-market transactions with competitive and cooperative behavior between individuals who may often know each other. In manufacturing, this combination might look like the decentralized networks of small producers discussed above: the flexible specialization of Emilia-Romagna. And for service industries? Consider the mutual respect accorded the pilots and air traffic controllers in Sweden. Respect for each other comes from knowing that the others are skilled professionals who gain their own feeling of self-respect from doing the job well. Could there not be a whole society of mutually respected service professionals, all doing their jobs well and all feeling good about it? It must be possible to de-velop such an economic equilibrium, because it benefits both the producer and the consumer. Who else is there?

In a society where human rather than physical resources were the pri-mary inputs to the production process, workers would no longer be forced to trade environmental harmony for job security in industries whose profit is calculated on the number of tons of natural resources transformed each day into market commodities. In a world where material possessions were justified primarily as tools for living, it might be easier to rationalize sane output levels for industrial production systems, which otherwise threaten to turn our most fundamental tool—the earth, with its green forests and blue skies and waters—against us.

In such a world, physical possessions such as homes, cars, and baby carriages are acquired as tools for living, not as symbols of material well-being. As tools, they are modified, added to, and embellished to suit the growing needs of their users, as we discussed in chapter 5, and discarded only when they can no longer support new growth. Computer software conceived in this manner is a tool for building the user's skills, instead of a regulating device through which the worker is owned and allocated like any other piece of capital equipment.

To support our society of good jobs, we might have to levy economic penalties against "stupidifying" products—products that through their use reduce skills instead of enhancing them, or products whose mindless, stressful, or physically debilitating production process amounts to an overall net loss of value rather than a value-adding process. These levies could be used to provide economic support for New Value industries: industries that make smart products with the labor of smart workers, for the smart customers who are needed to propel the economy along at an energetic pace.

We would need a society that invests in education and protects this investment by making certain that the jobs of its citizens are an extension of the classroom instead of the antithesis of it, the problem that now befalls many low-status workers, as we saw in chapter 2. It would be a society of active users, whose activity builds the culture. It would be a society safe for artists. This society might find much mass-produced culture uninteresting because it diminishes people's own capabilities and dilutes their local sense of identity rather than expanding them. In the case of music, for example, people might find that the greatest satisfaction comes to listeners who can also sing—a society where everyone becomes a singer.

Such a world would have communities in which stability is enhanced by the secure identities of people who know clearly what they can do well and whom they can do it for. Imagine communities where adult role models teach children to demonstrate their productivity by stimulating the growth of mutual capabilities, not by finishing the game with the most marbles. Imagine a society where the most stimulating social challenge is the mastery of the arts of competitive cooperation among institutions as well as individuals, a world where an air traffic controller and a pilot sharing control is the rule, not an exception. In such a world, the relation-building skills learned at work would strengthen family life.

If our hypotheses in chapter 3 are correct, the freedom from constant levels of high strain would make possible new levels of learning, not only at the individual level but at the organizational level. The learning organization so much discussed in the current management literature would become a reality. Imagine a community where scientists attempt to understand and master the complexities of interacting systems, to maintain a balance between equilibrium and the growth that is required to build a new layer of civilized behavior that we are only beginning to recognize as possible.

A fundamental premise of this society is that behavior among individuals is cooperative as well as competitive. In this society, private rewards are built on a platform of public institutions that are willingly supported, as has been the case in many of the Swedish examples we have reported. An understanding of how society has contributed to one's own well-being stimulates one to contribute to the society in return, to support the possibility of growth for all. The good jobs we have discussed, if our analyses in chapter 2 are correct, imply increasing participation in democratic institutions. Democratic experiences at work enhance participation in the community, building a society of active citizens, where communications are free and information is openly distributed.

The cooperative conflict-resolving skills imparted in the good jobs will make it more likely that difficult transitions and disputes can be handled successfully and will engender a feeling of confidence that issues will most likely be resolved fairly. A society that is seen to treat each of its members fairly does not engender extremes of violence or antisocial behavior. While conflicts would hardly disappear, the new social channels should reduce isolated individual terrors and foster a responsible citizenry, participatory leaders with the high social support and high decision latitude we discussed in chapter 2. Social stability and predictability could follow as consequences. Finally, although we have no evidence that such a social context would produce our ideal jobs, the constant monitoring of well-being at work, as discussed in chapter 6, could secure the base platform of health that makes feasible the enlightened functioning we have described here.

Speculations II: The Social Contexts of Bad Jobs

Or will other societal-level changes, such as the global division of labor, make bad jobs more likely and magnify their effects? Suppose instead of the small-scale, mixed-market relations discussed above we had a society of vast markets, huge firms, and minutely specified tasks? What kind of society is consistent with the high-strain, routinized jobs of the data entry clerk picking 18,000 keystrokes hour after hour on a meaningless blur of documents, or the autoworker wrestling with a set of misprogrammed, hydra-headed robotic welding machines, syncopated with the unyielding pace of the line? What larger social context is consistent with the commercialized and bureaucratized workers, who for so many reasons "Can't do that for you," workers who must constantly face the urge to transform their aggressions against a powerful management—which they cannot challenge—into surly barbs at powerless customers?

Could unrestricted, free-market global competition confirm the validity of Thomas Hobbes's seventeenth-century contention that life is really a controlled form of war, "All against all"? Could the societal stimulators of bad jobs be a global array of corporations with vast resources and no nationalistic dependencies, with capital installations that float from port to port securing the best exchange rate and the most accommodating labor force? These companies would turn out mass-produced commodities on a vast scale and employ laborers in whom no New Value would accumulate. Workers' low job-decision latitude and social isolation would be matched by powerlessness and fragmentation at the societal level. These huge conglomerates might contest economic turf like feudal lords with swords of instantaneous credit and debit, with power to wipe out the security of entitlements grounded in a generation of social agreement, all because of a new computation of break-up value in a merger battle. What might the workers think as they watched in awe the fateful outcome of unpredicted fights between multinational Titans, battles that might cost them their jobs?

What about social support? If social support at work were replaced by deciding whom one should know on the basis of cost-benefit computations, the worker collectivities described by Lysgaard and others in chapter 2 would be powerless. In a world where market behavior reigned supreme, even the family might mimic the production system and become no more than a unit for acquiring material possessions. Emphasis on the contract aspect of the marriage would weaken emotional and social ties. Emphasis on the custody of everything from children to kitchen tables would dilute the importance of trust, and all social relations would be reduced to cost-benefit calculations that could just as well be performed among strangers. The institution supposed to last until "death do us part" could be transformed into something like a real estate transaction, where social bonds depend on the market outlook. Readers who think we have finally gone too far might note that just such theoretical models have already long since been published in leading economic journals (Becker 1972).

For children raised in families where material possessions are everything, there would be two possible outcomes. For those who had little, hopelessness would be deeper, because they would have nothing to value. For those who had much, and had learned the skills of acquisition but not the skills of use, each new possession would soon be discarded for the next, in one endless, empty search for something new and pure in a land depleted of its natural beauty and inundated with half-used debris.

If there were no limits to the validity of market-based definitions of value, we would find not only huge inequalities of possession and control but vast inequalities of New Value knowledge as well. Luminous technopolises might stand amid cultural wastelands populated by a new second-class citizenry, poorly educated and doubly impoverished consumers valued only for their ability to buy ever-increasing amounts of ever-cheaper non-conducive products. Such second-class citizens would be limited to passive consumption that stimulated them to no new challenges. Their bad jobs would never encourage their skills but would turn over again and again, leading to no career.

Such uneducated multitudes, without a sense of social identity rooted in clear pride in their abilities, with no trust in the legitimacy of the society and no willingness to contribute to it, could be unruly and unpredictable. What kinds of militaristic population controls might these malcontented populations justify? Could they be the new computer-based Panopticon Prisons we saw arising in some centralized bureaucracies in chapter 8? The information system that would be needed to track offenses against the commercial state would certainly exceed the credit ratings, health liability records, tax records, police files, and national security files that are already monitored in our present society. In this version of the "1984" scenario, the single totalitarian people's state might be replaced by multiple corporate monoliths. For many, it would make little difference who fashioned the monitoring systems that never touched their bodies but maimed their psyches, violating the integrity of what had come to be understood as personal boundaries.

In a world where wealth is just a windfall transaction away, there might be little tranquillity. Winners could not stop, and losers could not even take food, health care, or shelter for granted. What would it be like to be in this world of constant threat of disruption, never able to relax? If our hypotheses from chapter 3 are correct, the lack of opportunity for true relaxation means that the system is never in a state of equilibrium. There would be no energy available for the creative synthesis; no comprehensive plans could be made; no lasting agreements to carry them out could be forged. The Disruption Police could continue to pursue the disrupters, but with ever more exhaustion and futility; order and future purpose might seem to lose ground to chaos.

We saw in chapter 2 that it is in high-strain populations that drugs are most commonly used, to assuage anxiety and induce some synthetic form of relaxation. But in a drugged society (whether by prescription or illegally), respite is never more than temporary; larger doses are always needed, and the side effects of reduced capacity to perform are almost unavoidable. A short-term cost-benefit focus for health care would lead to an endless set of symptom palliatives but little prevention, and thus the true health costs, along with psychiatric illness, suicide, accidents, and stress-related chronic disease, would continue to rise. The stress of life in such environments might also lead to aggressive violence when no satisfaction could be found. But the consequences would not be limited to sick individuals; the society itself would be sick, because it would not have the health to organize its growth. Material productivity might remain high, but the lack of health would be profound.

To conclude, our speculative extrapolations show that the contrasts between the bad-job and good-job societies could be much starker than the contrasts between their task structures. Of course, in reality we would not find such clear extremes but rather combinations of problems with specific causal factors harder to discern. And while the speculations above are, we hope, at least consistent with the material we have introduced so far, it would obviously take another book—or several—to discuss them satisfactorily and investigate their interconnections. One claim, however, is likely to go unchallenged: the context for good jobs is a society where healthy work means not just freedom from illness but a platform for growth. It may not be a society where all jobs are ideal, but at least it would be a society of creative and socially engaging work, where the family and community context would extend and integrate the implications of jobs designed on a new set of psychosocial principles. The second conclusion is that while there are strong arguments for psychosocial change, the totally unrestricted global market, with its expanded division of labor, its rigid, antidemocratic organizational structures, and its mass-produced products, is a major threat to making these changes. We stand at a fork in the road.

How Shall We Make the Choice?

We are in a time of transition between old models and new realities. How far have we come? While many decades of useful practice in alternative work design have been accumulated, the movements to address psychosocial factors associated with productivity and health are still young in the historical terms that measure industrial change. There is clearly an intellectual gap at present, and even opinions about where we stand are in a state of change. On the one hand, some will say that the new world of work has already been here for at least one decade—perhaps two. Indeed, we may be criticized by some management and work design professionals for attacking paper tigers: old models of economic and industrial organization that no longer represent modern practice, even in the United States auto industry. On the other hand, we definitely do not hear that opinion from workers, particularly in the United States, for whom our suggestions of work reorganization are more likely to be regarded as visionary. Many U.S. union members are certainly less hopeful now than they were a decade ago. They see old hierarchies unchanged, and there is evidence to support their perceptions (Lawler, Ledford, and Mohrman 1989). The old models live on in spite of changed practice because they form the ideology of our political debates and the educational curricula at our universities. Moreover, as we saw earlier in this chapter, these old models are actually thriving on the vibrant new realities of a global marketplace and of market-model information technologies. And in a complex world where uncertainty itself breeds anxiety, these models survive because no other equally comprehensive models have been advanced as alternatives. Our conceptual understandings and ideologies of work have lagged far behind our new practical examples.

We think we can see the outlines of a new coalition of forces that would make possible the changes we discuss on a large scale, affecting many companies in a number of countries. The rapid pace of innovations in industrial structure and the pace of research in social and medical science are placing us on the verge of some major changes in the new science of work design. Couldn't a new program of comprehensive work reconstruction derive the support, and wield the impact, that Taylor's did at the beginning of the twentieth century? We can consider two halves of such a new bargain that could mobilize the magnitude of support needed. Suppose, first, as we did in chapter 5, that job redesign solutions can be found that reduce job stress and also lead to increased worker skills. The losses that might be recovered from health promotion alone could be substantial both for the worker and for the firm. These costs are becoming major portions of company budgets. New linkages between previously separated professionals could yield cadres of facilitators for such redesigns.

Suppose further, now that we have sketched our image of a good job (actually, a good job in a world of material plenty), that the worker's skill development in good jobs is accompanied by an enhanced organizational potential for flexibility in production. Imagine that this flexibility in turn results in products that truly fit the customer's needs and are capable of stimulating the customer's own growth. A personal connection between a skilled worker with a responsible job and a consumer with evolving needs is an inseparable part—and a very strong advantage—of a new bargain that could take us into an economy where production is clearly based on human goals beyond survival needs alone. A key requirement for this bargain is an active customer who is also an active worker, not the disabled victim of stressful working life. Such people can participate in a full range of roles: active citizen, active family member, as well as engaged customer. There must also be a community context in which to capture these benefits. Indeed, in industries producing services, or service-like goods, the self-reinforcing quality of community-based production is clearest: the benefits to the client increase the sophistication of local demand ("smart customers"), and the increased participation at work spills over into increased community and family engagement. The switch from specialized, nonparticipatory work structures to active jobs would allow both the worker and the company to gain, just as they did with Taylor's Scientific Management, but now the worker, as consumer and citizen, could gain even more. Taylor's original coalition was enough to force an irresistible alliance for change during the early twentieth century, but this time the alliance could be even stronger, because it would include building broad patterns of social cohesion in the community that were lacking in that earlier bargain. The new scientific synthesis of job design and an expanded conception of economic life must be created to seal this new compact.

These changes above would, of course, represent the decentralized decisions of many separate firms. Earlier in this chapter, however, we noted the importance of establishing a favorable societal context for work reconstruction, as well as local solutions. Aren't the possibilities for such political change dim indeed? Isn't it true, for example, that no matter how many constituencies might be served by these changes, there is still no existing political structure that could mediate debate on this transformation? We would admit that at present there seems to be a discrepancy between the problems our present political structure is able to articulate and these important popular issues, which are emerging without vocabularies or institutional channels. One barrier, of course, is that our political, corporate, and even labor leaders, of both the left and the right, all have active jobs, which do not allow them the direct experience of the strain, isolation, or alienation that we have discussed. Where, then, are they to learn about these problems? We gather no statistics about them either nationally or locally. We have mountains of data on the economic indicators, but what measures inform our decision makers about the state of our psychosocial well-being or its causes? Many psychosocial issues exist in a shadowy area of problems whose existence is often denied altogether. In the area of psychosocial well-being we have leaders who speak but who cannot feel.

For many other people, the problem is that they can feel but have no voice with which to speak. For example, the present level of political aliena-

tion in the United States would appear to be shockingly high among bureaucratized, commercialized, and routinized workers. Meyerson (1989)
found that the service workers were less than one-fifth as likely to have
voted in the 1988 elections as managers and professionals and about one-
half as likely to have voted as the blue-collar workers who are sometimes
regarded as marginal participants in U.S. political processes* (not true of
Sweden; see p. 53n). The political dialogues have not begun for these
groups. What political stands should high-strain, isolated workers take?
Where are the forums for psychosocial issues? Which political party should
they join? Which newspapers should they read? This discrepancy is another indication of a time of transition, but its implication of disabled political institutions is very disturbing.

How shall new political institutions be built? A psychosocial perspective
on both the input and the output sides of working life suggests political
strategies that might build a new political consensus. On the input side the
issue is obtaining healthy conditions at work for the worker; on the output
side the issue is a healthy environment, based on human–capital intensive
instead of physical–capital intensive production. As we saw above, the production of services, broadly defined, raised common themes in several politically emergent areas: the alienated service worker frustrated by
unarticulated political concerns, and service-oriented production as a self-
sustaining, community platform that could facilitate both environmental
and workplace health. We saw in chapter 9 the numbers of bureaucratized,
commercialized, and routinized workers (the service workers discussed
above represented 28 percent of the U.S. voting-age population, but only
about 6 percent of the voters). Could these workers be united with other
groups by articulating common psychosocial hazards of work to build a
common political base? On the output side of industrial production, an appeal for environmental protection could surely be formulated on the basis
of an increasing orientation toward use of human resources, and a reduced
emphasis on physical resources. This would reduce the environmental risk
posed by industries whose revenue is dependent on transformation of natural resources into market-ready commodities.

A number of other political issues generally outside the scope of this
book might also be integrated with the theme above. At least half of the
New Value–disenfranchised workers are women, still underrepresented in
a broad range of working-life questions, but becoming ever more politically
potent. These issues provide men and women a common political agenda.
Second, the rapidly increasing political power of new environmentally fo-

*Meyerson analyzed U.S. Bureau of Labor Statistics data on work-force composition and
CBS/*New York Times* exit poll data from November 1988.

cused parties poses a political opportunity. Their value orientation toward health and the environment is the same as the focus of this book, but the environmental movement has as yet had relatively little contact with the Industrial Democracy constituencies noted at the end of chapter 9 (unions and joint management/labor groups). On the other hand, the Industrial Democracy movement, with its strong commitment to democracy and humanity of working life and with its creative record of industrial transformation, has not often moved beyond its base in large-scale, export-oriented, goods-producing industries. But a common set of healthy work/healthy environment interests might be found to link these two important political movements: perhaps a psychosocial focus on production which increases human capabilities, and a joint exploration of alternative social organizations for industry and the economy.

The handwriting for change is again on the wall, just as surely as it was at the turn of the twentieth century. By comparison with nineteenth-century industry, our present industries have increased overall economic prosperity for workers (and owners), and at the same time they have reduced physical health hazards for workers in mining, in foundries, and in construction, although they have certainly not eliminated hazards, as the main focus of the present-day occupational health and safety movement will attest. Of course, many of the employee benefits in this bargain were attained only after concerted organizational and political struggles by workers, involving the development of modern union structures in both the United States and Sweden. The struggles were difficult, but few would recommend turning the clock back to nineteenth-century industry. We now have a new set of health risks and a new set of industrial outputs based on the psychosocial structure of work. We probably also face a new set of struggles to achieve economic structures that fulfill the need for psychosocial well-being as well as the need for material satisfaction.

APPENDIX

Statistical Validity of Psychosocial Work Dimensions in the U.S. Quality of Employment Surveys

with Joe Schwartz and Carl Pieper

The Job Characteristic Data Surveys: The U.S. Quality of Employment Surveys

To assess the reliability of our psychosocial job measures, we chose the most comprehensive, nationally representative data base on job characteristics assembled in the United States: the three Quality of Employment Surveys (QES), developed for the U.S. Department of Labor by the University of Michigan Survey Research Center in 1969, 1972, and 1977. This is still the most recent, comprehensive, nationally representative set of data bases on job characteristics available in the United States—but it obviously needs to be supplemented with more current data. All respondents were working at least twenty hours per week, were between the ages of 18 and 65, and were chosen from randomly sampled U.S. households (for further detail, see Quinn and Staines 1979; Karasek, Schwartz, and Theorell 1982; and

Schwartz, Pieper, and Karasek 1988). A research group including Karasek, Schwartz, and Pieper was able to amalgamate all three national surveys into a single large data base of 4,503 respondents (2,946 men and 1,557 women [by year, N = 993 and 540 in 1969; 985 and 470 in 1972; and 968 and 547 in 1977]). In spite of some differences in detailed questions, we were able to develop consistent scales between surveys by utilizing factor analyses of roughly forty questions, separately for men and women in each survey.* The questions that were used to develop our scales are listed in table A–1, and reliability statistics are listed in table A–2 (correlations are available in Karasek, Schwartz, and Theorell 1982, table 3). While the data are self-reported, the data base as a whole allows more precise estimates of sources of error than the major alternative data base for U.S. job analysis: the expert assessments in the U.S. Dictionary of Occupational Titles (DOT) (see Spenner 1980). Although the DOT has much more detailed coverage (almost 12,000 titles), particularly for manufacturing, it is a much older data base, is very incomplete in the service industries and occupations, has unknown reliability, and is sometimes based on very few job descriptions (for 45 percent of the occupations, one observation or none at all; see discussion in Karasek, Schwartz, and Theorell 1982).

Revised 1970 U.S. Census Occupational Classification System

We have slightly modified the 1970 U.S. Census occupational classification system, based on 441 occupations, to produce 240 codes, because many of the 1970 census occupation groups are too rare to utilize. We have consolidated some very small occupations and have subdivided some very large ones. Figures A–1 and A–2, for men and women respectively, show almost all those occupations, scored for males, in which there were more than three men, and the computer-based labeling routine could fit approximately 80 percent of the labels on figure A–1 (only 38 selected occupations are shown in chapters 2 and 9 [selection discussed on p. 279]). We utilized the U.S. Census three-digit standard industry codes (S.I.C. codes) to break down several occupational codes with large populations (for example, managers are 11.9 percent of the male work force) into five to ten industry subcategories. Self-employment is used to subdivide managers further. Also, because almost 200 of the occupation codes refer to occupations rep-

*Mean scores for the national population did not change significantly between surveys on those decision latitude questions that were exactly the same across all three surveys (decision latitude: means = 37.59 in 1969; 37.92 in 1972; and 37.99 in 1977; S.D. = 6.70, 6.61, and 6.69 respectively). Standardized scores across the three surveys were combined (in one version, they were weighted by that year's scale reliability; see Karasek, Schwartz, and Theorell 1982 for further detail).

TABLE A–1

U.S. psychosocial job characteristic scales

The following job characteristic scales were compiled using factor
analysis of questions from the QES surveys 1969, 1972, 1977.*

A. Decision latitude (1 + 2)

1. Skill discretion
   Keep learning new things; can develop skills; requires high level of skill; job has
   variety; requires creativity; repetitious job (a negative indicator [−]).

2. Decision authority
   Have freedom to make my own decision; can choose how to perform work; have a
   lot of say on the job; take part in decisions that affect me.

B. Psychological job demands
   No excessive work [−]; no conflicting demands [−]; have time to do work [−]; work
   fast; work hard.

C. Job insecurity
   Steady job [−]; good job security [−]; likely to be laid off.

D. Physical exertion
   Job requires lots of physical exertion.

E. Hazardous exposure (1 + 2)

1. Hazardous condition exposure
   Dangerous equipment; dangerous work methods; things placed or stored dangerously; fires, burns, shocks; dirty, bad maintenance.

2. Toxic exposure
   Dangerous chemicals; air pollution (dusts, fibers, etc.); risk of catching disease.

F. Social support (1 + 2)

1. Supervisor social support
   Supervisor shows concern; supervisor pays attention; supervisor helpful getting
   work done; supervisor creates good teamwork.

2. Co-worker social support
   Co-workers friendly; co-workers helpful; co-workers personally interested; co-
   workers are competent.

---

*See Schwartz, Pieper, and Karasek 1988 and Karasek, Schwartz, and Theorell 1982 for more detailed
discussion of the component questions of each of the dimensions.

SOURCE: Karasek, Schwartz, and Theorell 1982.

resenting less than .1 percent of the male work force or .2 percent of the female work force (that is, fewer than three individuals in the QES male or female samples), we have combined a number of the smaller occupational
codes, but not those that seem incompatible on the basic job dimensions
listed in chapter 2. Those few individuals were dropped from our system,
leaving 98.5 percent of jobs scored for males and somewhat fewer for females. The final codes are listed in the Job Content Questionnaire User's

TABLE A-2
Reliability estimates and partitioning of variance:
Quality of Employment Surveys 1969, 1972, 1977

| | MEN | | | | | WOMEN | | | | |
| | Reliability | | | Between Occupation Variance | | Reliability | | | Between Occupation Variance | |
	Cross-Survey	Within Survey (Pooled)	Scale Reliability Total	% of Variance	% of Reliable Variance	Cross-Survey	Within Survey (Pooled)	Scale Reliability Total	% of Variance	% of Reliable Variance
Decision Latitude Skill	.965	.805	.776	.347	.447	.987	.772	.762	.388	.509
Discretion	.963	.766	.737	.349	.474	.988	.720	.711	.400	.562
Decision Authority	.970	.724	.703	.250	.356	.991	.710	.704	.270	.384
Psych. Demands	.961	.614	.591	.042	.071	.984	.704	.614	.033	.054
Job Insecurity	.907	.403	.366	.104	.286	1.000	.360	.360	.097	.269
Physical Exert.	1.000	**	1.000	.259	.259	1.000	**	1.000	.192	.192
Hazardous Exposure	.997	**	.997	.172	.172	1.000	**	1.000	.151	.151
Self-Income	1.000	**	1.000	.202	.202	.997	**	.997	.388	.388
Social Support	1.000	.831	.831	.040	.048	.463	.840	.809	.044	.054

**One-variable scale or logically dependent variables: no estimate of within-survey reliability.

Guide (Karasek 1985). In addition, job scores have been aggregated by 1972 S.I.C. three- and four-digit industry codes, by 1960 Census three-digit occupation codes, and by an aggregated version of the 1970 occupational codes with 80 categories.

Statistical Reliability of the Scales

One measure on which all the scales do remarkably well is test-retest reliability using occupation as the unit of analysis (cross-survey correlation, column 1 in table A–2). In all cases, this correlation is above .9, indicating that occupations that score high on a scale in one of the three QES national surveys score similarly high in the others as well, which strongly supports the validity of the scales. This repeatability of the job scores for occupations occurs in spite of the fact that different respondents rate the occupations in each of the surveys. The next measure, internal scale reliability as assessed by the Cronbach's alpha coefficient (table A–2, column 2), is related to the average internal correlations between the separate questions that make up the multiple-item scales (physical exertion is based on a single question and thus has no such measure). In this case, the scales do acceptably well, although the psychological demands scale is borderline and job insecurity is unacceptably low; the latter implies that several relatively independent aspects of job insecurity are being combined into a single scale.

BETWEEN-OCCUPATION VARIANCE: THE JOB VERSUS THE INDIVIDUAL AS CAUSE

As the discussion of the occupational maps in chapter 2 suggests, a very important determinant of job score reliability will be how much of the variance lies between occupational groups. This is a measure of presumably objective differences in jobs relevant to our job redesign goals. Table A–2 shows the percentage of reliable between-occupation variance for each job characteristic in columns 3 and 4. In general, the mean scores of a job dimension on each occupation do not account for the majority of the reliable scale variance; however, decision latitude, job insecurity, physical demands, are all better discriminated by occupation for men than is "take-home pay"—a clear indication of the potential utility of psychosocial job dimension analysis. On the other hand, psychological demands and social support are discriminated very poorly between occupation.

The remainder, the within-occupation variance, might be due to personal differences that occur in all occupations (age, genetic differences, or

FIGURE A-1

The occupational distribution of psychological demands and decision latitude for U.S. males (N = 2,897)

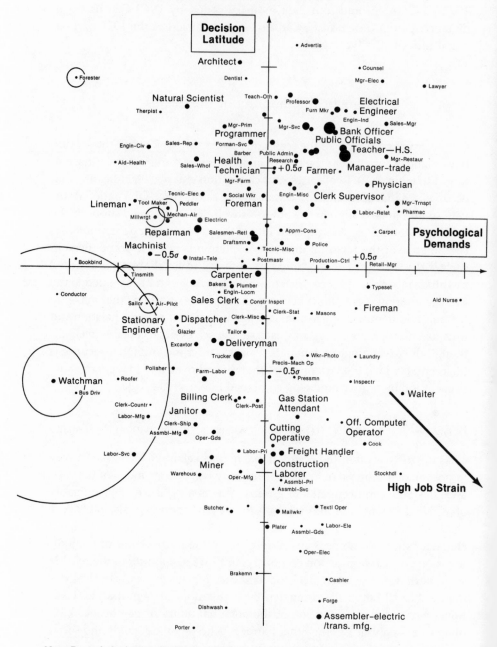

NOTE: Due to lack of space, the majority of labels have been abbreviated and 47 labels have not been printed.

SOURCE: Data from Quality of Employment Surveys 1969, 1972, 1977. Figure from Karasek et al. 1988. Reprinted by permission of the *American Journal for Public Health*.

FIGURE A–2

The occupational distribution of psychological demands and decision latitude for U.S. females (N = 1,387)

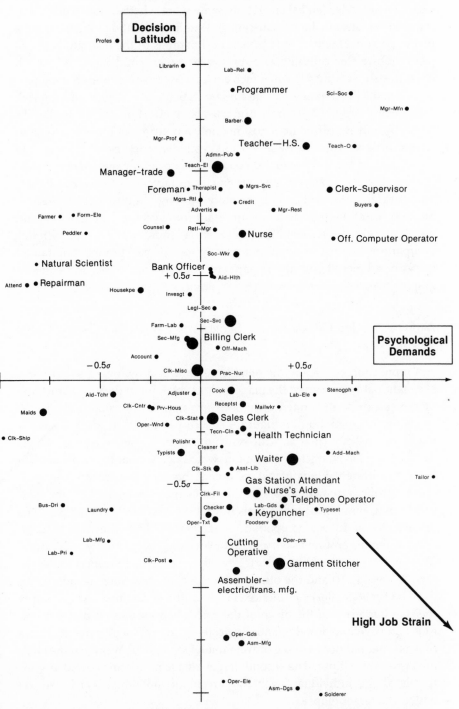

NOTE: Due to lack of space, the majority of labels have been abbreviated and 47 labels have not been printed.

SOURCE: Data from Quality of Employment Surveys 1969, 1972, 1977.

personality, for example) or simply to the breadth of even the three-digit U.S. Census codes (all bakers get the same score whether they work in automated factories or fancy patisseries). Within-occupation variance that is due to personal factors could bias our estimations of the magnitude of objective job-related causality, and for this reason a second version of the job characteristic scoring system, which corrects for this bias, is used in our analytic results in chapter 4 (see discussion in Schwartz, Pieper, and Karasek 1988). For example, age surely exerts a strong effect on cardiovascular illness risk, and age differences exist not only among job holders but even between some occupations (older doctors, younger orderlies). We can see the magnitude of these types of corrections for education, age, marital status, self-employment, religion, and urbanicity in table 3 of Schwartz, Pieper, and Karasek (1988). They are generally not large in absolute magnitude, but they are still relatively quite important for psychological demands and social support. Other troublesome potential sources of personal within-occupation variance—such as personality, genetic background, and family background (net of education)—are not as easily correctable as the demographic sources.

ACCURACY OF JOB CHARACTERISTIC SCORES FOR CENSUS OCCUPATION CODES ON THE PLOTS

A more concrete idea of the relative magnitude of within- and between-occupational variance and the magnitude of the error in the job characteristic scores can be illustrated using *watchman* on the decision latitude and psychological demand plot, figure A–1. Error in the position of this occupation on the plot (that is, scale error) may come from three sources: (1) variations in job characteristics among watchmen similar to the differences between different kinds of bakers noted above (within-occupation variance); (2) measurement errors in the scales themselves; and (3) the relatively small number of individuals in each occupation in the QES survey (an average of 15 per occupation for males). We have drawn two confidence intervals around *watchman* in the lower left corner of figure A–1, indicating the magnitude of uncertainty of job scores with respect to watchmen as a group (I) and the other with respect to watchmen as individuals (II). The first (smaller) confidence ellipse for the occupation level is simply the standard error of the mean of the watchmen's scores on decision latitude and psychological demands respectively; there is a 67 percent chance that another national sample of watchmen would yield average scores falling inside this ellipse. The second, larger ellipse represents confidence intervals at the individual level: 50 percent of individual watchmen are within the larger ellipse.

At the occupation level (the smaller ellipse), we can see that the error limits are relatively small (.22 individual population standard deviation units for decision latitude and .18 units for psychological demands). This means we could fairly easily make statistically significant predictions about differences in job characteristics between groups; that is, groups of watchmen differ significantly from groups of billing clerks. The larger confidence ellipse, however, implies much less precise estimates of job characteristics for individual watchmen; only half of watchmen would be expected to fall within even this large ellipse. This finding suggests that we may often not be able to significantly differentiate job experience between individuals based solely on their occupational title and that our inferences about the job characteristics of occupations will have to be based on rather large groups of individuals. This lack of precision should not be surprising because the occupational title alone represents rather little information about an individual's job. Much of the variation in job situation could easily occur within what are still quite broad occupational groupings even at the three-digit level.

Individual Scale Validity

DECISION LATITUDE

Column 1 in table A–2 shows that the decision latitude measure (as well as its components, decision authority and skill discretion) are highly reproducible across national samples. Also, columns 4 and 5 show that both scales clearly differentiate between occupations, indeed far better than income from the job. A correlation matrix also shows that decision latitude is rather highly correlated with social support and negatively correlated with physical demands. Because these correlations are well below the internal scale component correlations, however, the full set of scales is still validated as a set (see Karasek, Schwartz, and Theorell 1982). Content validation of the decision latitude scales comes from correlations with worker trait data on the DOT (Spenner 1980; Karasek, Schwartz, and Theorell 1982). A DOT estimate of Kohn and Schooler's (1973) "occupational self-direction" scale is correlated 0.77 with decision latitude; the DOT scores for "closeness of supervision" and our decision authority scale are correlated -0.65, while the DOT "routinization" scale and the often-utilized general education and specific vocational training time (GED, SVP) scales are highly correlated with our skill discretion scale (-0.54, 0.79, and 0.76 respectively). Convergent validity of our dimensions is also attested to by the high correlation between objective and self-report measures of decision latitude in a variety of studies (see p. 80). A Swedish self-reported skill discretion measure (Carlsson et al. 1974) correlates highly with expert ratings (r = .69 in 1968; r = .64 in 1974). High correlations between expert ratings and self-reports are corroborated in other findings (r = .78 in Kohn and Schooler [1973]; r = .87 average for autonomy and variety in Hackman and Lawler [1971] and Gardell [1971a]). All these findings make decision latitude (and its two components) the best understood and most statistically reliable of our job dimensions.

PSYCHOLOGICAL DEMANDS

The psychological job demands scores for each occupation are highly re-producible across occupations, but the U.S. QES psychological work load scale discriminates poorly between occupations, perhaps because broad questions about work load ("not enough time") are more likely than specific questions to be affected by self-report biasing factors (Lazarus 1966). This is a substantial shortcoming of the QES psychological demand scale. Nevertheless, there is evidence to suggest significant objective content for our measure in spite of this weakness. Similar measures have low correla-tions with the confounding factors that might lead to bias, such as stressors in other spheres of life (Karasek 1976), so there is little evidence of a halo effect in which strain from other spheres of life might be reported as strain due to job causes. Self-reports of psychological job demands correspond well with expert assessments in several other studies (Ager et al. 1975; Gardell 1971a; see also discussion of use of such measures in the role stress literature, p. 80). Finally, our occupation scoring method identifies occupa-tions that are plausibly high and low in psychological work load (for exam-ple, orderlies, lawyers, waiters, typesetters, and physicians score high, whereas rail conductors and bookbinders score low).

JOB INSECURITY

The low internal reliability of the job insecurity scales does not mean that the scale is inaccurate but that it is tapping several aspects of insecurity that are not very highly correlated. Indeed, the job insecurity scale plausibly lo-cates many occupations: job insecurity is high on our scale for artists, con-struction workers, and other workers in the building trades, and it is low for railroad engineers, mail carriers, telephone linemen, and bookkeepers. One improvement of this scale could come from utilization of publicly collected data on actual unemployment experience for each occupation (which, of course, is not necessarily the same as the threat of unemployment, as we noted above).

PHYSICAL EXERTION

Our physical exertion dimension in the next section is constructed from a single question on overall exertion, an unfortunately common limitation of exertion indicators in many large population studies of health status (Milvy, Forbes, and Brown 1977). Such measures probably affect exertion level and impulse loading dynamic effort combined, but probably convey little information about static loads (that is, uncomfortable positions) or exertion regularity. The accuracy of the physical exertion scale is attested to by the fact that it also plausibly locates occupations that rate high and low. Lumbermen, orderlies, and millworkers are high on our scale; occupations that are scored zero on our scale include a very large number of white-collar and professional workers (see figure 2–7). Our scale also correlates highly with the physical exertion worker trait data on the DOT ($r = .62$), a respectable validation given the limitations of the indicators in both data bases.

HAZARDOUS EXPOSURE

The validity of a combined general hazard indicator for rough testing of the presence of physical hazards (a self-reported safety hazards scale and a toxic exposure scale) is confirmed by its respectable correlation ($r = .60$) with the occupational hazard measure in the U.S. *Dictionary of Occupational Titles*. While such measures have proved useful in analysis of national population problems with physical hazards (Sundbom 1971), this measure of generalized physical hazard risk is far inferior to the physically monitored data in much occupational health research.

SOCIAL SUPPORT

Our measure of social support has high test-retest reliability at the occupation level. The scale reliabilities using the U.S. QES data for the co-worker, supervisor, and combined co-worker/supervisor measures are also quite high, but we find very little systematic difference between occupations for these scales, especially for supervisor support. Several studies have observed difficulty in finding strong correlations between self-reports and short-term expert observations of social support. Because these QES scales, when used at the individual level, clearly reveal the phenomenon of social-support buffering for psychological stress in a manner quite similar to that found in other data bases (Karasek, Triantis, and Chaudhry 1982), we have little reason to suspect that the problem lies in the substantive validity of the social support scales. We must simply conclude that there is wide variety in the level of social support in the majority of occupations. While this conclusion certainly weakens our ability to identify all occupations on a social support scale, we can still plausibly identify occupations that are very high or very low in social support across U.S. and Swedish data bases (see p. 73). Our analyses do not indicate that the scales are biased: a test of the occupation-level social support scores (estimated via job title) shows associations to psychological strain very similar to measures of social support based on the original individual-level data (Schwartz, Karasek, and Pieper 1982). In summary, social support scales are often highly reliable internally and are accompanied by a broad literature in the stress and behavior field, but their objective validity raises complex measurement questions.

The Job Content Questionnaire

The psychosocial job characteristic scales discussed above have been revised by adding roughly 50 percent more questions to those covered in table A–1, in order to address more precisely the issues noted in chapters 2, 3, 4, and 5. The result is the Job Content Questionnaire (JCQ) (Karasek 1985), which is now available in several languages. It is a short questionnaire with a basic 27-question format (Framingham version) and a recommended 49-question format. Additional scales are available to measure macro-level decision latitude, psychological strain, job satisfaction, the customer interface, and the human/computer interface. A major advantage of the JCQ is that scores obtained with it can be compared with national average scores in the United States from the QES survey questions, which are included as part of the new instrument. This feature provides a set of reference standards that have otherwise been lacking for psychosocial job measurement and are not available even for the widely used Job Diagnostic Survey (Hackman and Oldham 1975). Useful comparisons with full national population mean scores can be made with samples of as few as a dozen employees, detecting half a standard deviation difference on a medium powerful scale, but detailed occupational comparisons (to "male bakers," for example) can require samples of 75 or more. As of this writing, over forty research groups in seven countries were using the JCQ, and users have formed a network to circulate findings.

REFERENCES

Adler, P. 1985. New technologies, new skills. Department of Industrial Management and Engineering, Stanford University. Manuscript.

Ager, B., Aminoff, F., Bareryd, K., Englund, A., Nerell, G., Nilsson, G., Nilsson, C., Sareman, E., and Söderkvist, A. 1975. Arbetsmiljö i sågverk. En tvärvetenskaplig undersökning. (Work environment in sawmills. A cross-disciplinary study.) Undersöknings-rapport AM 101–75. Stockholm: Arbetarskyddsstyrelsen.

Agurén, S., Bredbacka, C., Hansson, R., Ihregren, K., and Karlsson, K. G. [1984] 1985. *Volvo Kalmar revisited.* Stockholm: Efficiency and Participation Development Council SAF, LO, PTK.

Agurén, S., and Edgren, J. 1980. *New factories: Job design through factory planning in Sweden.* Stockholm: Swedish Employers' Confederation.

Åhlström, P. 1980. Co-determination at work. Report no. 17, Working Life in Sweden. New York: Swedish Information Service. N.Y.

Åkerstedt, T., Knutsson, A., Alfredsson, L., and Theorell, T. 1984. Shift work and cardiovascular disease. *Scand J Work Environ Health* 10:409–414.

Aldag, R. J., Barr, S. H., and Brief, A. P. 1981. Measurement of perceived task characteristics. *Psychol Bull* 90:415–431.

Alfredsson, L. 1983. Myocardial infarction and environment: Use of registers in epidemiology. Acad. thesis, Karolinska Institute, Stockholm.

Alfredsson, L., Karasek, R., and Theorell, T. 1982. Myocardial infarction risk and psychosocial environment: An analysis of the male Swedish working force. *Soc Sci Med* 3:463–467.

Alfredsson, L., Spetz, C-L., and Theorell, T. 1985. Type of occupation and near-future hospitalization for myocardial infarction and some other diagnoses. *Int J Epidemiol* 14:378–388.

Alfredsson, L., and Theorell, T. 1983. Job characteristics of occupations and myocardial infarction risk: Effects of possible confounding factors. *Soc Sci Med* 17:1497–1503.

American Psychiatric Association, 1980. *Diagnostic and statistical manual of mental disorders* 3rd ed. Washington, D.C.

Antonovsky, A. 1968. Social class and the major cardiovascular diseases. *J Chron Dis* 21:65–106.

Antonovsky, A. 1987. *Unraveling the mystery of health.* San Francisco: Jossey-Bass.

Arbetsmiljölag 1976. Swedish Law on Work Environment, Stockholm: SOU 1976:1 (Ch 7; 176).

Argyris, C., and Schön, D. A. 1978. *Organizational learning: A theory in action perspective.* Reading, Mass: Addison-Wesley.

Arnetz, B. B. 1983. Psychophysiological effects of social understimulation in old age. Acad. thesis, Karolinska Institute, Stockholm.

Arnetz, B. B., Andreasson, S., Strandberg, M., Eneroth, P., and Kallner, A. 1987. Läkares psykosociala arbetsmiljö: Stress-hälsorisker-trivsel (The psychosocial work environment of physicians: Stress, health risks and work satisfaction). *Läkartidningen* 84(11): 816–824.

Arnetz, B. B., Eyre, M., and Theorell, T. 1982. Social activation of the elderly: A social experiment. *Soc Sci Med* 16:1685–1690.

Arnetz, B. B., Hörte, L. G., Hedberg, A., Theorell, T., Allander, E., and Malker, H. 1987. Suicide patterns among physicians related to other academics as well as to the general population. *Acta Psychiatr Scand* 75:139–143.

Arnetz, B. B., Theorell, T., Helström, L., Uddenberg, N., Allander, E., Unnegård, H., and Nyman, R. 1988. Läkarnas psykosociala arbetsmiljö (The psychosocial work environment of physicians). Stress research report. National Institute of Psychosocial Factors and Health, Stockholm.

Arnetz, B. B., and Theorell, T. 1987. Longterm effects of a social rehabilitation programme for elderly people: Physiological predictors and mortality data. *Clin Rehab* 1:225–229.

Arnetz, B. B., Wasserman, J., Petrini, B., Brenner, S-O., Levi, L., Eneroth, P., Salovaara, H., Hjelm, R., Salovaara, L., Theorell, T., and Petersson, I-L. 1987. Immune function in unemployed women. *Psychosom Med* 49:3–12.

Aronsson, G. 1984. Omstrukturering av kvalifikationskrav vid datorisering (Restructuring of qualification demands with computerization). Report no. 42, Department of Psychology, University of Stockholm.

Aronsson, G. 1987. *Arbetspsykologi: Stress—och kvalifikations—perspektiv* (Work psychology: Perspectives on stress and qualification). Lund: Studentlitteratur.

Ashford, N. 1973. *Crisis in the workplace.* Cambridge: MIT Press.

Åstrand, N. E. 1988. Prediction of sick leave, unemployment, labour turnover and mortality in a Swedish male working population. Acad. thesis. Department of Community Health Sciences, Lund University, Malmö.

Åstrand, I., and Lagerlöf, E. 1988. Arbetsmiljöinstitutet. Prioriterade forskningsområden— väg nå ökad kunskap om risker i arbetsmiljön (The Arbetsmiljö Institute. Research fields of high priority—a way to increased knowledge of risks in the occupational environment). *Läkartidningen* 85:2482–2487.

Averill, J. R. 1973. Personal control over aversive stimuli and its relationship to stress. *Psychol Bull* 80:286–303.

Axelsson, J-A., Björkegren, I., Moser, V., and Olsson, W. 1987. *Plan for less stress.* Stockholm: Statshälsan.

Bainbridge, L. 1974. Problems in the assessment of mental load. *Le Travail Humain* 37:279– 302.

Bajusz, E. 1965. The terminal electrolyte-shift mechanism in heart muscles: Its significance in the pathogenesis and prevention of necrotizing cardiomyopathies. In *Electrolytes and cardiovascular disease*, vol. 1, ed. E. Bajusz. New York: S. Karger.

Baker, D. 1985. The study of stress at work. *Ann Rev Public Health* 6:367–381.

Bales, R., and Slater, P. 1954. Role differentiation in small groups. In *Family socialization and interaction process*, ed. T. Parsons and R. Bales. Glencoe, Ill.: Free Press.

Bali, L. R. 1979. Long-term effect of relaxation on blood pressure and anxiety levels of essential hypertensive males: A controlled study. *Psychosom Med* 41:637–646.

Balint, M. 1964. *The doctor, his patient, and the illness.* London: Pitman Medical Publishing.

Bandura, A. 1977. Self-efficacy: Toward a unifying theory of behavioral change. *Psychol Rev* 84:191–215.

Bandura, A., Taylor, C. B., Williams, S. L., Mefford, I. N., and Barchas, J. D. 1985. Catecholamine secretion as a function of perceived coping self-efficacy. *J Consult Clin Psychol* 53:406–414.

Barklöf, K. 1988. Arbetsorganisatorisk förändring i svensk lokaltrafik (Change of work organization in Swedish public transportation). Report, Department of Environmental and Organizational Psychology, University of Stockholm.

Barnes, R. M. 1980. *Motion and time study design and measurement of work*, 7th ed. New York: Wiley.

Bazerman, M. H. 1982. The impact of personal control on performance: Is added control always beneficial? *J Appl Psychol* 67:472–479.

Becker, G. 1972. A theory of marriage. *J Polit Econ* 81:813–846.

Bejeroth, E. 1989. Tandvård på löpande band—om arbetsmiljön i den offentliga tandvården (Dental service on the assembly line—on the working environment in the public dental service). Stress research report. National Institute of Psychosocial Factors and Health, Stockholm.

Bentham, J. 1794. Panopticon, or, the Inspection House: Containing the Idea of a New Principle of Construction Applicable to Any Sort of Establishment, in Which Persons of any Description Are To Be Kept Under Inspection. Bentham Papers, c. 1794–1795; University College London, Rare Books and Manuscript Department.

Bentham, J. 1789. *Introduction to principles of morals and legislation.* London.

Berg, I. 1970. *Education and Jobs.* New York: Praeger.

Berg, I., Freedman, M., and Freeman, M. 1978. *Managers and work reform: A limited engagement.* New York: Free Press/Macmillan.

Berglund, B., Berglund, U., and Lindvall, T., eds. 1984. *Adverse effects of community noise: Research needs.* Oslo: Nordic Council of Ministers.

Berkman, L., and Syme, S. L. 1979. Social networks, host resistance and mortality: A nine-year study of Alameda county residents. *Am J Epidemiol* 109:186–204.

Berkowitz, B. 1965. Changes in intellect with age. Vol. 4, Changes in achievement and survival in older people. *J Genet Psychol* 107:3–14.

Bernier, M., and Avard, J. 1986. Self-efficacy, outcome, and attrition in a weight-reduction program. *Cognit Ther Res* 10:319–338.

Bernstein, P. 1974. Run your own business, Worker-owned plywood firms. *Working Papers for a New Society.* Summer: 24–34.

Bernstein, P. 1976. *Workplace democratization: Its internal dynamics.* Kent, Ohio: Kent State University Press.

Bikson, T. K., and Eveland, J. D. 1989. The interplay between work group structure and computer support. In *Intellectual teamwork*, ed. R. Kraut, J. Gallagher, and C. Egido. Hillsdale, N.J.: Erlbaum.

Blohmke, M., Schaefer, H., and Abel, H. 1969. Medical and social findings in coronary diseases. *Munchen Med Wschr* 11:701–710.

Blomqvist, M. 1981. *Vem bestämmer medbestämmandet?* (Who decides participation?) Stockholm: Arbetslivscentrum.

Boucher, T. 1988. Adam Smith and the humanists: An enquiry into the productivity of labor controversy. *I. E. Transactions*, 20:73–82.

Bourgeois, L. J. III, McAllister, D. W., and Mitchell, T. R. 1978. The effects of different organizational environment upon decisions about organizational structure. *Acad Manage J* 21:508–514.

Bowlby, J. 1969. *Attachment and loss*, vol. 1, *Attachment.* New York: Basic Books.

Bowles, S., and Gintis, H. 1987. *Democracy and capitalism: Property, community, and the contradictions of modern social thought.* New York: Basic Books.

Brady, J. V., Porter, R., Conrad, D., and Mason, J. 1958. Avoidance behavior and the development of gastro-duodenal ulcers. *J Exp Anal Behav* 1:69–72.

Brass, D. J. 1985. Technology and the structuring of jobs: Employee satisfaction, performance, and influence. *Organ Behav Hum Decis Processes* 55:216–240.

Braun, S., and Hollander, R. B. 1988. Work and depression among women in the Federal Republic of Germany. *Women and Health* 14:5–24.

Braverman, H. 1974. *Labor and monopoly capital: The degradation of work in the 20th century.* New York: Monthly Review Press.

Brayfield, A. H., and Crockett, W. H. 1955. Employee attitudes and employee performance. *Psychol Bull* 52:396–424.

Brenner, M. H. 1987. Relation of economic change to Swedish health and social well-being, 1950–1980. *Soc Sci Med* 25:183–195.

Brenner, M. H., and Mooney, A. 1983. Unemployment and health in the context of economic change. *Soc Sci Med* 17:1125–1138.

Brenner, S-O., and Levi, L. 1987. Long-term unemployment among women in Sweden. *Soc Sci Med* 25:153–161.

Brøchner, S. 1983a. Miljonbeløp er spilt pa spørgeleg (Millions of crowns wasted on question game). (*Jyllandsposten* Aarhus), October 10.

Brøchner, S. 1983b. Arbejdsgiverne klager over slagderiarbejder-undersøgelse (Employers complain about slaughter-work study). (*Jyllandsposten* Aarhus), October 18.

Brown, G. W. 1973. Life events and the onset of depressive and schizophrenic conditions. In *Life stress and illness*, ed. E. K. E. Gunderson and R. H. Rahe. Springfield, Ill.: Charles Thomas.

Bruhn, J., and Wolf, S. 1979. *An anatomy of health: The Roseto story.* Oklahoma City: University of Oklahoma Press.

Buck, V. E. 1972. *Working under pressure.* New York: Crane, Russek.

Buell, P., and Breslow, L. 1960. Mortality from coronary heart disease in California men who work long hours. *J Chron Dis* 11:615–626.

Business Week, 1972. 143–146, Sept. 9.

Califano, J. 1983. Can we afford one trillion dollars for health care? Speech delivered to Economic Club of Detroit, April 25.

Cannon, W. B. 1914. The emergency function of the adrenal medulla in pain and the major emotions. *Am J Physiol* 33:356–372.

Canton, J. 1984. The importance of worker involvement in program design. In *Health promotion in the workplace*, ed. M. P. O'Dounell and T. H. Ainsworth. New York: Wiley.

Caplan, G., Cobb, S., French, J. R. P., Harrison, R. V., and Pinneau, S. R., Jr. 1975. *Job demands and worker health: Main effects and occupational differences.* NIOSH publication no. 75–160, U. S. Department of Health, Education and Welfare.

Caplan, R. 1971. Organizational stress and individual strain: A social psychological study of risk factors for coronary heart disease among administrators, engineers, and scientists. Ph.D. diss., University of Michigan.

Caplan, R., Cobb, S., French, J. R. P. 1975. Relationship of cessation of smoking with job stress, personality and social supports. *J Appl Psychol* 60(2):211–219.

Carlsson, G. Eriksson, R. L., and Löfwall, C. 1974. Ekonomisk gruppering (Socioeconomic grouping). *Statistisk Tidskrift* 5:381–400.

Carlzon, J. 1987. *Moments of truth.* Cambridge, Mass.: Ballinger.

Carruthers, M. E. 1969. Aggression and atheroma. *Lancet* 2:1170–1171.

Cathey, C., Jones, H. B., Naughton, J., Hammarsten, J. F., and Wolf, S. 1962. The relation of life stress to the concentration of serum lipids in patients with coronary artery disease. *Am J Med Sci* 244:421.

Chadwick, J., Chesney, M., Black, G. W., Rosenman, R. M., and Sevelius, G. G. 1979. *Psychological job stress and coronary heart disease.* Menlo Park, Calif.: Stanford Research Institute.

Charlesworth, E. A., Williams, B. J., and Baer, P. E. 1984. Stress management at the work site for hypertension: Compliance, cost-benefit, health care and hypertension-related variables. *Psychosom Med* 46:387–397.

Cimons, M. 1987. Budget office impedes U.S. health studies, report says. *Los Angeles Times,* September 28.

Clack, G. 1974. The Topeka General Foods Plant. In *Job, safety and health,* ed. U.S. Department of Labor OSHA. July.

Cobb, S., and Kasl, S. 1977. The consequences of job loss. NIOSH publication no. 77-224. Cincinnati: National Institute for Occupational Safety and Health.

Cohen, S., and Syme, S. L. 1985. *Social support and health.* New York: Academic Press.

Collings, G., Jr. 1985. Stress management at work: The New York Telephone Company experiment. In *Behavioral medicine: Work, stress, and health,* ed. W. D. Gentry, M. Benson, and C. J. de Wolff. NATO, ASI series. Amsterdam: Martinus Nijhoff.

Conway, T. L., Vickers, R. R., Ward, H. W., and Rahe, R. H. 1981. Occupational stress and variation in cigarette, coffee, and alcohol consumption. *J Health Soc Behav* 22:155–165.

Cooper, C. L., and Marshall, J. 1976. Occupational sources of stress: A review of the literature relating to coronary heart disease and mental ill health. *J Occ Psychol* 49:11–28.

Costa, P. T., McCrae, R. R., and Holland, J. L. 1984. Personality and vocational interests in an adult sample. *J Appl Psychol* 69:390–400.

Courts, F. 1939. Relations between experimentally induced muscular tension and memorization. *J Exp Psychol* 25:235–256.

Cox, T. 1978. *Stress.* London: Macmillan.

Cranor, L., Karasek, R. A., and Carlin, C. 1981. Job characteristics and office work: Findings and health implications. Paper presented at NIOSH conference on Occupational Health Issues Affecting Clerical/Secretarial Personnel, Cincinnati, July 21.

Crozier, M. 1964. *The bureaucratic phenomenon.* Chicago: University of Chicago Press.

Csikszentmihalyi, M. 1975. *Beyond boredom and anxiety.* San Francisco: Jossey-Bass.

Cummings, T. 1978. Self-regulating work groups: A socio-technical synthesis. *Acad Manage Rev* 3:625–634.

D'Agostino, F., Smith, L., Leed, R., Fyn, T. 1988. The Framingham offspring cohort study: Preliminary report of the data. Dept. of Mathematics, Boston University.

Dahlström, E. 1965. *Industrin och arbetsorganisationen* (Industry and the organization of work). Stockholm: Scandinavian University Books.

Dahlström, E. 1969. *Intensifierad industriell demokrati (Intensified industrial democracy).* Stockholm: Prisma.

Dahlström, E., Eriksson, K., Gardell, B., Hammarström, O., and Hammarström, R. 1971. *LKAB och demokratin* (LKAB and democracy). Stockholm: Wahlström och Widstrand.

Danziger, S., and Gottschalk, P. 1987. Renewing the war on poverty: Target support at children and families. *New York Times,* March 22.

de Faire, U., and Theorell, T. 1984. *Life stress and coronary heart disease.* St. Louis: Warren H. Green.

Dement, W. 1969. The biological role of REM sleep. In *Sleep physiology and pathology: A symposium,* ed. A. Kales. Philadelphia: Lippincott.

Denney, N. W. 1982. Aging and cognitive changes. In *Handbook of developmental psychology*, ed. B. B. Wolman. Englewood Cliffs, N.J.: Prentice-Hall.

Dettleback, W. W., and Kraft, P. 1971. Organization change through job enrichment. *Train Dev J* 25:2–6.

Devereux, R. B., Pickering, T. G., Harshfield, G. A., Kleinert, H. D., Derby, L., Pregibon, D., Jason, M., Kleiner, B., Borer, J. S., and Laragh, J. H. 1983. Left ventricular hypertrophy in patients with hypertension. Importance of blood pressure response to regularly recurring stress. *Circulation* 68:470–476.

Dimsdale J. F., and Herd, J. A. 1982. Variability of plasma lipids response to emotional arousal. *Psychosom Med* 44:413–430.

Dobrzynski, J. 1988. Merger mania: Why it won't just stop. *Business Week*, March 21.

Dohrenwend, B. P., and Dohrenwend, B. S. 1969. *Social status and psychological disorder: A causal inquiry.* New York: Wiley.

Dohrenwend, B. S., and Dohrenwend, B. P., eds. 1974. *Stressful events: Their nature and effects.* New York: Wiley.

Doncevic, S., Theorell, T., and Scalia-Tomba, G. 1988. The psychosocial work environment of district nurses in Sweden. *Work and Stress* 2:341–351.

Dore, R. 1983. Goodwill and the spirit of market capitalism. *Brit J Sociol* 34:459–482.

Dubnoff, S. 1978. Inter-occupational shifts and changes in the quality of work in the American economy, 1900–1970. Paper presented at the Labor Studies Section of the Society for the Study of Social Problems, San Francisco, August.

Dumas, L. J. 1986. *The overburdened economy: Uncovering the causes of chronic unemployment, inflation and national decline.* Berkeley: University of California Press.

Duncan, O. D. 1961. A socioeconomic index for all occupations. In *Occupations and social status*, ed. A. J. Reiss. New York: Free Press.

Dunham, R. B., Aldag, R. J., and Brief, A. P. 1977. Dimensionality of task design as measured by the Job Diagnostic Survey. *J Appl Psychol* 20:209–223.

Durkheim, E. [1893] 1964. *The division of labor in society.* New York: Free Press.

Eaker, E. D., Packard, B., and Wenger, N. K., eds. 1988. *Coronary heart disease in women.* Proc. of an NIH Workshop. Washington, D.C.: Haymarket-Doyma.

Ebeltoft, A. 1986. *Fra muskelverk til miljøaktivitet* (From muscle aches to environmental activity). Oslo: Universitetsforlaget.

Edgren, B., and Ander, S. 1982. Arbetsfrånvaro. Sjukfrånvaro—en jämförelse mellan yrkesgrupper ur ett belastnings—och copingperspektiv (Work absenteeism. Sick leave—a comparison between occupations using a load and coping perspective). Report. Division of Work Science, Royal Techn. Institute, Stockholm.

Edgren, J. 1981. *Production and work organization in Sweden: Three development lines.* Stockholm: Management Press.

Edosomwan, J. A. 1986. A feasible methodology for assessing the impact of computer technology on productivity, production, quality, job satisfaction, and psychological stress in an assembly task. Ph.D. diss., George Washington University.

Edwards, R. 1979. *Contested terrain: The transformation of the workplace in the twentieth century.* New York: Basic Books.

Ehn, P. 1988. *Work-oriented design of computer artifacts.* Stockholm: Working Life Center and Almqvist and Wiksell International.

Eitinger, L. 1971. Acute and chronic psychiatric and psychosomatic reactions in concentration camp survivors. In *Society, stress and disease*, vol. 1, ed. L. Levi. Oxford: Oxford University Press.

Elden, M. 1981a. Political efficiency at work: The connection between more autonomous forms of workplace organization and more participatory politics. *Am Polit Sci Rev* 75:43–58.

Elden, M. 1981b. Sharing the research work: Participative research and its role demands. In *Human inquiry*, ed. P. Reason and J. Rowan. Chichester: Wiley.

Elden, M. 1983. Democratization and participative research in developing local theory. *J Occ Behav* 4:21–33.

Elmfeldt, D., Wilhelmsen, L., Wedel, H., Vedin, A., Wilhelmsson, C., and Tibblin, G. 1976. Primary risk factors in patients with myocardial infarction. *Am Heart J* 91:412–419.

Elvander, N. 1982. Kommunal demokrati och förvaltningsdemokrati (Community democracy and administrative democracy). In *Hotad sektor* (Threatened sector), ed. Arbetslivscentrum. Stockholm: Liber.

Emery, F. E., and Thorsrud, E. [1964] 1969. *Form and content in industrial democracy.* London: Tavistock, and Assen: Van Gorcun.

Ensinck, J. W., and Williams, R. H. 1974. Disorders causing hypoglycemia. In *Textbook of endocrinology,* 5th ed., ed. R. H. Williams. Philadelphia: W. B. Saunders.

Eriksson, R., and Åberg, R., eds. 1984. *Välfärd i förändring* (Changing welfare). Stockholm: Prisma.

Ewart, C. K., Taylor, C. B., Reese, L. B., and De Busk, R. F. 1983. Effects of early postmyocardial infarction exercise testing on self-perception and subsequent physical activity. *Am J Cardiol* 51:1076–1080.

Eyer, J. 1982. Changing trends in ischemic heart disease: Relations to cohort experience and economic trends in industrialized countries. *Adv Cardiol* 29:50–55.

Eyer, J., and Sterling, P. 1977. Stress-related mortality and social organization. *Rev Radical Polit Econ* 9:1–44.

Fain, J. N., Kovecev, V. P., and Scow, R. O. 1965. Effect of growth hormone and dexamethasone on lipolysis and metabolism in isolated fat cells of the rat. *J Biol Chem* 240:3522–3529.

Federal Energy Regulatory Commission. 1978. The Con Edison power failure of July 13 and 14, 1977. Final staff report. U.S. Department of Energy, Federal Energy Regulatory Commission.

Ferrarotti, F. 1980. *An alternative sociology.* New York: Irving.

Firth, R. 1939. *The primitive Polynesian economy.* London: Routledge and Sons.

Fiske, D. W., and Maddi, S. R. 1961. *Functions of varied experience.* Homewood, Ill.: Dorsey Press.

Fleischer, G. A. 1984. *Engineering economy capital allocation theory.* Belmont, CA: Wadsworth.

Floderus, B. 1974. Psychosocial factors in relation to coronary heart disease and associated risk factors. *Nordisk Hygienisk Tidskrift* Suppl. 6.

Foucault, M. 1979. *Discipline and punish: The birth of the prison.* New York: Vintage/Random House.

Frank, L., and Hackman, J. R. 1975. A failure of job enrichment: The case of the change that wasn't. *J Appl Behav Sci* 11:413–436.

Frankenhaeuser, M. 1980. Psychoneuroendocrine approaches to the study of stressful person-environment transactions. In *Selye's guide to stress research,* vol. 1, ed. H. Selye. New York: Van Nostrand Reinhold.

Frankenhaeuser, M., and Gardell, B. 1976. Underload and overload in working life: Outline of a multidisciplinary work. *J Human Stress* 2:34–46.

Frankenhaeuser, M., and Johansson, G. 1975. Behaviour and catecholamines in children. In *Society, stress and disease,* vol. 2, *Childhood and adolescence,* ed. L. Levi. Oxford: Oxford University Press.

Frankenhaeuser, M., and Johansson, G. 1986. Stress at work: Psychobiological and psychosocial aspects. *Int Rev Appl Psychol* 35:287–299.

Frankenhaeuser, M., Lundberg, U., and Forsman, L. 1980. Dissociation between sympathetic-adrenal and pituitary-adrenal responses to an achievement situation characterized by high controllability: Comparison between type A and type B males and females. *Biol Psychol* 10:79–91.

Franklin, J. 1986. *Molecules of the mind: The brave new science of molecular psychology.* New York: Atheneum.

Fredén, K., Åkerstedt, T., Olsson, K., and Orth-Gomér, K. 1986. Positive effects of displacing night work to the end of the shift cycle. In *Night- and shiftwork: Longterm effects and their prevention,* eds. M. Haider, M. Koller, and R. Cervinka. Proceedings of the VII international symposium on night- and shiftwork, Igls, Austria 1985. Frankfurt: Verlag Peter Lang.

Fredriksson, G., and Voight, P. 1979. Jämförande ergonomiska studier i olika komponenter i betongarbete (Comparative ergonomic study of concrete work components). Report R 147, Byggforskningen, Stockholm.

Freeman, H. J., and Jucker, J. 1979. Comparing the productivity of traditional and innovative work organizations. Paper presented at the Conference on Current Issues in Productivity, Columbia University, April 18. Stanford University, Department of Industrial Engineering and Engineering Management.

Freeman, R. B. 1976. *The overeducated American.* New York: Academic Press.

French, J. R. P., Jr. 1974. Person role fit. In *Occupational stress,* ed. A. McLean. Springfield, Ill.: Thomas.

French, J. R. P., Jr., Rodgers, W., Jr., and Cobb, S. 1974. Adjustment as person environment fit. In *Coping and adaptation*, ed. G. V. Coelho, D. A. Hamburg, and J. E. Adams. New York: Basic Books.

Frese, M. 1982. Occupational socialization and psychological development: An underemphasized research perspective in industrial psychology. *J Occ Psychol* 55:209–224.

Frese, M. 1987. A concept of control: Implications for stress and performance in human-computer interaction. In *Second international conference on human computer interaction*, ed. G. Salvendy. Amsterdam: Elsevier.

Frese, M. 1989. Theoretical models of control and health. In *Job control and worker health*, ed. S. L. Sauter, J. J. Hurrell, and C. C. Cooper. New York: Wiley.

Frese, M., and Sabini, J., eds. 1985. *Goal directed behavior: The concept of action in psychology*. Hillsdale, N.J.: Lawrence Erlbaum Associates.

Frese, M., and Semmer, N. 1986. Shiftwork, stress and psychosomatic complaints: A comparison between workers in different shiftwork schedules, non-shiftworkers, and former shiftworkers. *Ergonomics* 29:99–114.

Frese, M., and Stewart, J. 1984. Skill learning as a concept in life-span developmental psychology: An action theoretic analysis. *Human Devel* 27:145–162.

Frese, M., and Zapf, D. 1988. Methodological issues in the study of work stress: Objective vs. subjective measurement of work stress and the question of longitudinal studies. In *Causes, coping and consequences of stress at work*, ed. C. L. Cooper and R. Payne. New York: Wiley.

Freudenheim, M. 1987. Business and health. *New York Times*, May 26.

Friedman, M. 1962. *Capitalism and freedom*. Chicago: University of Chicago Press.

Friedman, M., and Rosenman, R. H. 1959. Association of specific overt behavior pattern with blood and cardiovascular findings. *JAMA* 169:1286–1297.

Friedman, M., Rosenman, R. H., and Carroll, V. 1958. Changes in serum cholesterol and blood clotting time in men subjected to cyclic variation of occupational stress. *Circulation* 17:852–873.

Funkenstein, D. H. 1956. Norepinephrine-like and epinephrine-like substances in relation to human behavior. *J Nerv Ment Dis* 124:58–73.

Ganster, D. 1989. Worker control and well-being: A review of research in the workplace. In *Job control and worker health*, ed. S. L. Sauter, J. J. Hurrell, and C. C. Cooper. New York: Wiley.

Gardell, B. 1971a. *Produktionsteknik och arbetsglädje* (Production technique and work satisfaction). Stockholm: Personaladministrativa Rådet.

Gardell, B. 1971b. *Technology, alienation and mental health*. Stockholm: Personaladministrativa Rådet.

Gardell, B. 1982. Worker participation and autonomy: A multilevel approach to democracy at the workplace. *Int J Health Serv* 12:527–558.

Gardell, B., and Gustavsson, R. A. 1979. *Sjukvård på löpande band* (Hospital care on the assembly line). Stockholm: Prisma.

Gardell, B., and Svensson, L. 1981. *Medbestämmande och självstyre: En lokal facklig strategi för demokratisering av arbetsplatsen* (Worker participation and autonomy: A local union strategy for democratization of the workplace). Stockholm: Prisma.

Gertler, M. M., and White, P. D. 1976. *Coagulation factors and coronary heart disease: A 25-year study in retrospect*. Oradell, N.J.: Medical Economics.

Gifford, S., and Gunderson, J. G. 1970. Cushing's disease as a psychosomatic disorder: A selective review of the clinical and experimental literature and a report of ten cases. *Perspect Biol Med* 13:169–221.

Gilbreth, F. B. 1909. *Bricklaying systems*. [SL]: Myron Clark Publ.

Gilmore, J. B. 1971. Play: A special behavior. In *Child's play*, ed. B. Herron and B. Sutton-Smith. New York: Wiley.

Ginzberg, E. 1987. Sounding board: A hard look at cost containment. *New Engl J Med* 316:1151–1154.

Gladstein, D. R., and Reilly, N. P. 1985. Group decision making under threat: The tycoon game. *Acad Manage J* 28:613–627.

Glass, D. C., and Singer, J. E. 1972. *Urban stress: Experiments on noise and social stressors*. New York: Academic Press.

Glynn, S. M., and Ruderman, A. J. 1986. The development and validation of an eating self-efficacy scale. *Cognit Ther Res* 10:403–420.

Goiten, B., and Seashore, S. 1980. *Worker participation: A national survey report*. Ann Arbor, Mich.: Survey Research Center, University of Michigan.

Golembiewski, R. T., Hilles, R., and Daly, R. 1987. Some effects of multiple O.D. interventions on burnout and worksite features. *J Appl Behav Sci* 23(3):295–314.

Golembiewski, R. T., Munzenrider, R., and Stevenson, J. 1984. Physical symptoms and burnout phases. Paper presented at the Second Annual Conference on Organizational Policy and Development, University of Louisville, Louisville, Kentucky, April.

Goodman, P. S. 1979. *Assessing organizational change: The Rushton Quality of Work experiment*. New York: Wiley.

Gordon, D., Edwards, R., and Reich, M. 1982. *Segmented work, divided workers: The historical transformation of labor in the United States*. New York: Cambridge University Press.

Gordon, T., and Shurtleff, D. 1973. Means at each examination variation of specified characteristics: Framingham Study Exam 1 to Exam 10. In *The Framingham study section 28*, ed. W. B. Kannel and T. Gordon. NIH publication no. 74-618, U.S. Department of Health, Education and Welfare.

Gough, R., and Vuonokari, T. 1988. *Långvårdens arbetsmiljö: En arbetsstudie* (The work environment in long-term care: A study of work sites). Stockholm: Arbetslivscentrum.

Gouldner, A. W. 1954a. *Patterns of industrial bureaucracy*. New York: Free Press.

Gouldner, A. W. 1954b. *Wildcat strike*. Yellow Springs, Ohio: Antioch Press.

Graveling, R. A. 1980. The modification of hormonal and metabolic effects of mental stress by physical exercise. In *Stress and tension control*, ed. F. J. McGuigan, W. F. Sime, and J. M. Wallace. New York: Plenum Press.

Gregory, D. 1987. Philosophy and practice in knowledge representation. In *Human productivity enhancement*, vol. 2, ed. J. Zeidner. New York: Praeger.

Griffin, R. W., Bateman, T. S., Wayne, S. J., and Head, T. D. 1987. Objective and social factors as determinants of task perceptions and responses: An integrated perspective and empirical investigation. *Acad Manage Rev* 30:501–523.

Grinker, R., and Spiegel, J. 1945. *Men under stress*. Philadelphia: Blakiston.

Grippa, A. J., and Durbin, D. 1986. Worker's compensation occupational disease claims. *Nat Coun Compens Ins Dig* 1(2):15–23.

Gryzb, G. J. 1981. Decollectivization and recollectivization in the workplace: The impact on informal work groups and work culture. *Econ Indus Democ* 2:455–482.

Gustavsen, B. 1976. Aktionsforskning (Action research). Report no. 13, Department of Psychology, University of Stockholm.

Gustavsen, B. 1985. Technology and agreements. *Ind Relat J* 16:3–26.

Gustavsen, B. 1987. Diffusion and discussion: National strategies for changing working life and the role of democratic dialogue. In *Future of work: A viewpoint of social sciences*, ed. K. Eklund. Helsinki: NIVA.

Gustavsen, B., and Hunnius, G. 1981. *New patterns of work reform: The case of Norway*. Oslo: Oslo University Press.

Guterl, F. 1984. Harris poll survey results: The job. *IEEE Spectrum* June:38–44.

Gyllenhammar, P. G. 1979. *Industripolitik för människor* (Industry politics for humans). Stockholm: Studieförbundet för Näringsliv och Samhälle.

Hacker, W. 1978. *Allgemeine Arbeits- und Ingenieurpsychologie* (General psychology of work and engineering). Bern: Huber.

Hackman, J. R. 1980. Assessment of QWL experiments. *Prof Psychol*.

Hackman, J. R. 1984. Psychological contributions to organizational productivity: A commentary. In *Productivity research in the behavioral and social sciences*, ed. A. Brief. New York: Praeger.

Hackman, J. R., and Lawler, E. E. 1971. Employee reactions to job characteristics. *J Appl Psych* 55:259–286.

Hackman, J. R., and Oldham, G. R. 1975. Development of the Job Diagnostic Survey. *J Appl Psychol* 60:159–170.

Hackman, J. R., and Oldham, G. R. 1976. Motivation through the design of work: Test of a theory. *Organ Behav Hum Perform* 16:250–279.

Hackman, J. R., and Oldham, G. R. 1980. *Work redesign*. Reading, Mass.: Addison-Wesley.

Haft, J. J. 1974. Cardiovascular injury induced by sympathetic catecholamines. *Prog Cardiovasc Dis* 17:73–86.

Hahn, M. 1985. Job strain and cardiovascular disease: A ten-year prospective study. *Am J Epidemiol* 122:532–540.

Hall, E. M., and Johnson, J. V. 1988. Depression in unemployed Swedish women. *Soc Sci Med* 27:1349–1355.

Hammarström, A., Janlert, U., and Theorell, T. 1988. Youth unemployment and ill health: Results from a two-year follow-up study. *Soc Sci Med* 26:1025–1033.

Hanlon, M. D., Nadler, D. A., and Gladstein, D. 1985. *Attempting work reform: The case of "Parkside" Hospital.* New York: Wiley.

Härenstam, A., Palm, U-B., and Theorell, T. 1988. Stress, health and the working environment of Swedish prison staff. *Work and Stress* 2:281–290.

Härenstam, A., and Theorell, T. 1988. Work conditions and urinary excretion of catecholamines: A study of prison staff in Sweden. *Scand J Work Environ Health* 14:257–264.

Härenstam, A., Theorell, T., Orth-Gomér, K., Palm, U-B., and Undén, A-L. 1987. Shift work, decision latitude, and ventricular ectopic activity: A study of 24-hour electrocardiograms in Swedish prison personnel. *Work and Stress* 1:341–350.

Harlan, W. R., and Shaw, W. A. 1972. Interpretation of hyperlipidemias. *Crit Rev Clin Lab Sci* 3:451–487.

Harrison, R. 1983. *Bentham.* London: Routledge and Kegan Paul.

Hartman, C., and Pearlstein, S. 1987. The joy of working. *INC.,* November.

Hartung, G. H., Foresyt, J. P., Mitchell, R. E., Vlasek, I., and Gotto, A. M. 1980. Relation of diet to high-density-lipoprotein cholesterol in middle-aged marathon runners, joggers, and inactive men. *New Engl J Med* 302:357–361.

Hatch, C. R. 1987. Learning from Italy's industrial renaissance. *Entrepren Econ* 6:4–11.

Hattis, D., Richardson, B., and Ashford, N. A. 1979. *General stress responses and cardiovascular disease processes: Review and reassessment of hypothesized relationships.* Cambridge: Center for Policy Alternatives, Massachusetts Institute of Technology.

Havlik, R. J., and Feinleib, M. D. 1979. *Proceedings of the conference on the decline in coronary heart disease mortality.* National Heart, Lung, and Blood Institute, National Institutes of Health, Bethesda, MD, October 1978. U.S. Department of Health, Education and Welfare, NIH publication no. 79-1610, May 1979.

Hayes, R., and Abernathy, W. 1980. Managing our way to economic decline. *Harv Bus Rev,* 58:67–77.

Haynes, S. G., Feinleib, M., and Kannel, W. B. 1980. The relationship of psychosocial factors to coronary heart disease in the Framingham study. Part III: Eight year incidence of coronary heart disease. *Am J Epidemiol* 3:37–58.

Hebron, M. E. 1966. *Motivated learning: A developmental study from birth to senium.* London: Methuen.

Hechinger, F. M. 1987. Pollster finds hope and confidence. *New York Times,* October 13.

Heimstra, N. W. 1973. The effects of smoking on mood change. In *Motives and incentives,* ed. W. L. Dunn. New York: Wiley.

Henry, J. P. 1988. The archetypes of power and intimacy and the aging process. Department of Physiology, University of Southern California. Manuscript.

Henry, J. P., and Cassell, J. 1969. Psychological factors in essential hypertension: Recent epidemiological and animal experimental evidence. *Am J Epidemiol* 90:171–200.

Henry, J. P., and Stephens, P. M. 1977a. The social environment and essential hypertension in mice: Possible role of the innervation of the adrenal cortex. *Prog Brain Res* 47:263–275.

Henry, J. P., and Stephens, P. M. 1977b. *Stress, health and the social environment: A sociobiologic approach to medicine.* New York: Springer.

Henry, J. P., Stephens, J., Axelrod, J., and Mueller, R. A. 1971. Effect of psychosocial stimulation on enzymes involved in the biosynthesis and metabolism of noradrenaline and adrenaline. *Psychosom Med* 33:227–237.

Herzlinger, R., and Calkins, D. 1986. How companies tackle health care costs: Part III. *Harv Bus Rev* January–February: 70–80.

Herzlinger, R., and Schwartz, J. 1985. How companies tackle health care costs: Part I. *Harv Bus Rev* July–August: 69–81.

Hiltzik, M. A. 1987. Exotic devices for investment techniques may hold potential for disaster. *Los Angeles Times,* October 29.

Hingley, P., and Cooper, C. L. 1986. *Stress and the nurse manager.* Chichester: Wiley.

Hinkle, L. E., Jr. 1974. The effect of exposure to culture change, social change, and changes in interpersonal relationships on health. In *Life events: Their nature and effects,* ed. B. S. Dohrenwend and B. P. Dohrenwend. New York: Wiley.

Hinkle, L. E., Jr., Whitney, L. H., Lehman, E. W., Dunn, J., Benjamin, B., King, R., Plakun, A., and Flehinger, B. 1968. Occupation, education and coronary heart disease. *Science* 161:238–248.

Hiroto, D. L. 1974. Locus of control and learned helplessness. *J Exp Psychol* 102:187–196.

Hirschorn, M. W. 1988. Medical discord. Some doctors assail quality of treatment provided by HMOs. *New York Times*, May 15.

Hjalmarson, A., Isaksson, O., and Ahren, K. 1969. Effects of growth hormone and insulin on amino acid transport in perfused rat heart. *Am J Physiol* 217:1795–1802.

Hjermann, I., Helgeland, A., Holme, I., Leren, P., and Lund-Larsen, P. 1980. A randomized intervention trial in primary prevention of coronary heart disease: The Oslo study. Paper presented at the Eighth European Congress of Cardiology, Paris, June 22–26.

Holland, T., Konick, A., Buffum, W., Smith, M. K., and Petchers, M. 1981. Institutional structure and resident outcomes. *J Health Soc Behav* 22:433–444.

Holme, I., Hegeland, A., Hjermann, I., Leren, P., and Lund-Larsen, P. G. 1977. Coronary risk factors in various occupational groups: The Oslo Study. *Brit J Prev Soc Med* 31:96–100.

Holmes, T. H., and Rahe, R. H. 1967. The social readjustment rating scale. *J Psychosom Res* 11:213–218.

Homans, G. 1950. *The human group.* New York: Harcourt, Brace.

House, J., and Cottington, E. 1986. Health and the workplace. In *Applications of social medicine to clinical medicine and health policy,* ed. L. Aiken and D. Mechanic. New Brunswick: Rutgers University Press.

House, J. S. 1981. *Work stress and social support.* Reading, Mass.: Addison-Wesley.

House, J. S., Strecher, V., Metzner, H. L., and Robbins, C. 1986. Occupational stress and health among men and women in the Tecumseh Community Health Study. *J Health Soc Behav* 27:62–77.

House, J. S., Wells, J., McMichael, A., Kaplan, B., and Landerman, L. 1979. Occupational health and stress among factory workers. *J Health Soc Behav* 20:39–160.

Howard, R. 1985a. *Brave new workplace.* New York: Viking.

Howard, R. 1985b. Utopia: Where workers craft new technology. *Technology Rev* (April): 43–49.

Hoxie, R. F. 1920. *Scientific management and labor.* New York: Appleton.

Hulin, C. L., and Blood, M. R. 1968. Job enlargement, individual differences and worker responses. *Psychol Bull* 69:41–55.

Hunter, J. E., and Schmidt, F. L. 1982. Fitting people to jobs: The impact of personnel selection on national productivity. In *Human performance and productivity,* vol. 1, *Human capability assessment,* ed. M. D. Dunnette and E. A. Fleishman. Hillsdale, N.J.: Erlbaum.

Ikard, F. F., and Tomkins, S. 1973. The experience of affect as a determinant of smoking behavior: A series of validity studies. *J Abnormal Psychol* 8:172–181.

Illich, I. 1977. *Medical nemesis.* New York: Bantam Books.

International Labour Office. 1979. *Introduction to work study,* 3rd rev. ed. Geneva: International Labour Office.

Jackson, S. 1983. Participation in decision making as a strategy for reducing job related strain. *J Appl Psychol* 68:3–19.

Jahoda, M., Lazarsfeld, P., Zeisel, H., 1971. *Marienthal: The sociography of an unemployed community.* Chicago: Aldine, Atherton.

Jamal, M. 1985. Relationship of job stress to job performance: A study of managers and blue-collar workers. *Human Relat* 18:409–424.

Janis, I., and Mann, L. 1977. *Decision making: A psychological analysis of conflict, choice, and commitment.* New York: Free Press.

Japanese Management Association. 1983. *Kanban: Just-in-time at Toyota.* Cambridge: Productivity Press.

Jenkins, G. D., and Gupta, N. 1985. The payoffs of paying for knowledge. *Nat Product Rev* 4:121–130.

Jersild, P. C. 1978. *Babels hus* (Babel's house). Stockholm: Bonniers.

Johansson, G., Aronsson, G., and Lindström, B. O. 1978. Social psychological and neuroendocrine stress reactions in highly mechanized work. *Ergonomics* 21:583–599.

Johansson, G., and Lindström, B. O. 1975. Paced and un-paced work under salary and piece-rate conditions. Report no. 459, Department of Psychology, University of Stockholm.

Johansson, S. 1971. Om Levnadsnivåundersökningen (On the National Survey of Level of Living). Stockholm: Låginkomstutredningen, Allmänna Förlaget.

Johnson, J. V. 1985. The effects of control and social support on work-related strain and adverse health outcomes. Research report 39, Department of Psychology, University of Stockholm, Stockholm.

Johnson, J. V. 1986. The impact of the workplace social support, job demands, and work control under cardiovascular disease in Sweden. Ph.D. diss., Johns Hopkins University. Distributed by Department of Psychology, University of Stockholm, Report no. 1–86.

Johnson, J. V., and Hall, E. M. 1988. Job strain, workplace social support and cardiovascular disease: A cross-sectional study of a random sample of the Swedish working population. *Am J Public Health* 78:1336–1342.

Johnson, J. V., Hall, E. M., and Theorell, T. In press. The combined effects of work strain and social isolation on prevalence and mortality in cardiovascular disease. *Scand J Work Environ Health.*

Johnson, J. V., and Johansson, G. 1988. The relationship between job design and health behavior: A cross-sectional study of smoking and physical exercise in a random sample of the Swedish male and female population. Manuscript.

Jonsson, A., and Hansson, L. 1977. Prolonged exposure to a stressful stimulus (noise) as a cause of raised blood pressure in man. *Lancet* 1:86.

Jönsson, B. 1980. The Volvo experiences of new job design and new production technology. In *Working Life.* Swedish Information Service, September.

Jorgensen, R. S., and Houston, B. K. 1986. Family history of hypertension, personality patterns and cardiovascular reactivity to stress. *Psychosom Med* 48:102–117.

Kahn, R. 1974. Conflict, ambiguity and overload: Three elements in job stress. In *Occupational stress,* ed. A. McLean. Springfield, Ill.: Charles Thomas.

Kahn, R. 1981. Work and health: Somatic and psycho-social effects of advanced technology. In *Working life,* ed. B. Gardell and G. Johansson. New York: Wiley.

Kahn, R., and Quinn, R. 1970. Role stress. In *Mental health and work organization,* ed. R. McLean. Chicago: Rand McNally.

Kahn, R., Wolfe, D., Quinn, R., Snoek, J., and Rosenthal, R. 1964. *Organizational stress: Studies in role conflict and ambiguity.* New York: Wiley.

Kannel, W. B., Feinleib, M., McNamara, P. M., Garrison, R. J., and Castelli, W. P. 1979. An investigation of coronary heart disease in families: The Framingham offspring study. *Am J Epidemiol* 110:281–90.

Kanner, A. D., Kafry, D., and Pines, A. 1978. Conspicuous in its absence: The lack of positive conditions as a source of stress. *J Human Stress* 4:33–39.

Karasek, R. A. 1976. The impact of the work environment on life outside the job. Ph.D. diss., Massachusetts Institute of Technology. Distributed by National Technical Information Service, U.S. Department of Commerce, Springfield, Va. 22161. Thesis order no. PB 263–073.

Karasek, R. A. 1978. Job socialization: A longitudinal study of work, political and leisure activity in Sweden. Paper presented at the Ninth World Congress of Sociology (RC30), Uppsala, Swedish Institute for Social Research, Stockholm University, August 15.

Karasek, R. A. 1979. Job demands, job decision latitude, and mental strain: Implications for job redesign. *Adm Sci Q* 24:285–307.

Karasek, R. A. 1981a. A new model of job characteristics and productivity. Task effectiveness as a function of skill utilization, motivation and job stress. Paper originally presented at the Conference on Current Issues in Productivity, Columbia University, April 18, 1978. [Revised stencil, Department of Industrial Engineering and Operations Research, Columbia University, New York.]

Karasek, R. A. 1981b. Job decision latitude, job design, and coronary heart disease. *Proceedings of the International Conference on Machine Pacing and Occupational Stress.* London: Taylor and Francis.

Karasek, R. A. 1981c. New value. Department of Industrial Engineering and Operations Research, Columbia University, New York. Mimeo.

Karasek, R. A. 1981d. Comparing job stress in white- and blue-collar work: Relationships between social class, job characteristics and psychological strain. In *Stress im Buro,* ed. M. Frese. Zurich: Huber.

Karasek, R. A. 1981e. Job socialization and job strain: The implications of two related psychosocial mechanisms for job design. In *Man and working life: Social science contributions to work reform,* ed. B. Gardell and G. Johansson. Chichester: Wiley.

Karasek, R. A. 1984. Critique of FAA training materials on job stress. U.S. Congressional Record. Committee on Public Works and Transportation, HR–98–83, 98th Congress, p. 787.

Karasek, R. 1985. Job content questionnaire. Department of Industrial and Systems Engineering, University of Southern California, Los Angeles.

Karasek, R. A. 1987a. Making customer-initiated variety feasible for CIM customer-oriented product design software. In *Social, ergonomic and stress aspects of work with computers,* ed. G. Salvendy, S. L. Sauter, and J. Hurrell. Amsterdam: Elsevier.

Karasek, R. A. 1987b. Method for assessing capability enhancement. Department of Industrial and Systems Engineering, University of Southern California, Los Angeles. Mimeo.

Karasek, R. A. 1989a. The political implications of psychosocial work redesign: A model of the psychosocial class structure. *Int J Health Serv* 19(3):481–508.

Karasek, R. A. 1989b. Control in the workplace and its health-related aspects. In *Job control and worker health,* ed. S. L. Sauter, J. J. Hurrell, and C. L. Cooper. Chichester: Wiley.

Karasek, R. A. In press. Lower health risk with increased job control among white-collar workers. *J Occ Behav.*

Karasek, R. A., Baker, D., Marxer, F., Ahlbom, A., and Theorell, T. 1981. Job decision latitude, job demands, and cardiovascular disease: A prospective study of Swedish men. *Am J Public Health* 71:694–705.

Karasek, R. A., Gardell, B., and Lindell, J. 1987. Work and non-work correlates of illness and behaviour in male and female Swedish white-collar workers. *J Occ Behav* 8:187–207.

Karasek, R. A., Russell, R. S., and Theorell, T. 1982. Physiology of stress and regeneration in job-related cardiovascular illness. *J Human Stress* 8:29–42.

Karasek, R. A., Schwartz, J., and Pieper, C. 1983. Validation of a survey instrument for job-related cardiovascular illness. Department of Industrial Engineering and Operations Research, Columbia University, New York. Mimeo.

Karasek, R. A., Schwartz, J., and Theorell, T. 1982. Job characteristics, occupation and coronary heart disease. Final report to National Institute of Occupational Safety and Health. New York: Columbia University.

Karasek, R. A., and Sioukas, A. 1990. Market scale, specialization, and job characteristics. Department of Industrial and Systems Engineering, University of Southern California, Los Angeles. Mimeo.

Karasek, R. A., Theorell, T., Alfredsson, L., Pieper, C., and Schwartz, J. 1982. Job psychological factors and coronary heart disease. *Adv Cardiol* 29:62–67.

Karasek, R. A., Theorell, T., Schwartz, J., Schnall, P., Pieper, C., and Michela, J. 1988. Job characteristics in relation to the prevalence of myocardial infarction in the U.S. HES and HANES. *Am J Public Health* 78:910–918.

Karasek, R. A., Triantis, K., and Chaudhry, S. 1982. Co-worker and supervisor support as moderators of associations between task characteristics and mental strain. *J Occ Behav* 3:147–160.

Karlsen, J. I., and Naess, R. 1978. *Arbeidsmiljø i hotell og restaurantnaeringen* (Work environment for hotel and restaurant workers). Arbeidsforsknings-instituttene, Oslo.

Kasl, S. V. 1979. Epidemiological contributions to the study of work stress. In *Stress at work,* ed. C. Cooper and R. Payne. New York: Wiley.

Kasl, S. V. 1989. An epidemiological perspective on the role of control in health. In *Job control and worker health,* ed. S. L. Sauter, J. J. Hurrell, and C. C. Cooper. London: Wiley.

Kasl, S. V., Cobb, S., and Brooks, G. W. 1968. Changes in serum uric and cholesterol levels in men undergoing job loss. *JAMA* 206:1500–1508.

Katz, D. and Kahn, R. 1966. *Social Psychology of Organizations.* New York: Wiley.

Katzell, R., Bienstock, P., and Faerstein, P. 1977. *A guide to worker productivity experiments in the United States 1971–75.* New York: New York University Press.

Katzell, R., and Yankelovich, D. 1975. *Work, productivity and job satisfaction.* New York: The Psychological Corporation.

Kauppinen-Toropainen, K. 1981. Job demands and job content: Effects on job dissatisfaction and stress. Department of Psychology, Institute of Occupational Health, Helsinki. Mimeo.

Kauppinen-Toropainen, K., and Hanninen, V. 1981. *Case studies on job reorganization and job redesign in Finland.* Helsinki: Työterveislaitos.

Keller, J. J. 1988. A scramble for global networks. *Business Week,* March 21.

Kemery, E. R., Bedeian, A. G., Mossholder, K. W., and Touliatos, J. 1985. Outcomes of role stress: A multisample constructive replication. *Acad Manage J* 28:363–375.

Kendrick, J. 1978. Special study on economic change: Hearing before the Joint Economic Committee, June, Washington, D.C. 95th Cong., 2d sess.

Kerckhoff, A., and Back, K. 1968. *The June bug.* New York: Appleton-Century-Croft.

Kern, H., and Schumann, M. 1984. *Das Ende der Arbeitsteilung? Rationalisierung in der industriellen Produktion* (The end of the division of labor? Rationalization in the industrial production). Munich: Verlag Ctl Beck.

Kiecolt-Glaser, J. K. 1985. Stress and the immune function. In *Measures of job stress: A research methodology workshop.* A NIOSH workshop conducted by Morris and McDaniel, Inc., New Orleans, LA.

Kiesler, D. J. 1983. The 1982 interpersonal circle: A taxonomy for complementarity in human transactions. *Psychol Rev* 90:185–214.

Kiesler, C. S., and Morton, T. L. 1988. Psychology and public policy in the "health care revolution." *Am Psychol* 43:993–1003.

Kihlbom, A. 1976. Circulatory adaptation during static muscular contractions: A review. *Scand J Work Environ Health* 2:1–13.

Killing, P. 1980. Technology acquisition, license agreement or joint venture. *Columbia J World Bus* Fall:38–46.

Kjeldsen, S. E., Eide, I., Aakesson, K., and Leren, P. 1983. Increased arterial catecholamine concentrations in 50-year-old men with essential hypertension. *Scand J Clin Lab Invest* 43:343–349.

Knox, S., Svensson, J., Theorell, T., and Waller, D. 1988. Emotional coping and elevated blood pressure. *Behav Med* 14:52–58.

Knox, S., Theorell, T., Svensson, J., and Waller, D. 1985. The relation of social support and working environment to medical variables associated with elevated blood pressure in young males: A structural model. *Soc Sci Med* 21:525–531.

Knutsson, A., Åkerstedt, T., and Jonsson, B. G. 1987. En jämförande tvärsnittsstudie av kroppsliga och psykosomatiska symptom bland dag- och skiftarbetare (Comparative cross-sectional study of physical and psychosomatic symptoms among day and shift workers). Stress research report no. 192. Stockholm: National Institute of Psychosocial Factors and Health.

Knutsson, A., Åkerstedt, T., Jonsson, B. G., and Orth-Gomér, K. 1986. Increased risk of ischaemic heart disease in shift workers. *Lancet*:89–92.

Koepp, S. 1987. Pul-eeze! Will somebody help me? *Time*, February 2.

Kohn, M. 1977. *Class and conformity: A study of values.* Chicago: University of Chicago Press.

Kohn, M. 1985. Unresolved interpretive issues in the relationship between work and personality. Department of Sociology, Johns Hopkins University. Manuscript.

Kohn, M., and Schooler, C. 1973. Occupational experience and psychological functioning: An assessment of reciprocal effects. *Am Sociol Rev* 38:97–118.

Kohn, M., and Schooler, C. 1978. The reciprocal effects of the substantive complexity of work and intellectual flexibility: A longitudinal assessment. *Am J Sociol* 84:24–52.

Kohn, M., and Schooler, C. 1982. Job conditions and personality: A longitudinal assessment of their reciprocal effects. *Am J Sociol* 87:1257–1286.

Koivisto, V. A., Soman, V., Conrad, P., Hendler, R., Nadel, E., and Felig, P. 1979. Insulin binding to monocytes in trained athletes: Changes in the resting state and after exercise. *J Clin Invest* 64:1011–1015.

Kopelman, R. E. 1985. Job redesign and productivity: A review of the evidence. *Nat Product Rev* (Summer): 237–255.

Kornhauser, A. 1965. *The mental health of the industrial worker: A Detroit study.* New York: Wiley.

Kornitzer, M., Kittel, F., Dramaix, M., and de Backer, G. 1982. Job stress and coronary heart disease. *Adv Cardiol* 19:56–61.

Koskenvuo, M., Kaprio, J., Kasaniemi, A., and Sarna, S. 1980. Differences in mortality from ischemic heart disease by marital status and social class. *J Chron Dis* 33:95–106.

Kraus, S., and Lilienfeld, A. M. 1959. Some epidemiologic aspects of the high mortality rates in the young widowed group. *J Chron Dis* 10:207–217.

Kristein, M. 1983. How much can business expect to profit from smoking cessation? *Prev Med* 12:358–381.

Kubicek, H. 1983. Glasfasenetze als Autobahnen zum elektronischen Büro an zum elektronischen Heim (Glass phase networks as highways to the electronic office and further to the electronic home). In *Medientag 1982*, ed. D. G. B. Landesbezirk. Rheinland-Pfalz: Mainz DGB.

La Croix, A. Z. 1984. Occupational exposure to high demand/low control work and coronary heart disease incidence in the Framingham cohort. Ph.D. diss., Department of Epidemiology, University of North Carolina.

Lader, M. H., ed. 1969. *Studies of anxiety. Br J Psychiatry*, special publication no. 3. Ashley, Kent: Headley Brothers.

Lag om medbestämmande. 1980. (Law on co-determination). Stockholm: SFS 620.

Lag om socialtjänst. 1980. (Law on social welfare). Stockholm: SFS 620.

Langner, T., and Michaels, S. 1963. *Life stress and mental health*. Glencoe, Ill.: Free Press.

Langosch, W., Brodner, B., and Borcherding, M. 1983. Psychosocial and vocational long-term outcomes of cardiac rehabilitation with postinfarction patients under the age of forty. *Psychosom Med* 40:115–128.

LaRocco, J., House, J., and French, J. 1980. Social support, occupational stress and health. *J Health Soc Behav* 21:202–218.

Lawler, E. E. 1986. *High-involvement management*. San Francisco: Jossey-Bass.

Lawler, E. E., and Ledford, G. E. 1982. Productivity and the quality of work life. *Nat Product Rev* 1:26–36.

Lawler, E. E., Ledford, J., and Mohrman, S. 1989. *Employee involvement in America: A study of contemporary practice*. Houston: American Productivity and Quality Center.

Lawler, E. E., and Mohrman, S. A. 1985. Quality circles after the fad. *Harv Bus Rev* 85:64–71.

Lawler, E. E., Nadler, D. A., and Cammann, C. 1980. *Organizational assessment*. New York: Wiley.

Lawrence, J. F. 1986. In take-overs, human toll is often ignored. *Los Angeles Times*, December 14.

Lazarus, R. S. 1966. *Psychological stress and the coping process*. New York: McGraw-Hill.

Lazes, P. 1978. Health workers and decision making. *Urban Health*, (April): 34–55.

Lazes, P., Wasilewski, Y., and Redd, J. D. 1977. Improving outpatient care through participation: The Newark experiment in staff and patient involvement. *Int J Health Educ* 20:61–68.

Leaf, A., and Liddle, G. W. 1974. Summarization of the effects of hormones on water and electrolyte metabolism. In *Textbook of endocrinology*, 5th ed., ed. R. H. Williams. Philadelphia: W. B. Saunders.

Lenin, V. I. [1917–1923] 1960–1970. *Collected works*, vol. 27. Moscow: Foreign Language Publishing House. As quoted by Bettelheim C. 1976. *Class struggles in the USSR. 1st period 1917–1923*. New York: Monthly Review Press.

Lenke, B., and Barklöf, K. 1988. Arbetsmiljö och hälsa hos motorbranschens tjänstemän och arbetsledare (Work environment and health in white-collar workers and supervisors in auto repair). Final report, no. 83–0261, to the Swedish Work Environment Fund, Stockholm.

Lerner, M. 1985. *Occupational stress groups and the psychodynamics of the world of work*. Oakland, Calif.: Institute for Labor and Mental Health.

Lesser, I. 1981. A review of the alexithymia concept. *Psychosom Med* 43:531–542.

Levi, L., ed. 1971. *Society, stress and disease*, 4 vols. Oxford: Oxford University Press.

Levi, L. 1972a. Conditions of work and sympathoadrenomedullary activity: Experimental manipulations in a real life setting. In *Stress and distress in response to psychosocial stimuli*, ed. L. Levi. *Acta Med Scand* Suppl 528, vol. 191.

Levi, L. 1972b. Introduction: Psychosocial stimuli, psychophysiological reactions and disease. In *Stress and distress in response to psychosocial stimuli*, ed. L. Levi. *Acta Med Scand* Suppl 528, vol. 191.

Levi, L. 1972c. Psychological and physiological reactions to and psychomotor performance during prolonged and complex stressor exposure. In *Stress and distress in response to psychosocial stimuli*, ed. L. Levi. *Acta Med Scand* Suppl 528, vol. 191.

Levi, L. 1972d. *Stress and distress in response to psychosocial stimuli. Acta Med Scand* Suppl 528, vol. 191.

Lewin, K. 1946. Action research and minority problems. *J Soc Iss* 2:34–46.

Lichtenstein, P., Pedersen, N. L., Plomin, R., de Faire, U., and McClearn, G. E. 1988. Type A behavior pattern, related personality traits and self-reported coronary heart disease. Department of Environmental Hygiene, Karolinska Institute, Stockholm. Manuscript.

Light, K. C., and Obrist, P. A. 1980. Cardiovascular response to stress: Effects of opportunity to avoid shock experience and performance feedback. *Psychophysiology* 17:243–252.

Lindell, J. 1982. Besvarsmönster och arbetsmiljökonstellationer i olika tjänstemannagrupper (Patterns of self-reported symptoms and work environments in different groups of white-collar workers). Bygghälsan, Stockholm. Mimeo.

Lindell, J. 1984. *Effektivitet, arbetsmiljö och hälsa* (Efficiency, working environment and health). Stockholm: Bygghälsan.

Locke, E. A., Shaw, V. N., Saari, L. M., and Latham, G. P. 1986. Goal setting and task performance: 1969–1980. In *Readings in industrial and organizational psychology,* ed. F. Landy. Chicago, Ill.: Dorsey Press.

Lov om arbeitervaern og arbeidsmiljø. 1977. (Law on occupational safety and environment). Norsk Lag Oslo: Norway's Law 4/2 nr4.

Lown, B., Verrier, R. L., and Corbalan, R. 1973. Psychologic stress and threshold for repetitive ventricular response. *Science* 182:834–837.

Lund, R. T., and Hansen, J. 1986. *Keeping America at work: Strategies for employing the new technologies.* New York: Wiley.

Lundberg, U., and Forsman, L. 1979. Adrenal-medullary and adrenal cortical responses to understimulation and overstimulation: Comparison between type A and type B persons. *Biol Psychol* 9:79–89.

Lundberg, U., and Frankenhaeuser, M. 1978. Pituitary-adrenal and sympathetic-adrenal correlates of distress and effort. Report no. 548, Department of Psychology, University of Stockholm.

Lundvall, B-A. 1985. *Product innovation and user-producer interaction.* Industrial Development Research Series. Aalborg: Aalborg University Press.

Lynch, J. J. 1977. *The broken heart.* New York: Basic Books.

Lysgaard, S. 1961. *Arbeiderkollektivet* (Workers' collectivity). Oslo: Universitets Forlaget.

Macy, B. A. 1979. A progress report on the Bolivar Quality of Work Life project. *Personnel* (August):527–559.

Macy, B., Peterson, M., and Norton, L. 1989. A test of participation theory in a work redesign field setting. *Human Relat* 42 (September).

Maddi, S., and Kobasa, S. G. 1984. *The hardy executive, health under stress.* Homewood, Ill.: Dow Jones-Irwin.

Maier, S. F., and Seligman, M. E. P. 1976. Learned helplessness: Theory and evidence. *J Exp Psychol [Gen]* 105:3–46.

Majchrzak, A., Chang, T. C., Barfield, W., Eberts, R. E., and Salvendy, G. 1987. *The human aspects of computer-aided design.* London: Taylor & Francis.

Manchester, K. L. 1972. Effect of insulin on protein synthesis. *Diabetes* 1:447–452.

Mann, E. 1988. Taking on General Motors: A case study of the UAW campaign to keep GM Van Nuys open. Los Angeles: Institute of Industrial Relations, University of California, Los Angeles.

March, J. G., and Simon, H. A. 1958. *Organizations.* New York: Wiley.

Marglin, S. A. 1974. What do bosses do? The origins and functions of hierarchy in capitalist production. *Rev Radical Polit Econ* 6(2):60–112.

Marmot, M. G. 1982. Socio-economic and cultural factors in ischemic heart disease. *Adv Cardiol* 29:68–76.

Marmot, M. G., and Syme, L. 1976. Acculturation and coronary heart disease in Japanese-Americans. *Am J Epidemiol* 104:225–247.

Marmot, M. G., and Theorell, T. 1988. Social class and cardiovascular disease: The contribution of work. *Int J Health Serv* 18:659–674.

Marris, P. 1975. *Loss and change.* Garden City, N.Y.: Anchor Press.

Marshall, R. 1988. Economic competitiveness, new technology, and participatory decision making for U.S. workers. Address to California Policy Seminar, Changing Technologies in the Workplace. University of California, Los Angeles, December 2.

Martin, R. P., Haskell, W. L., and Wood, P. D. 1977. Blood chemistry and lipid profiles of elite distance runners. *Ann NY Acad Sci* 301:346–360.

Marx, K. 1867. *Das Kapital,* vol. 1–3. Hamburg: Meissner.

Maslach, K. 1982. *Burnout: The cost of caring.* Englewood Cliffs, N.J.: Prentice-Hall.

Maslach, K., and Pines, A. 1977. The burnout syndrome in the day care setting. *Child Care Q* 6:100–113.

Mason, J. W. 1968. Organization of psychoendocrine mechanisms. *Psychosom Med* 30:565–808.

Matteson, M. T., and Ivancevich, J. M., eds. 1987. *Controlling work stress: Effective human resource and management strategies.* San Francisco: Jossey-Bass.

Matthews, K. A., and Haynes, S. G. 1986. Type A behavior pattern and coronary disease risk: Update and critical evaluation. *Am J Epidemiol* 123:923–960.

McAdams, D. P. 1985. *Power and intimacy and the life story: Personalogical inquiries into identity.* Homewood, Ill.: Dorsey Press.

McCright, P. R. 1988. The job control and job demand hypothesis in a laboratory setting. Ph.D. diss., Stanford University.

McDougall, M. M., Dembroski, T. M., Slaats, S., Herd, J. A., and Eliot, R. S. 1983. Selective cardiovascular effects of stress and cigarette smoking. *J Human Stress* 9:13–21.

McGrath, J. E. 1970. A conceptual formulation for research of stress. In *Social and psychological factors in stress,* ed. J. E. McGrath. New York: Holt, Rinehart and Winston.

McGregor, D. 1960. *The human side of enterprise.* New York: McGraw-Hill.

McMahon, P. 1987. Some jobs go begging. *Los Angeles Times,* September 20.

Mead, G. H. 1934. *Mind, self, and society.* Chicago: Univ. of Chicago Press.

Meade, W. J. 1987. *Mortal splendor: The American empire in transition.* New York: Houghton Mifflin.

Mechanic, D. ed. 1980. *Mental Health and social policy.* Englewood Cliffs, NJ: Prentice-Hall.

Medalie, J. H., Kahn, H. A., Neufeld, H. N., Riss, E., and Gouldborn, M. 1973. Five-year myocardial infarction incidence. *J Chron Dis* 26:329–341.

Meidner, R. 1981. *Om löntagarfonder* (On wage-earner funds). Stockholm: Tidens Debatt.

Meisner, M. 1971. The long arm of the job. *Ind Relat J,* October: 239–260.

Melman, S. 1958. *Decision making and productivity.* Oxford: Blackwell.

Melman, S. 1984. *Profits without production.* New York: Knopf.

Merton, R. K. 1940. Bureaucratic structure and personality. *Soc Forces* 18:560–568.

Metallarbetarförbundet. 1987. *Rewarding work.* Stockholm: Swedish Work Environment Fund.

Metallarbetarförbundet. 1985. *Det goda arbetet.* (The good work). Stockholm: Metallarbetarförbundet.

Meyerson, H. 1989. The incredible shrinking Democrats. *LA Weekly,* April 7–13.

Miles, R. H. 1976. Role requirements as sources of organizational stress. *J Appl Psychol* 61:172–179.

Miller, A. 1988. Stress on the job. *Newsweek,* April 25, 40–45.

Miller, D., and Swanson, G. 1960. *Inner conflict and defense.* New York: Holt, Rinehart and Winston.

Miller, K. I., and Monge, P. 1986. Participation, satisfaction and productivity: a meta analytic review. *Acad Manage Rev* 29:727–753.

Miller, M. W., and Winkler, M. 1988. A former trader aims to hook Wall Street on—and to—his data. *Wall Street Journal,* September 22.

Milvy, P., Forbes, W., and Brown, K. 1977. A critical review of epidemiological studies of physical activity. *Ann NY Acad Sci* 301:519–549.

Mischel, W. 1973. Towards a cognitive social learning reconceptualization of personality. *Psychol Rev* 80:252–283.

Moos, R. 1981. *Work environment scale manual.* Palo Alto, California: Consulting Psychologists Press.

Mortimer, J. T., and Lorence, J. 1979. Work experience and occupational value socialization: A longitudinal study. *Am J Sociol* 84:1361–1385.

Multiple Risk Factor Intervention Trial Research Group (MRFIT). 1982. Risk factor changes and mortality results. *JAMA* 248:1465–1477.

Nadler, G. 1981. *The planning and design approach.* New York: Wiley.

Nadler, G., Petersen, J., Hagel, M., and Chignell, M. 1989. Aids to the design process based upon techniques used by expert designers. Proceedings NSF Grantee Workshop on Design Theory and Methodology, Troy, NY. pp. 1.31–1.310.

Naisbett, J. 1984. *Megatrends: Ten new directions transforming our lives.* New York: Warner Books.

Naisbett, J., and Aburdene, P. 1985. *Reinventing the corporation: Transforming your job and your company for the new information service.* New York: Warner Books.

National Institute of Occupational Safety and Health. 1975. Problems in occupational safety and health. 75–124. Washington, DC: U.S. Government Printing Office.

National Insurance Bureau (Riksförsäkringsverket), Sweden. 1987. Official statistics.

Nesbitt, P. D. 1973. Smoking, physiological arousal, and emotional response. *J Pers Soc Psychol* 25:137–144.

Nirkko, O., Lauroma, M., Siltanen, P., Tuominen, S., and Vanhala, K. 1982. Psychological risk factors related to coronary heart disease: Prospective studies among policemen in Helsinki. *Acta Med Scand* (Suppl.) 660:137–154.

Noble, D. F. 1977. *America by design: Science, technology, and the rise of corporate capitalism.* New York: Knopf.

Noble, D. F. 1984. *Forces of production: A social history of industrial automation.* New York: Oxford University Press.

Noble, E. 1988. Life at Eastern Airlines: A lost sense of family. *New York Times,* April 29.

Norwegian Central Bureau of Statistics. 1976. *Yrke och dødlighet 1970–1973* (Occupation and mortality 1970–1973). Oslo: Statistisk Centralbyrå.

Obrist, P. A. 1976. The cardiovascular behaviour interaction: As it appears today. *Psychophysiology* 13:95–107.

O'Hanlon, J. F. 1981. Stress in short-cycle repetitive work: General theory and an empirical test. In *Machine pacing and occupational stress,* ed. G. Salvendy and M. J. Smith. London: Taylor and Francis.

Olsen, O., and Søndergaard-Kristensen, T. 1988. Hjerte/karsygdomme or arbejdsmiljø. Bind 3, Hvor stor betydning har arbejdsmiljøet for hjerte/karsygdomme i Danmark? (Cardiovascular illnesses and work environment. Part 3, What relative importance has the work environment to cardiovascular illnesses in Denmark?) Copenhagen: Arbejdsmiljøfondet.

Örebro Job Survey Instrument 1983. FHV 008 D Department of Occupational Medicine, Örebro County Hospital, Örebro.

Orth-Gomér, K. 1979. Ischemic heart disease and psychological stress in Stockholm and New York. *J Psychosom Res* 23:165–173.

Orth-Gomér, K. 1983. Intervention on coronary risk factors by adapting a shift work schedule to biologic rhythmicity. *Psychosom Med* 45:407–415.

Orth-Gomér, K., Hamsten, A., Perski, A., Theorell, T., and de Faire, U. 1986. Type A behaviour, education and psychosocial work characteristics in relation to ischemic heart disease—a case control study of young survivors of myocardial infarction. *J Psychosom Res* 30:633–643.

Oscarsson, B., Hammarström, O., Karlsson, G., and Lindholm, R. 1988. *A new world of work. The development programme.* Stockholm: Arbetsmiljöfonden.

Osler, W. 1910. The Lumleian lectures on angina pectoris. *Lancet* L:839–849.

Östberg, O., Whitaker, R., and Amick, B. 1988. *The automated expert.* Final report submitted to Teldok. Tarsta: Swedish Telecommunications Administration.

Ouchi, W. G. 1980. *Theory Z.* New York: Avon.

Paffenbarger, R. S., and Hyde, R. T. 1980. Exercise as protection against heart attack. *New Engl J Med* 302:1026–1027.

Paffenbarger, R. S., Jr., Laughlin, M. E., Gima, A. S., and Black, R. A. 1970. Work activity of longshoremen as related to death from coronary heart disease and stroke. *New Engl J Med* 282:1109–1114.

Page, L. B. 1976. Epidemiologic evidence on the etiology of human hypertension and its possible prevention. *Am Heart J* 91:527–534.

Paine, W. S. 1982. *Job stress and burnout.* London: Sage.

Papstein, P., and Frese, M. 1988. Transferring skills from training to the actual work situation: The role of task application knowledge, action styles and job decision latitude. Conference proceedings: Computer-Human interface 1988. Special issue of *SIGCHI Bull.*

Parker, M., and Slaughter, J. 1988. Managing by stress. The dark side of the team concept. *ILR Report* 24:19–23.

Parkes, C. M., Benjamin, B., and Fitzgerald, R. G. 1969. Broken heart: A statistical study of increased mortality among widowers. *Brit Med J* 1:740–743.

Pasmore, W., Francis, C., Haldeman, J., and Shani, A. 1982. Sociotechnical systems: A North American reflection on empirical studies of the seventies. *Human Relat* 35(12):1179–1204.

Pasmore, W. and Friedlander, F. 1982. An action-research program for increasing employee involvement in problem solving. *Adm Sci Q* 27:343–362.

Patel, C., Marmot, M. G., and Terry, D. J. 1981. Controlled trial of biofeedback-aided behavioral methods in reducing mild hypertension. *Brit Med J* 282:2005–2010.

Patel, C., Marmot, M. G., Terry, D. J., Carruthers, M., Hunt, B., and Patel, M. 1985. Trial of relaxation in reducing coronary risk: Four-year follow-up. *Brit Med J* 290:1103–1106.

Paykel, E. W. 1973. Recent life events and clinical depression. In *Life stress and illness*, ed. E. K. E. Gunderson and R. H. Rahe. Springfield, Ill.: Charles Thomas.

Payne, R. L., and Fletcher, B. 1983. Job demands, supports and constraints as predictors of psychological strain among school teachers. *J Voc Behav* 22:136–147.

Payne, R. L., Rick, J. T., Smith, G. H., and Cooper, R. G. 1984. Multiple indicators of stress in an active job: Cardiothoracic surgery. *J Occ Med* 26:805–808.

Pearlin, B., and Schooler, C. 1978. The structure of coping. *J Health Soc Behav* 19:2–21.

Pedersen, N. L., Gatz, M., Plomin, R., Nesselroade, J. R., and McClearn, G. E. 1988. Individual differences in locus of control during the second half of the life span for identical and fraternal twins reared apart and reared together. Department of Environmental Hygiene, Karolinska Institute, Stockholm. Manuscript.

Pell, S., and d'Alonzo, C. A. 1963. Acute myocardial infarction in a large employed population: Report of six-year study of 1,356 cases. *JAMA* 185:831–841.

Perrow, C. [1972] 1986. *Complex organizations: A critical essay.* New York: Random House.

Peters, T., and Waterman, R. H. 1981. *In search of excellence.* New York: Knopf.

Peterson, J. 1987. Global market: If Asia panics, Dow plummets. *New York Times*, October 27.

Piaget, J. 1932. *The moral judgment of the child.* Glencoe, Ill.: Free Press.

Pieper, C., La Croix, A. Z., and Karasek, R. A. 1989. Job strain and cardiovascular risk factors for male workers in the U.S. HES, HANES I and HANES II, Western Collaborative Group Study, and Exercise Heart Study. *Am J Epidemiol* 129:483–494.

Pierce, J. L., and Dunham, R. B. 1976. Task design: A literature review. *Acad Manage Rev* 1:83–97.

Piore, M. J., and Sable, C. F. 1984. *The second industrial divide: Possibilities for prosperity.* New York: Basic Books.

Piorkowski, P., Guther, K. H., Harig, H., Handreg, W., and Braun, H. 1981. Social factors correlating with coronary heart disease risk in a rural community of the GDR-model. Psychosocial stress, personality and occupational specificity. Paper presented at the International Conference on Psychophysiology, September 7–11. Karlovy Vary, Czechoslovakia.

Piotrokowski, C. S. 1979. *Work and the family system.* New York: Free Press.

Plate, R., Gall, I., and Schütz, F. 1985. Ny syn på produktionen (New view of production). In *En bok om Volvo (A book about Volvo)*. Göteborg: AB Volvo.

Pollack, A. 1988. Chip pact falls short of goals. *New York Times*, August 2.

Poulton, E. C. 1971. Skilled performance and stress. In *Psychology at Work*, ed. P. Warr. Harmondsworth: Penguin.

Prigogine, I. 1980. *From being to becoming: Time and complexity in the physical sciences.* San Francisco: W. H. Freeman.

Proudhon, P. J. [1851] 1923. *Systeme des contradictions economiques, ou philosophie de la misère*, 2 vol., ed. Roger Picard. Paris: Marcel Rivere.

Puska, P., Tuomilehto, J., Salonen, J., Neittaanmäki, L., Maki, J., Virtamo, J., Nissinen, A., Koskela, K., and Takalo, T. 1979. Changes in coronary risk factors during a comprehensive five-year community programme to control cardiovascular diseases (North Karelia Projekt). *Brit Med J* 2:1173–1178.

Pyörälä, K., Kärävä, R., Punsar, S., Oja, P., Teräslinna, P., Partanen, T., Jääskeläinen, M., Pekkarinen, M-L., and Koskela, A. 1971. A controlled study of the effects of 18 months' physical training in sedentary middle-aged men with high indexes of risk relative to coronary heart disease. In *Coronary heart disease and physical fitness*, ed. O. Andrée-Larsen and R. O. Malmborg. Copenhagen: Munksgaard.

Quinn, R. P. 1977. *Effectiveness in work roles: Employee responses to work environments.* Ann Arbor, Mich.: Survey Research Center, Institute for Social Research, University of Michigan.

Quinn, R. P., and Staines, G. L. 1979. *The 1977 Quality of Employment Survey: Descriptive statistics with comparison data from the 1969–70 and the 1972–73 surveys.* Ann Arbor, Mich.: Survey Research Center, Institute for Social Research, University of Michigan.

Raab, W. 1970. Myocardial electrolyte derangements. In *Preventive myocardiology: Fundamentals and targets*, ed. W. Raab. Springfield, Ill.: Charles Thomas.

Rafferty, Y. 1988. A survey of the working conditions and burnout in a human service agency: Report to the union. In *Psychology at Work*, 2d ed., ed. D. Bramel and R. Friend. Boston: Ginn.

Rahe, R. H. 1972. Subjects' recent life changes and their near-future illness reports. *Ann Clin Res* 4:250–265.

Rand, A. 1943. *The fountainhead*. Indianapolis: Bobbs-Merrill.

Reed, D. M., La Croix, A. Z., Karasek, R. A., Miller, D., and McLean, C. A. 1989. Occupational strain and the incidence of coronary heart disease. *Am J Epidemiol* 129:495–502.

Rehnström, P. 1987. Långsjönäs pappersbruk—Teknikrevolution i litet pappersbruk (Paper pulp factory in Långsjönäs, technical revolution in small paper pulp factory). Linköping University: Industriell teknik och arbetsorganisation.

Reichwald, R. 1983. Bürotechnik, Bürokratisierung und das Zentralisierungsproblem: Grundbelegungen vor Gestaltung der Büroarbeit. In *Bildschirmarbeit*, ed. A. Cakir. Berlin: Springer.

Relman, A. 1980. Mild hypertension. No more benign neglect. *New Engl J Med* 302:293–294.

Rissler, A., and Elgerot, A. 1978. Stressaktioner vid övertidsarbete (Stress reactions during overtime work). Report no. 23, Department of Psychology, University of Stockholm.

Ritti, R. 1971. Job enrichment in engineering organizations. In *New perspectives in job enrichment*, ed. J. Maher. New York: Van Nostrand.

Rizzo, J. R., House, F. J., and Lirtzman, S. I. 1970. Role conflict and ambiguity in complex organizations. *Adm Sci Q* 15:150–163.

Robbins, L., Helzer, J., Weissman, M., et al. 1984. Lifetime prevalance of specific psychiatric disorders in three sites. *Arc Gen Psychiatry* 41:949–958.

Robins, J., and Greenland, S. 1986. The role of model selection in causal inference from non-experimental data. *Am J Epidemiol* 123:392–402.

Rodin, J. 1986. Health, control, and aging In *The psychology of control and aging*, ed. M. M. Baltes and P. B. Baltes. Hillsdale, N.J.: Lawrence Erlbaum.

Rose, R. M., Hurst, L., and Jenkins, C. D. 1978. Air traffic controller health change study. Report, FFA contract no. DOT-FA 73WA–3211, Boston University School of Medicine.

Rosen, S. M. 1988. The Japanese model and the United States: Realities and possibilities in the 1980s. Paper presented at the International Workshop on the Japanese Model and Its Alternatives, FIOM-CGIL of Emilia-Romagna, Bologna, Italy, April.

Rosenbaum, J. 1976. *Making inequality: The hidden curriculum of high school marking*. New York: Wiley.

Rosenman, R. H. 1984. Health consequences of anger and implications for treatment. In *Anger and hostility in cardiovascular and behavioral disorders*, ed. M. A. Chesney and R. H. Rosenman. Washington, D.C.: Hemisphere Publishing.

Rotter, J. B. 1966. *Generalized expectations for internal versus external control of reinforcement*. Psychological Monographs, General and Applied, vol. 80, no. 1.

Rousseau, D. M. 1978. Characteristics of departments, positions and individuals: Contexts for attitudes and behaviours. *Adm Sci Q* 23:521–540.

Roy, A. 1987. Issues and guidelines for A.S.I.C. users. *Semiconductor Design Guide 1987*.

Rumberger, R. 1980. The economic decline of college graduates: Fact or fallacy? *J Human Resour* 15:99–113.

Russell, W. F., and Branch, T. 1979. The highs of the game. *New York Times Magazine*, September 16. Reprinted from W. Russell and T. Branch, *Second wind, The memoirs of an opinionated man*. New York: Random House, 1979.

Salancik, G. R., and Pfeffer, J. 1978. A social information processing approach to job attitudes and task design. *Adm Sci Q* 23:224–253.

Sales, S. M., and House, J. 1971. Job dissatisfaction as a possible factor in coronary heart disease. *J Chron Dis* 23:861–878.

Salonen, J. T., Puska, P., and Mustaniemi, H. 1979. Changes in morbidity and mortality during a comprehensive community programme to control cardiovascular diseases during 1972–1977 in North Karelia. *Brit Med J* 4:1178–1183.

Salvendy, G., and Smith, M. J., eds. 1981. *Machine pacing and occupational stress*. London: Taylor and Francis.

Samuelson, P. 1980. *Economics*, 11th ed. New York: McGraw-Hill.

Sandberg, A. 1976. *The limits to democratic planning: Knowledge, power and methods in the struggle for the future*. Stockholm: Liber.

Sandell, P., Bosrup, L., Söderberg, G., and Thulin, M. 1976. Kort beskrivning av Almex (Short description of Almex). In IVF, ed. Kundorderstyrd produktframtagning. Prodevent Stockholm: Mekanförbundet.

Sandén, P. O., and Johansson, G. 1987. Processövervakningens arbetsinnehåll och teknikförhållanden: Konsekvenser för mental belastning och arbetsengagemang (Job content and technology in process control: Consequences for mental load and job involvement). Report no. 52, Department of Psychology, University of Stockholm.

Sanger, D. E. 1987. Global markets' role widens. *New York Times*, October 28.

Sauter, S., Gottlieb, M., Jones, M., Dodson, V., and Rohrer, K. 1983. Job and health implications of VDT use: Initial results of the Wisconsin NIOSH study. *Commun Ass Comput Mach* 26:784–794.

Schleicher, R. 1973. Intelligenzleistungen Erwachsener in Abhängigkeit vom Niveau berufliche Tätigkeit (Intelligence performance in adults in relation to occupational level activity). *Probleme und Ergebnisse der Psychologie* 44:24–25.

Schnall, P. L., Pickering, T., and Karasek, R. 1988. Job characteristics and ambulatory blood pressure. Paper presented at the Twenty-eighth Annual Conference on Cardiovascular Disease Epidemiology, March, Sante Fe, New Mexico.

Schnall, P. L., Pieper, C., Karasek, R. A., Schwartz, J., Schlussel, Y., Devereux, R. B., Ganau, A., Alderman, M., Warren, K., and Pickering, T. G. 1989. The relationship between job strain, workplace diastolic blood pressure and left ventricular mass. Results of a case-control study. Cardiovascular and Hypertension Center, New York Hospital, Cornell Medical Center. Manuscript.

Schnorr, T. M., Thun, M. J., and Halperin, W. E. 1987. Chest pain in users of video display terminals. *JAMA* 257:627–640.

Schumacher, E. F. 1973. *Small is beautiful: Economics if people mattered.* New York: Harper and Row.

Schumann, M. 1974. Bestandaufnahme, Analyse und Entwicklungstrends in Produktionsbereich (Components, analysis and developmental trends in production). In *Humanisierung der Arbeit als gesellschaftliche und gewerkschaftliche Aufgabe* (Humanization of work as a societal and industrial task). Union conference in Frankfurt am Main.

Schwab, D. P., and Cummings, T. 1976. A theoretical analysis of the impact of task scope on employee performance. *Acad Manage Rev* 1:23–35.

Schwan, H. P. 1984. The development of biomedical engineering: Historical comments and personal observations. *IEEE Biomed Eng* 31:730–736.

Schwartz, C. C., Myers, J. K., and Astrachan, B. M. 1973. Comparing three measures of mental status: A note on the validity of estimate of psychological disorder in the community. *J Health Soc Behav* 14:265–273.

Schwartz, J., Karasek, R., and Pieper, C. 1982. A job characteristics scoring system for occupational analysis II: Demographic co-variation scoring system usage and reliability. Center for the Social Sciences, New York, Columbia University. Mimeo.

Schwartz, J., Pieper, C., and Karasek, R. 1988. A procedure for linking job characteristics to health surveys. *Am J Public Health* 78:904–909.

Scitovsky, T. 1976. *The joyless economy.* Oxford: Oxford University Press.

Scott, W. E. 1966. Activation theory and task design. *Organ Behav Hum Perform* 1:3–30.

Seashore, S. E., Lawler, E. E., Mirvis, P. H., and Cammann, C. 1980. *Observing and measuring organizational change: A guide to field practice.* New York: Wiley.

Seligman, M. E. P. 1975. *Helplessness: On depression, development and death.* San Francisco: W. H. Freeman.

Seligman, M. E. P. 1988. Why is there so much depression today: The waxing and waning of the commons. *G. Stanley Hall Lectures*, vol. 9. Washington, D.C.: American Psychological Association.

Selikoff, I. J., Churg, J., and Hammond, E. C. 1964. Asbestos exposure and neoplasia. *JAMA* 172:142–146.

Selye, H. [1936] 1976. *The stress of life.* New York: McGraw-Hill.

Selznick, P. 1949. *TVA and the grass roots: A study in the sociology of formal organization.* Berkeley: University of California Press.

Semmer, N. 1982. Stress at work, stress in private life and psychological well-being. In *Mental load and stress in activity: European approaches*, ed. W. Bachmann and I. Udris. Berlin: Deutscher Verlag der Wissenschaften; Amsterdam and New York: Elsevier–North Holland.

Semmer, N. 1984. Stressbezogene Taetigkeitsanalyse: Psychologische Untersuchungen zur Analyse von Stress am Arbeitsplatz Weinheim, Beltz. Department of Psychology, University of Bern. Manuscript.

References

Semmer, N., and Frese, M. 1988. Control at work as moderator of the effect of stress at work on psychosomatic complaints: A longitudinal study with objective measurement. Department of Psychology, University of Bern, Switzerland. Manuscript.

Semmer, N., and Pfafflin, M. 1978. Stress und das Training socialer Kompetenz. (Stress and the training of social competence.) In *Stress*, ed. E. Boesel. Hamburg: Hoffman and Campe.

Sennett, R., and Cobb, J. 1972. *The hidden injuries of class*. New York: Vintage.

Severo, R. 1980. Genetic tests by industry raise questions on rights of workers. *New York Times*, February 3.

Shaiken, H. 1984. *Work transformed: Automation and labor in the computer age*. New York: Holt, Rinehart and Winston.

Shaiken, H., Kuhn, S., and Herzenberg, S. 1983a. Automation and the workplace: Case studies on the introduction of programmable automation in manufacturing. Prepared for the Office of Technology Assessment. Massachusetts Institute of Technology, Cambridge. Summary.

Shaiken, H., Kuhn, S., and Herzenberg, S. 1983b. The effects of programmable automation on the work environment. A case study of auto assembly plant. In Automation and the workplace: Case studies on the introduction of programmable automation in manufacturing. Prepared for the Office of Technology Assessment. Massachusetts Institute of Technology, Cambridge.

Shaiken, H., Kuhn, S., and Herzenberg, S. 1983c. Case study of computer-aided automation. In Automation and the workplace: Case studies on the introduction of programmable automation in manufacturing. Prepared for the Office of Technology Assessment. Massachusetts Institute of Technology, Cambridge.

Shaw, A., and Riskind, J. H. 1983. Predicting job stress using data from the position analysis questionnaire. *J Appl Psychol* 68:253–261.

Shekelle, R. B., Schneider, A. S., Lin, S. C., Raynor, W. J., Garron, D. C., Ostfeld, A. M., and Paul, O. 1979. Work tension and risk of coronary heart disease (CHD). CVD Epidemiol. Newsletter no. 26. American Heart Association, National Center, 7320 Greenville Avenue, Dallas, Texas.

Shinn, M., Rosario, M., and Chestnut, D. E. 1984. Coping with job stress and burnout in the human services. *J Pers Soc Psychol* 46:864–876.

Siegrist, J. 1984. White-collar work setting and coronary-prone behaviour pattern. In *Breakdown in human adaptation to stress: Toward a multidisciplinary approach*, ed. J. Cullen and J. Siegrist. Amsterdam: Martinus Nijhoff.

Siegrist, J., Matschinger, M., Cremer, P., and Seidel, D. 1988. Atherogenic risk in men suffering from occupational stress. *Atherosclerosis* 69:211–218.

Siegrist, J., Siegrist, K., and Weber, I. 1986. Sociological concepts in the etiology of chronic disease: The case of ischemic heart disease. *Soc Sci Med* 22:247–253.

Silvestri, G. T., and Lukasiewics, J. M. 1985. Occupational employment projections: The 1984–85 outlook. *Monthly Labor Rev*, November 42–57.

Sims, H. P., Jr., Szilagyi, A. D., and Keller, R. T. 1976. The measurement of job characteristics. *Acad Manage J* 19:195–212.

Sinclair, U. 1906. *The jungle*. New York: Doubleday.

Sioukas, A., and Karasek, R. A. 1990. Market scale and specialization of labor in U.S. manufacturing industries: An empirical test and job design implications. Department of Industrial and Systems Engineering, University of Southern California. Manuscript.

Sloan, R. P., Gruman, J. C., and Allegrante, J. P. 1987. *Investing in employee health*. San Francisco: Jossey-Bass.

Smith, A. [1776] 1976. *An inquiry into the nature and causes of the wealth of nations*, 2 vols. Chicago: University of Chicago Press.

Smith, C. 1985. Sleep states and learning: A review of the animal literature. *Neurosci Biobehav Rev* 9:157–168.

Smith, M. J. 1985. Machine-paced work and stress. In *Job stress and blue-collar work*, ed. C. L. Cooper and M. J. Smith. Chichester: Wiley.

Smith, M. J., Cohen, B., Stammerjohn, J. B., and Happ, A. 1984. An investigation of health complaints and job stress in video display operations. *Human Factors* 23:387–400.

Soman, P., Koivisto, V. A., Diebert, D., Felig, P., and DeFronzo, R. A. 1979. Increased insulin sensitivity and insulin binding to monocytes after physical training. *New Engl J Med* 301:1200–1204.

Søndergaard-Kristensen, T., and Damsgaard, M. T. 1987. *Hjerte-karsygdomme og arbejdsmiljø* (Cardiovascular risk and job conditions). Copenhagen: Arbejdsmiljøfondet.

Søndergaard-Kristensen, T., and Lønnberg-Christensen, F. 1983. *Slagteriarbejde: En undersøgelse af arbejdsmiljø og helbred i slateri-og kødindustrien* (Slaughterhouse work: A study of work and health). Copenhagen: Arbejdsmiljøfondet.

Southwood, K. E. 1978. Substantive theory and statistical interaction: Five models. *Am J Sociol* 83:1154–1203.

Spaeth, J. L. 1979. Vertical differentiation among occupations. *Am Sociol Rev* 44:746–762.

Spenner, K. 1979. Temporal changes in work content. *Am Sociol Rev* 44:968–975.

Spenner, K. 1980. Occupational characteristics and classification systems: New uses of the Dictionary of Occupational Titles in social research. *Sociol Meth Res* 9:239–264.

Spillerman, S. 1977. Careers, labor market structure and socioeconomic achievement. *Am J Sociol* 83:551–593.

Starr, M. 1989. Innovazione e produtivita nelle impresse di medie dimensioni, in *Innovazione e Imprenditorialila*, ed. F. Corno. Padova, Italy: Centro Studi d'Impresa CEDAM.

Starrin, B., Larsson, G., Brenner, S-O., Levi, L., and Petterson, I-L. 1988. Samhällsförändringar, ohälsa och dödlighet: Sverige åren 1963–1983: En makrostudie (Societal changes, ill health and mortality: Sweden during the years 1963–1983: A macro-epidemiological study). Research report no. 13, Department of Community Medicine, County of Värmland, Karlstad, Sweden.

Statens Offentliga utredningar 1976. Lag om arbetsmijö (Law on work environment). Stockholm: SOU 1976:1.

Stauffacher, J. 1937. The effect of induced muscular tension on various phases of the learning process. *J Exp Psychol* 21:26–46.

Staw, B. M., Sandelands, L. E., and Dutton, J. E. 1981. Threat-rigidity effects in organizational behavior, a multilevel analysis. *Adm Sci Q* 26:501–524.

Stellman, J. M., and Daum, S. M. 1973. *Work is dangerous to your health.* New York: Random House.

Sterling, P., and Eyer, J. 1981. Biological basis of stress-related mortality. *Soc Sci Med* 15:3–42.

Sterling, T. D., and Weinkam, J. J. 1976. Smoking characteristics by type of employment. *J Occ Med* 18:743–754.

Stone, K. 1973. The origins of job structures in the steel industry. *Radical America* 7:19–64.

Sugimori, Y., Kusunoki, K., Cho, F., and Dehikawa, S. 1977. Toyota production system and Kamban system: Materialization of just-in-time and respect-for-human system. *Int J Prod Rese* Vol. 15:6, 553–564.

Sundbom, L. 1971. De förvärvsarbetandes arbetsförhållanden (Work site conditions for the working population). Stockholm: Låginkomstutredningen, Allmänna Förlaget.

Svensson, L. 1986a. Grupper och kollektiv: En studie av hemtjänstens organisation i två kommuner (Groups and collectivity: A study of the organization of home service in two communities). Stockholm: Arbetslivscentrum.

Svensson, L. 1986b. From management's control to workers' control—a case-study of a worker-initiated industrial democracy. In *Division of Labour, specialization and technical change.* Stockholm: Liber.

Swedish Central Bureau of Statistics. 1982. *Arbetsmiljö: Levnadsförhållanden 1979* (Work environment: Living conditions 1979). Sveriges officiella statistik, Report no. 32. Stockholm: Central Bureau of Statistics.

Swedish Central Bureau of Statistics. 1987. *Statistiska Meddelanden.* Report no. 10:8701. Stockholm: Central Bureau of Statistics.

Taber, T. D., Beehr, T. A., and Walsh, J. T. 1985. Relationships between job evaluation ratings and self-ratings of job characteristics. *Organ Behav Hum Decis Processes* 54:27–45.

Taggart, P., and Carruthers, M. 1971. Endogenous hyperlipidemia induced by emotional stress of racing driving. *Lancet* 1:363–366.

Tagliacozzo, R., and Vaughn, S. 1982. Stress and smoking in hospital nurses. *Am J Public Health* 72:441–446.

Tannenbaum, A. S. 1962. Control in organizations: Independent adjustment and organizational performance. *Adm Sci Q* 7:236–257.

Tannenbaum, A. S., Kavčič, B., Rosner, M., Vianello, M., and Wieser, G. 1974. *Hierarchy in organizations: A cross-cultural comparison.* San Francisco: Jossey-Bass.

Tata, J. R. 1970. Regulation of protein synthesis by growth and developmental hormones. In *Biochemical action of hormones*, ed. G. Litwack. New York: Academic Press.

Taylor, C. J. 1976. Experiments in work system design: Economic and human results. Working paper no. 76–7, Human Systems Development Study Center, Graduate School of Management, University of California, Los Angeles.

Taylor, F. [1911] 1967. *The principles of scientific management.* New York: Norton.

Temme, L. V. 1975. *Occupation: Meanings and measures.* Washington, D.C.: Bureau of Social Science Research, Inc.

Terkel, S. 1972. *Working.* New York: Pantheon.

The 9 to 5 Survey on Women and Stress, and Addendum. 1984. Cleveland, Ohio: 9 to 5 National Association of Working Women.

Theorell, T. 1989. Spontaneously occurring stressors. In *Frontiers of stress research,* ed. H. Weinter, I. Florin, R. Murison, and D. Hellhammer. New York: Huber.

Theorell, T. In press. Personal control at work and health. In *Stress, personal control and health,* ed. A. Appels and A. Steptoe. New York: Wiley.

Theorell, T., Ahlberg-Hulten, G., Berggren, T., Perski, A., Sigala, F., Soderholm, M., and Wallin, B-M. 1988. The worker's own exploration of work environment and cardiovascular risk: A way of stimulating discussion of improvements of the psychosocial work environment (in Swedish). Final report, no. 86–0406, to the Swedish Work Environment Fund, Stockholm.

Theorell, T., Ahlberg-Hulten, G., Berggren, T., Perski, A., Sigala, F., Svensson, J., and Wallin, B-M. 1987. Arbetsmiljö, levnadsvanor och risk for hjärtkärlsjukdom (Work environment, personal habits and risk of cardiovascular illness). Stress research reports, no. 195, National Institute for Psychosocial Factors and Health, Stockholm.

Theorell, T., and Åkerstedt, T. 1976. Day and night work: Changes in cholesterol, uric acid, glucose and potassium in serum and in circadian patterns of urinary catecholamine excretion. *Acta Med Scand* 200:47–57.

Theorell, T., Alfredsson, L., Knox, S., Perski, A., Svensson, J., and Waller, D. 1984. On the interplay between socioeconomic factors, personality and work environment in the pathogenesis of cardiovascular disease. *Scand J Work Environ Health* 10:373–380.

Theorell, T., Flodérus, B., and Lind, E. 1975. The relationship of disturbing life-changes and emotions to the early development of myocardial infarction and other serious illnesses. *Int J Epidemiol* 4:281–296.

Theorell, T., and Flodérus-Myrhed, B. 1977. "Workload" and risk of myocardial infarction: A prospective psychosocial analysis. *Int J Epidemiol* 6:17–21.

Theorell, T., Häggmark, C., and Eneroth, P. 1987. Psycho-endocrinological reactions in female relatives of cancer patients: Effects of an activation programme. *Acta Oncol* 26:419–424.

Theorell, T., Hamsten, A., de Faire, U., Orth-Gomér, K., and Perski, A. 1987. Psychosocial work conditions before myocardial infarction in young men. *Int J Cardiol* 15:33–46.

Theorell, T., Hjemdahl, P., Ericsson, F., Kallner, A., Knox, S., Perski, A., Svensson, J., Tidgren, B., and Waller, D. 1985. Psychosocial and physiological factors in relation to blood pressure at rest: A study of Swedish men in their upper twenties. *J Hypertens* 3:591–600.

Theorell, T., Karasek, R. A., and Eneroth, P. In press. Job strain variations in relation to plasma testosterone fluctuations in working men: A longitudinal study. *J Internal Med.*

Theorell, T., Knox, S., Svensson, J., and Waller, D. 1984. Final report, Project no. 80/77 and 80/3960, to the Swedish Work Environment Fund, Stockholm.

Theorell, T., Knox, S., Svensson, J., and Waller, D. 1985. Blood pressure variations during a working day at age 28: Effects of different types of work and blood pressure level at age 18. *J Human Stress* 11:36–41.

Theorell, T., Lind, E., Fröberg, J., Karlsson, C-G., and Levi, L. 1972. A longitudinal study of 21 coronary subjects: Life changes, catecholamines and related biochemical variables. *Psychosom Med* 34:505–510.

Theorell, T., Olsson, A., and Engholm, G. 1977. Concrete work and myocardial infarction. *Scand J Work Environ Health* 3:144–153.

Theorell, T., Perski, A., Ahlberg-Hulten, G., Berggren, T., Eneroth, P., Sigala, F., and Wallin, B. M. 1988. Om den psykosociala arbetsmiljön för läkare och andra utövare av serviceyrken (On the psychosocial situation of physicians and other men and women in service occupations). *Läkartidningen* 40:3268–3271.

Theorell, T., Perski, A., Åkerstedt, T., Sigala, F., Ahlberg-Hultén, G., Svensson, J., and Eneroth, P. 1988. Changes in job strain in relation to changes in physiological states: A longitudinal study. *Scand J Work Environ Health* 14:189–196.

Theorell, T., and Rahe, R. H. 1971. Psychosocial factors and myocardial infarction: An inpatient study in Sweden. *J Psychosom Res* 15:25–36.

Theorell, T., and Rahe, R. H. 1972. Behavior and life satisfaction characteristics of Swedish subjects with myocardial infarction. *J Chron Dis* 25:139–146.

Thibault, J., and Kelly, H. 1959. *The social psychology of groups.* New York: Wiley.

Thomas, J. and Griffen, R. 1983. The social information processing model of task design: A review of the literature. *Acad Manage Rev* 8:672–682.

Thompson, E. P. 1963. *The making of the english working class.* New York: Vintage.

Thornton, J., and Jacobs, P. 1971. Learned helplessness in human subjects. *J Exp Psychol* 87:369–382.

Thurow, L. C. 1984. *Dangerous currents: The state of economics.* New York: Viking Books.

Tichauer, E. 1973. Ergonomic aspects of biomechanics in the industrial environment: Its evaluation and control. NIOSH, U.S. Department of Health, Education and Welfare. Washington, D.C.: U.S. Government Printing Office.

Timio, M., Pede, P., and Gentili, S. 1977. Eliminazione urinaria di adrenalina, noradrenalina e 17-idrossicorticidi nello stress occupational (Urinary secretion of adrenaline, noradrenaline and 17-hydroxycorticoids in relation to occupational stress). *G Ital Cardiol* 7:1080–1087.

Toffler, A. 1981. *The third wave.* New York: Bantam Books.

Topping, D. L., and Mayes, P. A. 1972. The immediate effects of insulin and fructose on the metabolism of the perfused liver: Changes in lipoprotein secretion, fatty acid oxidation and esterification, lipogenesis and carbohydrate metabolism. *Biochem J* 126:295–311.

Trist, E. L. 1981. The evolution of sociotechnical systems: A conceptual framework and action research program. Issues in the Quality of Working Life No. 2, June, Ontario Ministry of Labor, Toronto.

Trist, E. L., and Bamforth, K. W. 1951. Some social and psychological consequences of the longwall method of coal getting. *Hum Relat* 4:3–38.

Trist, E. L., Jiggins, G., Murray, H., and Polliack, A. 1963. *Organizational choice.* London: Tavistock.

Trost, C. 1986. New-collar jobs: Unions pursue service workers in an effort to stem the decline in their ranks. *Wall Street Journal,* September 19.

Turnbull, C. M. 1972. *The mountain people.* New York: Simon and Schuster.

Turner, A. N., and Lawrence, P. R. 1965. *Industrial jobs and the worker.* Cambridge: Harvard University Press.

Turner, J. A. 1980. Computers in bank clerical functions: Implications for productivity and the quality of life. Ph.D. diss., Columbia University.

Turner, J. A., and Karasek, R. A. 1984. Software ergonomics: Effects of computer application design parameters on operator task performance and health. *Ergonomics* 27:663–690.

Umbers, I. 1979. Models of the process operator. *J Man-Machine Stud* 11:263–284.

U.S. Chamber of Commerce, Clearinghouse on Business Coalitions for Health Action. 1986. A guide to sources of health care data. Washington, D.C.: U.S. Government Printing Office.

U.S. Department of Defense. 1985. Applications Manual 12/85. MIL-STD 1567A. Washington, D.C.: U.S. Government Printing Office.

U.S. Department of Health, Education and Welfare. 1973. *Work in America: Report of a special task force to the Secretary of Health, Education and Welfare.* Cambridge: The MIT Press.

U.S. Department of Health, Education and Welfare. 1979a. Coronary heart disease in adults: U.S. 1971–1973. DHEW Public Health Series 1,000, Series 11, no. 10. Washington, D.C.: U.S. Government Printing Office.

U.S. Department of Health, Education and Welfare. 1979b. Plan and operation of the Health and Nutrition Examination Survey, U.S. 1971–1973. DHEW Pub. 79-1310, Series 1, no. 10b. Washington, D.C.: U.S. Government Printing Office.

U.S. Department of Health and Human Services, Health Care Financing Administration. 1988. Washington, D.C.: National Health Spending Report. Washington, D.C.: U.S. Government Printing Office.

U.S. Office of Disease Prevention and Health Promotion. 1987. National Survey of Worksite Health Promotion Activities. Washington, D.C.: U.S. Government Printing Office.

U.S. Office of Technology Assessment. 1984. Computerized manufacturing, automation education and the workplace. OTA-CIT-235. April 1984. Washington, D.C.: U.S. Government Printing Office.

U.S. Office of Technology Assessment. 1985. Automation of America's offices. OTA-CIT-287. December 1985. Washington, D.C.: U.S. Government Printing Office.

U.S. Office of Technology Assessment. 1986. Technology and structural unemployment: Reemploying displaced adults. OTA-ITE-250. February 1986. Washington, D.C.: U.S. Government Printing Office.

U.S. Office of Technology Assessment. 1987. Report on electronic work monitoring. Committee on Civil Liberties and Civil Service Management. Washington, D.C.: U.S. Government Printing Office.

Vågerö, D., and Olin, R. 1983. Incidence of cancer in the electronics industry: Using the new Swedish cancer environment as a screening instrument. *Brit J Ind Med* 40:188–192.

Van Maanen, J., and Schein, E. H. 1979. Toward a theory of organizational socialization. In *Research in organizational behavior*, vol. 1, ed. B. M. Staw. Greenwich, Conn.: JAI Press.

Volpert, W. 1974. *Handlungsstrukturanalyse* (Analysis of the structure of acting). Köln (Cologne): Pahl-Rugenstein.

Volpert, W. 1989. Work and personality development from the viewpoint of the action regulation theory. In *Socialization at work—a new approach to the learning process in the workplace and society*, ed. H. Leymann and F. Kornbluh. London: Glower.

Volpert, W., Oesterreich, R., Gablenz-Kolakovic, S., Krogoll, T., and Resch, M. 1983. Verfahren zur Ermittlung von Regulationserfordernissen in der Arbeitstätigkeit (VERA): Analyse von Planungs- und Denkprocessen in der industriellen Produktion (Method of measuring regulation demands at work: Analysis of the planning and thinking process in industrial production). Köln (Cologne): TüV.

von Otter, C. 1985. Storskalighet och småskalighet inom sjukvården (Large and small scale in hospital care). In *Privat och offentlig sjukvård. Samverkan eller konkurrens.* (Private and public care. Coordination or competition.), ed. E. Jonsson and D. Skalin. Stockholm: SPRT.

Vroom, V. 1964. *Work and motivation.* New York: Wiley.

Wagner, J. A., and Gooding, R. Z. 1987. Shared influence and organizational behavior: A meta-analysis of situational variables expected to moderate participation-outcome. *Acad Manage J* 30:524–541.

Wahlstedt, K. 1988. Sömnstörningar och magtarmbesvär under skiftarbete (Sleep disturbance and gastrointestinal symptoms during shift work). Department of Psychosocial Research, National Board of Occupational Health and Safety, Stockholm. Manuscript.

Wahlund, I., and Nerell, G. 1976. Tjänstemännens arbetsmiljöer (The work environment of white-collar workers). Report no. 1, The Federation of Salaried Employees (TCO) Stockholm.

Wainwright, H., and Elliott, D. 1982. *The Lucas plan.* London: Allison and Busby.

Waldron, I. 1976. Why do women live longer than men? Part 1. *J Human Stress* 2:2–18.

Waldron, I. 1979. A quantitative analysis of cross-cultural variations in blood pressure and serum cholesterol. *Psychosom Med* 41:582–602.

Walker, C. R., and Guest, R. H. 1952. *The man on the assembly line.* Cambridge: Harvard University Press.

Wall, T. P., and Clegg, C. W. 1981. A longitudinal study of group work design. *J Occ Behav* 2:31–49.

Wallin, L., and Wright, I. 1986. Psychosocial aspects of the work environment: A group approach. *J Occ Med* 28:384–393.

Wall Street Journal. 1987. Glutted markets. A global overcapacity hurts many industries. No easy cure is seen. March 9, leading article.

Watson, F. M. C., and Henry, J. P. 1977. Loss of socialized patterns of behavior in mouse colonies following daily sleep disturbance during maturation. *Physiol Behav* 18:119–123.

Weber, M. [1922] 1947. *The theory of social and economic organization.* New York: Free Press.

Weil, S. [1949] 1952. *The need for roots. Prelude to a declaration of duties towards mankind.* London: Routledge and Kegan Paul.

Weiner, H. 1977. *Psychobiology of human disease.* New York: American Elsevier.

Weis, W. L. 1981. No ifs, ands or buts: Why workplace smoking should be banned. *Management World*, September: 39–44.

Weiss, J. 1971. Effects of coping behaviour. *J Comp Physiol* 77:1–10.

Welford, A. T. 1976. *Skilled performance in perceptual and motor skills.* Glenview, Ill.: Scott, Foresman.

Welford, A. T., Brown, A., and Gabb, J. 1950. Two experiments on fatigue as affecting skilled performance in civilian air crews. *Brit J Psychol* 40:195–211.

Welin, L., Tibblin, G., Svärdsudd, K., Tibblin, B., Ander-Peciva, S., Larsson, B., and Wilhelmsen, L. 1985. Prospective study of social influences on mortality: The study of men born in 1913 and 1923. *Lancet* 1:915–918.

Wendeberg, B. 1982. *Gnosjöandau: myt eller verklighet?* (The spirit of gnosjö: myth or truth?). Värnamo: Wendeberg.

Westcott, B. J., and Eisenhart, K. M. 1986. The dynamics of process innovation in manufacturing. Paper presented at the meeting of the Academy of Management, Chicago.

White, R. 1959. Motivation reconsidered: The concept of competence. *Psychol Rev* 66:297–333.

Whyte, W. F. 1948. *Human relations in the restaurant industry.* New York: McGraw-Hill.

Wiggins, J. S., and Broughton, R. 1985. The interpersonal circle: A structural model for the integration of personality research. *Perspect Personality* 1:1–47.

Williams, R. H., and Porte, D. 1974. The pancreas. In *Textbook of endocrinology,* 5th ed., ed. R. H. Williams. Philadelphia: W. B. Saunders.

Williams-Ashman, H. G. 1979. *Endocrinology,* vol. 3, *Biochemical features of androgen physiology,* ed. L. J. DeGroot, G. F. Cahill, W. D. Odell, L. Martini, J. T. Potts, Jr., D. H. Nelsson, E. Steinberger, and A. I. Winegrad. New York: Grune and Stratton.

Wolf, S. 1969. Psychosocial forces in myocardial infarction and sudden death. *Circulation* Suppl. 4:74–82.

Wolf, W. C., and Fligstein, N. D. 1979a. Sex and authority in the workplace: Causes of sexual inequality. *Am Sociol Rev* 44:235–252.

Wolf, W. C., and Fligstein, N. D. 1989b. Sexual stratification: Differences in power in the work setting. *Soc Forces* 58:94–107.

World Health Organization, European Collaborative Group. 1984. Multifactorial trial in the prevention of coronary heart disease, 3: Incidence and mortality results. *Eur Heart J* 4:141–159.

Wright, I. 1985. Psychosocial aspects of the work environment: A group approach. Göteborg: AB Volvo.

Wundt, W. 1922. *Einleitung in die Philosophie.* (Introduction to philosophy.) Leipzig: Alfred Kröner.

Yerkes, R. M., and Dodson, J. D. 1908. The relation of strength of stimulus to rapidity of habit-formation. *J Comp Neurol Psychol* 18:459–482.

Young, M., and Willmott, P. 1957. *Family and kinship in East London.* London: Routledge and Kegan Paul.

Young, M., and Willmott, P. 1973. *The symmetrical family.* London: Routledge and Kegan Paul.

Yrkesmedicinska Kliniken Örebro. 1983. Questionnaire 8309, FHV 008 D/2.

Zaleznik, A. M., de Vries, K., and Howard, J. 1977. Stress reactions in organizations: Syndromes, causes and consequences. *Behav Sci* 22:151–162.

Ziegarnik, B. 1927. Das Behalten erledigter und unerledigter Handlungen (On finished and unfinished tasks). *Psychologische Forschung* 9:1–85.

Zola, E. [1885] 1952. *Germinal,* trans. H. Harris. London: Dent.

Zuboff, S. 1982. New worlds of computer-mediated work. *Harv Bus Rev* September–October: 142–152.

Zuboff, S. 1988. *In the age of the smart machine: The future of work and power.* New York: Basic Books.

INDEX

Absenteeism, 49, 168, 259; and job redesign outcomes, 183–87; and productivity, 182–83

Accumulated strain, 98–99

Action regulation theory, 171–72

Action research, 204

Active behavior mechanism, 51–54, 70

Active jobs, 94, 103; characteristics of, 32, 35–36, 43, 44; gender differences in distribution of, 42, 46; and leisure behavior, 52–54

Active-learning hypothesis, 91–94, 170–74

Administrators, 278–85, 295

Adrenaline, 100, 104–7, 111, 116, 201

Adrenal medullary and adrenal cortical systems, 104–7

Affiliation, 97–98, 312

Aggression, 33

Air traffic controllers, 84, 105, 120, 142, 157, 295–96, 325; health information feedback study involving, 208, 212, 213, 214; humane future jobs for, 315, 318–19

Alcohol consumption and alcoholism, 141, 151; economic costs of, 166; and unemployment, 307

Alexithymia, 99, 102, 115, 116; and heart disease, 114

Almex AB, 253–55, 256, 258

Anabolic response, 104, 107–9, 110, 116, 195, 196

Anticipatory worrying, 96

Anxiety, 93, 102–3; and drug use, 329; and high-stress jobs, 31–34; and job insecurity, 305–7; and learning, 100; and Type A behavior, 113

Apprenticeship, 312

Arousal, 32–34, 90–91; acute and chronic, 106; physiological responses to, 105, 106, 109

Arrhythmia, 110–11, 118, 201. *See also* Heart disease

Artificial intelligence, 270

Asbestos, 4, 66, 286

Assembly line work, 23, 88, 108; decision latitude and social support levels low for, 74; and job redesign, 278–85, 288; psychosocial characteristics of, 33, 34, 37, 39, 44, 65; and technological innovation, 251, 253, 257, 266–67, 268, 272

Atherosclerosis, 106, 109, 111, 112

Automation, 46, 251, 253–59. *See also* Technology

Autonomous work groups, 101, 192, 253–54, 288, 297

Bandura, Albert, 171

Batch-processing computer systems, 252

Behavior modification, 8

Bentham, Jeremy, 21, 163, 194, 265, 291

Biofeedback, 217

Biological control systems, 86, 87

Blood pressure, 112, 116, 117, 122; and exercise, 109; and heart disease, 141–42, 155–56; and impact of health feedback, 208–20; and job strain, 142–46. *See also* Hypertension

Blue-collar work: and heart disease, 135–40; physical demands of, 65–66. *See also* Assembly-line work; Low-status jobs; Social class

Boredom, 149, 150, 314; and computer-based work, 264, 268; and smoking, 146

Buffer stocks, 267

Bureaucratic hierarchies, 10, 59, 244, 293

Burnout, 39, 51, 100, 240, 241